Projections

Brief Readings on American Culture

Second Edition

J. STERLING WARNER
Evergreen Valley College

BILL SWANSON
South Puget Sound Community College

THOMSON

HEINLE

Australia • Canada • Mexico • Singapore • Spain • United Kingdom • United States

THOMSON

HEINLE

Projections, Second Edition
Brief Readings on American Culture
Warner, Swanson

Publisher: *Michael Rosenberg*
Acquisitions Editor: *Stephen Dalphin*
Development Editor: *Helen Triller*
Production Editor: *Matt Drapeau*
Marketing Manager: *Ken Kasee*
Manufacturing Manager: *Marcia Locke*

Compositor: *UG / GGS Information Services, Inc.*
Project Manager: *Heshy Rosenwasser*
Cover Designer: *Diane Levy, DFL Publications*
Cover photo: *David Mendelsohn/Masterfile*
Printer: *Transcontinental*

Printed in Canada.
1 2 3 4 5 6 7 8 9 10   06 05 04 03 02

For more information contact Heinle,
25 Thomson Place, Boston, MA 02210 USA,
or you can visit our Internet site at
http://www.heinle.com

For permission to use material from this text or product contact us:

Tel:	1-800-730-2214
Fax:	1-800-730-2215
Web:	www.thomsonrights.com

ISBN: 0-15-504219-X

Copyrights and Acknowledgements appear on page 398, which constitutes a continuation of the copyright page.

Preface

Aims and Philosophy

Projections: Brief Readings on American Culture, Second Edition, provides a thorough overview of the reading, studying, and writing processes in combination with a thematic anthology designed to stimulate discussion, critical thinking, and writing. We wrote this book with several basic premises in mind. First, we believe that students bring different kinds of cultural literacy into the writing classroom. These literacies are rooted in pop culture, television, computers, and movies. Although these aspects of American culture are often seen as distractions from conventional literacy, they can—when skillfully used in curriculum—prove helpful to students working their way through the essays, aphorisms, photographs, and cartoons in this volume as well as its scattering of short stories and poems.

Literacy usually refers to the ability to read written texts, but in recent years it has been used in other contexts as well—computer literacy, multicultural literacy, and media literacy, to name but a few. Almost anything can be considered a "text," that is, an object that requires interpretation. For writing classes, this suggests an opening out of the curriculum as the topics for essays range over new issues and new cultural materials. Our goal here is to couple innovation with tradition in writing instruction so as to meet the learning needs of students and to promote skills that lead to persistence and success in the writing classroom. To these ends, we have provided many connections in the book to cultural influences beyond the printed media. All chapters feature film links, and some chapters explore a reservoir of cultural material that can energize our quest for a better understanding of American culture. Most students today have spent more time watching television and movies than reading. This experience is part of the culture they bring into the classroom. These same students have no idea what postmodernism is; they just live it. This book will help them understand it a little better by writing about it.

We know that teaching styles differ; we have, therefore, presented approaches to reading and writing that instructors may use in part or in whole, as appropriate. We have written questions following every type of text presented and then added some extra questions to stimulate still more connections to related issues. Each chapter is designed with the principle of theme and variation in mind. Each selection is strong enough to stand alone as a coherent statement of some kind. If a whole chapter is assigned, the thematic material expands outward, forming a cluster of related topics. This is meant to provide a flexible text that can be used in many different ways.

New to the Second Edition of *Projections*

The second edition of *Projections: Brief Essays on American Culture* offers many new features, including over a dozen new readings by various authors; three new student essays; and nine new "Observations and Opinions" quotations. In addition, we have expanded our material on writing summaries and paraphrasing; inserted Kathleen Hudson's interview of legendary blues artist, Stevie Ray Vaughan, following our discussion on how to write interviews; included Compositions and Films: Frequently Asked Questions' as an adjunct piece in our 'Writing about Films' Appendix; and updated our 'Glossary of Literary, Rhetorical, and Cultural Terms. Also new to the second edition of *Projections* is Chapter 12, The Body: Language, Ritual, and Wellness, a casebook study of body enhancement, modification, and health.

Organizations

This book is divided into two parts. The first, Communication Skills: Reading and Writing, offers a base that students and instructors may return to later as they move from one group of thematic readings to another. In addition to providing a review of major forms of composition (narration, description, exposition, and argumentation) that pervade all types of writing, Part One also presents a brief discussion of rhetorical modes of development. The first chapter in Part One, The Reading/Studying Process, contains reading and studying tips, a sample annotated essay, a discussion of summary writing and paraphrasing, and treatment of the collaborative approach: writing in groups.

Chapter 2, The Writing Process: An Overview, examines prewriting, writing paragraphs, drafting essays, revising essays, and editing. The discussion of strategies for development emphasizes how methods of development often overlap. Chapter 2 also contains sections on argumentation and persuasion and diction and style, as well as a sample student essay.

Part Two, Thematic Readings, consists of ten chapters of readings organized in thematic groupings examining the following themes: The American Family; Stereotypes and Social Barriers; Media: Controversies and Celebrities;

Environments; Cyberspace and Technology; Popular Culture; Television; Music; Movies; and The Body: Language, Ritual, and Wellness—A Casebook. We have structured essays, fiction, and even a few poems into units that focus on different aspects of the writing process.

Reading Selections

Each thematic chapter contains four or five reading selections, including works by writers such as Louise Erdrich, Alice Walker, Martin Scorsese, Barbara Ehrenreich, Stanley Crouch, Amy Tan, Toni Morrison, Oscar Hijuelos, Ishmael Reed, Rose Anna Higashi, Garrison Keillor, Kurt Vonnegut, Terry McMillan, and Dave Barry. Essays treat such diverse topics as the changing role of the family in American society, the effects of technology and cyberspace on our lives, the role of the media in society, "Reality TV," body piercing, sports, amusement parks, plastic surgery, the power of television, street musicians, and hiphop, among others. Essays are arranged from least to most challenging, the later readings being ideal for use toward the end of the semester or quarter in order to prepare students for the more complex reading they will be encountering in later college writing courses.

Selection Apparatus

Each thematic chapter features the following elements in conjunction with the readings:

Observations and Opinions: These sections contain brief quotes or aphorisms that provide introductory glimpses of the chapter's theme. These quotes can be used to initiate thinking, discussion, and writing about the appropriate theme and are accompanied by brief sets of reading and writing activities that draw on student responses to the quotes or prompt a thematic journal entry.

Observations and Opinions sections are followed by a thematic introduction that touches on some of the issues involved in each chapter's theme and a description of each of the chapter's reading selections.

Gathering Thoughts: Prewriting Inquiries: Found in a shaded box after the thematic introduction to each chapter, these questions are designed to function equally well for each reading in the chapter and may be returned to frequently to generate new ideas and to reexamine old ones, generating fresh dialogue and lively writing.

Allusions: Allusions to people, places, and events in the readings that readers may not recognize are presented at the beginning of the reading, immediately after the headnote. Sometimes a brief exercise is incorporated into the Allusions section.

Afterwards (Vocabulary, Content, Style and Structure, Collaborative Explorations, and Writing Assignments): The post-reading apparatus deals with the reading/writing process and is subdivided into several subcategories:

- *Vocabulary* entries consist of word lists and related exercises.
- *Content* sections contain comprehension questions that invite the exploration of one's personal, cultural, or historical knowledge.
- *Style and Structure* questions focus on how a work is structured and why certain strategies the authors have used are more effective than others.
- *Collaborative Explorations* are group activities (adaptable for use in the electronic classroom) that provide students with opportunities to work together and to explore thematic topics and issues as members of a group rather than as isolated individuals. Such explorations include collaborative essays, panel presentations, and group debates.
- *Writing Assignments* serve as prompts for various types of essays.
- *Cross-Links* follow many of the readings. Boxes following the readings list thematic reading cross-links and film cross-links. These entries are cross-references to other readings in the book or to films listed at the end of each chapter. These entries show how readings in one chapter can be connected to readings in other chapters and how the film lists can be used to develop the themes suggested by the readings. Cross-Links can also be used to open up new avenues of discussion and to encourage writing on topics that connect one form of communication to another.

End-of-Chapter Apparatus

The Visual Connection: These sections contain photographs and cartoons that serve as complementary pieces to thematic chapters. Such visual aids are useful in opening class discussion because—for many—the immediacy of visual images is an instantaneous stimulus for thinking.

Film Links: In these sections, students are encouraged to draw from their film-viewing experiences to make connections with the themes dealt with in this book. Writing prompts here are followed by the names of ten to twelve films that students may wish to write about or to link to the thematic topic under discussion. (Instructors who would like to take a multimedia approach to composition should refer to the appendix entitled Writing about Films, which follows Chapter 12. Instructors who may have some reservations about using films in class are referred to the Appendix, where they will find answers to frequently asked questions about teaching writing through use of films.)

Additional Writing Assignments: The writing prompts in these sections encourage the use of cultural literacy, personal observations, and experiences as well as traditional methods of expository and argumentative writing to help generate critical thinking and to sharpen writing skills.

Appendix on Writing about Films, Glossary of Terms

Films represent an international and historical spectrum of works that present diversity of culture with an immediacy that is not always available in the translation of written texts. Americans now have thousands of choices available to them at video stores, which have become commercial archives of popular culture. The availability of films on video makes responding to them critically or assessing them in essays ideal tasks for the college writing classroom. The Appendix, located at the back of this book, offers students and instructors information about an alternative approach to some of the other writing assignments in this book. Finally, a glossary of common literary, rhetorical, and cultural terms is included at the back of the text.

Acknowledgements

In the field of composition and rhetoric, all comers have very definite ideas about how to best instruct students. This makes writing a textbook a delicate balancing act in which fine distinctions need to be weighed with patience, subtlety, and attentiveness to detail. We would like to gratefully acknowledge the contributions of those instructors and reviewers whose constructive suggestions helped shape this second edition: Amy Anderson, *Powell, California State University, Sacramento*; Gordon Anderson, *Delgado Community College*; Rebecca Belcher, *Olivet Nazarene University*; Mary Fitz Simmons, *College of Saint Rose*; Joel B. Henderson, *Chattanooga State Technical Community College*; Shirlee McGuire, *Olivet Nazarene University*; Mark Medvetz, *University of Montana, Missoula*; and Kashama Mulamba, *Olivet Nazarene University*.

Finally, we would like to express continued thanks to Developmental Editor Helen Triller, who worked as patiently through the second edition of *Projections* as she did on the first. In addition, we would like to offer our thanks to Heinle Acquisitions Editor Steve Dalphin; our Projection Editor, Matt Drapeau; and our Project Manager, Heshy Rosenwasser, for championing our project and giving us their encouragement, insight, and judgment while supporting it through its various stages of vision and revision.

J. Sterling Warner
Evergreen Valley College

Bill Swanson
South Puget Sound Community College

To The Student

Projections is a word that suggests varied meanings. It comes from the Latin prefix *pro*, which means "forward", and the verb *jacere*, which means "to throw." This relates to the writing process and to this book in particular, if you think about how the mind projects thoughts onto a blank piece of paper every time you sit down to write. Or you could think about how culture projects itself upon the world or about how movies are projected onto a blank screen. Perceptions, words, and ideas come from within ourselves and are projected outward, toward other people in various forms—speech, writing, music, videotapes, films. When we have something we want to say, we "toss some ideas around" in our heads; then we throw them out into the world in one form or another. This "throwing forward" is a creative act that is usually aimed at a target like a jump shot lofted toward a basketball hoop. Sometimes we connect—swish!—other times we miss. This is the challenge of communicating with words. We need to project what we think and feel out there where it can become part of the game called "American culture."

The word "projections" also contains the noun "project" within it. A project is an ongoing activity with a definite goal. A piece of writing is a type of project. It requires planning, organization, and perseverance. A project moves in stages from brainstorming to production to evaluation. Every time you sit down to write, you start a project.

Finally, projection is actually a job title; projectionists literally put movies on to the screens in theaters. In this book we have put together some readings with some film lists to show it is possible to make connections between these two types of projections.

We write in order to understand our place within the vast web of cultural relationships. *Projections: Brief Readings on American Culture,* Second Edition, is an introduction to ways of developing basic critical and analytical skills that we all need to make sense out of our own experience and the world around us.

Brief
Contents

Detailed
• • • • • • • • • • Contents • • • • • • • • • •

Part Two
·············

Thematic Readings   **67**

3. The American Family   **68**

As the kitten scrambled away, Native American poet/author
Louise Erdrich "went down to the basement, looking for it
with a flashlight, but . . . the untamed creature fled from
the concrete-floored area and off into the crawl space—
draped with spider webs as thick as cotton . . . " There, in
her effort to rescue the kitten, she comes to recognize the
house as the "husk" of herself, "an empty double."

"Sassafrass, with his thick, lush, white coat, his hand
grenade solidarity, was nothing if not cooperative; he

recognized a good deal. And he'd surely live forever. He was smart enough to outwit death. Hide in the pillows of the couch when it came by to pick up white rats. Since all three of us Johns stand firm on each other's shoulders, we know we too will live forever, just like Sass."

Poet, essayist, and Pulitzer Prize-winning novelist Alice Walker finds it more difficult to write about her father than her mother, but because "writing about people helps us to understand them," she also explains that "coming to terms with what he meant to my life is crucial to a full acceptance and love of myself."

How true is the idea that "God could not be everywhere, so he made mothers"? Is motherhood really the ultimate experience for a woman? Anna Quindlen definitely believes that too many people have bought into the Hallmark Card version of motherhood and fail to realize that raising children is not always romantic, "often hard, and sometimes even horrible."

"I grew up listening to my father play the steel guitar. It was his pastime and passion. Once or twice a month our front room would fill with fiddlers and guitar pickers who had come west from Texas and Oklahoma and Arkansas and other places farther south to make money in the fields and in the shipyards of World War Two."

Amy Tan reflects on the fact that her mother, an immigrant
from China, has long realized the limitations of her
English, and she says, "it has continued to disturb me how
much my mother's English still limits people's perceptions
of her. I think my mother's English almost had an effect on
limiting my possibilities as well."

Author/artist Guillermo Gómez-Peña welcomes a borderless society and says we need to cease to characterize
immigration as a "unilateral 'problem'." Indeed, "it is time
for the facts: Anglos won't go back to Europe, and
Mexicans and Latinos (legal or illegal) won't go back to
Latin America. We are all here to stay."

Morrison explains that, historically, immigrants to the
United States have been encouraged to perceive African

Americans as their primary rivals for social, political, and economic power. In time, this practice "shaped by film, theater, advertising, the press, television and literature," reinforced race talk, "the mindless linguistic and cultural symbols which demonize American Blacks."

Poet/author Rose Anna Higashi has a profound aversion to mediocrity and believes that "Americans can do better than drivel dished up to us routinely on daytime T.V. and passed off as food and fashion." Indeed, she contends that "the mass media have corrupted American culture by robbing us of our ability to discern excellence, to make moral judgements, and to appreciate our own self-worth."

Author/poet Victor Martinez recalls how the Vietnam portrayed in the news media was quite different than the Vietnam he remembers. It's as if he and his compadres had never been there—so thorough is the lack of representation of Chicanos in the armed forces during the Vietnam War.

In August of 1997, the death of Diana, Princess of Wales, was a profoundly sad and sobering event. "Unfortunately, the incident provoked a good deal of indiscriminate condemnation of photographers who cover celebrities— whether these photographers call themselves paparazzi or not. From our perspective, much of the criticism was hasty—and sometimes shamelessly self-serving."

"To me, anyone who does what should be done is not a hero," says physically assisted voluntary euthanasia proponent, Jack

Kevorkian. He feels that, "as a physician," he is doing only what he should do and that is ethically caring for patients—in some cases terminally ill patients who are in extreme pain and wish to end their lives in dignity—not as vegetables supporting a medical profession which has become a commercial enterprise.

Leora Broydo questions whether "the fashion conscious have an ecoconscience. By dividing and classifying types of cloth and the fabric-finishing processes they go through, Broydo offers some interesting advice for those who want to wear "green" clothes.

Beat-poet, naturalist Gary Snyder responds to an article, "There's No Going Back to Nature, " written by Walter Truett Anderson (*Mother Jones*, September/October 1996) claiming people can—and sometime do—get in touch with their immediate environment. "With homebased knowledge, it is then within our power to get a glimpse of the planet as home."

Nature plays a prominent role in author, essayist, and film-maker Jeanne Wakatsuki Houston's short story. Indeed, her immediate, manmade environment, an internment camp during World War II, juxtaposed against a natural environment where "snow fell in sheets of lace, a translucent curtain swirling and fluttering with the wind."

According to Andrew Lam, there are some things far worse than the disastrous effects of warfare on a country. In Vietnam, the "Vietnamese Communist regime, long weakened by regionalism and corruption, can barely control the relentless destruction of the country's forests." Shrinking forests will lead to "soil erosion, dwindling mangrove groves, mudslides and weakening harvests." These, combined with heavy monsoons, will lead to an ecological cataclysm.

Garrison Keillor offers a "tongue-in-cheek" proposal, which would make Minnesota an extremely wealthy state by selling the water from its Great Lakes to the south. "Overnight Minnesota will be transformed from corn belt to money belt. Gigantic glass skyscrapers will rise in downtown St. Paul…and as the money floods in, Minnesotans will look for acquisitions: IBM, UPS, USX, GTE, Time Warner, Minnecorp, J. P. Olson, Chase Minnesota."

Kurt Vonnegut is by no means against technology and
computers. As he put it, "I work at home, and if I wanted
to, I could have a computer right by my bed, and I'd never
have to leave it. But I use a typewriter, and afterward
I mark up the pages with a pencil." Though he acknowledges
that technological advances can save time in doing something, he insists that "we are on earth to fart around, and
don't let anybody tell you any different."

Grace Mateo acknowledges that "Technology is a many-
splendored thing. Of its many innovations that have affected our lives, the development of cyberspace is arguably the
most far reaching." However, she also realizes that "the
ability to cyberspace to convey information in 'real time'
has become a boon and a curse."

"At first, the ridiculous efforts of the students to emulate
robots were merely amusing and perhaps a little irritating.

Young people, calling themselves 'robotniks,' began to talk about themselves as they would normally talk about cybernetic systems: 'This book fed me approximately so many units of new information . . . ' "

Reporter Joshua Quittner explains that "Every time this country extrudes any significant bit of evil at its fringes, my editors dispatch me to the Internet to look for its source." However, every time he "dutifully" logs on and goes hunting for information, he rarely locates "anything more than the usual Internet chatter."

In the past, sports fans seldom attracted attention unless they got violent, "hurling missiles at 'enemy' players, rushing the field, brawling after the game. But in the last three decades, in a trend almost unnoticed by sports commentators and sociologists, fans have been expressing themselves in more colorful and peaceful ways, potentially even upstaging the games themselves." Nonetheless, whether people wear absurd hats, paint themselves team colors, or cheer on players, Barbara Ehrenreich insists that the antics of today's sports fans hearken back to older social traditions.

Pulitzer Prize-winning author/humorist Dave Barry satirizes "sports," a very big part of American culture—especially for men. "What inner force" pushed the first athlete? Barry says, "Your guess is as good as mine. Better, probably, because you haven't had four beers. All I know is whatever the reason, Mankind is still nuts about sports."

"As an extreme sport, snowboarders can begin to shun the safety of the baggy-pant uniform. Likewise, riders can shun the comfort of our culture's 'normal' behavior—moving beyond our inherited aggression, competition and individualism." Martha Henning, a "gray on a tray," should know; she defies the idea that snowboarders must be "young, daring, and strong."

Amusement parks—what are they, and how do we respond to them going into the 21st century? Journalist T. Trent Gegax reflects that "after *Jurassic Park*, ordinary amusement parks looked so . . . ordinary. But fear not, adrenaline junkies: at the total-immersion theme parks of the future, guests will get to play pulse-quickening roles."

Extremism pervades all aspects of popular culture today from fashions to sports, hairstyles to political slogans, television programs to stand-up comedians. Yet "the very success of the word extreme spells its doom" because what once meant the "total commitment of a samurai warrior"

9. Television   254

Richard Zoglin rings an alarm: "If it frightens you to think of how much TV has affected out cultural habits in just a few decades, then get ready for another zap to your system. In the future, what we know as TV will have been transmogrified from a box in the corner into a ubiquitous, wall-to-wall bath of infotainment."

Former talk-show host Jane Whitney explains how and why she became disgusted with the exploitive nature of most popular talk-show formats. She points out: "Increasingly, the audience and I saw the same guest through different lenses. They saw entertainment—I saw exhibitionism . . . "

"TBS stands officially for Turner Broadcasting System, but Testosterone Broadcasting System would be more to the point. Superstation, which TBS bills as its flagship, and which reaches (according to its publicity) 81 million households, markets itself as 'the TV haven for the Regular Guy.' "

Oscar Hijuelos reminisces about an event that will forever be etched in his memory: "When I heard the opening strains of the *I Love Lucy* show I got excited because I knew she was referring to an item of eternity, that episode in which my dead father and my Uncle Cesar had appeared, playing Ricky Ricardo's singing cousins, fresh off the farm in Oriente Province, Cuba, and north in New York for an engagement at Ricky's nightclub, the Tropicana."

Legendary cartoonist of such counterculture comics as *Mr. Natural* and *Zap Comix*, Crumb offers a look at street

How do movie poster artists know what to design in order
to attract motion picture audiences? "How do movie studios come up with designs for the posters they use to lure
us into theaters?" An American Institute of Graphic Arts
member claims, "Film advertisers will tell you that every
poster has got to have a gun or a naked woman on it—
period." However, it's not that simple.

Stanley Crouch's essay focuses on the portrayal of African
Americans in motion pictures, from early depictions of
black Americans on film as minstrels to black exploitation
films of the 1970s. All in all, he notes the "absence of
human complexity—regardless of race in Hollywood
films"—because quality film writing and production tend
to be secondary to "big business" at the box office.

According to Jessica Yellin, "With the demise of the Soviet
Union, Hollywood found itself out in the cold with no one
to hate. Now, all of a sudden, it's warmed up to a new crop
of bad guys—ranging from giant bugs to supernovas."

Comparing his childhood ambitions and adult achievements in the film business, Martin Scorsese states, "The
quiet concentration and sense of fulfillment I felt drawing
my own movies as a child I can now find only in the editing room. It's where you deal with the very essence of
film."

As Linda Hogan reflects on her participation in a spiritual
healing ceremony—a Native American sweat lodge—
she explains its components, its ritual procedures, and its

ultimate purpose. The ceremony puts people "back together by restructuring the human mind." In doing so, Hogan says that "we bring together the fragments of our lives in a sacred act of renewal, and we reestablish our connections with others."

Traditionally, the ancient practice of mehendi—henna painting—decorated a bride's "hands and feet in order to beautify her, but most importantly, at a marriage ceremony, mehendi is used to bring happiness to the bride and her future family." In the United State, such body art became mainstream when Madonna started decorating herself with intricate henna patterns.

Have you ever considered body piercing or wondered about the potential health risks involved in doing so? Soppie Phipps, a fan of body piercing, once had many such questions, but after researching body beautification, she concludes that as long as piercings are "carried out under the correct conditions, the world is your oyster—the only limit is your imagination."

Nichole Overman, a student writer, examines how self-images of women are influenced by popular culture, especially the media, even going so far as to get breast implants and other types of plastic surgery that are sometimes dangerous.

Joe Woodward examines the growth of "so called body arts" in North America and expands his discussion to a comparison of cosmetic mutilation worldwide. He further suggests that the current popularity of body piercing,

Rhetorical Contents

I. Argumentation and Persuasion

II. Cause and Effect

III. Comparison and Contrast

IV. Definition

V. Description

VI. Division and Classification

VII. Exposition (Combined Strategies)

VIII. Fiction and Poetry

XII. Process Analysis

Part One

Communication Skills: Reading and Writing

The Reading/Studying Process

Reading Essays

Good writers are good readers.

Learning to get inside a piece of writing, to inhabit it like a small and interesting house, is the first act of a skillful reader. When you are having trouble getting interested in something you are reading, it's a little like standing outside a house where a party is going on. You have the vague sense that something exciting might be happening in there, but you are not really part of it. You can see from the window that small groups of people are clustered together in animated conversations, some earnest, some mostly joking around. You wonder, what are they talking about? What do these people find so stimulating?

When you open a book, you are answering an invitation to a social engagement, a party for the mind that has been going on for over three thousand years. Everyone is invited. The invitation says: What are you waiting for? This is a party that invites you to have conversations with some of the most stimulating people this planet has produced so far. If you are looking for quick wit, fantastic stories, philosophical arguments, or just a little pleasant diversion, these are the people to get to know. Writers will say anything. Pick up a magazine, a newspaper, or a best-selling novel at any supermarket, bookstore, or library and flip through the pages, observing articles, stories, and other printed material. You may find yourself in a variety of worlds because writers have a special talent: They create reality with words. Often they do their work in solitude, but they do not lock their ideas away in a secret diary. They crave an audience. Deep down, they all really want to be the life of the party. They want to hold your attention. They want to please you with words, to get you to think, to imagine, to remember, to become one of *their* readers.

The essays in this anthology are varied. Some will relate familiar ideas and experiences; others may seem strange and challenging. Some will make you nod in agreement; some will make you want to argue with the writer. Your job as a reader is to give the writer a fair hearing and to keep an open mind, but, ultimately, you must evaluate the quality of the ideas and the form of the writing itself.

Active Reading Tips

To keep your mind actively engaged with the material when you are reading, you should choose a time and place to read when you can concentrate and read the whole essay straight through. Reading an essay is different from watching a television program or a movie. Like running uphill, it takes more energy and at first may seem exhausting. You may try reading the essay straight through once and fairly quickly just to get the feel for it as a whole piece; then read it a second time and mark it and study it.

Try to do your reading as early in the day as possible.   If you wait until after dinner, after work, or after the kids are put to bed, you simply may not have the energy left for this kind of mental work. Try not to underestimate how difficult the reading is; even a short essay can be very demanding of your attention. Also, you should look up any word that is new to you and even those that are familiar but not completely clear in your own mind. Good writers try to choose exactly the right words, and you have to be just as exact in your understanding of them.

Have a definite plan for where and when you plan to do your reading.
Seek solitude and quiet. If you find it difficult to locate such a place, you might try using earplugs that you can get at most drugstores to block out distracting noise. As much as possible, give the reading your complete, undivided attention. Some people say they study better with the TV or headphones on. This is mostly just *rationalizing* and really just an elaborate way of kidding yourself. Give solitary, quiet reading a chance. Find a quiet place in the library away from the foot traffic and give your mind a chance to focus on one thing at a time.

You might also write down some of your impressions of the essay while you are reading it.   Whatever ideas, feelings, memories, associations, or questions pass through your mind while you are reading are relevant to your response. Your instructors are not looking for a certain response or a right answer; they do not expect you to have exactly the same insight into readings that they have. This is why discussion is so important. By comparing our various responses, we can get some sense of who we are in relation to the reading and to each other.

It is important to understand what you read, but you must go beyond this. You need to consider what the implications are, what could have been said but wasn't, what the writer's assumptions are, where there are gaps in the reasoning or where evidence has or hasn't been provided, how the essay is organized, how it manages to communicate.

When asked to read an essay, actively involve yourself in the reading process—that is:

Scan the reading, noting titles, subtitles, and headings (they are signals).

Circle unfamiliar words and references; look up their meanings and jot them down in the margins for reference.

Read the essay carefully and underline key passages that are either particularly important points or points that you would like to clarify or dispute.

Jot down notes in the margins of your text—impressions and questions about the piece you are reading.

Take the reading seriously and don't dismiss it before thinking about it. You should have something to say about what you have read.

Make connections between the issues you read about and real-life situations.

Overall, come to class prepared to say something about what you've read. Think of yourself as an active participant in the class.

A Sample Annotated Reading

Now, take a look at some active reading strategies in action. Observe how Michael, a student, took strategies of active reading to heart and exhaustively marked Stewart Brand's "We Owe It All to the Hippies," an essay suggesting that people "forget the war protests, even long hair. The real legacy of the sixties generation is the computer revolution."

We Owe It All to the Hippies

Stewart Brand

Author STEWART BRAND created the *Whole Earth Catalog* and co-founded the Hackers Conference and the WELL teleconference system. His books include *How Buildings Learn: What Happens after They're Built* and *The Clock of the Long Now.* The following essay appeared in the Spring 1995 Special Issue of *TIME* magazine.

The web

Newcomers to the Internet are often startled to discover themselves not so much in some soulless colony of technocrats as in a kind of cultural Brigadoon—a flowering remnant of the '60s, when hippie communalism and libertarian politics formed the roots of the modern cyber-revolution. At the time, it all seemed dangerously anarchic (and still does to many), but the counterculture's scorn for centralized authority provided the philosophical foundations of not only the leaderless Internet, but also the entire personal-computer revolution.

We—the generation of the '60s—were inspired by the "bards and hot-gospellers of technology," as businessman historian Peter Drucker described media maven Marshall McLuhan and technophile Buckminister Fuller. And we bought enthusiastically into the exotic technologies of the '60s, such as Fuller's geodesic domes and psychoactive drugs like L.S.D. We learned from them, but ultimately they turned out to be blind alleys. Most of our generation scorned

[Handwritten margin notes:]

One who follows freedom of will instead of necessity

Belief that a country or town should be self-governed

State of lawlessness

A curious claim... why should I believe it?

Geometric shapes fit together to form an organic dome

Mind Expansion?

the roots of cyber-punk fiction?

computers as the embodiment of centralized control. But a tiny contingent—later called "hackers"—embraced computers and set about transforming them into tools of liberation. That turned out to be the true royal road to the future.

to incite or appeal by argument, especially good deeds

"Ask not what your country can do for you. Do it yourself," we said, happily perverting J.F.K.'s Inaugural exhortation. Our ethic of self-reliance came partly from science fiction. We all read Robert Heinlein's epic *Stranger in a Strange Land* as well as his libertarian screed-novel, *The Moon is a Harsh Mistress.* Hippies and nerds alike reveled in Heinlein's contempt for centralized authority. To this day, computer scientists and technicians are almost universally science-fiction fans. And ever since the 1950s, for reasons that are unclear to me, science fiction has been almost universally libertarian in outlook.

is this true?

As Steve Levy chronicled in his 1984 book, *Hackers: Heroes of the Computer Revolution,* there were three generations of youthful computer programmers who deliberately led the rest of civilization away from the centralized mainframe computers and their predominant sponsor, IBM. "The Hacker Ethic," articulated by Levy, offered a distinctly countercultural set of tenets. Among them:

(Power to the People?)

"Access to computers should be unlimited and total."

"All information should be free."

"Mistrust authority—promote decentralization."

definitely '60s philosophy

"You can create art and beauty on a computer."

"Computers can change your life for the better."

a political declaration indicating measures or intentions ← Nobody had written these down in manifestoes before; it was just the way hackers behaved and talked while shaping the leading edge of computer technology.

In the 1960s and early '70s, the first generation | *1st generation of hackers* of hackers emerged in university computer-science departments. They transformed *Big Computers* ← mainframes into virtual personal computers, using a technique called time sharing that provided widespread access to computers. Then in the late | *2nd generation of hackers* '70s, the second generation invented and manufactured the personal computer. These non-academic hackers were hard-core counter-culture types—like Steve Jobs, a Beatle-haired hippie who had dropped out of Reed College, and Steve Wozniak, a Hewlett-Packard engineer. Before their success with Apple, both Steves developed and sold "blue boxes," outlaw devices for making free phone calls. Their contemporary and early collaborator, Lee Felsenstein, who designed the first portable computer, known as the Osborne 1, was a New Left radical who wrote for the renowned underground paper the *Berkeley Barb*.

Chant ← As they followed the mantra "Turn on, tune in and drop out," college students of the '60s also dropped academia's traditional disdain for business. "Do your own thing" easily translated into "Start your own business." Reviled by the broader social establishment, hippies found ready acceptance in the world of small business.

Was getting into the world of small business really that easy?

They brought an honesty and a dedication to service that was attractive to vendors and customers alike. Success in business made them disinclined to "grow out of" their counterculture values, and it made a number of them wealthy and powerful at a young age.

3rd generation of hackers

The third generation of revolutionaries, the software hackers of the early '80s, created the application, education, and entertainment programs for personal computers. Typical was Mitch Kapor, a former transcendental-meditation teacher, who gave us the spreadsheet program Lotus 1-2-3, which insured the success of IBM's Apple-imitating PC. Like most computer pioneers, Kapor is still active. His Electronic Frontier Foundation, which he co-founded with a lyricist for the Grateful Dead, lobbies successfully in Washington for civil rights in cyberspace.

Transcendentalism: doctrine that knowledge is outside experience

In the years since Levy's book, a fourth generation of revolutionaries has come to power. Still abiding by the Hacker Ethic, these tens of thousands of netheads have created myriad computer bulletin boards and a nonhierarchical linking system called Usenet. At the same time, they have transformed the Defense Department–sponsored ARPAnet into what has become the global digital epidemic known as the Internet. The average age of today's Internet users,

4th generation of hackers

Play on the word "deadhead"

(interesting reference to 3rd & 4th generation of hackers as "revolutionaries")

who number in the tens of millions, is about 30
years. Just as personal computers transformed the
'80s, this latest generation knows that the Net is
going to transform the '90s. With the same ethic
that has guided previous generations, today's
users are leading the way with tools created
initially as "freeware" or "shareware," available to
anyone who wants them.

Of course, not everyone on the electronic
frontier identifies with the counter-cultural roots of
the '60s. One would hardly call Nicholas
Negroponte, the patrician head of M.I.T.'s Medical
Lab, or Microsoft magnate Bill Gates "hippies." Yet
creative forces continue to emanate from that
period. Virtual reality—computerized sensory
immersion—was named, largely inspired and
partly equipped by Jaron Lanier, who grew up in
a geodesic dome in New Mexico, once played
clarinet in the New York City subway and still
sports dread-locks halfway down his back. The
latest generation of supercomputers, utilizing
massive parallel processing, was invented,
developed and manufactured by Danny Hillis, a
genial longhair who set out to build "a machine
that could be proud of us." Public-key encryption,
which can ensure unbreakable privacy for anyone,
is the brainchild of Whitfield Diffie, a lifelong
peacenik and privacy advocate who declared in a
recent interview, "I have always believed the
thesis that one's politics and the character of one's
intellectual work are inseparable."

Our generation proved in cyberspace that where self-reliance leads, resilience follows, and where generosity leads, prosperity follows. If that dynamic continues, and everything so far suggests that it will, then the information age will bear the distinctive mark of the countercultural '60s well into the new millennium.

is this the logic of a "hippie" or a "yuppie"?

Reading Aloud

What has reading aloud got to do with basic writing? Plenty. Reading aloud engages multiple senses in the reading process, most notably, listening, speaking, and thinking in addition to viewing (the standard mode of reading). "We read to write, and we write to be read." Part of reading includes processing information, assessing it, and coming to an understanding on a topic or an issue. Reading aloud can clarify relationships between words, phrases, sentences, and entire concepts.

The following essay by Ursula K. Le Guin, "Read My Lips: On the Joys—and the Necessity—of Reading Aloud," touches on some of the advantages of reading works aloud, encouraging writers to read their own work and the work of others aloud to appreciate the richness of the written language. Le Guin's language-oriented essay also offers an opportunity to practice several of the active reading strategies discussed earlier in this chapter, including: (1) scanning the reading, (2) noting titles, subtitles, and headings, (3) circling unfamiliar words or references, (4) reading material carefully, (5) underlining key words and phrases, (6) jotting down notes—both observations and questions, and (7) making connections between issues and real-life situations.

Exercise #1:   Go through "Read My Lips: On the Joys—and the Necessity—of Reading Aloud," applying every active reading strategy mentioned above as well as any active reading technique you have personally devised. (Refer to Stewart Brand's essay, "We Owe It All to the Hippies," for a model annotated essay.) Compare your annotated essay to what others did in class.

Exercise #2:   Reread Le Guin's essay aloud, either individually or in groups. What information "jumps out" at you? Does Le Guin say anything that makes more sense when spoken? How? Why?

Read My Lips: On the Joys—and the Necessity—of Reading Aloud

Ursula K. Le Guin

A native of Berkeley and current resident of Portland, Oregon, URSULA K. LE GUIN is the author of over thirty books. She received her Bachelor of Arts degree from Radcliffe and her Master of Arts degree from Columbia University; then, on a Fulbright Scholarship, she moved to Paris, France, where she met and married her future husband, Charles Le Guin, a historian. After publishing *Rocannon's World* (1964), Le Guin wrote a succession of books for all age groups. She became particularly well known for her science fiction and fantasy stories. Some of her science fiction novels include *Planet of Exile* (1966), *City of Illusions* (1967), *The Left Hand of Darkness* (1969), *The Dispossessed* (1974), *Very Far from Anywhere Else* (1976), and *The Water Is Wide* (1976). Her works of fantasy include *A Wizard of Earthsea* (1968), *The Tombs of Atuan* (1972), *The Farthest Shore* (1972), *Malafrena* (1979), *The Beginning Place* (1980), and *Always Coming Home* (1985). Le Guin also wrote three volumes of short fiction: *The Wind's Twelve Quarters* (1975), *Orsinian Tales* (1976), and *The Compass Rose* (1982). *The Language of the Night: Essays on Fantasy and Science Fiction* (1979)—the source of the following essay—and *Dancing on the Edge of the World: Thoughts on Words, Women, and Places* (1989) represent her two collections of essays. Le Guin originally presented this essay as a lecture for Composers Inc. on the campus of the University of California at Berkeley in the fall of 1986. It appeared in its present form in the July/August 1989 edition of the *Utne Reader.*

1   The printed word is reproducible. You can type the word surprise or print it in type or on a computer screen or printout, and it's the same word reproduced. But if you say "sunrise" and then I say "sunrise," yes, it's the same word we're saying, but we can't speak of reproduction, only of repeating, a very different matter. It matters who said it. Speech is an event. Events aren't reproducible. To say that the letters *o* and *m* "make" the word *om* is to confuse sign and event, like mistaking a wristwatch for the rotation of the planet. The word *om* is a sound, an event: it "takes" time to say it; its saying "makes" time. The instrument of that sound is the breath, which we breathe over and over, by way of being alive. Indeed the sound can be reproduced mechanically, but then it has ceased to be, as we say, live. It's not the event, but a shadow of it.

2   Writing of any kind fixes the word outside of time, and silences it. The written word is a shadow. Shadows are silent. The reader breathes back life into that unmortality, and maybe noise into that silence.

3   People used to be aware that the written word was the visible sign of an audible sign, and they read aloud—they put their breath into it. Apparently if the Romans saw somebody sitting reading silently to himself they nudged each other and sniggered. Abelard and Aquinas moved their lips while they read, like louts with comic books. In a Chinese library you couldn't hear yourself think, any more than you can in Chinese opera.

4   So long as literacy was guarded by a male elite as its empowering privilege, most people knew text as event. What we call literature was recitation: the speaking and hearing, by live people gathered together, of a more or less fixed narrative or other formal structure, using repetition, conventional phrases, and a greater or lesser amount of improvisation. That's the *Odyssey,* the *Bhagavad-Gita,* the *Torah,* the *Edda,* all myths, all epics, all folktales, the entire literature of North America, South America, and much of Africa before the white conquests, and still the literature of many cultures and subcultures from New Guinea to the slum streets.

5   We call the art of language, language as an art, "writing." I'm a writer, right? Literature literally means letters, the alphabet. The oral text, verbal art as event, as performance, has been devalued as primitive, a "lower" form, discarded, except by babies, the blind, and people who come to hear people give lectures.

6   What, in fact, are we doing here—me lecturing, you listening? Something ever so ethnic. We're indulging in orality. It isn't illegal, but it's pretty kinky. It's disputable because oral text is held to be "inferior" to written—and written really now means printed. We value the power of print, which is its infinite reproducibility. Print is viral. The model of modern Western civilization is the virus: the pure bit of information which turns its environment into endless reproductions of itself.

7   I'm not complaining, you know. If it weren't for writing, for books, how could I be a novelist married to a historian? Written language is the greatest single technology of the storage and dissemination of knowledge, which is the primary act of human culture. It gives us all the libraries full of books of science, reference, fact, theory, thought. It gives us newspapers, journals. It gives us interoffice memos, catalogs of obscure forms of potholder and electric tempeh shredder, and the reports of federal committees on deforestation printed on paper that used to be a forest. That's how it is—we're literate. And we're word processors now too, since information theory and the computer are hooked up together. That's dandy. But why do we lock ourselves into one mode? Why either/or? We aren't binary. Why have we replaced oral text with written? Isn't there room for both? Spoken text doesn't even take storage room: It's self-recycling and does not require wood pulp. Why have we abandoned and despised the interesting things that happen when the word behaves like music and the author is not just "a writer" but the player of the instrument of language?

8   Where have I *heard* language as art? In some, some few speeches—Martin Luther King, Jr. . . . In some well-told ghost stories at the campfire, and some really funny dirty jokes, and from my mother at 80 telling us her experience in the 1906 earthquake when she was nine. From comedians with a great text, like Bill Cosby's *Chickenheart,* or Anna Russell's version of *The Ring,* aesthetically far superior to

Wagner's. From poets reading, live or on tape, and writers performing—prose pros, you might call them. But from amateurs too. People reading aloud to each other. And here's a point I've been aiming at: If you can read silently you can read aloud. It takes practice, sure, but it's like playing the guitar: You don't have to be Doc Watson; you can get and give pleasure just pickin'. And a second point: A lot of the stuff we were taught to read silently—Jane. You are moving your lips!—reads better out loud.

9   Reading aloud is of course the basic text of a kid's book. If you apply it to literary works written for adults reading in the silent-perusal mode—that is, in prose—the results can be positively, or negatively, surprising. An example: the present-tense narrative so much in vogue, particularly in "minimalist" fiction, seems more casual and more immediate than the conventional narrative past-tense; but read aloud, it sounds curiously stilted and artificial; its ultimate effect of distancing the text from the reader becomes clear. Another example: Last spring after reading Jane Austen's *Persuasion* to each other, my partner and I decided tentatively and unhopefully to have a bash at Virginia Woolf's *To the Lighthouse*. When Austen wrote, people still read aloud a great deal, and she clearly heard her text and suited its cadences to the voice; but [with] Woolf, so cerebral and subtle . . . , we found our only problem was that our reading got impeded by tears, shouts of delight, and other manifestations of intellectual exhilaration and uncontrollable emotion. I will never read Virginia Woolf silently again, if I can help it; you miss half of what she was doing.

Active reading techniques engage the senses and reinforce comprehension. Reading aloud helps a reader to recollect and sort out facts and details. The act of reading itself requires more concentration, and simply hearing the words spoken out loud increases retention and memory. Readers are then better able to reflect upon the relationships between major and minor points of a work. Recollection is the key to clarification and comprehension of a work as a whole. Beyond reading aloud, writing summaries and paraphrases can often put material into a new light and offer you, the writer, a valuable exercise in rewording what you understand based on what you have read.

Writing Summaries of Readings

Writing a summary forces you to condense what you've read into some coherent, short form. It is a very helpful way to make sure you have understood what you've read and that you haven't forgotten any of the main points. It will also improve your memory of what you've read. Often our first impressions of a piece of writing, no matter how powerful or favorable, fade rather rapidly and sometimes disappear altogether in sleep. The more you write about what you've read, the greater the impression the reading leaves on your mind and memory. All professional writers keep notes on what they've read. These notes help reduce the complexity of an essay to manageable mental impressions that you can move around in your own mind and memory. After all, it is impossible to remember every single word of what you have read, so you have to *decide* what it is you want to take away from it and remember.

Summarizing is really a matter of choosing the significant points and arranging them in a way that will bring back as much of the original as possible without having to reread the whole thing. This is especially handy when it comes to writing papers of your own. The summaries can remind you of what you have read and act as points of departure for developing your own ideas. As a general rule of thumb you might go through an essay or any other written text, and then, taking a paragraph or two at a time, state the author's major point without getting tangled up in details. A summary is an overview—not a detailed outline in prose form. The same principle applies to entire books; take a chapter at a time, imitating the structure or flow of information of the original. Strive to be accurate. Again, a summary places another's ideas in a condensed form; it does not require interpretation.

In the following summary of Stewart Brand's annotated essay, "We Owe It All to the Hippies," note how Jarrett, a student, summarizes the basic thrust of the essay:

Sample Summary

The counterculture of the 1960s introduced a lifestyle into mainstream American life that was not merely based on protest; the so-called 'hippies' also represented a libertarian scorn for centralized authority and control that provided the philosophical foundation for the personal computer revolution. Though LSD and geodesic domes turned out to be "blind alleys," the computer revolution has proven to be a truly successful movement, a road to the future. This new ethic—often reflected in works of science fiction—is based on self-reliance, the old American desire to "do it yourself." According to Brand, there were four generations of revolutionaries—hackers who were responsible for promoting and developing computers, software, and the Internet. The first generation of hackers came from computer-science departments in universities in the late sixties and early seventies, and were responsible for making big mainframe computers into "virtual personal computers" through "timesharing"; the second generation of hackers "invented and manufactured" personal computers; the third generation of revolutionary hackers was responsible for developing

software packages that provided entertainment and
education; the fourth generation has provided the creative
energy that has made the Internet a tool for "leaderless"
personal and global communication. More innovations are on
the way—virtual reality, supercomputers, public-key
encryption. Brand concludes that an ethic based on the
idea that "where self-reliance leads, resilience follows,
and where generosity leads, prosperity follows" will
continue to support the information age into the next
millennium.

Although by strict definition, a summary does not include editorial comments or student opinions, it is a good idea to place them down on paper *after you write your summary.* Why? Thoughts and ideas generated from readings—sharp and fresh in your mind and accessible on paper—may form the basis of a future essay. To ensure clarity, skip a line or so between (1) the formal summary and (2) your opinions and insights. Your opinions are a by-product of a summary rather than the actual summary itself. For example, after writing the above summary, Jarrett skipped two lines and wrote:

I have always been what I considered knowledgeable about
computers, but never in my life did I think of the
computer revolution as a counterculture movement. Although
intrigued, I cannot help but feel that the author is
asking me to suspend any suspicions I may have about the
truth of his conclusions and just believe his analysis.

Read the following essay, "On My Own Terms," by Terry McMillan, highlighting its key points with a pen or marker. Then, read its summary. Note how the student writer stays focused on main points in order to present the big picture when she summarizes McMillan's essay. Also, compare the overall length of McMillan's essay to the student's summary of it.

On My Own Terms

Terry McMillan

1   I didn't grow up with any ambitions or fantasies of one day being a writer. It wasn't some carefully calculated or planned goal I had set for myself. As a matter of fact, it was much more organic than that. When I was 19, some guy—whose name I can't

remember—broke my heart and my reaction surfaced in the form of a poem. No one was more shocked than I at those words on that yellow pad, but there they were. I had written them, and they were honest. I didn't even know how hurt I was until read it. I remember placing that piece of paper on the kitchen table and feeling a sense of relief that I had given my heart permission to scream.

2   That's how it started. More poems came. Tacky, corny, phony, maudlin, sophomoric poems. During the seventies, while at the University of California, Berkeley, I felt personally affected by much of the sociopolitical and racial activity that was going on. No one asked me for my opinions, but I had many of them, and I had to let them out. I started writing editorials for our college newspaper. I was not solving the world's problems, but I was acknowledging them. This is when I discovered that writing had started to become an outlet, a place where I could blow off steam and not feel so helpless. I often felt a little better afterward because, in most cases, I didn't know exactly how I felt until I had written it down.

3   What bothered me then—and still does today—was injustices of any kind. I've always had a romantic notion about life, that it was meant to be good; that we have to find our own way; that God puts obstacles in our path to test us, to see what we're made of, to make us pay attention and take notice. If we pass these series of tests we will experience joy, love, a sense of accomplishment, spiritual enlightenment, perhaps even peace.

4   But sometimes things get ugly. How we treat each other. What we care about. Our priorities. I hate pain. I hate feeling hurt, disappointed, brokenhearted. And I take it personally when people I care about and love have to go through it too. It irks me no end when I think I can see the whys and how-comes. In a fantasy world, all I'd have to do is twitch my nose or snap my fingers and I could make it all right. But in this real world, I found out that I could create real, lifelike worlds where Black people would encounter some of these injustices and undergo a variety of tests. I could make these characters stronger, more resilient, so that they could at least acknowledge and face some of their problems— along with their strengths and weakness—and figure out what steps to take to tackle them.

5   I believe this is why most artists create the work that we do: We want to see more beauty. More balance. We want everything to be all right. Shoot, I want to be all right. I want my friends and family members to be all right. Too often we're not. We all know that life is hard. But as artists, what drives us, what propels us, is the desire to make our lives run more smoothly, with less angst, fewer voids and a minimum of gray.

6   A lot of folks think you get a notion to write a book and then you mosey on over to the computer and pow! In a matter of weeks or months you've written the megabook and are on your way to the top. It didn't happen that way. First of all, let's rewind the tape back to 1985 when I had to teach myself how to juggle. I had a nine-month-old baby and a full-time job and had just sold a novel that needed to be rewritten. How was I going to do it? I couldn't quit my job, that was for sure.

Couldn't give my son away, either. I decided that I had to get up a little earlier and write as much as I could in the time that I had. I discovered what the world was like at 5:00 A.M. Quiet. Still. Dark. I would write for two hours, then pack Solomon into his stroller, push him to the babysitter's by 8:00, get on the subway, edit in red ink as the train shook, and revise during my lunch hour and on the way home.

7   I did this for nine months until the book was finished. It was called Mama. What I learned from that experience was very simple: You can make time to do anything you really want to do. I also discovered that, besides men, writing was the one thing I truly felt passionate about. After a while I didn't even need an alarm clock to get up. Some mornings, when I was geeked about what I might be in for the next day on the job, I would find myself at my typewriter as early as 4:00.

8   I never thought I could make a clock stop based on a story I'd written. But there comes a time in your life when you have to take yourself seriously. I could've gotten a regular job (and I did, as a word processor), and I could've worked for a television station (I got an offer), and I probably could've made "good" money. But my mother taught me to stick my neck out and not listen to what other folks told me to do. Always trust your instincts. Listen to your heart, your gut. I was warned that I'd starve writing fiction. Have no illusions about folks reading your books, I was told, let alone buying them. Get your degree because if all else fails, you can always teach. Well, I got my degree. And I taught. It was not exciting for me.

9   It never mattered whether any of my books would make the best-seller list. My stories and the people that inhabited them were of foremost importance to me. I cared about them, loved them, worried about them. When I finished Mama, I understood what my mother had gone through raising five kids. When I finished Disappearing Acts, I understood better how hard it is to love somebody under adverse conditions. Waiting to Exhale helped me get stronger as a woman living on my own. The fact that others ended up identifying with and, to some extent, appreciating these stories has been a great source of satisfaction. But if only 10,000 folks had read them, instead of millions, I'd still feel the same sense of gratification, because I didn't write these stories for millions of people I don't know. I wrote them because I needed to write them. Had to.

10   God has blessed me a million times over. He gave me the courage to stop drugging, 13 years ago, and drinking, 12 years ago. Last year I lost the most important person in my life: my mama. Recently, my best friend in the world died. I didn't think I could handle the grief, the empty feeling of loss, because I wasn't prepared for either of them to leave. But I've had to learn to deal with their absence even though it hurts, and I don't like it.

11   I've learned to cope with uncomfortable things in a number of different ways. One way is simply to face them, no matter how much uneasiness it may cause. I've also finally started exercising and found out that it's not all that bad. And last, my computer beckons when I need to make sense of it all. I don't have to have the answers. I'm just grateful that the questions continue to pop up. Finding resolutions is the best part. And it usually takes a while.

Summary: "On My Own Terms"

Terry McMillan did not start out to be a writer, but in college she discovered that writing about her personal frustrations gave her an outlet for her pent-up feelings. Later, writing for a college newspaper, she began to express herself about racial and political issues. She was inspired by her desire to meet life's challenges and by her perception of injustice and the pain it causes. She wanted to write stories that would show how Black people especially deal with setbacks in the real world—she wanted to show both their strengths and weaknesses. Like other artists, she was motivated by a desire to make the world a little better place to be. She learned that writing takes dedication and self-discipline. While working full-time and raising her small son, she revised her first novel by getting up at 5:00 A.M. and writing for two hours a day. Despite the pessimism from others about the chances of writing a best-seller, McMillan followed her gut feelings, her passion for writing. She wasn't writing just to sell books; she wrote because she had to. Her books were stories she wanted to tell. She has had financial success and has experienced grief at the loss of her mother, but, come what may, she returns still to her computer to write, to try and make sense of it all.

Paraphrasing Readings

When you paraphrase someone else's work, you put what another person has written into your own words. Paraphrasing quoted material or complex thoughts from another's writing—acknowledging your sources—can be beneficial in your own work. First, your composition will sound like it was written by a single person with a unified voice rather than a patchwork quilt of your own insights and quotes by another author. Second, since you will be somewhat an authority on your writing topic, you will be able to place difficult words and concepts into language anyone can understand; that is, you will provide clarity and coherence to information. Compare the quote below from Jane Whitney's essay, "When Talk Gets Too Cheap," to Allen Garner's paraphrase of it:

Quotation

Increasingly the audience and I saw the guests through different lenses.
They saw entertainment; I saw exhibitionism—albeit committed by

consenting adults. It was worse when children were hauled into the fray. Whenever possible, youngsters and especially infants were used to hook the viewer by upping the emotional ante. On one show, an eight-year-old boy listened wide-eyed as his aunt announced that he had been abandoned by his mother because she didn't want him. On another, as a bitter ex-wife delivered a diatribe about her daughters' "dead beat dad," the camera dollied in for close-ups of the girls in tears.

```
                  Paraphrase of quotation
Jane Whitney observes that she began to see her guests on
her talk show as people who seem to enjoy revealing tragic
and unpleasant aspects of their personal lives in public,
but her audience continued to see her guests as
entertainment. Whitney was especially disturbed by her
guests' willingness to drive their own children to tears
in order to put on a good show, whether it was finding out
that they were unwanted or the children of a "dead beat."
```

Unlike a summary, a paraphrase is generally around the same length as the original work, and it should include the major points as well as details. To put it another way, a paraphrase does not attempt to compress another person's thoughts so much as to restate them clearly and effectively. However, merely putting what someone else has written in your own words does not make it "yours." That's why if you paraphrase someone else's ideas, you must give credit to the author. In an actual essay, for instance, you might preface the paraphrase with something like:

"According to Elanye Rapping . . . ,"

"Guillermo Gómez-Peña explains that . . . ,"

"Carol Squire argues . . . ,"

"Kori Quintana asserts . . . ,"

"As Steve Levy chronicled . . . ,"

"As Joel Cohen so aptly put it . . . ,"

The following two exercises based on Ursula K. Le Guin's essay, "Read My Lips: On the Joys—and the Necessity—of Reading Aloud," and Stewart Brand's essay, "We Owe It All to the Hippies," will provide you with some practice in summarizing and paraphrasing someone else's work.

Exercise #1:   Now that you have actively read and marked up "Read My Lips: On the Joys—and the Necessity—of Reading Aloud," review your annotations and determine the major idea of Le Guin's essay; then, write a summary of it.

Exercise #2:   Paraphrase a paragraph or so of Stewart Brand's essay. When were you able to "use your own words" most freely? When did you feel compelled to use the words or examples that Brand used in his essay? What might your answers suggest about the nature of a paraphrase? Compare your conclusions to those of your classmates.

Working in Groups: The Collaborative Approach

Although reading, writing, and thinking are often solitary activities, the purpose of all these activities is to communicate. Group work, therefore, represents a social activity. It informs, stimulates, enlightens, and activates other people. Professional writers are often solitary and *gregarious* by turns. That is, they spend time alone, but they also spend time discussing their ideas with others who share their interests or concerns. Most books, regardless of subject matter, have an acknowledgment page at the beginning where the author thanks his or her friends and acquaintances who have been kind enough to listen, talk, and read along with the writer in the process of producing a finished work. Authors choose the friends and colleagues whose opinions they value to respond to their writing, to say what they think and offer suggestions for revision.

In a class there isn't enough time to wait for these editorial groups to develop over a long period of time, so we form them on a more short-term basis. This means you will be working with people you hardly know and whose views may be quite different from your own. In group situations, it is natural to feel rather guarded about expressing anything that might seem antagonistic or judgmental. Most of us are much more candid with friends than with people we've just met. In groups it helps to have some rules or agreed-upon ways of communicating that make it easier to have interaction develop in an honest and helpful way. You could discuss among yourselves how to formulate specific rules for special purposes, but, in general, groups function best (1) when everyone gets a chance to participate, (2) when everyone listens to what each is saying, and (3) when you can agree to disagree in a way that does not lead to negative, personal feelings. Above all, give each other permission to be honest about what you think and feel and to be fair and considerate. You need to have good manners. It is just that easy and that complex.

Studying Tips

- Studying involves many activities: reading, thinking, talking to yourself, rereading certain passages out loud, underlining in books, making lists, daydreaming, remembering other things you've read or written, imagining just what the words suggest and contemplating it, arguing with what you've read, writing comments in the margin, looking things up, memorizing, following little digressions that come up and stimulate your curiosity.

- Studying is not just cramming for a test or doing your homework exactly as assigned. It is a way of using your mind so that you begin to see the interrelationships between ideas and the things you've studied.

- Studying is what you do on your own, beyond what any teacher would require. If you want to be good at anything, you need to act on your own initiative, use your own judgment, and take the time necessary to master whatever it is you're trying to learn. Some people can read an essay in half an hour; someone else might spend five hours on it.

- Studying requires patience and stamina and creativity. If you're reading something and it doesn't make sense or bores you, try to figure out why. Identify the specific words or passages that trouble you or displease you. Work with it. Respond as though challenged, and exert whatever energy is required. It won't be the same for any two people. No one can tell you how hard you need to work while studying. At this level in your education, you should give it everything you've got. The skills you develop in a college writing class can form a strong foundation for every piece of writing you do for the rest of your life.

The Writing Process: An Overview

Once you decide or have been assigned to write something, you next have to figure out where to start. This is usually called the prewriting stage of preparing to write and writing the first draft. Just getting started is the most difficult step for many writers. The difficulty has its source in various states of mind. The first is uncertainty. We often don't know what we think about a particular issue. We are reluctant to start putting words on paper until we've done more thinking or more reading. Or we may feel confusion because our minds feel flooded with ideas, possibilities, and half-understood insights. We feel we need time to digest our thoughts more fully before starting to write. Or we may see the whole process of planning, writing, revision, and editing as so time-consuming and laborious that we may simply want to put it off in order to do other less frustrating things. Whatever the causes, some genuine, some merely rationalizations, we must eventually pick up our pen or turn on our computer and start putting some words down in some meaningful order.

Prewriting

This stage in writing is traditionally referred to as "invention" because writers must invent both the form and content of what they plan to express. There are formal and informal strategies.

Formal Prewriting: Answering Questions

Formal prewriting strategies employ a structured set of questions that are designed to produce writing. This guide—called a heuristic—usually consists of a set of questions that will generate responses. The most famous of these guides is the one used by journalists who must supply basic information in the lead paragraph of a news story by answering these questions: Who? What? When? Where? How? and Why? Before starting to write, you can compose your own list of questions. If they are arranged in a logical sequence, then simply answering them will begin to give a structure to your essay. Each paragraph is essentially the answer to a question, whether or not the question has been explicitly stated.

Look at how Naomi Wolf generates ideas for her book *The Beauty Myth*, challenging her readers to rethink their assumptions about women by simply asking good questions. Toward the end of her excerpt, which is really a list of questions, she comes to the conclusion that women are beautiful but that it will be necessary to move beyond the beauty myth before anyone truly believes it. This becomes the controlling idea, or thesis, she will use when developing her work, in this case, an entire book:

> What is a woman? Is she what is made of her? Do a woman's life and experience have value? If so, should she be ashamed for them to show? What is so great about looking young?
>
> The idea that a woman's body has boundaries that must not be violated is fairly new. We evidently haven't taken it far enough. Can we extend that idea? Or are women the pliable sex, innately adapted to being shaped, cut, and subjected to physical invasion? Does the female body deserve the same notion of integrity as the male body? Is there a difference between fashions in clothing and fashions in women's bodies? Assuming that someday women can be altered cheaply, painlessly, and with no risk, is that to be what we must want? Must the expressiveness of maturity and old age become extinct? Will we lose nothing if it does? Does a woman's identity count? Must she be made to want to look like someone else? Is there something implicitly gross about the texture of female flesh? The inadequacy of female flesh stands in for the older inadequacy of the female mind. Women asserted that there was nothing inferior about their minds; are our bodies really inferior?
>
> Is "beauty" really sex? Does a woman's sexuality correspond to what she looks like? Does she have the right to sexual pleasure and self-esteem because she's a person, or must she earn that right through "beauty," as she used to through marriage? What is female sexuality— what does it look like? Does it bear any relation to the way in which commercial images represent it? Is it something women need to buy like a product? What really draws men and women together?
>
> Are we beautiful or aren't we?
>
> Of course we are. But we won't really believe it the way we need to until we start to take the first steps beyond the beauty myth.
>
> Does all this mean we can't wear lipstick without feeling guilty?
> —Naomi Wolf, from *The Beauty Myth: How Images of Women Are Used Against Women*

By no means should an essay simply consist of a series of questions, of course. Rather, questions should direct the writer towards answers, "particular" facts and details that readers will want and need to know in order to understand and appreciate the subject of an essay.

Informal Prewriting

The informal methods of prewriting employ various types of free association in order to "break the ice" in your own mind and get the ideas flowing. These methods include freewriting, brainstorming, clustering, listing, and looping. The idea here is to open your mind to word associations and to visualize freely until you come up with some ideas, words, and details that make you want to get started writing. You know you are ready to start when you get a strong sense of your point of view on a subject. Usually when people argue heatedly, their pulses beat faster, their minds race ahead, and they begin to speak loudly. Words come quickly to the tongue when the adrenaline is flowing. This is partly because when you get into an angry dispute with someone, you usually have a strong sense of your own convictions and goals. You know what you're arguing for and why.

Freewriting

Freewriting lets writers examine what they may have to say about a topic or an issue by freely associating words, phrases, and thoughts to get the mind focused on a topic. Simone, for instance, freewrote on the topic of videos to arrive at a position on that broad topic. Without concerning herself about grammatical or mechanical correctness, she wrote one word group after another, exploring a topic she realized she knew well:

> Videos. It seems wherever you turn, somebody's got a video camera. If no reporters are at the scene of the crime, no problem. Someone's sure to have a Camcorder going. Shopping, I hate to go to the Quick Mart, especially late at night cause the video recorder is always on. Americans actually send videos of themselves to television shows . . . ah, fame. I'd like to be famous—a musician. Musicians are on video. There are entire channels of music videos. Why? They project a kind of drama through sight, sound, lighting, and movement. *Musical videos will be a major art form in the 21st century.* Will VHS still be around? How about laser disks?

Although Simone rambled around a bit, she did tend to return to the key word, video, and although she initially seemed to have a lot to say about how videos are such a large part of our daily lives, it wasn't until she wrote "Musical videos will be a major art form in the 21st century" that she realized her position on music videos and what she would end up explaining and justifying in the body of her essay.

Brainstorming

Brainstorming is a technique of prewriting that allows writers to test an idea—to think through a topic a bit before committing to writing about it. Some people talk out loud or into a tape recorder when brainstorming ideas. Others use a set of questions or free associations to trigger thoughts; the technique is not so much concerned with a rigid set of steps. Rather, brainstorming serves as a means to an end: generating topics to write about while avoiding "writer's block."

Clustering

In many ways, clustering is a form of brainstorming or listing that allows readers to visualize the relationships among people, places, and things that evolve as a result of this method of prewriting. To cluster, select a key focusing word (or word group) and then begin to establish relationships, drawing circles around each word you list and lines between related items. Note how the writer clustered "tabloid news" in the following:

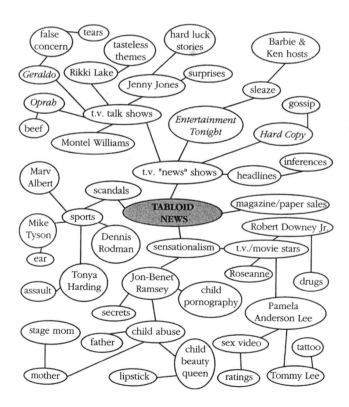

After clustering freely around the words "tabloid news," Megan realized that she seemed to have a lot of details and associations with "sensationalism," so she crossed out several clusters unrelated to sensationalism such as the "Barbie and Ken hosts," "tattoo," and "surprises," and then she reconsidered her ideas: How and why do tabloid news shows feed viewers sensationalized scandals and half-truths? Ultimately, Megan turned the answers to her questions into a declarative statement—the controlling idea for her essay: Today, television talk shows center on tabloid news in response to the viewing public's insatiable appetite for gossip and sensationalized scandals. She then devoted the body of her paper to justifying her thesis.

Listing

Listing, yet another way to prewrite, means that the writer jots down lists—words, phrases, and short sentences under a heading instead of freely associating words and ideas in a paragraph. Many people like to prewrite by "listing" because, on one hand, the technique triggers both major points for discussion and details/associations. On the other hand, the compressed nature of a list is easily transformed into a scratch outline for an entire paper, minus the free associations that end up having no bearing on the essay. Listing generates any number of thoughts and in numerous formats. In her poem, "Me," poet and songwriter Jewel uses a form of listing, for instance, to observe herself initially and then to reflect upon what she's said (e.g., "I like the color of wine," but "I probably won't always like the color of wine").

ME

Jewel

Jewel's poem "Me" appears on the inside CD jacket of *Pieces of You.*

I
I have blonde hair
I pluck my eyebrows
I have my father's nose,
my mother's hands
I have crooked teeth
and green eyes
I play guitar

I used to get sick a lot
I like the color of wine
I've cheated on boyfriends
I've owned fake ID
But my hair is still blonde
and my teeth are still crooked
and I probably won't always like
the color of wine

II
I have firm breasts
I have lips that always smile
I have veins that bleed
I laugh when I'm nervous
I feel the pain of others
but cry for no reason
I like open flame
I've been selfish since a child
I'm from Alaska
but hate the cold
I've cheated on diets
I've faked applications
But I still bleed
and my lips still smile
and my breasts won't always be firm

III
I have strong shoulders
I have olive skin
I have a Swiss face
borrowed from my grandmother
I have long nails on my right hand
which I break regularly
my little toe is strange
I write
I used to make wreaths from dandelions
brush my hair before bed
cheated on tests
faked flirtatious French accents
But I still have gold skin
and my nails still break
and I probably won't always have
strong shoulders

and I may not always write
but maybe I'll start making wreaths
from dandelions again

Exercise: Experiment with the prewriting technique called listing by writing
"ME" at the top of a piece of paper and listing your associations with the word
in one to three columns as Jewel did. What personal observations could you
organize and develop in an essay?

Looping

Looping is a prewriting method in which authors write a series of short freewriting exercises. After you complete one exercise, step back and think a moment
about what you said. Perhaps you'll want to turn to someone in the class or at
home and tell him what you just wrote without looking at your paper. Then, take
the best idea from one exercise and write it at the top of a clean piece of paper;
this idea will serve as the "focusing word" for your next round of freewriting.
Keep up the looping exercises, refining and sharpening your topic's focus, until
you feel like you have arrived at a controlling idea for an entire essay. The following illustrates the process of looping:


```
                    Freewrite #1
Traveling. Ever since I can remember I have loved taking
off on a trip. When we moved to California when I was a
child, I remember sitting in the back seat of the car with
my sister and staring out the window at the passing
landscape. We drove south from Seattle along the coast
highway and we stopped often to eat or stretch our legs or
to look at tourist sights. The sea lion caves! Drive
through a redwood tree! See a live octopus! We were really
suckers for all the tourist traps. It took us two weeks to
travel from Seattle to San Francisco. I remember
especially Seaside, Oregon, because we stopped for two
days, and my sister and I got to play on the beach and eat
saltwater taffy and cotton candy and cheeseburgers.


                      Loop #1
                Seaside-Beach towns
Some of my best memories from childhood come from my visits
to beach towns. The thing that really sticks in my mind is
how nobody seems to have a real job in these places. Plenty
of money changes hands, of course, but you never see any
```

canneries or steel mills or insurance company headquarters. These towns, like Seaside, Oregon, or Santa Cruz, California, or Long Beach, Washington, usually have a main street filled with little shops that sell nothing but useless junk: souvenirs, T-shirts, bumper stickers, bracelets, chess sets made out of quartz rocks, that sort of stuff. The sunlight and the wind and the ocean give the place a special feeling. The rules of everyday life are temporarily suspended. You have permission to goof off, to spend your money in a whimsical way. There are often carnival rides—roller coasters, bumper cars, unicycles—that add the lure of adventure and danger. Also, the arcades are filled with shrewd and nimble kids who think they can beat the pinball machine or the video game.

Loop #2

Vacations

Vacations are not so much about traveling to new places as they are a chance to live by slightly different rules. Whether you go to a beach town or a campground or stay in a hotel in a big city, the thing to remember is let go of your everyday habits. A vacation is really a state of mind more than it is a journey to some place. This state of mind allows you to be slightly impractical, somewhat lazy and goofy. It means you don't have to worry about what clothes you wear or what you look like. A vacation is a psychological carnival that we all need to visit from time to time, even when we don't have the money to go anywhere.

From Prewriting to the Paragraph

Printers devised the practice of indenting words at the beginning of a paragraph in order to make written documents easier to read. Imagine what books would look like if the entire text was printed as one unbroken body of words. You would feel lost in an ocean of words. The purpose of a paragraph, then, is to indicate to the reader when one idea begins and when it ends. A paragraph is a logical unit of thought. It has a beginning, a middle, and an end. It makes a point, explains it, and illustrates it. Paragraphs are the building blocks of an essay and have a structure very similar to a whole essay. Typically, paragraphs have the following features:

A Topic Sentence.   The central purpose or controlling idea of a paragraph is written as a statement of some kind. It should be an idea worth examining and explaining in some detail. Ideally, a topic sentence clearly defines a discussion point, giving it some sort of "edge" to guide development and promote reader interest.

Unity.   The topic sentence establishes the discussion point that will be explained, argued, analyzed, or proven through the use of representative examples and details as well as sound reasoning. To maintain unity in a paragraph, make a point and support it without wandering off target.

Coherence.   Writers initially achieve paragraph coherence by careful sentence organization. For instance, a writer would want to provide a specific topic sentence prior to details and examples because otherwise the sentence relationships would not make sense. Writers also achieve paragraph coherence by using transitions and linking devices—words or word groups that indicate the relationship between other words, phrases, clauses, or entire paragraphs.

Details and Examples.   Representative examples and details help writers to support their claims, illustrate their points, and argue their issues. "Showing" promotes greater understanding and greater credibility than "telling" because readers consider or reconsider information in light of detailed facts and evidence—not because of an author's claims.

Focusing the Topic Sentence

Always remember that a reader cannot read your mind and that in order for your ideas to be appreciated, you need to state them as clearly and precisely as possible. Your topic sentence should be neither too narrow (e.g., I own a dog) nor too broad or vague (e.g., The United States needs to take care of its problems). Notice the difference between the following topic sentences:

> **Weak topic sentence**: "Skiing is fun" is a topic but neither very interesting nor sufficiently focused. Who would disagree with it? What thoughts does it provoke? It is simply a commonplace observation.

> **Improved topic sentence**: "The Winter Olympics improves international cooperation." This is slightly better since it suggests a direction of development. The writer would have to define "international cooperation," explain why it is important, and give examples of how this is demonstrated by the games. Though this topic is better, it is still a commonplace thing to say.

> **Revised version of the improved topic sentence**: Your final revision of the sample topic sentence might say, "Though the Winter Olympics were conceived as a way to promote international cooperation, they also arouse strong feelings of nationalism and reinforce long-standing rivalries." This sentence suggests a wider range of discussion and introduces a note of

controversy. It is a more thoughtful observation and suggests various methods of development: definition, narration, comparison/contrast. Compare this topic sentence (twice revised) to the initial version of it.

Drafting Essays

Once you actually start producing words, it is a good idea to give yourself permission to write freely and expressively without worrying too much about what others will think. A certain tone will emerge in writing as you begin to understand your own point of view. A first draft can be both messy and slightly disorganized. The cutting, shaping, revising, and editing can come later.

Introductory Paragraphs

The first paragraph of an essay has several functions: (1) it tells the reader what the topic of the essay is; (2) it provides some provocative statements, definitions, or examples that will "hook" the reader's interest; (3) it establishes the tone and point of view of the essay; and (4) it usually contains the thesis that states the overall plan and purpose of the essay. Alice Walker illustrates all four functions of an introductory paragraph in the opening paragraph of "Father" (see Chapter 3, The American Family, for her entire essay):

> Though it is more difficult to write about my father than about my mother, since I spent less time with him and knew him less well, it is equally as liberating. Partly this is because writing about people helps us to understand them, and understanding them helps us to accept them as part of ourselves. Since I share so many of my father's characteristics, physical and otherwise, coming to terms with what he has meant to my life is crucial to a full acceptance and love of myself.

Although this introduction is brief, notice how it immediately lets the reader know that Walker will be writing about her father. Then she "hooks" the reader by suggesting that this is not merely a personal reminiscence but a process that illustrates how writing and remembering is a way to discover ourselves. Her statement of purpose establishes her meditative and personal tone: "coming to terms with what he has meant to my life is crucial to a full acceptance and love of myself." This paragraph shows how a good writer can get an essay started quickly and elegantly.

Body Paragraphs

Most of us have been told more than once that paragraphs consist of topic sentences and supporting statements; this is not a complete description but a way of simplifying the structure of paragraphs for the sake of clarity. It is supposed to make it seem simple to write a paragraph, but we all know that it is a much more complex process. Our purpose here is to show how paragraphs move through various levels of thought in order to develop a point: (1) controlling ideas, (2) explanations, (3) evidence and support, and (4) transitional links. You might think of it this way: a paragraph consists of four levels of thought, and this results in four types of sentences.

The body paragraphs in Alice Walker's essay fulfill readers' needs and expectations by using topic sentences, explanatory sentences, evidence sentences, and transitional sentences to develop the controlling idea explained in her thesis paragraph. For instance, in paragraph 14 Walker says:

> For years I have held on to another early memory of my life between the ages of two and four. Every afternoon a tired but jolly very little black man came up to me with arms outstretched. I flew into them to be carried, to be hugged, to be kissed. For years I thought this black man was my father. But no. He was my oldest brother, Fred, whose memories of my father are, surprisingly, as painful as my memories of him, because as my father's first child, and a son, he was subjected to my father's very confused notions of what constituted behavior suitable for a male. And of course my father himself didn't really know. He was in his late teens, a child himself, when he married. His mother had been murdered, by a man who claimed to love her, when he was eleven. His father, to put it politely, drank, and terrorized his children.

Notice how Walker opens the paragraph with very specific observations that are summarized at the end of the sixth sentence when she says about her brother, "he was subjected to my father's very confused notions of what constituted behavior suitable for a male." Here she is giving her observations meaning by explaining their significance. This is the central idea that gives the paragraph coherence. All the sentences that follow give further explanation of the causes for both her father's and her brother's behavior.

Types of Sentences Used in Paragraph Development

1. **Topic sentences**: This may consist of more than one sentence, and the sentences may appear in different parts of the paragraph. They may be at the beginning or end, but where they appear varies—in good writing—from paragraph to paragraph.

2. **Explanatory sentences**: These sentences make connections between general ideas and specific illustrations. These are the statements that give a paragraph coherence and substance.

3. **Evidence sentences**: These sentences provide facts, statistics, and descriptive details. They contain concrete nouns and other words that speak to the senses (e.g., "wet towel," "weeping guitars," and "crackling leaves").

4. **Transitional sentences**: These sentences are simple guideposts that link the other sentences together and let us know the level of abstraction is going to change.

Concluding Paragraphs

The last paragraph of an essay should give a reader a sense of closure, a sense that the writer's promise to discuss a certain topic has now been fulfilled. This is the paragraph in an essay that ties up all its loose ends. It is also where the writer draws some conclusions, that is, derives the final observations and reflections from the essay as a whole. It is a place to recapitulate the main ideas of the essay, to remind the reader about what has already been said. It is the final impression the essay will leave upon the reader.

> My father was never able to vote for a black candidate for any national or local political office. By the time black people were running for office and occasionally winning elections, in the late sixties and early seventies, he was too sick to respond with the exhilaration he must have felt. On the night of Jackson's speech, I felt it for him; along with the grief that in neither of our lifetimes is the United States likely to choose the best leadership offered to it. This is the kind of leader, the kind of ever-growing, ever-expanding spirit you might have been, Daddy, I thought—and damn it, I love you for what you might have been. And thinking of you now, merging the two fathers that you were, remembering how tightly I hugged you as a small child returning home after two long months at a favorite aunt's, and with what apparent love you lifted me beside your cheek; knowing now, at forty, what it takes out of a body and spirit to go and how much more to stay, and having learned, too, by now, some of the pitiful confusions in behavior caused by ignorance and pain, I love you no less for what you were.

In this paragraph, Walker brings together her childhood memories, her political consciousness as a black woman, a new sense of reconciliation with her father, and her declaration of love for her father. The final long sentence seems to weave together by its very structure the various essential thoughts and feelings of the essay.

Revising Essays

Revising material to make it more comprehensible is a must; however, revision is more than simply correcting mechanical or grammatical errors. One should strive for effective organization, not just grammatical correctness. Repetitious sentence patterns become monotonous and boring. To increase reader interest in what you have to say, go through your composition and combine related material and remove unnecessary, redundant information. Eliminate words that do not support your argument or explain and justify your position. Wordiness may confuse or frustrate a reader. If this occurs, you may lose the momentum you were building in your composition, as well as your reader's interest.

During the revision stage of writing, you will want to add transitional words and linking devices to establish relationships clearly between words, sentences, paragraphs, and sections. Clear organization creates coherence, a sense that the ideas are arranged in an orderly and easy-to-follow way. Also, this is the time to add supporting details and examples to strengthen the content of your paper. As indicated in the following section, you might want to break down the steps in the revising process into several stages, in order to make what you write unified, coherent, and well supported with specific examples.

Stages of Revision

1. **Revise for Organization** of material. Begin with the big picture; that is, check the progression of your paragraphs. Place your least significant information or weakest argument first and then develop subsequent paragraphs in order of importance (emphatic order). Next, go through the sentences in each paragraph in a similar manner; what logical order do they follow? Do details follow facts? Does each paragraph have a clear controlling idea or topic sentence? If not, what statement would clearly phrase the controlling idea of each respective paragraph? The following outlines the initial draft and the revised progression of an essay, arguing and explaining the essential ingredients for a successful party.

   ### Revising for Organization: Example (draft)
   ¶1 Introductory paragraph leading to thesis
   ¶2 Live music
   ¶3 People

¶4 Food and drinks

¶5 Stimulating conversation

¶6 Concluding paragraph placing all the major discussion points back into focus with the thesis of the essay

Revising for Organization: Example (revision)

¶1 Introductory paragraph leading to thesis

¶2 Food and drinks

¶3 People

¶4 Stimulating conversation

¶5 Live music

¶6 Concluding paragraph placing all the major discussion points back into focus with the thesis of the essay

2. **Revise for Content**. When you revise for content, begin by going through your topic sentences and make certain that they express clear and distinct ideas. Check on the accuracy of your word choices. Have you put the right words in the right places? Do your sentences answer the questions who, what, when, where, why, and how?

   REVISING FOR EMPHASIS: EXAMPLE (DRAFT):
   Jason works at the shopping mall. Tina works at the shopping mall. Chenelle sells pets in the shopping mall. Brett also works at the shopping mall.

   REVISING FOR EMPHASIS: EXAMPLE (REVISED):
   Jason, Tina, Chenelle, and Brett work at the shopping mall. (parallel structure)

3. **Revise for Coherence**. Here your objective will be to review the relationship between your sentences and paragraphs to determine if the relationships between them create a clear sequence. Use transitional expressions and linking words such as however, on the other hand, therefore, furthermore, in addition, on the contrary, nonetheless, first, second, third, and finally.

   REVISING FOR COHERENCE: EXAMPLE (DRAFT):
   Turn everything on. Wire the VCR box and the TV. Also don't forget to plug in the other wires to get electricity.

   REVISING FOR COHERENCE: EXAMPLE (REVISION):
   Hooking up a VCR is an easy task requiring no special skills or tools. First, take your VCR out of its packing material. Plug the coaxial

cable onto the back of the television set terminal in the site labeled "video out" and connect it to the back of the VCR in the site labeled "video in." Lock down both terminals with the nut around the cable by hand. Take the electrical wire from the back of the television and put it into the outlet in the back of the VCR. Plug the electrical wire from the back of the VCR into the wall socket.

4. Revise for Emphasis.

There are many ways of achieving emphasis when you write besides exclamation marks. Something as simple as putting items in a series using the same grammatical (parallel) structure can show the relative importance of each item. In a series, the last item is usually perceived to be the most important.

REVISING FOR CONTENT EMPHASIS: EXAMPLE (DRAFT):
John drove to Washington in 1998.

REVISING FOR CONTENT EMPHASIS: EXAMPLE (REVISION):
On January 10, 1998, John drove to Seattle, Washington, for a conference on Language Arts in the middle of the biggest snowstorm to hit the area in twenty years.

5. Revise for Style.

The best writing does not call attention to itself. It seems to be as transparent as a newly washed window. The reader simply sees what the writer is trying to say. Good style results from simple, clear language, active verbs, and creative observations and ideas. This is not easy to do. As a writer you need to know what you are trying to say and how best to say it.

REVISING FOR STYLE: EXAMPLE (DRAFT):
Lydia has put her stuff into the drawer along with her other things.

REVISING FOR STYLE: EXAMPLE (REVISED):
Lydia placed her collection of photographs in her top dresser drawer, along with her love letters and her diary.

Editing Essays

The final step in the composition process consists of editing and proofreading your work so that careless errors will not distract or confuse your readers. However, editing deals with far more than simply "retyping" a rough draft or making a messy-looking composition appear "neat and orderly." Proofreading requires going over the whole essay and checking for spelling, grammar, and punctuation errors. You need to make use of a dictionary, handbook, or software that will help you identify errors and correct them. Then you should reread your essay from start to finish and:

Make sure that the body of your essay does what your thesis says it will do.

Check for transition words and phrases that link paragraphs together.

Look for repetitious sentence patterns that can be condensed and rewritten using parallel structure.

Go over each paragraph to be sure that you have provided relevant and appropriate examples to support your main points.

Be sure that the essay has a conclusion that reminds the reader of your main points and brings a sense of closure to your discussion as a whole.

Save yourself a lot of time and anxiety by writing the first draft from start to finish without editing. You can always sort out and eliminate unnecessary information after you have finished the first draft; however, it is not as easy to recapture the inspiration that guided you in writing about a topic in the first place.

Remember that editing your work is the last stage in the writing process. It is time to polish what you have said and how you have said it. Proofreading is a mechanical rather than a creative process; it requires close attention to detail. Revision, on the other hand, may require rethinking the controlling ideas and structure of your essay. You may find gaps in your thinking that need to be filled in by fuller development and explanation, or you may get new ideas that need to be added and integrated into what you have already written. Put yourself in the place of the reader. Think of reasonable questions that a reader might have about what you have written and try to answer those questions in advance.

Editing for Grammatical Errors

- Subject–Verb Agreement in Number (match singular subjects with singular verbs and plural subjects with plural verbs)

  Example:

  My *dog scare* most of my neighbors. (singular subject/plural verb)

  My *dog scares* most of my neighbors. (corrected with singular verb)

- Consistent Point of View (first, second, or third person)

  Example:

  We always enjoy the circus because *you* like to watch tight-rope walkers. (shift from first person plural to second person)

> *We* always enjoy the circus because *we* like to watch tight-rope walkers.
> (match first-person plural pronouns)

- Pronoun Agreement in Number (singular or plural)

Example:

> *Everybody* put *their* coats on my bed. ("their" is a plural reference to
> a singular pronoun; change words like "everybody" and "every-
> one" to their plural equivalent)
>
> *They* put *their* coats on my bed.

- Faulty Use of Participles

Example:

> Elvis *had drank* too much coffee that morning. (faulty past participle)
>
> Elvis *had drunk* too much coffee that morning. (corrected by
> changing a past-tense verb with the past participle form of the
> word)

Editing for Mechanical Errors (punctuation)

- Complete Sentences and Fragmented Thoughts: A sentence is a complete
  thought; it contains a subject and a complete verb.

Dependent Word Fragment

Example:

> *Because Lynda was sick.*
>
> *Ryan stayed home* because Lynda was sick. (add an independent
> clause to the fragmented thought)

Added Details Fragment

Example:

> *Especially swimming.*
>
> The Nguyens enjoy water activities, especially swimming. (insert
> the added detail fragment after the independent clause to correct
> the above example. In other instances, insert the added details
> to the sentence before or after it—whichever makes better
> sense)

Missing Subject Fragment

Example:

> Makes a good friend and dependable companion. (no subject)
>
> *My dog* makes a good friend and dependable companion. (add sub-
> ject: dog)

Incomplete Verb Fragment

Example:

Denzel *going* to the football game tomorrow night with Harvey.

Denzel *is going* to the football game tomorrow night with Harvey.
(add the linking verb "is" after Denzel and before the present participle "going")

Run-on Sentences and Comma Splices

Run-on sentences are two complete sentences punctuated as one.   The Manor Theater was my favorite place to spend Saturday afternoon it has been converted into a real estate office and a food co-op now. (problem: no punctuation between complete sentences)

The Manor Theater was my favorite place to spend Saturday afternoon, but it has been converted into a real estate office and a food co-op now. (add a comma and the coordinating conjunction "but" between the independent clauses)

The Manor Theater was my favorite place to spend Saturday afternoon; it has been converted into a real estate office and a food co-op now. (separate "afternoon" and "it" with a semicolon)

The Manor Theater was my favorite place to spend Saturday afternoon. It has been converted into a real estate office and a food co-op now. (separate "afternoon" and "it" with a period, and capitalize the first letter, "i" in the second sentence)

Comma splices are two complete sentences separated by only a comma.

Example:

The soccer tournament ended on a bad note, a riot broke out after the final game. (comma splice)

The soccer tournament ended on a bad note; a riot broke out after the final game. (separate independent clauses with a semicolon)

The soccer tournament ended on a bad note when a riot broke out after the final game. (make one independent clause dependent)

The soccer tournament ended on a sour note. A riot broke out after the final game. (correct by punctuating each independent clause as a simple sentence)

- Commas
  Commas serve many purposes, but their most important function is to clarify information. Following are some of the most common uses of commas; they are used

To Separate Items in a Series

Example:

Levon, Rick, Garth, and Robbie climbed onto the bus headed for Lake Charles.

To Set Off Parts of an Address or Date

Example:

He was born in Baltimore, Maryland, on July 10, 1973, and moved to San Jose, California, former "Prune Capital of the Western World."

To Interrupt a Sentence

Example:

Frank stared at the chandelier, a gaudy contraption of plastic and brass, and sighed.

To Open a Sentence

Example:

After waxing his mustache, Geraldo glanced in the mirror with approval.

While planning for the graduation party, they forgot to invite the college president.

To Separate Independent Clauses When Used Along with One of the Seven Coordinating Conjunctions (and, but, for, or, nor, so, yet)

Example:

I wanted to go to bed early, but I had too much homework to complete by tomorrow.

Dashes

Use a dash where you would otherwise use a comma to emphasize your point. The most important thing about the dash is not to overuse it; if you do, it will lose its rhetorical impact.

Example:

Last night I watched *Diva*—an excellent French film.

■ Semicolons

Semicolons separate complete ideas—sentences—but indicate a closer relationship between independent clauses than a period.

Example:

Vernell's feet ache; however, he still plans to play soccer for two hours.

Semicolons separate items in a series when information in the parallel clauses already contain commas.

Example:

> Kevin has lived in Olympia, Washington; Campbell, California; Fargo, North Dakota; and Atlanta, Georgia. (Note how confusing these sentences would have been if all items in the series had been separated by a comma: Kevin has lived in Olympia, Washington, Campbell, California, Fargo, North Dakota, and Atlanta, Georgia.)

- Capital Letters
Capitalize the first word in each new sentence, along with proper nouns (names, places, historical periods).

Example:

> Yesterday, I spent the entire morning wandering around the Louvre Museum in Paris, France.

- End Punctuation Marks

Periods

A period indicates the end of a complete thought.

Example:

> The Mercedes rolled into the parking lot around midnight.

Exclamation points

An exclamation point, used sparingly, draws emphasis to a point.

Example:

> I have had enough of this heat!

Question marks

A question mark is used in a sentence to indicate a query.

Example:

> What is the purpose of life?

Editing for Spelling Errors

- Run the spell check on your word processor to locate typos like "bkan" instead of "bank" or "masshysteria" instead of "mass hysteria."
- Proofread the spelling of all words yourself. In particular, look for words that your spell check recognized as legitimate words but are not the words you intended to use to convey information to your readers (e.g., "top" instead of "tap," "money" instead of "honey," "steak" instead of "steal," "master" instead of "muster").
- Proofread your vocabulary words to locate "homophones," words that are pronounced the same way but are spelled differently and have dissimilar definitions ("two" and "too," "accept" and "except," "four" and "for," "blew" and "blue").

Methods of Exposition: Strategies for Development

Writers are explainers, and when they explain something or expose information on paper, they compose expository essays. In the process of doing so, writers can make a topic more intelligible by providing explanations that clarify relationships that are not immediately obvious or understandable. We call the various methods of developing material *rhetorical modes*. The logical development of an explanation often depends on one's purpose for writing (e.g., to define a concept, to compare and contrast two colleges in order to determine which one would best meet your academic and/or vocational needs and interests). Often writers use some sort of cause/effect reasoning to get started—although there are other "natural" and "logical" methods for developing material. Some of the writing strategies writers refer to as expository modes of development include:

> *Cause and effect* (moving many causes to single effect; one cause with several effects).
>
> *Classification and division* (employing a clear principle for breaking down a topic into smaller units for discussion).
>
> *Comparison and contrast* (showing similarities and contrasting differences for a particular reason).
>
> *Definition* (providing clear distinctions between what something is and is not).
>
> *Description* (applying specific, visual explanations that feature concrete nouns and active verbs).
>
> *Illustration and example* (using multiple examples and illustrations to actively "show" your readers what you mean and how you arrived at your present point of view).
>
> *Narration* (telling a story).
>
> *Process analysis* (relaying how to do something or how something was done).

The following paragraphs offer a more detailed definition, a representative example, and sample questions about each method of expository development.

Cause and Effect

When we don't understand "why" a certain thing has happened—a stock market crash, a sudden upsurge in unemployment, or a world war—we attempt to find out what caused it. The causes are usually numerous, with some having more impact than others. A causal (cause/effect) analysis sorts all this information out and shows which causes are most significant. When writers propose a solution to a problem, they also need to predict consequences. Once we understand what caused a stock market crash, we might make some proposals that would prevent another one. This means we need to predict the effects of particular proposals. The credibility of any proposal often depends upon how plausible an argument a writer can make about the flow of effects that will follow from any hypothetical suggestion.

> All immigrants fight for jobs and space, and who is there to fight but those who have both? As in the fishing ground struggle between Texas and Vietnamese shrimpers, they displace what and whom they can. Although U.S. history is awash in labor battles, political fights and property wars among all religious and ethnic groups, their struggles are persistently framed as struggles between recent arrivals and blacks. In race talk the move into mainstream America always means buying into the notion of American blacks as the real aliens. Whatever the ethnicity or nationality of the immigrant, his nemesis is understood to be African American.
>
> —Toni Morrison, from "On the Backs of Blacks"

Cause and Effect Sample Paragraph Questions

What does Morrison think causes the conflict between immigrant groups? What effect has the competition between immigrant groups had on the way African Americans are perceived?

Cause and Effect Paragraph Exercise

Write a well-organized, fully developed paragraph in which you explain the causes, the effects, or both causes and effects of doing something for someone else when you were neither expected nor asked to do anything at all. Remember, the details and examples in your paragraph should work together to answer the question "why."

Classification and Division

Most essays use some aspect of classification and division. Its usefulness comes from taking a large or complex subject and simplifying it by reducing it to component parts; that is, classification and division breaks down material into manageable units that can be discussed coherently and effectively.

> Alicia [from *Clueless*] is the It Girl of '95, and not by accident. We trend watchers in the media aren't as dumb and dumber as we seem,

either. We've been analyzing the data, and folks, we can safely tell you, cute is a trend. It's all over the movies: Sandra Bullock fumbled, giggled and gollied her way to the big time with this year's *While You Were Sleeping*. Drew Barrymore has perfected her Lolita impersonations to such a degree that in *Mad Love* her acting amounted to raising her pencil-drawn eyebrows, pursing her beestung lips and tossing her ringlet curls. Cute is tricky. Not just anyone can do it. Meg Ryan de-cutified herself for mature, serious roles in *When a Man Loves a Woman* and *Flesh and Bone*, and audiences thought the unbubbly Meg tasted flat. Then she tried to bounce back with pratfalls over giant plants in *French Kiss*, and she pretty much fell flat. Marisa Tomei tried cute in *Only You*—hated it. Debra Winger, cute in *Forget Paris?* As if.

—Karen Schoemer and Yahlin Chang, from "The Cult of the Cute"

Classification and Division Sample Paragraph Questions

What is classified and divided in this paragraph?

Classification and Division Paragraph Exercise

In a brief paragraph, classify and divide (1) types of people (e.g., movie stars, college professors, employers), or (2) methods of learning (e.g., books, interactive television, computers).

Comparison and Contrast

The techniques used for comparing similarities and contrasting differences for a particular purpose (e.g., the best price for a new car that meets all your needs—and your budget) are frequently useful in expository and argumentative writing. Just remember, comparing and contrasting people, places, or things is a method for arriving at some conclusion—not an end in itself.

The defining characteristic of Martin's relationship with the Beatles was his vastly different musical background; their partnership was almost a case of opposites attracting. While the Beatles were musical illiterates who could neither read nor notate music, Martin had graduated from London's prestigious Guildhall School of Music, where he had studied musical theory, composition, orchestration, piano, and oboe. And although Martin came from a modest background—his father was a carpenter who was reduced to selling newspapers on the street during the Depression of the 1930s—he looked and sounded distinctly upper class, thanks to a self-possessed bearing and polished accent. What

Martin had in common with the Beatles, however, besides musical talent, was an open-minded eagerness to explore new ideas and unconventional means of expression. This freethinking attitude, combined with his unimpeachable classical background, made George Martin an ideal collaborator for the Beatles.

—Mark Hertsgaard, from *A Day in the Life:*
The Music and Artistry of the Beatles

Comparison and Contrast Sample Paragraph Questions

Why is it effective to place the similarities between George Martin and the Beatles at the end of this paragraph?
What effect does it have?
Why does contrast heighten your interest in this famous musical collaboration?

Comparison and Contrast Paragraph Exercise

In a brief paragraph, compare and contrast two songs, two people, two cars, or two employers. In your final sentence or so, come to some sort of conclusion about your topic. Have a reason for comparing similarities and contrasting differences.

Definition

A definition essay explains a concept or idea. Definition tends to be used in most compositions because a clear definition of terms is essential for exploring and analyzing your main idea. The following paragraph, for instance, clearly explains the meaning of film noir, a concept crucial to an audience's appreciation and understanding of the American crime film.

Film noir is a descriptive term for the American crime film as it flourished, roughly, from the early forties to the late fifties. It embraces a variety of crime dramas ranging from claustrophobic studies of murder and psychological entrapment to more general treatments of criminal organizations. From stylized versions of the city at night to documentary-like reports of the city at midday, from the investigations of the wry, cynical sleuth to the "innocent" man momentarily and fatally tempted by luxury, to the desperate flailings of the confirmed and inveterate criminal, the genre covers a heterogeneous terrain. In range of theme and in visual style, it is both varied and complex, and in level of achievement it is consistently high. Film noir is one of the most challenging cycles in the history of films.

—Foster Hirsch, from *Film Noir: The Dark Side of the Screen*

Definition Sample Paragraph Questions

What are the various parts of this definition? Why is the definition mode of writing useful for introducing a complex term like film noir?
How many different characteristics are brought together to define this style?

Definition Paragraph Exercise

Limiting yourself to only a paragraph or so, use the rhetorical strategy of definition to explain your understanding of a concept like honesty, intelligence, poverty, responsibility, loneliness, happiness, or good fortune. You might also define your topic by negation; that is, define your topic by explaining what it is not.

Description

Descriptive essays use significant details, especially concrete nouns and active verbs (verbs that "show" rather than "tell"). Descriptive essays also inform or expose information to readers through words and phrases that appeal to the senses (e.g., taste, touch, smell, sight, sound). Sensory details make compositions come alive.

> On a summer evening in Berkeley, California, circa 1984, a tradition is about to recur. Across the usually staid campus of the University of California, ritually costumed celebrants, young and old, are arriving and beginning to gather in and around the stately Greek Theater. Pastels and intricate patterns of flowing garb flutter and fly in a warm breeze that whispers across campus from the Golden Gate, swirling through the gathering throng in quiet greeting. A boyish young man, his face tanned and radiating pristine health, reveals his calm yet clear anticipation; he blesses each passer-by with a quiet, "Welcome home, sister. Welcome back, brother." I return his beatific smile. Around me, the crowd is growing; we have been gathering since mid-day, arriving by foot or in cars, vans, or converted school buses, all bedecked with innumerable and intricate variations of the symbols of our tribe: skeletons and skulls, roses, lightning bolts. And tie-dye-brazenly multicolored tie-dyed everything, everywhere. Tonight, the rites of the Grateful Dead will be celebrated once again, and we, the Deadheads, are beginning the ritual preparations.
> —Susan Dobra, from "The Rites of the Dead"

Description Sample Paragraph Questions

How many sense impressions does Dobra work into this paragraph?
What specific words stand out as memorable details? How and why can you visualize the event she is describing?

Description Paragraph Exercise

Depending on where you are when you read and do this exercise, describe the classroom you are sitting in, the student center, the library, your home, and so on. Include all of the people, places, and things around you. What sounds do you hear, sights do you see, scents do you smell, and so on? Use imagery and details that will appeal to your reader's five senses.

Illustration and Example

Showing rather than telling readers what you want them to know is one of the strengths of illustration and example. A few representative examples can take the place of long lists.

> In many of these late-80's films, men and women not only have quit trying to hash things out, they don't even keep company on the same film reel. Like the '50s backlash cinema, independent women are finally silenced by pushing them off the screen. In the tough-guy films that proliferated at the end of the decade, male heroes head off to all-male war zones and the Wild West. In the escalating violence of an endless stream of war and action movies—*Predator, Die Hard, Die Harder, RoboCop, RoboCop 2, Lethal Weapon, Days of Thunder, Total Recall*—women are reduced to mute and incidental characters or banished altogether. In the man-boy body-swapping films that cropped up in the late '80s—*18 Again, Like Father, Like Son*, and, the most memorable, *Big*—men seek refuge in female-free boyhoods. And male characters in another whole set of films retreat even further, to hallucinatory all-male fantasies of paternal renewal. In such films as *Field of Dreams, Indiana Jones and the Last Crusade, Dad*, and *Star Trek V: The Final Frontier*, mother dies or disappears from the scene, leaving father (who is sometimes resurrected from the dead) and son to form a spiritually restorative bond.
>
> —Susan Faludi, from *Backlash: The Undeclared War Against American Women*

Illustration and Example Sample Paragraph Questions

How many of the films Faludi mentions have you seen? How does this knowledge help you to understand her points? What is she trying to illustrate? What specific terms help to distinguish the different types of films from one another?

Illustration and Example Paragraph Exercise

Faludi uses examples to show how certain types of films fit into categories. Take a subject that you are familiar with—motorcycles, restaurants, music groups, anything—and write a paragraph in which you put these things into categories and then provide plenty of examples to show what you mean.

Narration

Essentially, a narrative tells a story and has an easy-to-follow sequence—often chronological—with dialogue. Although narrative is usually referred to as a method of development in and of itself, its role in exposition cannot be ignored.

> It was a Saturday afternoon on La Salle Street, years and years ago when I was a little kid, and around three o'clock Mrs. Shannon, the heavy Irish woman in her perpetually soup-stained dress, opened her back window and shouted out into the courtyard, "Hey, Cesar, yoo-hoo, I think you're on television, I swear it's you!" When I heard the opening strains of the *I Love Lucy* show I got excited because I knew she was referring to an item of eternity, that episode in which my dead father and my Uncle Cesar had appeared, playing Ricky Ricardo's singing cousins fresh off the farm in Oriente Province, Cuba, and north in New York for an engagement at Ricky's nightclub, the Tropicana.
> —Oscar Hijuelos, from *The Mambo Kings Play Songs of Love*

Narration Sample Paragraph Questions

How does Hijuelos use details to create a strong sense of chronological coherence? What happened first, second, third?
What does dialogue add to Hijuelos's narrative?

Narration Paragraph Exercise.   Write a narrative paragraph in which you recall a memorable moment in your life. Where were you? Who were you with? What did you do? Why was the occasion or event memorable? Provide transitions and linking words to help establish the chronology of what took place. Also, use dialogue if at all possible.

Process Analysis

Process analysis is a technique that explains how something is or was done (informational process analysis) or how to do something (directive process analysis). Either method relies heavily on precise transitions and linking words to indicate "steps" in the process under discussion. When explaining a topic using "process analysis," make sure you show—don't just tell—your readers who or what you want them to understand.

> The explosion was having its effect on animal life also. Specialized groups of insects were arising to feed on the new sources of food and, incidentally and unknowingly, to pollinate the plant. The flowers bloomed and bloomed in ever larger and more spectacular varieties. Some were pale unearthly night flowers intended to lure moths in the evening twilight, some among the orchids even took the shape of female spiders in order to attract wandering males, some flamed redly in the light of noon or twinkled modestly in the meadow grasses. Intricate mechanisms splashed pollen on the breasts of hummingbirds, or stamped it on the bellies of black, grumbling bees droning assiduously from blossom to blossom. Honey ran, insects multiplied, and even the descendants of that toothed and ancient lizard-bird had become strangely altered. Equipped with prodding beaks instead of biting teeth they pecked the seeds and gobbled the insects that were really converted nectar.
>
> —Loren Eiseley, from "How Flowers Changed the World," *The Immense Journey*

Process Analysis Sample Paragraph Questions

How many steps are implied in the transformation of nature Eiseley describes? What are his most impressive details and links between steps?

Process Analysis Paragraph Exercise

What steps did you take to register for this and other classes at this college? What did you have to do in order to begin selecting classes? Write a process analysis paper either explaining how to register for college classes (a how-to paragraph) or else how your registration was done (a directive process analysis paper). Make sure to address the key purpose of using process analysis to develop topics and issues; answer the question "how."

Argumentation and Persuasion

Why Study Argumentation?

In a democratic society it is necessary to engage in public thinking, to reflect upon the issues that affect us all, *and* to debate what should be done about them.

No one person or group can claim a monopoly on knowledge or the truth. We live in a diverse society with many interests contending with one another in order to achieve their goals. As a result, we as a society need to discuss and debate issues that have impact on the whole society. This huge discussion that is going on all the time through the media and all other forms of communication creates the discourse of American society. Argumentation provides the guidelines for participating in these communities of discourse.

We need to think about the consequences of the collective decisions we make regarding public issues like nuclear power, saving endangered species, health insurance, airline safety, and military spending. When you present an argument, you use facts and evidence, much like a lawyer, to make proposals that will solve problems. Since controversial issues usually call for decisions about right and wrong, ethical reasoning must be used to make these kinds of decisions. When you try to explain what *should* be done and why, you are making an argument. When the issue pertains to consequences that could result in harm to other people, you are having a debate about ethics. The hardest issues in our society—stem cell research, capital punishment, gun control—all require reasoning about fundamental assumptions that are the basis for laws and codes of behavior.

Argumentation provides a way to discuss difficult ethical problems without resorting to violence. Argumentation is important because it provides a reasonable way for people who disagree with one another to make the best case for their own interests while recognizing the legitimate concerns of others. The best arguments are ethical in the sense that they account for the consequences for all concerned and admit to unforeseen consequences and the possibility of revision.

In contrast to expository writing, which seeks to "explain" or "expose" readers to specific information on a topic, or to narrative writing, which relates a story, argumentation and persuasion attempt to influence readers through a combination of ethical (ethos), emotional (pathos), and logical (logos) appeals. These appeals, when successful, convince readers that their attitudes about a topic are worth reexamining. Although some claim that all writing is argumentative since writers must support what they say with evidence or proof, the essential goal of exposition is to explain, not to argue. You should be aware that methods of development tend to blend together and that expository and argumentative techniques reinforce one another.

Inductive and Deductive Logic

Often, textbooks make a distinction between argumentative and persuasive writing, with argumentative writing relying on an ethical stance and good, clear reasoning (induction and deduction). Inductive logic moves from several specific facts to a general statement or conclusion based on those facts. The more facts you can offer your readers the better. A wide selection of facts and details shows readers that you drew your conclusion from a fair sampling of material.

I tend to get invigorated when I watch old *Friends* reruns on television. (**fact**)

My next-door neighbor chuckles from the moment *Friends* begins until it concludes. (**fact**)

Courteney Cox and Jennifer Aniston are Diane's favorite actors, and *Friends* is her favorite television program. (**fact**)

Friends and its respective actors are definitely entertaining. (**conclusion**)

Whenever you move from facts to generalizations, you make what is referred to as an inductive conclusion. That is, even though your facts are representative, the moment you ask readers to arrive at a conclusion based on your facts, you request that they suspend their doubts, put their faith in you, and step forward—somewhat blindly. Therefore, the more examples you offer readers of friends and family who find *Friends* entertaining, the smaller the inductive leap of logic.

In contrast, deductive logic follows a process of evaluating general points, divided into major and minor premises (information and evidence); in turn, these premises lead to some sort of conclusion. The truth of your deductive conclusions depends on the validity of its premises. For example, if you begin your deductive analysis with a sentence like, All piano players enjoy listening to old Fats Waller tunes (major premise), and Carole plays the piano (minor premise), then you would probably deduce that Carole likes to listen to old Fats Waller records. Although the deductive process observed here is faultless, the mere fact that not all piano players have ever heard of—let alone listened to—Fats Waller makes the conclusion indefensible. To correct such an oversight, make sure to use qualifying words and phrases like "many," "most," "some," "several," "usually," or "for the most part" to acknowledge exceptions to general rules and to qualify general remarks.

In addition to a blend of logical reasoning and ethical appeals, persuasive writing engages readers through their emotions. That is, authors who want to persuade people through irrational but effective logic often use an emotionally charged word or phrase such as "money," "sex," or "free food." People can carefully reason what they "need" to survive in today's world, but it is far more difficult for them to get a grasp on the practicality of their "wants." Like emotionally charged words, "wants" tend to defy logic.

On Logic, Reasoning, and Fallacies

Just because we believe something is true doesn't mean that it is true. Often our wishes influence our beliefs. We want something to be true, so we believe that it is. This decision to accept certain things as true is not always a conscious or rational one. Our feelings, hopes, desires, prejudices, and fears strongly influence what we believe to be true. In order to justify beliefs that may not be true, we invent rationalizations that appear reasonable but are often a form of self-deception meant to defend our own ego rather than determine what is actually true or not true. Rationalizations are a way of making excuses for ourselves so that we can defend ourselves from ideas that would humiliate us to admit are true.

Logic and reasoning are mental tools for examining the validity (truth) of ideas, assumptions, beliefs, and the relationships between them. Logic is a kind of word game based on definitions and their implications. Informal logic refers to the everyday application of this game. It is not "formal" like mathematics or computer programming, which attempt to adhere strictly to the conclusions that can be drawn from their highly artificial definitions. "Informal logic" is based upon meanings (definitions, premises) and inferences rather than the purely logical structure of an argument, and it may be true or false, depending on the evidence that supports it. An argument can be logically coherent but untrue because it is based on false premises.

Logic also provides a method for sorting out various claims. Fallacies are errors in reasoning; they are sometimes unintentional (unconscious rationalizing) or intentional (propaganda, advertising). They also can be very persuasive because they help us to rationalize; after all, nothing makes us feel better than to hear an argument that reaffirms what we already believe is true. Feeling good about ourselves will not strengthen an argument, however, particularly when it is riddled with logical fallacies. Therefore, take time to proofread, locate, and correct errors in reasoning when you write. The following list of "informal fallacies" is by no means exhaustive, but they represent the types of reasoning errors that, if left unchecked, could undermine and invalidate the sort of argumentative papers written for the college classroom or an employer.

Logical Fallacies

Attacking the Person ("Ad Hominem")

This fallacy uses personal insult as a way to weaken an opponent's argument. It replaces reasoning with name-calling.

Rush Limbaugh referred to Hillary Clinton as a "femiNazi."

Ronald Reagan was referred to as an "empty suit."

Republicans call Democrats "tax-and-spend liberals."

Democrats call Republicans "right-wing extremists."

Insults, whether clever or crude, never add any truth to an argument, and they frequently backfire by making the person who uses them seem desperate to win an argument by any means possible. A solid argument is always more persuasive than a good insult.

Appeal to the Mob ("Ad Populum")

This is a fallacy that makes use of highly volatile and emotional language that is meant to stir up a crowd and sometimes inspire violent actions. This strategy usually involves demonizing a particular group of people so that they are seen as evil, amoral, and threatening. When a crowd of people feels threatened, it easily becomes angry, agitated, and hostile. Racist ideologies, for example, usually claim that other races are deceitful, selfish, dangerous, aggressive, and sub-human. These claims are clothed in various labels and characterizations, but they amount to an attempt to arouse base feelings of distrust, hostility, and revenge.

Argument to Pity

This fallacy attempts to win an argument by appealing for sympathy, by influencing our feelings rather than our thinking.

> A student says to a professor, "You can't give me a C in this course. I'll never get accepted into the Nursing program. Don't you want to help me?" (A professor can only give a grade based on a student's performance in the class.)

> An ad might say, "If you really care about your children's future, you'll buy them a personal cellular phone. They can call you when they need you." (This says nothing about the cost of the phone or the limitations of its use.)

Begging the Question, or Circular Reasoning

A sound argument makes points not already contained in the conclusion. A circular argument attempts to prove a statement is true by simply repeating the statement in other words. Consider the following statements:

- Bernard Hermann lost the Union election in 1998 because he didn't get enough votes. (*Losing an election and not getting enough votes mean the same thing. We still don't know why Hermann lost the election.*)
- Abortion should be illegal because it takes the life of a baby. (*The whole debate over abortion has to do with the legal rights of a person. Pretending that the distinction between a fetus and a baby can be overlooked is an attempt to win an argument by avoiding the central point at debate. Those who support legalized abortion believe that a fetus does not have the same legal standing as a baby.*)

- Free-trade agreements are good because they lead to the increased buying and selling of goods. (*Trading is the buying and selling of goods.*)
- The *Bible* is true because it is the Word of God. How do we know it is the Word of God? The *Bible* says so. (*To prove that the Bible is the Word of God would require confirmation from some other source than the Bible. On the other hand, holy texts are usually said to be the word of God; how do we know? The holy texts like the Bible—the Koran, the Bhagavad-Gita, the Tibetan Book of the Dead—tell us so.*)
- Greg's pit bull is mean because it is vicious. (*If it is in a dog's nature to be vicious, the dog can just as easily be mean; in either case, the dog is destructive and dangerous.*)

In each case a point is simply restated in a new way. No new information has been introduced to show the validity of the premise.

Circular reasoning looks like this: X is true if Y is true. Y is true only if X is true.

Either/Or Fallacy

This is a fallacy that there are only two possible points of view on any possible issue and that these two opposing views do not allow for any gradations between them.

- If you're not part of the solution, you're part of the problem. (*This implies there is only one solution and that no debate about possible alternatives is required.*)
- If you love your parents, then you must never criticize them. (*This suggests that criticism and love are necessarily opposed to one another. Constructive criticism can be an expression of both concern and caring, usually considered aspects of love.*)
- America, love it or leave it. (*This implies that one cannot have mixed feelings about America and still want to remain.*)

Causal Fallacy ("Post Hoc Ergo Propter Hoc")

A causal fallacy—post hoc ergo propter hoc—literally means, "After this, therefore because of this." This fallacy arises from the confusion between a temporal relation between events and a causal relation. In other words, just because Event B comes after Event A does not mean it was caused by Event A.

During the presidential campaign of 1992, the George Bush ads reminded voters that George Bush was elected president in 1988 and that the Soviet Union collapsed and the Berlin Wall came down in 1989. *(This ad was meant to imply that the election of George Bush in 1988 had somehow caused these other two momentous events to occur. Actually, these events might have had very little to do with who was elected president in 1988. Their historical causes are numerous, complex, and rooted in circumstances beyond the borders of the United States.)*

Sweeping Generalizations and Stereotypes

This fallacy disregards the need for verifiable facts and a broad sampling of evidence. A sweeping generalization simply makes claim after claim without ever justifying the remarks. Writers who use sweeping generalizations expect readers to trust them.

People enjoy riding roller coasters and visiting the penny arcade when they go to an amusement park. *(The mere fact that one person may dislike going to places where people are visiting arcades or riding roller coasters is enough to make this statement untrue.)*

Before and after making broad claims, provide readers with plenty of representative details and examples as well as some qualifying words such as often, usually, most of the time, and so on.

Remember, locating fallacies, half-truths, and distorted facts in what others write may very well sharpen the argumentative edge or point of attack in your own composition. In a well-written argument, logic functions like a solid foundation for a building: It stabilizes what you say. Once the logic becomes tainted or expressed in faulty terms, however, the strength and power of the structure weakens and falls apart. Therefore, when you revise your essay, eliminate logical fallacies and add carefully reasoned remarks to qualify a generalization.

Choosing Just the Right Words: Diction and Style

Precise word choice is yet another important item to strive for as you edit successive drafts of an essay. Conveying exactly what you mean and nothing more or less, however, is not as easy as it sounds. Diction (word choice) can often miss its intended mark when shaded by connotations—associations with a word—or imprecise, indirect words. In the essay that follows, John Leo discusses two different styles of word choice: euphemisms and doublespeak. Euphemism is a word of Greek origin that means "good sound"; it refers to words that are used in specific situations because they are less offensive or are less likely to arouse strong feelings. For example, after an airplane accident, the news reporters would likely say that the "remains" were removed from the site of the crash rather than the "corpses" or "dead bodies." The bathroom is often referred to as "the john," "the powder room," or "the rest room." New taxes have been called "revenue enhancers"; civilians killed as a result of military combat have been called "collateral damage."

Doublespeak, a word invented by George Orwell and used in his novel *1984*, refers to language used by a totalitarian (authoritarian) government to conceal its actions and to confuse its citizens. Phrases like "War is peace" or "Freedom is slavery" have this effect. Some groups today often use words to conceal or misrepresent their stated goals. A pro-pesticide lobbying group might call itself "Friends of the Forest," or a group of property owners who want to resist environmental regulations might call themselves "The Save Our Rivers Foundation." To use language in this way creates confusion because the words themselves cannot be trusted.

Leo's essay points out that euphemisms and doublespeak are two examples of how word choice can create bad style—that is, language that conceals more than it reveals. In recent years, "political correctness" has also become a style issue because various groups have sought to remove the built-in biases in language. The desire to use words that are not offensive has led to new words like "fireperson," "chairperson," and "mentally challenged." Will nonbiased language lead to less prejudice in our society, or will it merely provoke a backlash of resistance and ridicule? These are some of the questions raised by Leo's essay. When you read this essay, you should underline the words that have the strongest effect on you.

Who's for a Little Tongue Violence?
Euphemism and Doublespeak

John Leo

JOHN LEO frequently comments on language, the media, and communication in the United States. His latest book is entitled *Incorrect Thoughts: Notes on Our Wayward Culture*. A staff writer for *U.S. News and World Report*, Leo wrote "Who's for a Little Tongue Violence" for publication in the On Society section of that magazine in the April 15, 1996, issue. His article considers the negative aspects of euphemism and doublespeak in the English language, since they both make communication less exact and frequently "conceal" information or confuse readers.

1   Some recent bulletins from the language wars:

2   There are no more girdles left in the world—they are all "shapewear" now. "Homosexual marriage" is gone too, replaced by the more abstract and perhaps more soothing "same-sex marriage." Childless couples have all been replaced by "child free" ones. Nudists have virtually disappeared, though there are many practitioners of clothing-optional lifestyle. And at Stanford University, nobody ever fails a course. Instead of getting an F, a dedicated campus underachiever gets an NP—no pass. (Last season the Stanford football team had 7 wins, 3 no-wins and a tie.)

3   Sex and death are the natural producers of gassy euphemisms. The Navy's "swimmer nullification program" turns out to be a program to teach our frogmen how to kill other countries' frogmen. Drag queens, as common these days as table salt, are mutating upscale into "gender illusionists," and the removal of a man's genitals in an effort to convert him into a woman is now "gender reassignment," formerly transsexual surgery. ("Hopkins, up 'til now, you've been a male and a darned good one, but now we have a new assignment for you. . . .")

4   In the multicultural wars, one of the clever moves by the multiculturalists was simply to add an "s" to the term "American people." This apparently harmless plural effortlessly removed the unum from e pluribus unum in the state history standards of Colorado and in the first and very controversial version of the national history standards. As John Fonte of the American Enterprise Institute said, this was a "revolutionary" step, implying that America is a loose multinational confederation of separate peoples, something like the former Yugoslavia. In the new and much better national standards, released last week, all the "American peoples" have been changed back to "American people."

5   "Third World," the cold-war term for nonaligned nations, now increasingly means "non-whites." In William Kunstler's obituary, the *Los Angeles Times* reminded us that in defending a black New Yorker, he deplored "how the police treat young Third World people in the depressed communities of our city." Brown University has a Third World Center, though many of the alleged third-worlders who use it are actually from New York or Los Angeles.

6   Co-opt the Media. In advocacy language, the first rule of thumb is: Remove the operative word and get the media to use your new term. "Choice" was a brilliant verbal maneuver. It avoided the operative and emotive word "abortion" and positioned what is, after all, a killing procedure as a simple matter of preference, just one more purely commercial transaction in a market economy based on choice. Bill Clinton, arguing in 1991 that Bush administration officials "want to expand opportunity for choice in education and every other area but want to restrict it on abortion," was not just backing abortion-rights advocates. He was buying into the argument embedded in the polemical word "choice."

7   A lot of verbal gamesmanship now surrounds euthanasia and assisted suicide. The Ninth Circuit Court of Appeals suggests we talk about "hastening death" rather than assisted suicide. "Aid in dying" is a failed euphemism (Derek Humphry, founder of the Hemlock Society, says so). "Death with dignity" successfully eliminates any reference to suicide or mercy killing. But the pesky D-word is still in there. The perfect death-free euphemism is yet to be found. In his book, The Inarticulate Society, Tom Schactman points out that many schools now refer to their charges as "clients" rather than "students," and often talk about "success" and "accomplishment" rather than learning. He thinks this is a strategic move reflecting the intention to give the young what they want (i.e., serving a client) at the expense of what most of us would call education.

8   Politically correct language has given us the terms visual rape (staring), mental rape (lying or confusing someone to gain sexual consent), educational genocide (the schools are terrible), cultural genocide (the ban on fur is hurting the economy of Canada's native people), environmental child abuse (they are building an incinerator next door). In all these cases, the aim is to take a perceived offense and ratchet it up into a more serious category of offense, thus inflaming the issue and gaining more attention.

9   The best example of this is the tendency to regard words as actions. (If words are acts, presumably they can be punished without raising traditional First Amendment issues.) Words and violent actions are lumped together into statistics on "ethnoviolence." "Violence of the tongue," a phrase used by Martin Luther King Jr., has become extremely popular for its linking of vile talk and vile action. Sometimes it appears in an improbable form: "tongue violence."

10   Back to the euphemism frontier. To the amazement of all, pedophiles and some sex researchers now refer to adult sex with children as "intergenerational intimacy." ("Officer, one of these children has just been groped by this intergenerational intimate, formerly a child molester.") It would be interesting to speculate how the rest of the perversions could be brightened up with spiffy new language. Perhaps necrophilia would emerge as "post-terminal intimacy."

Questions for Discussion or Writing

1. What is Leo trying to say in this essay about word choices? Why does he object to some words and not others?

2. Can you think of situations in which euphemisms might be appropriate? When? Where? Why?

3. Can you find examples of doublespeak in your own environment?

4. What do you think "political correctness" means? Why does the attempt to find nonoffensive language seem to offend some people? Think of some examples of political correctness and analyze them.

Vocabulary Logs

A "vocabulary log" is a place to keep new, unfamiliar words and their definitions. Beginning with John Leo's essay, "Who's for a Little Tongue Violence? Euphemism and Doublespeak," record new words and their definitions (both look them up in a dictionary and review how they were used in the piece that you read) in your personal vocabulary log. At least once a week, review all the words in your vocabulary log, and look for them in future readings. Your objective here is not only to increase your vocabulary but also to develop an awareness of when and where you might use newly acquired words correctly in your own writings.

The Grading Standards Form:
A Student/Instructor Checklist

The following form summarizes the characteristics of a college essay in an evaluative scheme. It can be used to help you evaluate your own papers before turning them in. This "self-grading" method is a way to remind yourself of all the parts of a paper that need to be checked over before you turn it in. It outlines the three major components of an essay: rhetoric, style and diction, and editing. It lists positive and negative traits associated with each aspect of an essay. This form can be read over before you start writing to remind you of the goals to be achieved in writing; also, it can be used when you have finished a first draft to evaluate your own work. Furthermore, your instructors may also wish you to attach a copy of this form to the compositions to provide them with a means of evaluating and encouraging the ongoing development of your composition skills.

Both students and instructors may modify a grading standards chart or a checklist for drafting, revising, and editing papers, of course, but in any case, it should serve as a positive indicator of your progress in writing skills as well as what you need to work on. Moreover, an equal amount of attention should be paid to what you do well when you write as well as to the respective aspects of writing (drafting, revising, editing). That way, you will develop as a "whole writer" instead of one who excels only in a single area of concern such as rhetoric, style and diction, or editing.

Writing is a solitary task, but it is not a lonely one. No one else can do your writing for you, but, on the other hand, whatever you choose to write is part of a network of connections you have established in your own mind with other

---

GRADING STANDARDS: COMPOSITION

---

1 = Very Weak   2 = Weak   3 = Adequate   4 = Strong   5 = Very Strong

Rhetoric

Thesis: (+) a thoughtful, perceptive, and focused generalization; a point worth making; a clear plan for development

(−) vague or commonplace statements; topic needs to be narrowed

1 2 3 4 5

Unity: (+) maintenance of focus; each paragraph relates to the thesis; key terms have been defined; thorough explanations

(−) insufficient explanation; straying from main point

1 2 3 4 5

Coherence: (+) logical order; effective use of transition words and statements

(−) abrupt and unexplained transitions; difficult to see connection between ideas

1 2 3 4 5

Completeness: (+) solid evidence; specific and concrete details; relevant examples

(−) insufficient development due to lack of quotes, facts, examples, details

1 2 3 4 5

Style and Diction

Persona & Readability: (+) engaging voice; and tone sentence variety; parallel structure; appropriate vocabulary; clarity of expression

(−) distracting or untrustworthy voice; awkward sentence structure; wordiness; inaccurate word choices; confusing word order

1 2 3 4 5

Individuality: (+) independent thinking; freshness; lively and varied vocabulary

(−) stereotyped thinking; truisms; clichés; received ideas; lack of analysis

1 2 3 4 5

Editing

Grammar: (+) error-free sentences; correct usage

(−) fragment, run-ons, comma splices, improper verb forms, pronoun-antecedent agreement

1 2 3 4 5

Punctuation: (+) correct usage

(−) commas, quotation marks, possessive apostrophes, semicolons, capitalization

1 2 3 4 5

Spelling: (number of errors: _____)

1 2 3 4 5

Manuscript Form: (+) typed; double-spaced; standard margins

(−) not typed or poorly typed; nonstandard format

1 2 3 4 5

writers and other potential readers. As soon as you start to write, you begin to think about who you are writing for, who your future readers—your audience—might be. Writing is a very particular form of communication. It is more formal and more exact than daily conversation. It can be read and reread. It has to get along without gestures, facial expressions, and tone of voice. You have to think about how to put your words together on a page so that something interesting will happen in the mind of the reader. This is challenging, frustrating, exciting, and satisfying all at the same time. It is very common to hear writers complain in interviews about how difficult it is to write, but very few of them want to give it up to do other kinds of work. Writing is work. There is no getting around that; but it is creative work, work that starts out with a blank sheet of paper or a blank screen and develops slowly into something that has form, content, and a life of its own.

Sample Student Essay

The following student essay on college athletics represents a series of steps in the writing process. The author first interviewed a former college athlete and then read several articles about the special issues related to college athletics. Next he wrote a rough draft that was rewritten twice before this final version was finished. The essay shows how a college writer can take a topic with some personal interest but go beyond merely personal writing. By making research an integral part of developing his topic, the student writer has included points of view and information that give his argument greater credibility. The essay is organized in sections of two to three paragraphs that develop separate parts of his argument. This gives the essay more breadth and shows the relationship between a range of related topics.

College Athletics: Not What It Appears to Be

Keith Sego

Keith Sego, a student at Eastern Washington University, wrote the following expository essay to examine the image and the reality of college athletics. His assignment was to find information about his topic from articles and an interview.

(1) Professional athletes receive enormous wealth and recognition. Many young people fantasize about what a

Continued

life it would be—to have all the things you want and
to have everyone know who you are; after all, money
and fame are powerful motivators. What does it take
to make it though? There isn't a class to teach you
how to become a super athlete. Only for the lucky few
does this become a reality. Athletes are admired, but
there is a dark side to the dream. Besides the
physical demands, there are others as well: coaches
and scouts pursue young athletes, sportswriters track
their behavior on and off the field, and others try
to become their friends hoping to receive something
in return. A young athlete must make many decisions
under academic, social and economic pressure. These
decisions can make or break an athlete's future. In
order to understand the complexity of this situation,
college athletics can be broken down into several
components: the recruitment of athletes and the
financial fundraising required; the education of
athletes and how they cope with academic life; and
the steps that organizations like the NCAA must take
to regulate the practices of colleges.
(2) College sports have become so popular and so
profitable for the colleges that coaches and programs
will do almost anything to recruit the best possible
team. The demand for all-star college athletes is
very high, but there are only a few who fit the
qualifications. Recruiting used to be simpler decades
ago when a coach would ask a player to go to his
college, and in return the student would receive a
scholarship or some financial aid. With gratitude,
the student would accept and become a "student-
athlete," but today everyone is more interested in
being an "athlete-student." Athletics comes first.
Most importantly, recruitment was done legally
because there wasn't such a bidding war. The stakes
were not so high. Today, a hot prospect can expect
many kinds of offers, both legal and illegal. The
National Collegiate Athletic Association (NCAA)
clearly states that no athlete is allowed to receive
any gifts other than financial aid for attending
school, but in many cases prospects receive cars,

money, houses, and clothes. Not only is recruiting done illegally, but the pressure sometimes amounts to psychological harassment. Coaches will send letters, talk to the player's current coach, and visit the player's home in order to sign an athlete. Illegal recruiting takes place with foreign players as well. Rules regarding citizenship, student admission, and academic eligibility are broken. When colleges recruit players from countries such as Nigeria, Russia, or Japan, the athletes receive visas, which allow them to enroll in school for a certain period of time. Many times these visas contain false information, or, if the athlete is not successful, they expire and are not renewed. This results in termination of the visa and deportation of the player.

(3) College sports have become a business. It has become the minor league for professional sports, especially football and basketball. The NCAA is such a big business that it has talked about paying athletes for their duties as though it were a job. This is on top of the incentives they already receive both legally and illegally. I interviewed Peter Shaw, a former football player for Washington State University. According to him, players were not allowed to have jobs while participating in sports because there is not enough free time. Therefore, if they could not work and did not receive any illegal incentives, the athletes would not have a financial means of supporting themselves. He believes that college athletes are exploited, especially when they do not receive anything but their scholarship money. Major universities with sports reputations such as Duke, North Carolina, Michigan, and Florida State rack up hundreds of thousands of dollars on ticket sales each year and millions more from television revenues. CBS paid close to $200 million a year for the rights to NCAA basketball, and has just signed a $6 billion contract for the exclusive rights to broadcast their basketball games over the next

Continued

thirteen years. Only a tiny fraction of this money goes to athletes. What happens to the athletes who compete for four years and don't get drafted by a professional team? These athletes often fail to receive a degree because they are strongly encouraged to be athletes first and students second. They return home, their eligibility used up, their scholarship terminated, and their college career over. Meanwhile, the colleges that recruited them feel no obligation to help them return to school. The athletes feel they have been used up and thrown away.

(4) Other problems come from "boosters." Boosters are loyal fans or local supporters who donate time and money to help a school's sports program. But these "boosters" break the NCAA rules when their "honest gifts" are used in illegal recruiting schemes that provide athletes with "gifts" like automobiles, free apartments, and clothes. A survey showed that one third of athletes questioned said they had received some sort of illegal payment provided by boosters. In some cases, the schools knew about this and decided not to do anything about it. Sometimes boosters almost seem to be running the athletic department, and even worse, they appear to be doing it with the encouragement of the college administration. In a recent study, sixty schools had been cited for violating NCAA rules, and of these sixty, forty-nine involved violations related to boosters.

(5) College *education* for athletes appears no longer to be a priority. In fact, not only is the education not taken seriously, but also coaches and programs play a role in the schemes to give out grades to athletes who do not deserve them. Many college athletes do not enroll in college-level classes, nor do they live on campus. They are kept separate from the mainstream of college life. The University of Miami once recruited a football player who received a 200 on the verbal section of his SAT. This is just about the lowest score possible; nevertheless, over 150 colleges attempted to recruit this athlete.

(6) A college *education* may be exactly what athletes need. Instead of blaming the low SAT scores and GPAs on the players, these scores may come from poor teaching, cultural differences, or underprivileged backgrounds. A study showed that from 1994 to 1996, 58% of student athletes graduated compared to the general student body's 57%. This suggests that teachers are dishing out unearned grades, and players enroll in a steady stream of "cupcake classes." Though this number includes both male and female athletes, female athletes apparently come into college with a different mindset. Their minds aren't necessarily focused exclusively on professional teams, and they concentrate harder on their studies and achieve more academic success. In 1996, a study showed that 68% of women athletes graduated after six years compared to only 54% of men.

(7) Although it may be true about some grades being given away, some college athletes have the opportunity to get academic help if they wish to use it. In 1991, the NCAA made it a requirement for all colleges to have tutoring and academic counseling centers for student athletes to get independent help with work they might not understand, or with classes they might have missed. Michigan State University recently opened the Clara Belle Smith Student-Athlete Academic Center to help student athletes with their schoolwork. It is the latest and arguably the most elaborate example of an academic facility for athletes. Sundays through Thursdays, about two-hundred-and-fifty students fill two computer labs with sixty computers, and one-hundred-and-seventy tutors who provide approximately one thousand tutoring sessions per week. Why is all this necessary? Basketball, for example, with its daily practice, weeknight games, long schedules and constant traveling takes its toll on players' academics (Scott interview).

(8) Despite these controversies, more and more is being done by the NCAA to limit the amount of

Continued

corruption. The NCAA has established a few more rules to regulate recruiting and academic processes. These rules (1) limit the number of days coaches are allowed to attend summer camps and tournaments for scouting, (2) take scholarships away from teams that fail to graduate at least 33% of their players, (3) award scholarships to teams that graduate at least 75% of their players, and (4) limit teams to recruiting only eight players every two years (no more than five in one year) in order to cut down on the number of athletes who are forced to quit or transfer because of bigger and better players being brought in, and athletes would have to pass at least 12 hours of course work with at least a 2.0 GPA at the end of their first term in college to be eligible. With these new rules, NCAA officials are trying to avoid the demands of tracking down complex cases of academic fraud which are costly and time consuming to prove. They believe that the institutions themselves have been doing a very good job of monitoring the academic eligibility of their athletes. The most popular target is recruiting violations.

(9) College athletes receive benefits and, in some cases, illegal benefits. This has made college athletics the target for the media and for officials suspicious of successful and popular athletic programs. Because of the recognition and demand for these talented athletes, it appears that no one cares what the ordinary student is doing—only the athlete. We may envy the abilities of athletes, their privileges, or their accomplishments, but the athletes go through a lot more than people know to get where they are and to succeed in school without upsetting officials or violating any rules. It is not as easy to be a college athlete as it seems.

Part Two

Thematic Readings

The American Family

Observations and Opinions

When I was a boy of fourteen, my father was so ignorant I could hardly stand to have the old man around. But, when I got to be twenty-one, I was astonished at how much he had learned in seven years."

—MARK TWAIN

. . . the extended family can resolve at a stroke all the problems of unequal talents and unequal success which otherwise arouse that devastating emotion—human egoism. The function of the family is to level out inequality.

—HAN SUYIN FROM "THE FAMILY OF TOMORROW"

Come mothers and fathers
Throughout the land
And don't criticize
What you can't understand
Your sons and your daughters
Are beyond your command
Your old road is
Rapidly agin'.
Please get out of the new one
If you can't lend your hand
For the times they are a changin'.

—BOB DYLAN FROM "THE TIMES THEY ARE A-CHANGIN' "

While entertaining a visitor, one hears some servants chatting
without any restraint in one of the back rooms. It is embarrassing to
know that one's visitor can overhear. But how to stop them?
   A man whom one loves gets drunk and keeps repeating himself.
   To have spoken about someone not knowing that he could overhear. . . .
   To hear one's servants making merry. This is equally annoying if
one is on a journey and staying in cramped quarters or at home and
hears the servants in a neighboring room.
   Parents, convinced that their ugly child is adorable, pet him and
repeat the things he has said, imitating his voice.
   An ignoramus who in the presence of some learned person puts
on a knowing air and converses about men of old.
   A man recites his own poems (not especially good ones) and tells
one about the praise they have received—most embarrassing.
   Lying awake at night, one says something to one's companion,
who simply goes on sleeping.
   In the presence of a skilled musician, someone plays a zither just
for his own pleasure and without tuning it.
   A son-in-law who has long since stopped visiting his wife runs
into his father-in-law in a public place.

—Sei Shonogon, "Embarrassing Things" from *The Pillow Book*

Observations and Opinions: Reading/Writing Activities

1. What does Han Suyin mean by "extended family"? Contrast her sincere words with Mark Twain's ironic remarks about his father. What point is Twain trying to make? Write your response to these questions using a variety of sentence patterns.

2. Write your own definition of an American family in your journal, considering gender roles and family structure. You might then reflect on Bob Dylan's appeal to parents to understand rather than criticize their children. Do times ever change with regard to parent/child relations?

3. Reread the list of "Embarrassing Things" by Sei Shonogon and take another look at the cartoon following it. Then, write a two-part journal entry. First, write your own list of embarrassing things. Next, reflect back on your list and Sei Shonogon's list of embarrassing things, and comment on why looking back at an embarrassing moment often can be funny. You might want to draw an original cartoon, along with captions, of one of your own embarrassing moments. Then, look at the elements of your cartoon (e.g., frame, caption, content—what is happening and to whom), and try to reconstruct it as a brief paragraph, making extensive use of concrete nouns and active verbs. What might this activity suggest about the challenge of painting a picture with words?

Introduction

How would you define a "family"? Is there a model for the American family? What values do you associate with the word "family"? Is discussion of family values merely political campaign banter or a reflection of deeply felt human needs? Discussions about family bring in other words like love, nurturing, support, devotion, loyalty, and care, but these words are abstractions, and family life consists of many specific actions, the particular things you do or don't do for the people you live with. Family life can mean staying up with a sick child, shopping for dinner, picking up someone from school, helping with homework, or watching a movie together. These specific activities represent patterns of behavior, patterns that can become almost rituals, that create a predictable emotional order in our lives. A family could be defined as any group of people who know each other well because they spend a lot of time together and care about each other, but there is more to it than this.

Families are a source of values, but they are also a source of conflict. The negative side of family life brings to mind words like neglect, rivalry, unrealistic expectations, control, and abuse. Leo Tolstoy, the Russian novelist, began *Anna Karenina* with, "All happy families are the same, but every unhappy family is unhappy in its own way." Unhappy family life has provoked writing for thousands of years. In one of the earliest stories in the Old Testament, Cain kills Abel, his brother; in Greek mythology, Chronos, the father of the gods, tries to kill his sons and is, in turn, killed by one of them. Think of the strange story of Oedipus, the king who killed his father and married his mother without knowing it, or of Shakespeare's King Lear, abandoned by his daughters. Stories like this express the tension and the power of the psychological bonds that develop within a family. When they are broken, the consequences can be devastating.

Peer groups, congregations, political parties, and generation members can also function like a family. Even sports teams and television newscasting crews refer to themselves as families. Why? A family and its members nurture, support, defend, and comfort each other.

All of the following readings reveal something about identity and family. Louise Erdrich recalls retrieving a stray kitten from beneath her house and meditates upon motherhood, emptiness, and premonitions of death. In contrast, Anna Quindlen presents a picture of motherhood far from the romanticized image one finds on a Hallmark card. John Marlowe thinks about the way generations pass on what they know to one another in lifetimes that pass by all too quickly. Alice Walker regrets not knowing her father better while he was alive. She speculates about what a difference knowing him might have made for her. James Houston, on the other hand, explains that he resisted much in his father's world—especially music—as a youth. Nonetheless, Houston shows how families "pass on" music from generation to generation, creating a heritage and a tradition that ultimately become the memories that define who and what we are.

The following authors rely on storytelling, or narration, because it offers them a method of communicating through a chronological sequence of events. Louise Erdrich recalls an event so common that ordinarily it barely would be worth mentioning; John Marlowe reminisces about his son's pet rat; Alice Walker rethinks her relationship with her father; and James Houston explains how returning to country music created a loving, appreciative bond between him and his father.

Gathering Thoughts: Prereading Inquiries

Consider the following questions and respond to them informally in your journal or writing log. You might return to these questions after reading this chapter and note what, if anything, you understand from a different point of view and how and why some responses were confirmed by the section authors, individual assignments, and collaborative activities.

1. What is the duty or responsibility of a family? Has your understanding of family obligations ever changed (e.g., for a single-parent family, for an extended family)?

2. Do you think mothers and fathers mirror child-rearing practices and behavior patterns of their own parents? Would you choose to be just like your parents if and when you have children?

3. James Baldwin once said, "Children have never been very good at listening to their elders, but they have never failed to imitate them." What did he mean by that, and what does it suggest about family communication?

4. What is meant by "human nature"? How does your definition of human nature affect your beliefs about families and the role they play in human development?

5. Does living in a family teach you anything about the relationship between freedom and responsibility? Do families give us more freedom or less? Is "freedom" just an illusion? Explain.

6. How should parents discipline their children, on one hand, and show respect for them on the other? Is such a relationship even possible? How should parents use authority within the family?

7. Someone once said, *"children love to learn but hate to be taught."* Reflect on your childhood and prove or disprove this quote with two concrete examples.

8. What sacrifices do you think a person should make for his or her partner and family to ensure a healthy relationship?

9. Will individual relationships become more or less important to you in the 21st century? How or why will father/son, father/daughter,

> mother/son, mother/daughter relationships change or remain the same? Why?
>
> **10**. How do you plan to share quality time with your own children if and when you have a family? What lessons did you learn from your parents? When you raise children of your own, what might you emphasize differently than your parents, and how might this meet the immediate needs of our youth?

Beneath the House

Louise Erdrich

Of Chippewa and German American descent, **LOUISE ERDRICH** is both a poet and a novelist and frequently writes about the Native American experience. Erdrich's published works include *Jacklight* (1984), *Baptism of Desire* (1989), and *Fishing for Myth* (1997), collections of poetry, and several novels: *Love Medicine* (1984), *The Beet Queen* (1986), *Tracks* (1988), *The Bingo Palace* (1994), and *Tales of Burning Love* (1996). Erdrich's newest novel, *The Last Report on the Miracles at Little No Horse* (2001), has been described as "not so much a novel, but a study of passion" since it "explores the possibilities of love through a collection of reminiscences of four women who have been married to the same man." Other works include *The Antelope Wife: And Other Short Stories* (1998). *Erdrich* co-authored *The Crown of Columbus* with her husband, Michael Dorris (1992), now deceased, and her collection of nonfiction, regarding large and small events that every parent may face, appeared in *The Blue Jay's Dance: A Birth Year* (1995) and is also the source of this essay.

ALLUSIONS

Many of the allusions (casual references) to motherhood expressed here use figurative speech (nonliteral use of language); see the Glossary for a more detailed explanation of figuratively talking about something or someone and literally referring to one or the other.

1   It was as if the house itself had given birth. One day the floor cried where I stepped on it, and I jumped back. I was near a heating vent, and when I bent and pried the cover off and thrust my hand in, I briefly grabbed a ball of fur that hissed and spat.

I heard the kitten scrambling away, the tin resounding like small thunder along the length of its flight.

2   I went down to the basement, looking for it with a flashlight, but, of course, at my step the untamed creature fled from the concrete-floored area and off into the earthen crawl space—draped with spider webs as thick as cotton, a place of unpeeled log beams, the underside of the house. I put out milk in a saucer. I crouched on the other side of the furnace, and I waited until I fell half-asleep. But the kitten was too young to drink from a dish and never came. Instead, she set up, from just beyond where I could catch her, a piteous crying that I could hardly stand to hear.

3   I went after her. The earth was moldy, a dense clay. No sun had fallen here for over two centuries. I climbed over the brick retaining wall and crawled toward the sound of the kitten. As I neared, as it sensed my presence was too large to be its mother, it went silent and scrabbled away from the reach of my hand. I brushed fur, though, and that slight warmth filled me with what must have been a mad calm because when the creature squeezed into a bearing wall of piled stones, I inched forward on my stomach. My back was now scraping along the beams that bore the weight of the whole house above me. Tons and tons of plaster, boards, appliances, and furniture. This was no crawl space anymore. I could hardly raise my shoulders to creep forward, could move only by shifting my hips up and down. On the edge of panic—I had never before been in a space so tight—one thought pressed in: if it settled very suddenly upon my back, my last crushed words would be, "Shit! I don't even like cats." Because I don't like cats, just find their silken ways irresistible.

4   Its face popped out right in front of me, and vanished. How far back did the piled rock go? If I moved a rock, would the whole house fall on me? I reached for the kitten, missed, reached again, missed. I tried to breathe, to be patient. Then, after a time, the kitten backed toward me, away from a clump of dirt I managed to throw at the far wall. Its tail flicked through a space in the rock, and I snatched it. Held it, drew it toward me. Out it came with a squeak of terror, a series of panting comic hisses, and a whirl of claws and teeth, tiny needles it didn't yet know how to use.

5   She is a pretty cat, a calico, marbled evenly with orange and black. Rocky. She sits near as I write, leaps into the warmth of my chair when I leave, and is jealous of the baby.

6   The night after I pulled her from the house, the darkness pressed down on me until I woke. I'd swum weightlessly into a smaller and smaller space. What the body remembers of birth, it anticipates as death. In the house of my dreams the basement is the most fearful: the awful place filled with water, the place of both comfort and death. I fear in particular the small space, the earth closing in on me, the house like a mother settling its cracked bones and plumbing.

7   That afternoon, from underneath, I had heard the house all around me like an old familiar body. I hadn't told anybody else that I was going after the kitten, so nobody knew I was below. The normal sounds of my family's daily life were magnified. Their steps trailed and traveled around me, boomed in my ears. Their voices jolted me, their words loud but meaningless, warped by their travel through the walls and beams. Water flowed through invisible pipes around me, hitched and gurgled. It was like being dead, or unborn. I hadn't thought about it then, but now I could clearly see

part of me, the husk of myself, still buried against the east wall: a person sacrificed to ensure the good luck of a temple, a kind of house god, a woman lying down there, still, an empty double.

AFTERWARDS

Vocabulary

The vocabulary words are rather simple in Erdrich's essay, but they definitely serve an important function. Here, Erdrich uses personification (attributing human qualities to things that are not human) by giving the house human characteristics. What words and phrases does she use to accomplish this? In addition to personification, what other types of figurative speech (a word suggesting a figurative rather than a literal meaning) does Erdrich use here?

Content

1. After reading the title "Beneath the House," what do you expect the essay to be about and why? What clues did Erdrich's title offer? Briefly summarize the controlling idea and experience described in her essay.

2. Erdrich notices many fine details as she ventures into the basement; cite some of them.

3. What is beneath your own house? Does the structure (building foundation) allow it to have a life of its own?

4. What role does the kitten play in Erdrich's narrative? Why does Erdrich feel "on the edge of panic" while reaching for the kitten? How does she calm herself?

Style and Structure

1. How does the opening sentence, "It was as if the house itself had given birth," set the stage for the rest of the narrative?

2. Why does the author structure her essay as two distinct units?

3. How does Erdrich use transitions and linking words in this essay? How do they assist her in writing a clear narrative? In what way does Erdrich's use of details create a "special" atmosphere under her house?

Collaborative Explorations

1. Locate and visit a place below ground level. Record your thoughts in one column and your observations in another. When you return to the

classroom, write short individual compositions explaining when and where thoughts and observations mesh together. Finally, compare and contrast your short compositions with those of other class members. How were your experiences similar to and yet different from each other?

2. Personification is often useful when describing something in a narrative. In small groups, write a long paragraph in which you personify a place in your community, such as a museum. As a group, visit a place in your community, take notes, and then determine what images can give life to the place you have visited. Finally, write and revise your paragraph together.

Writing Assignments

1. Write a narrative about a discovery you made, or a time you journeyed into a place you had not previously explored. Within your narrative, describe what you found or where you journeyed, and explain what you learned from your experience.

2. Compose a narrative detailing a time when you rescued your pet from underneath a house, on top of the roof, or a similar experience. Pay particular attention to "time transitions," words that help your reader to move clearly from one moment to the next (e.g., the beginning, middle, and end of your rescue).

Thematic Reading Cross-Links: See Chapter 4, Stereotypes and Social Barriers, for other readings on people and their reaction to their immediate surroundings, especially Ishmael Reed's essay, "Ground Zero."

Movie Cross-Links: View *My Family*, mentioned on the Film Links list at the end of the chapter for a look at an extended family over the years.

I'll Do It for You

John Marlowe

JOHN MARLOWE, a former educator and high school principal at Northgate High School in Walnut Creek, California, is now a freelance writer. He and his wife live in the San Francisco Bay area and Greece. In the following essay, which initially appeared in *Phi Delta Kappan* in April 1979, Marlowe explains how both he and his son gained an increased understanding of and appreciation for life from a most unlikely source: Sassafrass, their pet rat.

ALLUSIONS

John Dewey: American philosopher who believed that education should be based upon "learning by doing."

Clark Kent: Superman's name or alias on the planet Earth (Kal-El was his name on his home planet, Krypton).

> *"All those things I can do, all those powers I have,*
> *I couldn't save him. . . ."*
>
> —A TEEN-AGE CLARK KENT AT HIS EARTH FATHER'S DEATH

1   Sassafrass, a white rat, a hefty, friendly rodent, lived with us for two years. My son, who is also named John, like me and my father, brought him home, and my wife and I immediately disliked the creature. He was too long of fang, too beady and quick in the eye department.

2   But we let the kid have his way. Especially since we argued so much lately about school. He didn't do well all the time, and the current theory was that rather than compete with a school administrator father, he'd take a dive. I hoped he'd see value in school, even though much of what he was assigned was a waste of his time and the teachers' as well. So we let a white rat into our lives and soon we were figuratively eating out of his hands as he literally ate out of ours.

3   Like all good pets he had the apparent ability to think rationally. He would do Bugs Bunny cartoon tricks, cut anthropomorphic capers around the couch at night. He'd hustle around us as we watched TV on the occasional nights I didn't have meetings or writing deadlines. He was a reasonable, responsible, white-furry participant in the family.

4   He'd sneak popcorn out of our communal bowl and burrow back into the pillows of the sofa, a friendly cave-rat in our midst. Now and then he'd run sway-butted across the back of the couch, as if he were on his way to an appointment. He'd never leave the furniture for the floor.

5   He'd stop by, take a break from his self-appointed rounds, and sniff around us with his long, thin, dignified nose with its white-pink rubbery tip constantly twitching, only to snuggle into one of our laps and take a ratnap.

6   Other times when my son would work on his electric trains or listlessly poke at his homework and listen to records, Sass would prowl around the premises, exploring, checking, and rechecking. Never trying to run away. No reason to. Content to sniff around our house and furniture as if it were truly his turf that he was more than willing to share with the rest of his pets.

7   We'd jokingly warn visitors to be careful around him because he carried a knife. Though we joked, there was that about him. A little shifty, a little more zip than the situation required. But he would make up for that minor criminality by sitting up at

your feet so you could pick him up and scratch him under the chin while he narrowed his red eyes with pleasure. Or he'd lie flat on his back in the palm of your hand, close his eyes, and luxuriate in a good old-fashioned belly scratch. You expected him to purr.

8   Sassafrass, with his thick, lush, white coat, his hand grenade solidity, was nothing if not cooperative; he recognized a good deal. And he'd surely live forever. He was smart enough to outwit death. Hide in the pillows of the couch when it came by to pick up white rats. Since all three of us Johns stand firm on each other's shoulders, we know we too will live forever, just like Sass. My father gets strength and continuity from a son and a grandson. I get it from both ends from a living father and a growing son. My son has two strong connections with the past, and his whole future ahead.

9   I knew the familiar white flash was quick enough to dart in between the raindrops of death.

10   Wrong.

11   He lost weight. With alarming rapidity, his once solid body grew skinny and trembly. Instead of running, taking deer like leaps, he'd shiver in place, cold from the draft of impending death.

12   I asked a biology teacher who seemed to favor animals what might be wrong— hoping it was something we could cure. She calmly asked his age, and when I told her, she coldly answered, "He's dying of old age."

13   "That's not possible. He's young," I argued. "He'll live for another four or five years." We had a dog's lifespan in mind.

14   "I'm sorry about what you planned," she said, but I felt she was mocking our attachment to an animal. "He's old. If he were in his natural habitat . . ."

15   "What the hell is a natural habitat any more?" I asked, though my argument was not with her.

16   "I'm not being philosophical, I'm just telling you that your white rat is dying and the kindest thing for you to do is put him to sleep."

17   "To sleep?"

18   "I can do it for you."

19   "How?"

20   "Chloroform. Simple. I'll do it for you."

21   "Can't we just let him die?"

22   "Sure, but he's in a lot of pain. In the real world . . ."

23   The real world, I thought. What is the real world if this wasn't it?

24   She continued, ". . . in the real world he would have been killed by natural enemies."

25   Not Sass. He was too smart, too agile, too quick, too personable, too much like the three of us. He'd organize other rats to save himself; they'd rally to his defense. He'd outlast them all.

26   "He isn't very pleasant to have around now. I'll do it for you."

27   "Are you sure he's hurting?"

28   "Positive."

29   I knew John's decision would be for the chloroform if there were pain. I thought of the poor rat shivering in his dank skin that was losing hair, which had turned yellow and sticky. "We can do it."

30   John and I stood in his room. He held the trembling, blind animal gently to his chest; I held a coffee can, a wad of cotton, and the bottle.

31   "Will it hurt him?"

32   "I don't think so. If it does, it won't be much more than the pain he is already feeling. She said it would be just like going to sleep for him."

33   "He won't be running around my room any more."

34   "That's right."

35   "And he won't be sneaking around the couch while we all watch TV."

36   "I guess not."

37   "He won't be stealing popcorn."

38   "No, he won't."

39   "Will it hurt?"

40   "I don't know . . . I don't know . . . It should be just like going to sleep. Do you want me to do it, John?"

41   "No. Maybe we both should."

42   "O.K. We can help each other." John's throat was moving and he was taking long blinks to keep back the tears. So was I.

43   "Put him in the can," I said. He kissed the poor, dying rodent on the top of its head, then gently slid it into the hideously shining interior of the can while I saturated the cotton with chloroform.

44   Sass, in the bottom of the reflecting container, panted weakly. I dropped the wet cotton in and snapped the plastic cover on tightly. We held the can firmly in our four hands.

45   And then Sass shook violently with a final fury. The can jumped in our grip from his frantic death throes, a last dodge away from what must hit us all, Sass and all three Johns.

46   And I felt the shiver go through me and my son, and we both knew that, some day, we would each do the same. I have to protect him from it as best I can, and he has to protect me. And though we never said the words, we realized the implications of our deed.

47   The can stopped quivering and we held it, our fingers entwined, both learning more about our future than any school could ever teach.

AFTERWARDS

Vocabulary

anthropomorphic, communal, luxuriate, chloroform. Look up the suffixes and/or prefixes for three of these words, and then write a short paragraph explaining how knowing the meaning of a prefix (e.g., bio, meaning "life") or a suffix (e.g., -ist, meaning "one who") can help you to predict the meanings of some words when used in context.

Content

1. Who or what was Sassafrass? What does Marlowe call Sassafrass for short? How might this nickname connote one of Sassafrass's character traits? Offer some examples.

2. Describe Marlowe and his wife's immediate impression of Sassafrass. How and why does this initial impression change as time passes?

3. What does Sassafrass teach Marlowe and his son about themselves and their future? When, where, why, and how do they reach a greater understanding of life?

Style and Structure

1. Analyze the emotional impact of the final five paragraphs in Marlowe's essay. How do they express sensitivity and appeal to a reader's emotions?

2. Illustrate how readers learn about Marlowe, the speaker, through his dialogue with his son and the biology instructor. What do both conversations reveal about the speaker? Why do you think Marlowe felt dialogue would communicate some ideas better than a narrative?

3. Compare and contrast your reaction to "I'll Do It for You," the title of Marlowe's essay, before and after you read the piece. How does the title capture the essence of Marlowe's essay? What takes place, and who is involved? Why do you imagine he chose that particular phrase?

Collaborative Explorations

Select a recorder for your group to take notes, and then discuss the general idea of Marlowe's narrative essay. Summarize it. Next, take paragraphs 1–7 and rewrite them, inserting occasional dialogue. That is, take some of the facts and details the author tells you and activate them by using dialogue. Each paragraph will still contain a degree of narration, of course, but rather than telling readers,

"My son, who is also named John, like me and my father, brought him home, and my wife and I immediately disliked the creature," you would show your feelings in a line of dialogue such as, "John! What do you think you're doing bringing a rat home? We better not see it running loose in the house!" Pass the rough copy of the assignment from one group member to another, making suggestions and correcting careless errors. Discuss the individual critiques of the assignment and then prepare a final draft of it to (1) read to the rest of the class and (2) submit to your instructor.

Writing Assignments

1. Write an essay describing the life and death of the first pet you or someone you know owned. Begin your composition with some sentences that "lead in" to the controlling idea of your essay. Then develop it by offering some detailed descriptions of memorable activities with the pet (e.g., when you first got it, how it grew over the years, and when it died). You might conclude your essay by explaining how the questions asked and the confusion felt at the time of the pet's death have now become clarified.

2. Have your librarian or English instructor help you to locate a copy of E. B. White's essay "Once More to the Lake" in your library. Then read it, assess it (what happens in the narrative essay? what is the relationship between the father and the son?), and then write an essay comparing and contrasting the father/son experiences expressed by Marlowe and White. How do both essays conclude with insights into the temporary nature of life and the bonds between generations?

Thematic Reading Cross-Links: See Chapter 9, Television, for an alternative look at the most influential force shaping attitudes toward death and illness.

Movie Cross-Links: Several movies on the film list in the Film Links section of this chapter touch on the fragility of life and the grieving process, including *Men Don't Leave* and *Yi-Yi.*

Father

Alice Walker

ALICE WALKER was born in Eaton, Georgia in 1944 and was the eighth child of African American sharecroppers. Her works include *The Third Life of Grange Copeland* (1970), *Revolutionary Petunias* (1973), *Meridian* (1976), *You Can't*

Keep a Good Woman Down (1981), *The Color Purple*, for which she won the Pulitzer Prize and National Book Award for Fiction (1983), *In Search of Our Mother's Gardens* (1984), *Horses Make a Landscape Look More Beautiful* (1984), *Temple of My Familiar* (1989), *Possessing the Secret of Joy* (1992), *The Same River Twice: Honoring the Difficult* (1996), *Anything We Love Can Be Saved* (1997), *By the Light of My Father's Smile* (1998), and *The Way Forward Is with a Broken Heart* (2000). In addition to her own work, Walker writes and lectures on African American authors like Zora Neale Hurston, Jean Toomer, and Langston Hughes—individuals who provided some of the models and inspiration for her own writing. In *Living by the Word: 1983–87* (1988), for instance, Walker explains that she has always found it difficult to write about her father, who is so much like herself "physical and otherwise," but that she must acknowledge what he has meant to her in order to fully accept and love her "self."

ALLUSIONS

Civil Rights Movement: National movement calling for equal civil rights for all United States citizens, regardless of ethnic origin, sex, or religion.

Roosevelt: Democrat Franklin Delano Roosevelt, the architect of "the New Deal" following the stock market crash of 1929 and the 31st president of the United States.

Jehovah's Witness: American Protestant sect that believes that its members are the elect of God and prophets of the coming millennium. Throughout their history, Jehovah's Witnesses have striven to have as little contact as possible with established government and religious institutions.

Jesse Jackson: African American reverend and renowned rhetorician; Jackson unsuccessfully ran for the United States presidency in 1984, yet he receives wide recognition and respect.

Rastafarians: Jamaican religious group.

Jah: Rastafarian word, derived from the Hebrew, for God or spiritual being.

hippies: Members of a countercultural group in which young people stereotypically wore beads, grew their hair long, protested the Vietnam War, championed civil rights, and rejected the values of the dominant culture. The media portrayed hippies as confused youths, lost in a haze of drugs, sex, and rock and roll.

1   Though it is more difficult to write about my father than about my mother, since I spent less time with him and knew him less well, it is equally as liberating. Partly this

is because writing about people helps us to understand them, and understanding them helps us to accept them as part of ourselves. Since I share so many of my father's characteristics, physical and otherwise, coming to terms with what he has meant to my life is crucial to a full acceptance and love of myself.

2   I'm positive my father never understood why I wrote. I wonder sometimes if the appearance, in 1968, of my first book, *Once*, poems largely about my experiences in the Civil Rights movement and in other countries, notably African and Eastern European, surprised him. It is frustrating that, because he is now dead, I will never know.

3   In fact, what I regret most about my relationship with my father is that it did not improve until after his death. For a long time I felt so shut off from him that we were unable to talk. I hadn't the experience, as a younger woman, to ask the questions I would ask now. These days I feel we are on good terms, spiritually (my dreams of him are deeply loving and comforting ones), and that we both understand our relationship was a casualty of exhaustion and circumstances. My birth, the eighth child, unplanned, must have elicited more anxiety than joy. It hurts me to think that for both my parents, poor people, my arrival represented many more years of backbreaking and spirit-crushing toil.

4   I grew up to marry someone very unlike my father, as I knew him—though I feel sure he had these qualities himself as a younger man—someone warm, openly and spontaneously affectionate, who loved to talk to me about everything, including my work. I now share my life with another man who has these qualities. But I would give a lot to be able to talk grownup to grownup with Daddy. I'd like to tell him how hard I am working to understand. And about the humor and solace I occasionally find (while writing *The Color Purple*, for instance, in which some of his early life is imagined) in the work.

> My father
> (back blistered)
> beat me
> because I
> could not
> stop crying.
> He'd had
> enough "fuss"
> he said
> for one damn
> voting day.

5   In my heart, I have never wanted to be at odds with my father, but I have felt, over the years, especially when I was younger, that he gave me no choice. Perhaps if I could have relaxed and been content to be his favorite, there would have been a chance for closeness, but because a sister whom I loved was clearly not favorite material I did not want to be either. When I look back over my life, I see a pattern in

my relationships going back to this, and in my love relationships I have refused men who loved me (at least for a time) if they in turn were loved by another woman but did not love her in return. I am the kind of woman who could positively forbid a married lover to leave his wife.

6   The poem above is one of my earliest as an adult, written after an abortion of which my father would not have approved, in which I felt that visceral understanding of a situation that for a poet can mean a poem. My father far away in the South, me in college in the North—how far away from each other! Yet in the pain of the moment and the illumination of some of what was wrong between us, how close. If he ever read the poem, I wonder what he thought. We never discussed my work, though I thought he tended to become more like some of my worst characters the older he got. I remember going home once and being told by my mother of some of the curses he was capable of, and hardly believing her, since the most I'd ever heard my father say was "God damn!" and I could count the number of times on toes and fingers. (In fact, his favorite curse, when a nail refused to go in straight or he dropped the hammer on his sore corn was "God damn the god dam luck to the devil!" which always sounded rather ineffectual and humorous to me, and which, thinking of it, I hear him say and see his perspiring dark face.)

7   Did he actually beat me on voting day? Probably not. I suppose the illegal abortion caused me to understand what living under other people's politics can force us to do. The only time I remember his beating me was one day after he'd come home tired and hungry from the dairy (where he and my brothers milked a large herd of cows morning and afternoon), and my brother Bobby, three years older than me and a lover of chaos, and I were fighting. He had started it, of course. My mother, sick of our noise, spoke to my father about it, and without asking questions he took off his belt and flailed away, indiscriminately, at the two of us.

8   Why do certain things stick in the mind? I recall a scene, much earlier, when I was only three or so, in which my father questioned me about a fruit jar I had accidentally broken. I felt he knew I had broken it; at the same time, I couldn't be sure. Apparently breaking it was, in any event, the wrong thing to have done. I could say, Yes, I broke the jar, and risk a whipping for breaking something valuable, or, No, I did not break it, and perhaps bluff my way through.

9   I've never forgotten my feeling that he really wanted me to tell the truth. And because he seemed to desire it—and the moments during which he waited for my reply seemed quite out of time, so much so I can still feel them, and, as I said, I was only three, if that—I confessed. I broke the jar, I said. I think he hugged me. He probably didn't, but I still feel as if he did, so embraced did I feel by the happy relief I noted on his face and by the fact that he didn't punish me at all, but seemed, instead, pleased with me. I think it was at that moment that I resolved to take my chances with the truth, although as the years rolled on I was to break more serious things in his scheme of things than fruit jars.

10   It was the unfairness of the beating that keeps it fresh in my mind. (And this was thirty-seven years ago!) And my disappointment at the deterioration of my father's ethics. And yet, since I am never happy in my heart when estranged from my father,

any more than I would be happy shut off from sunlight, in writing this particular poem I tried to see my father's behavior in a context larger than our personal relationship.

11   Actually, my father was two fathers.

12   To the first four of his children he was one kind of father, to the second set of four he was another kind. Whenever I talk to the elder set I am astonished at the picture they draw, for the man they describe bears little resemblance to the man I knew. For one thing, the man they knew was physically healthy, whereas the man I knew was almost always sick; not sick enough to be in bed, or perhaps he was but with so many children to feed he couldn't afford to lie down, but "dragging-around" sick, in the manner of the very poor. Overweight, high blood pressure, diabetes, or, as it was called, "sugar," rotten teeth. There are certain facts, however, that identify our father as the same man; one of which is that, in the 1930s, my father was one of the first black men to vote in Eatonton, Georgia, among a group of men like himself he helped organize, mainly poor sharecroppers with large families, totally at the mercy of the white landlords. He voted for Roosevelt. He was one of the leading supporters of the local one-room black school, and according to everyone who knew him then, including my older brothers and sister, believed in education above all else. Years later, when I knew him, he seemed fearful of both education and politics and disappointed and resentful as well.

13   And why not? Though he risked his life and livelihood to vote more than once, nothing much changed in his world. Cotton price continued low. Dairying was hard. White men and women continued to run things, badly. In his whole life my father never had a vacation. (Of course my mother had less of one: she could not even get in the car and drive off to town, as he could.) Education merely seemed to make his children more critical of him. When I went south in the mid-sixties to help register voters, I stopped by our house to say hello but never told either of my parents what I planned to do. I didn't want them to worry about my safety, and it never occurred to me that they cared much about the vote. My father was visibly ill, paranoid, complaining the whole time of my mother's religious activities (she had become a Jehovah's Witness). Then, for no apparent reason, he would come out with one of those startlingly intelligent comments about world affairs or some absolutely clear insight into the deficiencies of national leaders, and I would be reminded of the father I didn't know.

14   For years I have held on to another early memory of my life between the ages of two and four. Every afternoon a tired but jolly very black man came up to me with arms outstretched. I flew into them to be carried, to be hugged, to be kissed. For years I thought this black man was my father. But no. He was my oldest brother, Fred, whose memories of my father are, surprisingly, as painful as my memories of him, because as my father's first child, and a son, he was subjected to my father's very confused notions of what constituted behavior suitable for a male. And of course my father himself didn't really know. He was in his late teens, a child himself, when he married. His mother had been murdered, by a man who claimed to love her, when he was eleven. His father, to put it very politely, drank, and terrorized his children.

15   My father was so confused that when my sister Ruth appeared in the world and physically resembled his mother, and sounded like his mother, and had similar expressions, he rejected her and missed no opportunity that I ever saw to put her down. I, of course, took the side of my sister, forfeiting my chance to be my father's favorite among the second set of children, as my oldest sister, Mamie, was favorite among the first. In her case the favoritism seemed outwardly caused by her very light color, and of course she was remarkably intelligent as well. In my case, my father seemed partial to me because of my "smartness" and forthrightness, but more obviously because of my hair, which was the longest and "best" in the family.

16   And yet, my father taught me two things that have been important to me: he taught me not to bother telling lies, because the listener might be delighted with the truth, and he told me never to cut my hair. Though I have tried not to lie, the sister he rejected and I loved became a beautician, and one of the first things she did—partly in defiance of him—was to cut my shoulder-blade-length hair. I did not regret it so much while in high school and college (everyone kept their hair short, it seemed), but years later, after I married, I grew it long again, almost as long as it had been when I was grown up. I'd had it relaxed to feathers. When I walked up to my father, as he was talking to a neighbor, I stooped a little and placed his hand on my head. I thought he'd be pleased. "A woman's hair is her glory," he'd always said. He paid little attention. When the black power movement arrived, with its emphasis on cropped natural hair, I did the job myself, filling the face bowl and bathroom floor with hair and shocking my husband when he arrived home.

17   Only recently have I come to believe he was right in wanting me to keep my hair. After years of short hair, of cutting my hair back each time it raised its head, so to speak, I have begun to feel each time as if I am mutilating my antennae (which is how Rastafarians, among others, think of hair) and attenuating my power. It seems imperative not to cut my hair anymore.

18   I didn't listen to my father because I assumed he meant that in the eyes of a man, in his eyes, a woman's hair is her glory (unfortunately, he wore his own head absolutely clean-shaven all his life); and that is probably what he did mean. But now I begin to sense something else, that there is power (would an ancient translation of glory be power?) in uncut hair itself. The power (and glory) perhaps of the untamed, the undomesticated; in short, the wild. A wildness about the head, as the Rastas have discovered, places us somehow in the loose and spacious freedom of Jah's universe. Hippies, of course, knew this, too.

19   As I write, my own hair reaches just below my ears. It is at the dangerous stage at which I usually butt my forehead against the mirror and in resignation over not knowing "what to do with it" cut it off. But this time I have thought ahead and have encased it in braids made of someone else's hair. I expect to wear them, braces for the hair, so to speak, until my own hair replaces them. Eventually I will be able, as I was when a child, to tie my hair under my chin. But mostly I would like to set it free.

20   My father would have loved Jesse Jackson. On the night Jesse addressed the Democratic convention I stayed close to my radio. In my backwoods cabin, linked to the world only by radio, I felt something like my father must have, since he lived

most of his life before television and far from towns. He would have appreciated Jesse's oratorical gift, and, unlike some newscasters who seemed to think of it primarily as technique, he would have felt, as I did, the transformation of the spirit of the man implicit in the words he chose to say. He would have felt, as I did, that in asking for forgiveness as well as votes and for patience as well as commitment to the Democratic party, Jackson lost nothing and won almost everything: a cleared conscience and peace of mind.

21   My father was never able to vote for a black candidate for any national or local political office. By the time black people were running for office and occasionally winning elections, in the late sixties and early seventies, he was too sick to respond with the exhilaration he must have felt. On the night of Jackson's speech, I felt it for him; along with the grief that in neither of our lifetimes is the United States likely to choose the best leadership offered to it. This is the kind of leader, the kind of ever-growing, ever-expanding spirit you might have been, Daddy, I thought—and damn it, I love you for what you might have been. And thinking of you now, merging the two fathers that you were, remembering how tightly I hugged you as a small child returning home after two long months at a favorite aunt's, and with what apparent joy you lifted me beside your cheek; knowing now, at forty, what it takes out of body and spirit to go and how much more to stay, and having learned, too, by now, some of the pitiful confusions in behavior caused by ignorance and pain, I love you no less for what you were.

AFTERWARDS

Vocabulary

spontaneously, visceral, ineffectual, indiscriminately, deterioration, diabetes, resemblance, paranoid, spacious, oratorical, implicit, exhilaration, constituted, beautician, forthrightness, defiance, mutilating, antennae, attenuating, imperative. Notice how many of the descriptive vocabulary words create a particular tone or voice as the author speaks to readers. Add the above words and their definitions to your vocabulary log. Then explain which words could have been replaced by a simpler word (e.g., using important instead of imperative) and which words really have no acceptable substitute (e.g., antennae).

Content

1. Why does Walker find it difficult, yet comforting, to write about her father? What can be the effect of writing and speaking to people who upset or confuse us?

2. What were the two important things Walker's father taught her? Explain the significance of each in her life.

   3. Describe Walker's growth and development, especially as it relates to her father. How was he actually "two fathers"? What does Walker regret most about her relationship with her father?

Style and Structure

   1. Why do you imagine Walker used only a single sentence in paragraph 11? What strategic function does it serve? Why are single-sentence paragraphs generally not used in formal writing? Would paragraph 11 have been more or less effective if Walker had used several single-sentence paragraphs in her essay? Why?

   2. Citing specific examples, show how Walker uses transitional devices (linking words) to move the discussion of her father, the subject of her essay, from past to present perceptions of him.

   3. In what way does Walker's conclusion demonstrate that she has come to terms with her father? Considering the number of unflattering remarks she makes about him, how did she manage to lead her readers from the first until the final sentence of her essay? How did she establish trust? What methods of persuasion did she use outside of reasoning?

Collaborative Explorations

Brainstorm a list of father "types," as portrayed in films, on television, in advertisements, and in pieces of fiction and nonfiction. Begin the assignment by having each group member individually create a list of a father figure's responsibilities. Then compare your lists and note which "responsibilities" the majority of your peers mentioned. Next, write a master list of father-figure types portrayed in film, television, fiction, and nonfiction. Present your group insight to the rest of the class.

Writing Assignments

   1. Freewrite about the phrase, "important lessons my parents taught me." What sort of lessons come to mind? Who taught you the lessons you recall? Narrow your freewriting down to a specific focus, a controlling idea or angle on the topic of "important lessons." Then write an essay demonstrating how and why the lessons you generated through freewriting (a prewriting activity) have been memorable and instructive. If you have only recently placed value on these lessons, clarify that point in your introductory sentences or thesis statement itself.

   2. Write an essay where you discuss difficult times, as well as positive occasions with your mother, father, or parent figure (e.g., an older

brother or a sister and so on). What do you regret about your relationship with the person? Were there things you did not care about in your youth that, looking back, you wish you could have done differently? Like Walker, conclude your essay with some sort of statement clarifying how and/or what you feel about your mother, father, or parent figure today.

Thematic Reading Cross-Links: See Chapter 6, Environments, to observe how people's surroundings can influence their growth, physically and emotionally. Another interesting essay to read along with Walker's piece is "How Playing Country Music Taught Me to Love My Father" by James D. Houston, the last essay in this chapter.

Movie Cross-Links: See *To Kill a Mockingbird* and *The Joy Luck Club* on the film list in the Film Links section at the end of this chapter to gain perspectives on family and gender relationships.

Playing God on No Sleep

Anna Quindlen

An author of fiction and nonfiction, **ANNA QUINDLEN** has written articles for *Newsweek* and other magazines for many years. Her nonfiction books include *Living Out Loud* (1992), *Thinking Out Loud: On the Personal, the Political, the Public, and the Private* (1994), and *How Reading Changed My Life* (1994). Among her best-known novels are *Object Lessons* (1992), *One True Thing* (1994), and *Black and Blue* (1998). The following essay appeared in the July 7, 2001, edition of *Newsweek*; Quindlen suggests the article's tone with the following subheading: *"Isn't motherhood grand? Do you want the real answer or the Hallmark-card version?"*

ALLUSIONS

Andrea Yates: A mother who flipped out and killed her five children.

The Exorcist: A movie from the 1970s in which a young girl becomes possessed by the devil; Quindlen refers to the pea-green vomit scene from the movie in her essay.

1   Isn't motherhood grand? Do you want the real answer or the official Hallmark-card version? So a woman walks into a pediatrician's office. She's tired, she's hot and

she's been up all night throwing sheets into the washer because the smaller of her two boys has projectile vomiting so severe it looks like a special effect from "The Exorcist." Oh, and she's nauseated, too, because since she already has two kids under the age of 5 it made perfect sense to have another, and she's four months pregnant. In the doctor's waiting room, which sounds like a cross between an orchestra tuning loudly and a 747 taking off, there is a cross-stitched sampler on the wall. It says GOD COULD NOT BE EVERYWHERE SO HE MADE MOTHERS.

2   This is not a joke, and that is not the punch line. Or maybe it is. The woman was me, the sampler real, and the sentiments it evoked were unforgettable: incredulity, disgust and that out-of-body feeling that is the corollary of sleep deprivation and adrenaline rush, with a soupçon of shoulder barf thrown in. I kept reliving this moment, and others like it, as I read with horrified fascination the story of Andrea Yates, a onetime nurse suffering from postpartum depression who apparently spent a recent morning drowning her five children in the bathtub. There is a part of my mind that imagines the baby, her starfish hands pink beneath the water, or the biggest boy fighting back, all wiry arms and legs, and then veers sharply away, aghast, appalled.

3   But there's another part of my mind, the part that remembers the end of a day in which the milk spilled phone rang one cried another hit a fever rose the medicine gone the car sputtered another cried the cable out "Sesame Street" gone all cried stomach upset full diaper no more diapers Mommy I want water Mommy my throat hurts Mommy I don't feel good. Every mother I've asked about the Yates case has the same reaction. She's appalled; she's aghast. And then she gets this look. And the look says that at some forbidden level she understands. The look says that there are two very different kinds of horror here. There is the unimaginable idea of the killings. And then there is the entirely imaginable idea of going quietly bonkers in the house with five kids under the age of 7.

4   The insidious cult of motherhood is summed up by the psychic weight of the sampler on that doctor's wall. We are meant to be all things to small people, surrounded by bromides and soppy verse and smiling strangers who talk about how lucky we are. And we are lucky. My children have been the making of me as a human being, which does not mean they have not sometimes been an overwhelming and mind-boggling responsibility. That last is the love that dare not speak its name, the love that is fraught with fear and fatigue and inevitable resentment. But between the women who cannot have children and sometimes stare at our double strollers grief-stricken, and the grandmothers who make raising eight or 10 sound like a snap and insist we micromanage and overanalyze, there is no leave to talk about the dark side of being a surrogate deity, omniscient and out of milk all at the same time.

5   The weight was not always so heavy. Once the responsibility was spread around extended families, even entire towns. The sociologist Jessie Bernard has this to say: "The way we institutionalize motherhood in our society—assigning sole responsibility for child care to the mother, cutting her off from the easy help of others in an isolated household, requiring round-the clock tender, loving care, and making such care her exclusive activity—is not only new and unique, but not even a good

way for either women or—if we accept as a criterion the amount of maternal warmth shown—for children. It may, in fact, be the worst."

6   It has gotten no better since those words were written 25 years ago. Worse, perhaps, with all the competing messages about what women should do and be and feel at this particular moment in time. Women not working outside their homes feel compelled to make their job inside it seem both weighty and joyful; women who work outside their homes for pay feel no freedom to be ambivalent because of the sub rosa sense that they are cutting parenting corners. All of us are caught up in a conspiracy in which we are both the conspirators and the victims of the plot. In the face of all this "M is for the million things she gave me" mythology it becomes difficult to admit that occasionally you lock yourself in the bathroom just to be alone.

7   The great motherhood friendships are the ones in which women can admit this quietly to one another, over cups of tea at a table sticky with spilt apple juice and littered with markers without tops. But most of the time we keep quiet and smile. So that when someone is depressed after having a baby, when everyone is telling her that it's the happiest damn time of her life, there's no space to admit what she's really feeling. So that when someone does something as horrifying as what Andrea Yates did, there is no room for even a little bit of understanding. Yap yap yap, the world says. How could anyone do that to her children?

8   Well, yes. But. I'm imagining myself with five children under the age of 7, all alone after Dad goes off to work. And they're bouncing off the walls in that way little boys do, except for the baby, who needs to be fed. And fed. And fed again. And changed. The milk gets spilled. The phone rings. Mommy, can I have juice? Mommy, can I have lunch? Mommy, can I go out back? Mommy, can I come in? And I add to all that depression, mental illness, whatever was happening in that house. I'm not making excuses for Andrea Yates. I love my children more than life itself. But just because you love people doesn't mean that taking care of them day in and day out isn't often hard, and sometimes even horrible. If God made mothers because he couldn't be everywhere, maybe he could have met us halfway and eradicated vomiting, and colic too, and the hideous sugarcoating of what we are and what we do that leads to false cheer, easy lies and maybe sometimes something much, much worse, almost unimaginable. But not quite.

AFTERWARDS

Vocabulary

micromanage, omniscient, ambivalent, insidious, eradicated. After checking the definitions of each of these vocabulary words in your dictionary, reread and locate where they appear in the essay. What other words might the author have substituted for *omniscient, ambivalent, insidious,* and *eradicated?*

Content

1. What seems to be Quindlen's attitude toward motherhood? Why?

2. Comedian/sitcom personality Roseanne once said, "There's a lot more to being a woman than being a mother, but there's a hell of a lot more to being a mother than most people suspect." To what extent does Quindlen echo Roseanne's sentiments? How does Quindlen's knowledge add authority to claims that might be misunderstood as merely "attitude"?

3. Why might an extended family—as the author implies—offer mothers a way of spreading around the responsibility for child rearing?

Style and Structure

1. To the best of your ability, describe the tone of Quindlen's essay.

2. What incidents, words, and phrases does Quindlen use in "Playing God on No Sleep" to illustrate that motherhood may not be the greatest thing to ever happen to a woman? Why might childless women romanticize the reality of raising children?

3. How does the reference to Andrea Yates's grisly murder of her five children make a larger point about the demands of motherhood?

Collaborative Explorations

In small groups, discuss the extent to which you agree with the concept that a "large family is not a fortress but rather an access route to everyone and thus, the true cradle of society." Have each group member discuss his or her knowledge of and contact with extended families. Then, go back and answer three questions based on your collective experiences. (1) Do large families "shelter" or "protect" their members from the real world? (2) How can an extended family provide its members access to people, groups, events, and opportunities? (3) How might the extended family spread responsibility for child rearing (see content question #3)? Your group's concluding insights may be used later on for writing assignments.

Writing Assignments

1. Write an essay wherein you defend your point of view regarding the ethics involved in motherhood or fatherhood. When are ethics solely a matter of tradition, and when are they genuinely a matter of commitment?

2. In a well-reasoned, thoroughly supported argumentative essay, agree or disagree with the author's belief that while a woman may love her

children "more than life itself," that does not mean the responsibility of "taking care of them day in and day out isn't often hard, and sometimes even horrible."

Thematic Reading Cross-Links: For a contrasting look at motherhood as the ultimate female experience, compare Quindlen's essay to Louise Erdrich's "Beneath the House," the first essay of this chapter.

Movie Cross-Links: Contrast movies like *The Joy Luck Club* that present positive mother/daughter relationships to more disturbing portrayals of mothers as found in *What's Eating Gilbert Grape* or *American Beauty.*

How Playing Country Music Taught Me to Love My Dad

James D. Houston

An author of fiction and nonfiction, **JAMES D. HOUSTON** has written a variety of books about the Pacific West in general and California in particular. A former creative writing instructor at the University of California at Santa Cruz, Houston remains active reading his works at colleges and speaking at local and national conferences. Houston's writings include *Gig* (1988), *The Men in My Life: And Other More or Less True Recollections of Kinship* (1994), *Continental Drift* (1996), and *The Last Paradise* (1997). In addition to his own work, he coauthored *Farewell to Manzanar* (1973) with Jeanne Wakatsuki Houston, his wife. Then in 1988, they collaborated again on *One Can Think About Life After the Fish Is in the Canoe: Beyond Manzanar.* The Houstons also worked on film projects together, such as *Barrio* (1978) and *The Melting Pot* (1980).

ALLUSIONS

Bob Wills: Singer and fiddle-playing leader of Bob Wills and the Texas Playboys, a group that epitomized the western swing style of the 1930s and 1940s.

Louis Armstrong: Jazz singer and trumpeter who personally created many of the innovations that came to define jazz as a style of music.

Jack Teagarden: Texas-born singer and trombonist who combined blues, jazz, and western elements in his music.

Turk Murphy: Jazz trombonist and band leader who perpetuated the Dixieland style.

Red Nichols: Trumpeter and band leader of Red Nichols and His Five Pennies.

Elizabethan: Refers to the reign of Elizabeth I of England (1533–1603).

Roy Acuff: Country singer/songwriter who appeared for many years on The Grand Ole Opry radio show.

Jimmie Rodgers: Country singer/songwriter known for his railroad songs and yodeling singing style.

> *Deep within my heart*
> *lies a melody,*
> *a song of old San Antone . . .*
>
> —BOB WILLS

1   I grew up listening to my father play the steel guitar. It was his pastime and his passion. Once or twice a month our front room would fill with fiddlers and guitar pickers who had come west from Texas and Oklahoma and Arkansas and other places farther south to make money in the fields and in the shipyards of World War Two. Dad was more or less the leader, since he had the most equipment—a little speaker, two mikes, an old Westinghouse recording machine. From upstairs, with my head and my radio under pillows and covers, where I was trying to concentrate on *The Shadow*, I could hear them ripping into San Antonio Rose or Detour—There's a Muddy Road Ahead. Clutching the radio I would groan and burrow deeper and, to fend off the guitars, imagine the look of The Shadow himself, my sinister and worldly night-time companion.

2   I thought I was groaning about the music. But it was dad who made me cringe. Coming of age in San Francisco, I was a smartass city kid, cool and sullen, and ashamed of all his downhome tastes and habits. During those years I lost a tremendous amount, resisting the things he cared about and denying who he was. At the time I had no way of knowing how much was working against us. No two points of origin could have been farther apart.

3   His hometown was not a town at all. It was an east Texas village called Pecan Gap, where kids grew up chopping cotton. To escape he dropped out of high school in the tenth grade and joined the Navy, on a hitch that sent him to Honolulu in the mid-1920s, for two years of submarine duty at Pearl Harbor. That was where he learned half the music he knew. In Texas he had learned enough rhythm guitar to accompany singing. Some Hawaiian taught him the flat-lap style, the right hand flashing with silver picks, the left moving its little steel bar across the strings, sliding, whining, yearning, dreaming. Until the day he died, the two tunes he played most, and loved most, were The Steel Guitar Rag and The Hilo March.

4   He also learned the ukulele over there. When I was fourteen I found one hanging in his closet. My first hour of aimless plinking jangled his nerves. I knew this, and I kept it up until he grabbed the uke and told me to sit still while he taught me three chords and a basic strum, which he described as "tryin to shake somethin off the end of your fanger."

5   I started practicing that strum and those chords about two hours a day. After a week he hid the ukulele. One afternoon I came home from school and it was gone. First I accused my sister. Then I confronted my mother. When I told dad that his ukulele had disappeared he pursed his lips judiciously and said, "Gone, you say. Imagine that."

6   Who knows why he hid it? Maybe the sound I had been making, akin to the squawk of a rusty clothesline wheel, was too big a price to pay to have another musician in the family. Maybe he was getting even with me for refusing to listen to his band. I'm still not sure. We were both inexperienced at this game. He was my first and only father. I was his first and only son.

7   For two days I searched, and finally found the uke between the ceiling and the roof beams, shoved back under some insulation. When I came strumming into the front room, he turned red. His jaws bunched in the classic, teeth-grinding, Dust Bowler's way of holding it all inside. Then he tried to grin. With eyes lowered, he jerked his face sideways in that other classic gesture that can signify all moods from outrage to wonder. He said, "Looks like you scared it up."

8   Maybe this had been a little test, to measure my commitment. Before long he showed me the rest of his chords, another strum, a simple way to pick the melody to Lovely Hula Hands. About the time I had practiced all this to death, I graduated to the four-string banjo. I was in a neighborhood music store eyeing the long neck and stretched head and gleaming strings of a brand-new instrument, when the owner's seductive voice, from somewhere behind me said I was welcome to do more than look. From there it was a short step to Dixieland Jazz which, in those days, around 1950, was the hottest sound in northern California. My songs were The Muskrat Ramble and The Rampart Street Parade. My new-found heroes were Louis Armstrong, Jack Teagarden, Turk Murphy, Red Nichols and His Five Pennies.

9   Sometimes, say late on a Saturday afternoon, I would be practicing, and I would hear dad in the front room tuning up, as if by chance. Begrudgingly I would find myself in there with him, running through the changes for one of his big production numbers, The Steel Guitar Rag, the Cow Cow Boogie. But I was arrogant about these little rehearsals. His arrangements, his slides and flourishes, his idea of an impressive finale—this was ancient history. It was beneath me. It was worse than hicksville. It was Okie music. And I was anything but an Okie.

10   From Dixieland I soon moved toward modern jazz, and now my instrument was the upright bass. How High The Moon, Darn That Dream, Willow Weep For Me. These were the songs you had to know, and how could dad and I even talk about such music? The tunes we listened to placed us on opposite sides of an uncrossable chasm, a Grand Canyon of taste—the augmented seventh chord as far from his vocabulary as a queen's pawn, or existentialism.

> Goin down to Cripple Creek,
> Goin on the run,
> Goin down to Cripple Creek
> To have a little fun . . .

11   Though music has never been my main line of work, I have always kept some gig or another going on the side, found some combo to sit in with. I inherited this from him, of course, a connection so obvious it eluded me for half my life. I have played in dance bands and in piano bars, at New Years Eve parties and for weddings in June. I have played in total release sessions where anyone can get into the act, with any horn or rhythm-maker handy, to do whatever comes to mind.

12   For several years I spent half my mornings on classical and flamenco guitar. By that time he had pretty much quit playing. After the family moved down to Santa Clara Valley, his old picking buddies were too far away to meet with. Most of them had packed up their instruments anyhow, when their fingers gave out. And by that time I was married, living here in Santa Cruz, starting my own family, taking on a few guitar students for the extra cash, and trying to go the distance with classical repertoire—Villa-Lobos, Tarrega, Fernando Sor. Those days now stand for what pushed me farthest from him. Call it my own yearning for sophistication. I was never much good at sophistication. It runs right against the grain. But I confess that I have hungered for it. In the preludes and the nocturnes, I could taste it, and in the numerous baroque guitar suites I tried to master, in the Elizabethan galliards, in the Fantasía written by some 16th century lutenist whose three surviving works had recently been transcribed from nearly indecipherable tablatures.

13   I still love the galliards. I always will. But it took me twenty years of part-time music life to discover, or rather to quit being ashamed of the fact and come right out and admit that I love San Antonio Rose more. If I am sitting in a honky tonk when the pedal steel begins to whine the opening bars of that song, I have no choice but to surrender. I hear a calling in the blood. It launches me. It fills me with unabashed glee.

14   I can now trace this change in outlook to a bluegrass band I happened to join, during the very year dad passed away. At the time I told myself I was "between gigs," looking for new musical allies and looking for something I had not tried. But I am convinced that more than coincidence brought this group together. It was another version of the ancient maxim: when the musician is ready, the band will appear.

15   Everyone else had played a lot of country music. The mandolin picker was a graduate student from North Carolina. The banjo player came from Knoxville, Tennessee, by way of Viet Nam, discovering California like my dad did, passing through. I was the novice, and the first night we got together I was stupefied with boredom. One of the pleasures of playing string bass is working through a good set of chord changes, the challenging progression, the little surprise moves that have to be memorized. In bluegrass there are many tricky melodies to be executed by fiddle and banjo and mandolin, but no changes to speak of, three or four in most tunes, two in a lot of them, in some tunes no changes at all.

16   "Just hang on to that A minor, Jim baby!" the mandolin picker told me, as we began to play a modal breakdown featuring his shiny Gibson. "And for God sake, let me hear that A!"

17   It took some getting used to. It took a while to hear what was really going on with five stringed instruments, all acoustic, all made of wood. They wove a tapestry of sound, a tight braid of mountain counterpoint, and I found that I could squeeze inside the braid, pushing notes up from underneath for the fiddle and banjo to loop around. The best way to feel it is to stand in a circle, get moving on a song like Blackberry Blossom or Cripple Creek. Then all the strings and resonating chambers pulse at one another in intricate, skin-whiffling ways.

18   I told myself that bluegrass is rural chamber music, which, in a certain sense, is true. But those were mainly academic words I needed, to talk myself into it.

19   I soon discovered, or remembered, that my head was full of songs I had grown up hearing on "The Grand Ole Opry" out of Nashville. Dad used to listen to that show every Saturday night. I started taking vocals on some of Roy Acuff's great hits, Wreck on The Highway, The Wabash Cannonball. The other guys were bringing in truck driving songs, gospel numbers, old Jimmie Rodgers yodels, anything that tickled us, as long as we could call it "country," as long as we could do it acoustically and without piano and drums. We could afford to be purists because we all made our money other ways. We dressed up in boots and string ties and colored shirts and drank whiskey in the parking lot. I would often think of dad while we were playing, wishing he could have seen and heard all this, sometimes wondering why he had to pass away before I could embrace what I had resisted for so long.

20   I guess this band had been together for a couple of years when he finally turned up, very briefly, at a country fair outside of town.

21   There's a long low valley winding inland from the ocean and the coast road called Highway One. About five miles back, in a big open meadow, wooden booths had been nailed up out of rough-hewn planks and hung with flags and banners. The meadow was recently mowed. Hay was raked into mounds for picnickers to loll against. Steep stands of madrone and bay and redwood sloped away on both sides and seemed to gather all the sunlight into this grassy basin. It wasn't hot. Little breezes eddied through there all day long. But from noon on, the sun was so bright, the haystacks shimmered so, you could hardly look at them with the naked eye.

22   There were clay pots for sale, and embroidered shirts, and buffaloes of welded iron, and roasting corn, and ice cream, and free draft beer for the band, to chase down the Jim Beam we had stashed behind our sound system. By the end of the second set we were so loose we played Foggy Mountain Breakdown faster than we ever thought we could. Not one of us missed a note. We all agreed it was the best we had sounded. The scene had lifted us to its own excellence. And it was just then, as I stepped back into the shade, looking for a drink, high from the music, yet already wistful, afraid we might never be that good again, that I spotted him leaning against one of the hay bales, in between our bandstand and the curving line of booths.

23   He looked mighty comfortable, like this was how he had hoped to spend the day. His legs were stretched in front of him, ankles crossed, hands behind his head. He

wore white shoes, white duck pants, a white shirt open at the collar, and a white, broad-brim plantation owner's hat, watching me carefully and almost smiling. He never had smiled much. Somehow it was difficult for him. He gave me as wide a smile as he'd ever been able to deliver, followed by his ultimate statement, that all-purpose sideways twist of the head, which in this case signified approval, and perhaps a hint of true delight. Then a strolling couple passed between us, and he was gone.

24   I stared at the hay mound until my eyes blurred, trying to conjure him up again and wishing to hell I had been born ten years before World War One, so we could have toured east Texas together, around 1928, when he first got back from Honolulu, out of the Navy and looking for some action. He and his pals had about twenty-five tunes between them and an old bathtub Model T. They hit all the towns between Fort Worth and Corpus Christi, actually played for a couple of months on a radio station out of Texarkana, two guitars and a country fiddle. He wore that white plantation owner's hat everywhere he went in those days, twenty-four years old at the time and a singing fool.

AFTERWARDS

Vocabulary

ukulele, repertoire, baroque, galliards, lute, maxim, counterpoint, yodel, eddied. Houston uses a number of vocabulary words to refer to specific types of music. Define each word and categorize them (e.g., a list for types of music, a list for aspects of music, and so on).

Content

1. How many instruments has Houston learned to play in the course of this story? How does each instrument represent a change of direction in music and his life?

2. What does this essay reveal about some father-son relationships? Why did Houston's father hide the ukulele? Why did Houston avoid playing his father's type of music for so many years? Why does Houston wish his father could hear him in the bluegrass band?

3. What are the social and cultural associations with country music that make Houston not want to be part of it?

Style and Structure

1. How do various categories of music help Houston to tell his story? How do the song titles serve as significant details?

2. Toward the end of the essay, Houston says his father "finally turned up" at a country fair one day. What effect does this observation have on the essay? How does the subjective "vision" help to shift the mood of the whole essay?

3. What transition statements help to signal turning points in the essay?

Collaborative Explorations

Have group members list their parents' favorite music, being as specific as possible. Next, have them list their own music preference, including recording artists, genres, and so on. How many types of music are mentioned? How many parents and children share musical tastes? How do the differences in taste seem to reflect differences in beliefs as well?

Writing Assignments

1. Write a descriptive portrait of one of your parents by focusing on the types of music they like and don't like. Give specific examples and link them to stories about your parents.

2. How does Houston's evolving openness toward new types of music help us to understand his changing attitude toward the lives of country music performers listed in the Film Links at the end of this chapter?

Thematic Readings Cross-Links: Relate Houston's narrative to *The Mambo Kings Play Songs of Love* in Chapter 10, Music. Also compare Houston's essay to Alice Walker's essay, "My Father."

Movie Cross-Links: See *Coal Miner's Daughter* and *Sweet Dreams*, two films tracing the lives of country music performers, in the Film Links at the end of Chapter 10, Music.

The Visual Connection: Photograph Writing Activities

1. To what extent is the following photograph of mothers and their children typical of mother/child "family" pictures? Do you think the children in the picture would pose any differently if they were with their fathers? Why or why not?

Mothers and Their Children

2. How would you characterize the nature of gender roles in the following photo, The Kiss? Study the photograph for a bit, and note the details that suggest the couple's relationship—as well as their individual identities. To what extent is affectionate behavior influenced through the immediate family, and what do you believe is acquired through personal experience? Write a paragraph describing the photograph, using concrete nouns and active verbs, and try to capture its details, as well as its emotional context.

The Kiss

How to Conduct an Interview
••••••••••••••••••••••••••••••••••

Interviews provide a fertile basis for learning about people and generating writing ideas. People who need to do interviews as part of their job include newspaper reporters, magazine writers, talk-show hosts, biographers, psychologists, personnel managers, social scientists, poll takers, and marketing researchers. Learning how to ask questions in a structured but informal way is a valuable skill to have no matter what career you plan to enter. Here are some guidelines that may assist you:

1. Display a genuine interest in the person you are interviewing. Show by your eye contact and tone of voice that you are interested in what he or she has to say.

2. Treat the person you interview with respect. If you want to be a trusted listener, then you should display an open and nonjudgmental attitude. Your first task is to get the person you interview to open up and speak freely in an honest, spontaneous way.

3. Write out questions in advance that lead to specific issues— yet trust yourself to abandon prewritten questions as well. Genuine connection with the person interviewed—and the dialogue between you two—should take precedence over process. True, television interviewers like Larry King, Oprah Winfrey, or Charlie Rose always have a script for an interview. They know in advance that there are certain subjects they want their guests to talk about, but they usually don't start out by asking these questions; they gradually work toward them. Once a person starts talking, a conversation usually warms up and becomes less formal and inhibited. You have to have follow-up questions that will take you deeper and deeper into a subject. Say you were going to interview a mayor who had just been defeated for reelection. You might make a list of questions like this:

   How did you get started in politics?

   Who helped you become a success?

   What goals have you achieved while in office?

   What groups have been your best supporters?

   What were the special challenges in your last campaign?

In retrospect, what would you have done differently?

What are your plans for the future?

The most interesting and revealing part of the interview would come from the ex-mayor's response to his own defeat. Listeners on both sides politically would probably want to know what his perceptions are regarding his own failed campaign and whether or not he plans to remain in politics. Although this is the central focus, notice that it is not the first question asked. The first few questions are designed to get the mayor to reflect on his accomplishments and goals. After having an opportunity to express the more positive aspects of his career, he would probably feel less defensive and evasive about discussing his defeat.

4. Use your intuition to ask spontaneous questions. Let your own curiosity guide you in following directions that you had not anticipated. If you listen closely and have a genuine interest in the subject, then you may temporarily abandon your plan and explore interesting digressions that just come up in the conversation. Comic talk-show hosts like David Letterman and Jay Leno constantly look for chances to turn an interview into comedy. They have questions prepared, but they know a straight interview can be too predictable. They ask questions that are surprising, strange, off-the-wall. Their goal is to get their guests to loosen up a bit and feel relaxed and make casual jokes. They have a plan, but they improvise as well because a spontaneous question is more likely to evoke a spontaneous response. A good conversation is made up of give-and-take responses that follow an internal logic of their own. The goal of an interview is to turn it into a conversation that just "happens."

5. Take notes or use a tape-recorder. Accuracy is very important in recounting an interview in writing. If you take notes, you may want to go over the notes before you leave and confirm with the interviewee that your notations are accurate. A tape-recorder allows you more freedom to enter into the give-and-take of the conversation and makes it possible to transcribe the interview later. In some cases you may simply want to publish the interview word-for-word as it was spoken. Observe how Kathleen Hudson wrote out the following excerpt from her interview of "Stevie Ray Vaughan."

KATHLEEN HUDSON: INTERVIEW
EXCERPT OF "STEVIE RAY VAUGHAN"

A professor of writing and literature at Schreiner University, Kathleen Hudson is the founder/director of the Texas Heritage Music Foundation, home for her oral history archives, a collection of 300 interviews with Texas songwriters and musicians. The following interview excerpted from her book about Texas song writers, *Telling Stories, Writing Songs: An Album of Texas Songwriters* (University of Texas Press, 2001), illustrates her write-up of a recorded interview with blues guitar legend, Stevie Ray Vaughan. Note how she moves between prepared questions and open-ended dialogue, permitting Vaughan to address more than merely pre-planned questions.

Hudson: I'm so overwhelmed by your performance, and the stories you told about in each song. I'm sure we can add much by talking about the music, since the performance speaks for itself.

Vaughan: That's the best I could do today. That's how I do it everyday now.

Hudson: I heard you first at Aqua Fest several years ago. You blazed under a full moon that night. Something real was happening.

Vaughan: We were having fun.

Hudson: Let's talk about that song you played toward the end of the set tonight. You talked a little about your own feelings as an introduction.

Vaughan: The song was called "Life Without You." It was written when a friend of ours died. I was trying to talk about what drugs do to people. It kills people in their heart, and sometimes it's bad enough to kill them physically. You know when I say heart, I mean soul.

Hudson: The song portrayed pain in some places and then suddenly I felt this burst of celebration that came into it. There was so much intensity; it's hard to differentiate between the intense pain and the intense happiness that sometimes overlap or go hand in hand.

Vaughan: Sometimes no pain, no gain.

Hudson: Are there any special circumstances that drive you to put pen to paper?

Vaughan: Sometimes it's easy to write about something, sometimes it's not; I just hope it continues. It's a gift. I'm trying to do the best that I can with the gifts I've got. And not try to stand there and say it's all me, 'cause it's not.

Hudson: Is there one performer that has influenced your style?

Vaughan: I can't nail down one. If I hadn't heard Hendrix and Clapton or others, I wouldn't be able to do what I'm doing now. What we all do is try to pay attention to what we've heard and give it back our own way.

Hudson: Is there any particular song you like to play more than another?

Vaughan: Which night are you talking about?

Hudson: I like that.

Vaughan: I like "the next one." What is it going to be? I keep doing the best I can to keep going with it.

Hudson: You're well respected and loved by many other performers.

Vaughan: I'm just glad to be alive and be playing and know about these people as well. I played a set with Otis Rush the other night. Just being there playing along with him and being able to stand right next to him, feel what he is doing; it was like coming home. He invited me to come home and hold on to a note and see where it goes. Thank God for people like Otis Rush.

Hudson: Chris Holzhaus said a turning point in his career was "tonight, playing on the same stage as Stevie Ray Vaughan."

Vaughan: Well, I thank him. We've got to hold hands and keep walking.

Hudson: I loved the ending of your show where the band lined up, throwing their arms around each other, saying, "Hey, we're a family."

Vaughan: We are.

Film Links: The American Family

1. How is "family life" often presented in films? First, brainstorm the word "parents" and examine your own experience with them or parent figures. Next, watch as many of the movies on the following list as you can, paying special attention to the relationship between couples and parents and their children. Finally, write an essay arguing that crisis situations as experienced in life and demonstrated in movies provide the basis for parent/child bonding. Support your argument with examples drawn from personal experience, observation, readings, and films (analyze references to films).

2. Referring to Writing about Films, the questions (heuristics) listed in the appendix, generate a particular focus on the topic of "American Families" and develop it in a well-supported essay. Your observations and insights gleaned from films may be useful in "showing" rather than simply "telling" your readers what you have to say.

Rebel Without a Cause (USA, Nicholas Ray, 1955). Three teens discover stronger bonds between themselves than their families.

To Kill a Mockingbird (USA, Robert Mulligan, 1962). Children in a small southern town grow up in a hurry when their father defends a black man accused of raping a white woman.

To Sleep with Anger (USA, Chester Burnett, 1990). An African American family in Los Angeles gets a visit from an old friend who has a strange effect on the whole family.

Men Don't Leave (USA, Paul Brickman, 1990). A young widow moves her family to Baltimore in search of a new life and finds more difficulties than she had imagined.

The Joy Luck Club (USA, Wayne Wang, 1993). Two generations of Chinese women—mothers and daughters—relate their personal stories of life and its trials.

What's Eating Gilbert Grape? (USA, Lasse Hallström, 1994). A young grocery clerk finds ways to support his eccentric family.

My Family (USA, Gregory Nava, 1994). Sixty years in the life of a Mexican family that settles in Los Angeles at the turn of the 20th century.

Flirting with Disaster (USA, David O. Russell, 1995). A young father who was adopted in infancy goes on a cross-country search for his biological mother with unforeseen and ridiculous results.

Ulee's Gold (USA, Victor Nunez, 1998). A father, a beekeeper by profession, finds himself entangled in the world of drugs and unpaid debts to criminals after his son-in-law is jailed.

American Beauty (USA, Sam Mendes, 1999). A middle-class man has a midlife crisis that unleashes the repressed impulses of his whole family and leads to revelation and catastrophe.

Limbo (USA, John Sayles, 1999). A single mother with a teenage daughter tries to survive as a saloon singer in Alaska. She's looking for a chance to start over and finds an out-of-work fisherman in a similar condition.

October Sky (USA, Joe Johnston, 1999). True story of a young boy living in West Virginia in the 1950s who feels pressure from his family to go to work in the coal mines when his ambition is to build rockets.

Yi-Yi (Taiwan, Edward Yang, 2000). An extended family in Taipei struggles to stay together despite a death and a divorce.

Additional Writing Assignments

1. Many people argue that there is no longer any such thing as a typical American family. Explain how and why such things as cultural differences and lifestyles make it impossible to generalize the "typical" American family. Bear in mind that "typical" means "representative," not "ideal." ("Ideal" implies a preference over how things really are.)

2. Do children really "yearn to belong to a great family" as many social critics claim? Write a brief composition citing your own reasons and providing your own examples and observations to argue for the truth or falsity of such a position. You might want to consider the concept of family in a figurative sense. That is, do people consider their coworkers as part of their professional family? Is the 'hood or a street gang a family? Are the people living on a commune or playing in the same music group part of a "figurative family"?

3. Compare and/or contrast how your parents, guardians, or authority figures followed some sort of dream (American or otherwise) to attain a goal and how you plan to "prosper" because of or in spite of it in the future. What distinguishes your way of achieving success?

4. Although gay couples still cannot be legally married in the United States, several states like Hawaii have introduced bills that would provide them with medical and dental benefits formerly reserved for traditional couples. Excluding any political or religious biases you may have

on the issue, write an argumentative paper persuading your readers that it is (or is not) logical and fair for two human beings living together like a married couple to enjoy the same health benefits as traditional couples.

5. Research and write a three- or four-page family history (this could be the start of a long, ongoing project!). Begin by interviewing relatives on both sides of the family and getting the last known mailing addresses for relatives you have never met. Next, explain how your family came to live where you are today; stick to showing readers how your family came to call a particular city "home," even if you are in another state attending college. You might conclude your essay by projecting future research into your family's history. (See the earlier section of Chapter 3, How to Conduct an Interview, to review effective interview techniques.)

Chapter Four

Stereotypes and Social Barriers

Observations and Opinions

*When I was playing synthesizer in Barefoot & Pregnant, a mostly
female band in New York that attempted to defy the stereotypes of
women in rock, the sexism we encountered came from well-meaning
fools whose compliments were always qualified with "for a girl."
Our drummer was always "a good drummer—for a girl." She was
more inventive than any of the male drummers who traveled our
club circuit, which made us wonder how much she would have to
practice before she would be deemed a good drummer, period.*

—MARGOT MIFFLIN FROM "THE FALLACY OF
FEMINISM IN ROCK" IN *KEYBOARD*

*The United States exists as a sovereign nation. "America," in
contrast, exists as a myth of democracy and equal opportunity to
live by, or as an ideal goal to reach.*

—BHARATI MUKHERJEE ON "AMERICA"

*The loneliness of Americans does not have its source in xenophobia;
as a nation we are an outgoing people, reaching always for
immediate contacts, further experience. But we tend to seek out
things as individuals, alone.*

—CARSON MCCULLERS, FROM "LONELINESS . . . AN AMERICAN MALADY"

*Chicanos and other people of color suffer economically for not
acculturating. This voluntary (yet forced) alienation makes for a
psychological conflict, a kind of dual identity—we don't identify*

*with Anglo-American cultural values and we don't totally identify
with Mexican cultural values.*

—GLORIA ANZALDÚA, FROM *HOW TO TAME A WILD TONGUE*

*I have a dream that my four little children will one day live in a
nation where they will not be judged by the color of their skin but by
the content of their character.*

—MARTIN LUTHER KING, JR. FROM "I HAVE A DREAM"

Observations and Opinions: Reading/Writing Activities

1. How do Margot Mifflin and Bharati Mukherjee both touch upon the contrast between the ideal of equality in the United States and the reality? To what extent might an ideal become a stereotype?

2. Compare and contrast Carson McCullers's perception about American loneliness to Dr. Martin Luther King, Jr.'s dream of social unification. How might King's "dream" be an answer to the cause of American loneliness and/or social alienation?

3. How does Gloria Anzaldúa's explanation of the dual identity of Chicanos and other people of color reveal how both Anglo-American and Mexican cultures produce stereotypes?

Introduction

Differences between people can cause tension, misunderstanding, distrust, and controversy. What makes conversations between men and women, or between people from different ethnic, religious, or political groups awkward, strained, or annoying? Most people are more at ease when they are in a familiar situation around friends they know and trust. New people and new situations can cause uncertainty and fear. These feelings give rise to mental images that represent such people or situations. At such moments, we no longer see other people as individuals but as *stereotypes*. When people think they have other individuals "all figured out," they feel in control—no surprises. Unfortunately, the desire to anticipate what others believe, think, say, do, and like can become unfair, judgmental exercises.

Think of words and phrases like redneck, skater, conservative, Ivy Leaguer, feminist, day trader, illegal alien, lawyer, felon, soccer mom, Baby Boomer, reliable source, homeboy, and community college student. Each of these is loaded with pictorial meaning; we picture someone in our imagination and take that image to be true. All of the images reduce the complexity of individual human beings to a shorthand system of types. This kind of thinking leads to racial profiling, stereotyping, and various other forms of prejudice and discrimination. The complex variety of human beings defies strict definition; there always will be exceptions to a generalized image.

Today, geographical borders have been replaced by political, cultural, ethnic, and gender boundaries. As a result, people tend to have to overcome obstacles imposed by stereotypes—stereotypes that limit social mobility. Why? Stereotypes are often sexist, racist, ageist, and demeaning; they are labels meant to represent a certain set of beliefs, and these form the basis for thinking about what is important and what is not; who is qualified for a job and who lacks experience; or why "blue" is a color for boys and "pink" is more appropriate for girls. The struggle of being recognized for who and what we are, instead of how others typecast or perceive us, seems unending. Our strongest sense of who and what we are may have been established through our earliest relationships—with our parents, friends, family members, teachers, spiritual leaders, and so on. Still, early influences on one's attitude do not justify ongoing prejudice or stereotyping.

Stereotyping imposes social borders that are illogical, unreasonable, unfair, and immoral. They tend to trap and dehumanize particular social, economic, religious, ethnic, gender, and age groups. Senior citizens are not all bad drivers; Koreans do not all own convenience stores; African Americans are not all rappers; English instructors don't all go home and read Shakespeare; Appalachian residents do not all play banjos, make moonshine, and dress like hillbillies; Chicanos are not all mechanics or gang members; women are not all good mothers; and men do not all watch football. The list of stereotypes goes on and on, but none is justified. Anybody who pretends to know or understand others through a stereotype exhibits ignorance rather than insight.

The articles in this section examine some of the social barriers and misunderstandings caused by prejudging and stereotyping. In "One of the Bad Guys?" for instance, Ray Hanania questions the logic behind depicting all Arabs and Muslims as terrorists. He highlights the absurdity behind presenting only one image for millions of human beings. Keeping focused on his topic—the media, movies, television—he shows how even supposedly unbiased news agencies fuel false perceptions and reinforce existing stereotypes of people from the Middle East.

According to Toni Morrison, today's stereotyping results from the fact that "popular culture, shaped by film, theater, advertising, the press, television, and literature is heavily engaged in race talk." In her essay, "On the Backs of Blacks," she reminds us that social stratification, the need for each group to "get ahead," sometimes at the expense of others, has resulted in the mean-spirited discrimination that has been an endless source of frustration for African Americans. She asks us to remember our history and to tell the truth.

Amy Tan presents a different look at barriers—especially those barriers confronting the children of immigrant families. These obstacles result from assumptions that are more perceived than real. Tan views her mother's struggle to be seen as a whole person, despite her imperfect English, as profoundly shaping her mother's experience.

Guillermo Gómez-Peña describes himself as a resident of two cultures—both the United States and Mexico: "The border became my home, my base of operations, and my laboratory of social and artistic experimentation. My art, my dreams, my family and friends, and my psyche were literally and conceptually divided by the border." He contemplates the "borderless" consciousness that results when cultures spill over political borders.

Finally, Ishmael Reed describes his city, a neighborhood in Oakland, California. He calls it "Ground Zero," a phrase generally used to designate a bombing site. This is definitely a man-made world of crack dealers and "drug fascists," as he calls them, and it imposes definite physical borders, compromising one's chances for advancement and success in society. He finds this urban world of asphalt, concrete, glass, steel, and chemicals inhospitable because of the threat of violence that hangs in the air wherever drug traffic flourishes, but what should he do? Move to the country? Is it that easy? One's social and economic situation may make such an option impossible. Reed strives to get beyond stereotypes and describe his immediate world in all its frightening detail.

Where and how we find ourselves places to live and prosper in the future will be determined by how well we learn to appreciate the rich mixture of human cultures and ways of living in America while avoiding the temptation to stereotype.

Gathering Thoughts: Prereading Inquiries

Examine the following questions individually or collaboratively to generate ideas and consider the multiple issues involved with stereotypes and social barriers. At this point, base your responses on personal experience, observations, or readings; at a later date, you may want to research questions of fact in your college library or online. How did your individual or group findings compare with those of others?

1. Why are Americans so interested in meeting aliens from outer space and so suspicious, if not intolerant, of humans from different social, economic, ethnic, and religious backgrounds?

Continued

2. How has popular culture affected your perception of diversity?

3. Are your attitudes toward the opposite sex or attraction to the same sex shaped by cultural, religious, and political beliefs, or are they the result of independent reasoning?

4. When have you "prejudged" a person's ability to do something for one reason or another?

5. What social, family, and peer pressures might encourage people to act or say something contrary to their better judgment? Illustrate your points with specific examples.

6. What are the benefits of a society that is tolerant toward human diversity? Give two or three examples.

7. How have you been stereotyped in your lifetime? Did the way others stereotype you create opportunities or barriers? Why?

8. How might victims of stereotypes actually be seen as prophets of an emerging world, a world where overlapping economies cease to regard difference as justification for suspicion, distrust, and fear?

9. Does it make any sense to deny anyone equal medical care and education? How might social barriers imposed by political agendas favor some people while harming many others?

10. In previous decades, assimilation was considered to be the goal of all immigrants. Is it still? Should we adopt a more multicultural perspective? If so, what would it be? What message would this give to all future immigrants?

Mother's English

Amy Tan

Born in Oakland, California, AMY TAN was a graduate of San Jose State University and a freelance writer before publishing her prize-winning book *The Joy Luck Club* (1989). Tan's stories have been published in numerous popular magazines, including *The Atlantic*, *Grand Street*, *Lear's*, and *McCall's*. Her second novel, *The Kitchen God's Wife* (1992), was followed by two children's books illustrated by Gretchen Schield: *The Moon Lady* (1992) and *The Chinese*

Siamese Cat (1994). Tan completed her third novel, *The Hundred Secret Senses* (1995), and she lives in San Francisco. In addition to writing, Tan sings for The Rock Bottom Remainders, a rock group including such popular writers as Dave Barry and Stephen King. (Their motto is "We play music as well as Metallica writes novels.")

ALLUSIONS

The Joy Luck Club: A reference to Amy Tan's first novel about four mother/ daughter relationships.

YMCA: An acronym (a word formed by combining initial letters) meaning Young Men's Christian Association.

Forbes Report: A money magazine—capitalist news.

"Wall Street Week": A PBS TV show dedicated to discussing investment planning.

1   As you know, I am a writer and by that definition I am someone who has always loved language. I think that is first and foremost with almost every writer I know. I'm fascinated by language in daily life. I spend a great deal of time thinking about the power of language—the way it can evoke an emotion, a visual image, a complex idea, or a simple truth. As a writer, language is the tool of my trade and I use them all, all the Englishes I grew up with.

2   A few months back, I was made keenly aware of the Englishes I do use. I was giving a talk to a large group of people, the same talk I had given many times before and also with notes. And the nature of the talk was about my writing, my life, and my book *The Joy Luck Club*. The talk was going along well enough until I remembered one major difference that made the whole thing seem wrong. My mother was in the room, and it was perhaps the first time she had heard me give a lengthy speech, using a kind of English I had never used with her. I was saying things like "the intersection of memory and imagination," and "there is an aspect of my fiction that relates to this and thus." A speech filled with carefully wrought grammatical sentences, burdened to me it seemed with nominalized forms, past perfect tenses, conditional phrases, all the forms of standard English that I had learned in school and through books, a form of English I did not use at home or with my mother.

3   Shortly after that I was walking down the street with my mother and my husband and I became self-conscious of the English I was using, the English that I do use with her. We were talking about the price of new and used furniture and I heard myself saying to her, "Not waste money that way." My husband was with me as well, and he didn't notice any switch in my English. And then I realized why: because over the twenty years that we've been together he's often used that English with me and I've used that with him. It is sort of the English that is our language of intimacy, the English that relates to family talk, the English that I grew up with.

4   I'd like to give you some idea what my family talk sounds like and I'll do that by quoting what my mother said during a recent conversation which I video-taped and then transcribed. During this conversation, my mother was talking about a political gangster who had the same last name as her family, Du, and how the gangster in his early years wanted to be adopted by her family which was by comparison very rich. Later the gangster became more rich, more powerful than my mother's family and one day showed up at my mother's wedding to pay his respects. And here's what she said about that, in part, "Du Yu Sung having business like food stand, like off the street kind; he's Du like Du Zong but not Tsung-ming Island people. The local people call him Du, from the river east side. He belong that side, local people. That man want to ask Du Zong father take him in become like own family. Du Zong father look down on him but don't take seriously until that man become big like, become a Mafia. Now important person, very hard inviting him. Chinese way: come only to show respect, don't stay for dinner. Respect for making big celebration; he shows up. Means gives lots of respect, Chinese custom. Chinese social life that way—if too important, won't have to stay too long. He come to my wedding; I didn't see it I heard it. I gone to boy's side. They have YMCA dinner; Chinese age I was nineteen."

5   You should know that my mother's expressive command of English belies how much she actually understands. She reads the Forbes Report, listens to Wall Street Week, converses daily with her stock broker, reads all of Shirley MacLaine's books with ease, all kinds of things I can't begin to understand. Yet some of my friends tell me that they understand 50% of what my mother says. Some say they understand maybe 80%. Some say they understand almost nothing at all. As a case in point, a television station recently interviewed my mother and I didn't see this program when it was first aired, but my mother did. She was telling me what happened. She said that everything she said, which was in English, was subtitled in English, as if she had been speaking in pure Chinese. She was understandably puzzled and upset. Recently a friend gave me that tape and I saw that same interview and I watched. And sure enough—subtitles—and I was puzzled because listening to that tape it seemed to me that my mother's English sounded perfectly clear and perfectly natural. Of course, I realize that my mother's English is what I grew up with. It is literally my mother tongue, not Chinese, not standard English, but my mother's English which I later found out is almost a direct translation of Chinese.

6   Her language as I hear it is vivid and direct, full of observation and imagery. That was the language that helped shape the way that I saw things, expressed things, made sense of the world. Lately I've been giving more thought to the kind of English that my mother speaks. Like others I have described it to people as broken or fractured English, but I wince when I say that. It has always bothered me that I can think of no other way to describe it than broken, as if it were damaged or needed to be fixed, that it lacked a certain wholeness or soundness to it. I've heard other terms used, "Limited English" for example. But they seem just as bad, as if everything is limited, including people's perceptions of the Limited English speaker.

7   I know this for a fact, because when I was growing up my mother's limited English limited my perception of her. I was ashamed of her English. I believed that her English reflected the quality of what she had to say. That is, because she expressed it imperfectly, her thoughts were imperfect as well. And I had plenty of empirical evidence to support me: The fact that people in department stores, at banks, at supermarkets, at restaurants did not take her as seriously, did not give her good service, pretended not to understand her, or even acted as if they did not hear her.

8   My mother has long realized the limitations of her English as well. When I was fifteen she used to have me call people on the phone to pretend I was she. In this guise, I was forced to ask for information or oftentimes to complain and yell at people that had been rude to her. One time it was a call to her stock broker in New York. She had cashed out her small portfolio and it just so happened that we were going to New York the next week, our very first trip outside of California. I had to get on the phone and say in my adolescent voice, which was not very convincing, "This is Mrs. Tan." And my mother was in the back whispering loudly, "Why don't he send me check already? Two weeks late. So mad he lie to me, losing me money." Then I said in perfect English, "Yes I'm getting rather concerned. You had agreed to send the check two weeks ago, but it hasn't arrived." And she began to talk more loudly, "What you want—I come to New York, tell him front of his boss you cheating me?" And I was trying to calm her down, making her be quiet, while telling this stock broker, "I can't tolerate any more excuses. If I don't receive the check immediately I'm going to have to speak to your manager when I arrive in New York." And sure enough the following week, there we were in front of this astonished stock broker. And there I was, red-faced and quiet, and my mother the real Mrs. Tan was shouting at his boss in her impeccable broken English.

9   We used a similar routine a few months ago for a situation that was actually far less humorous. My mother had gone to the hospital for an appointment to find out about a benign brain tumor a CAT scan had revealed a month ago. And she had spoken very good English she said—her best English, no mistakes. Still she said the hospital had not apologized when they said they had lost the CAT scan and she had come for nothing. She said that they did not seem to have any sympathy when she told them she was anxious to know the exact diagnosis since her husband and son had both died of brain tumors. She said they would not give her any more information until the next time; she would have to make another appointment for that, so she said she would not leave until the doctor called her daughter. She wouldn't budge, and when the doctor finally called her daughter, me, who spoke in perfect English, lo-and-behold, we had assurances the CAT scan would be found, they promised a conference call on Monday, and apologies were given for any suffering my mother had gone through for a most regrettable mistake. By the way, apart from the distress of that episode, my mother is fine.

10   But it has continued to disturb me how much my mother's English still limits people's perceptions of her. I think my mother's English almost had an effect on

limiting my possibilities as well. Sociologists and linguists will probably tell you that a person's developing language skills are more influenced by peers. But I do think the language spoken by the family, especially immigrant families, which are more insular, plays a large role in shaping the language of the child. . . . [While this may be true, I always wanted, however,] to capture what language ability tests can never reveal—her intent, her passion, her imagery, the rhythms of her speech, and the nature of her thoughts. Apart from what any critic had to say about my writing, I knew I had succeeded where it counted when my mother finished reading my first book and gave me her verdict. "So easy to read."

AFTERWARDS

Vocabulary

belies, intersection, nominalized, wrought, transcribed, empirical, portfolio, CAT scan, linguists. Look up the words above and check to see the meanings in their original languages. Do they mean something different in English? Write a brief explanation showing how the meaning has either remained stable or has taken on new significance.

Content

1. How is the conversational tone of Tan's essay appropriate to listeners as well as to readers?

2. What makes Tan's mother uncomfortable with her English? As a result, what does she ask her teenage daughter, Amy, to do?

3. Explain what you think Amy Tan means when she writes, "I think my mother's English almost had an effect on limiting my possibilities as well." What does this statement reveal about her awareness of prejudice?

Collaborative Explorations

Form a group and list all the possible meanings and associations you can think of for the words "immigration" and "alien" (including "alienation"). Look them up in the dictionary and see where the words come from. What borders and social barriers do you relate with each word? Finally, write a short collaborative paper in which your group takes all the material it brainstormed and reflects upon what it is to be an "immigrant" and an "alien" in every sense of the words.

Style and Structure

1. How and why did Tan's mother influence her style of writing? What, even in her broken English, could Tan's mother effectively express? Why does Tan value this?

2. In detail, discuss the different types of Englishes Tan's mother speaks. When and where is each of her mother's Englishes appropriate? Give some representative examples of these Englishes.

3. How does Tan build her essay to its conclusion? Why do you imagine she chose to arrange her narrative events in their present order? Why does she mention her experience with her mother at the hospital last? What effect would paragraph 9 have on a reader if it had been placed in the first or second paragraph? Explain.

Writing Assignments

1. Write a paragraph or so where you explain what you have often observed or personally experienced because of "imperfect English" or another language difficulty (stuttering, dyslexia). How were you, or someone you know, denied access to opportunities because another person prejudged your skills based on how you speak?

2. In April 1998, Marcia Mogelonski published an article called "Watching in Tongues" in *American Demographics*. Therein, Mogelonski noted that leading advertisers see a rare opportunity to claim a fast-growing, long-ignored market—38 million Americans whose native tongue is not English. Do you agree with her? Briefly respond to her belief, offering some of your own observations. If you owned your own cable or digital company, how would you take advantage of the current situation? How might you get 38 million people to subscribe to your service?

Thematic Reading Cross-Links: For an interesting contrast to a mother/daughter relationship, see Alice Walker's essay, "Father," from Chapter 3, The American Family.

Movie Cross-Links: See the movie version of Amy Tan's novel, *The Joy Luck Club,* and consider her portrayal of all four mothers and their daughters, noting how they all confront social barriers—sometimes imposed on each other—and adjust.

Beyond the Tortilla Curtain
Guillermo Gómez-Peña

In addition to his writings, **Guillermo Gómez-Peña** works as a visual performance artist in Los Angeles, California. Gómez-Peña edited *Made in Aztlan: Centro Cultural de Raza* (1987), and his other works include *Warrior for Gringostrokia* (1993) and *The New World Border: Prophecies, Poems, & Loqueras for the End of the Century* (1996). *Friendly Cannibal* (1996), co-authored with Enrique Chagoya, and *Temple of Confessions: Mexican Beasts and Living Santos* (1996), written with Roberto Sifuentes, represent Gómez-Peña's major collaborations.

ALLUSIONS

Möbius strip: Discovered by a German mathematician, August Möbius, in 1858, a Möbius strip is a continuous loop with one surface and one edge formed by twisting one end of a long, thin rectangular strip 180 degrees (1/2 twist) and attaching this end to the other. Used by artists and environmentalists as a symbol of continuous transformation.

NAFTA: The North American Free Trade Agreement with Mexico.

1   From 1978 to 1991, I lived and worked in and among the cities of Tijuana, San Diego, and Los Angeles. Like hundreds of thousands of Mexicans, I was a binational commuter. I crossed that dangerous border regularly, by plane, by car, and by foot. The border became my home, my base of operations, and my laboratory of social and artistic experimentation. My art, my dreams, my family and friends, and my psyche were literally and conceptually divided by the border. But the border was not a straight line; it was more like a *Möbius strip*. No matter where I was, I was always on "the other side," feeling ruptured and incomplete, ever longing for my other selves, my other home and tribe.

2   Thanks to my Chicano colleagues, I learned to perceive California as an extension of Mexico and the city of Los Angeles as the northernmost barrio of Mexico City. And in spite of many California residents' denial of the state's Mexican past and their bittersweet relationship with contemporary Mexicans, I never quite felt like an immigrant. As a mestizo with a thick accent and an even thicker moustache, I knew I wasn't exactly welcome; but I also knew that millions of Latinos, "legal" and "illegal," shared that border experience with me.

3   Then in 1991 I moved to New York City, and my umbilical cord finally snapped. For the first time in my life, I felt like a true immigrant. From my Brooklyn apartment, Mexico and Chicanolandia seemed a million light years away.

4   I decided to return to Southern California in 1993. Since the riots, Los Angeles had become the epicenter of America's social, racial, and cultural crisis. It was, unwillingly, the capital of a growing "Third World" within the shrinking "First World." I wanted to be both a witness and a chronicler of this wonderful madness.

5   I found a city at war with itself; a city gravely punished by natural and social forces; a city that is experiencing in a more concentrated manner what the rest of the country is undergoing. Its political structures are dysfunctional and its economy is in shambles; cutbacks in the defense budget have resulted in increased unemployment; and racial tensions are the focus of daily news reports. Crime rates and poverty levels can be compared to those of a Third World city. All this coincides with an acute crisis of national identity. Post–Cold War America is having a very hard time shedding its imperial nostalgia, embracing its multiracial soul, and accepting its new status as the first "developed" country to become a member of the Third World.

6   Perhaps what scared me more than anything was to realize who was being blamed for all the turmoil. The Mexican/Latino immigrant community was the scapegoat and was being singled out by both Republican and Democratic politicians, fanatic citizen groups like SOS (Save Our State), and sectors of the mainstream media as the main cause of our social ills. The racist Proposition 187, which denies nonemergency medical services and education to illegal aliens, passed with 60 percent of the vote on November 8, 1994, and turns every doctor, nurse, pharmacist, police officer, schoolteacher, and "concerned citizen" into a de facto border patrolman. Furthermore, the very same people who supported Prop 187 [now held up in court] also opposed women's and gay rights, affirmative action, bilingual education, freedom of expression, and the existence of the National Endowment for the Arts. Why? What does this mean? What are we all losing?

7   Despite the fact that the United States has always been a nation of immigrants and border crossers, nativism has periodically reared its head. American identity has historically depended on opposing an "other," be it cultural, racial, or ideological. Americans need enemies against whom to define their personal and national boundaries. From the original indigenous inhabitants of this land to the former Soviets, an evil "other" has always been stalking and ready to strike.

8   Fear is at the core of xenophobia. This fear is particularly disturbing when it is directed at the most vulnerable victims: migrant workers. They become the "invaders" from the south, the human incarnation of the Mexican fly, the subhuman "wetbacks," the "aliens" from another (cultural) planet. They are always suspected of stealing "our jobs," of shrinking "our budget," of taking advantage of the welfare system, of not paying taxes, and of bringing disease, drugs, street violence, foreign thoughts, pagan rites, primitive customs, and alien sounds. Their indigenous features and rough clothes remind uninformed citizens of an unpleasant pre-European American past and of mythical lands to the south immersed in poverty and political turmoil, where innocent gringos could be attacked for no apparent reason. Yet these invaders no longer inhabit the remote past, a banana republic, or a Hollywood film. They actually live down the block, and their children go to the same schools as do the Anglo kids.

9   Nothing is scarier than the blurring of the border between them and us; between the Dantesque South and the prosperous North; between paganism and Christianity. For many Americans, the border has failed to stop chaos and crisis from creeping in (the origin of crisis and chaos is strangely always located outside). Their worst nightmare is finally coming true: The United States is no longer a fictional extension of Europe, or the wholesome suburb imagined by the screenwriter of Lassie. It is

rapidly becoming a huge border zone, a hybrid society, a mestizo race, and, worst of all, this process seems to be irreversible. America shrinks day by day, as the pungent smell of enchiladas and the volume of quebradita music rise.

10   Authoritarian solutions to "the problem" of immigration can only make things worse. Further militarizing the border while dismantling the social, medical, and educational support systems that serve the immigrant population will only worsen social tensions. Denying medical services to undocumented immigrants will result in more disease and more teenage pregnancy. Throwing 300,000 kids out of the schools and into the streets will only contribute to crime and social disintegration. Not only will these proposals backfire, they also will contribute to a growing nationalism in the Latino and Asian communities and repoliticize entire communities that were dormant in the past decade.

11   So what to do with "the problem" of immigration? First of all, we need to stop characterizing it as a unilateral "problem." Let's be honest. The end of the century appears scary to both Anglos and Latinos, to legal and illegal immigrants. Both sides feel threatened, uprooted, and displaced, to different degrees and for different reasons. We all fear deep inside that there won't be enough jobs, food, air, and housing for everybody. Yet we cannot deny the processes of interdependence that define our contemporary experience as North Americans. In a post–NAFTA, Post–Cold War America, the binary models of us/them, North/South, and Third World/First World are no longer useful in understanding our complicated border dynamics, our transnational identities, and our multiracial communities.

12   It's time to face the facts: Anglos won't go back to Europe, and Mexicans and Latinos (legal or illegal) won't go back to Latin America. We are all here to stay. For better or worse, our destinies and aspirations are in one another's hands.

13   For me, the only solution lies in a paradigm shift: the recognition that we all are protagonists in the creation of a new cultural topography and a new social order, one in which we all are "others" and we need the other "others" to exist. Hybridity is no longer up for discussion. It is a demographic racial, social, and cultural fact. The real tasks ahead of us are to embrace more fluid and tolerant notions of personal and national identity and to develop models of peaceful coexistence and multilateral cooperation across boundaries of nationality, race, gender, and religion. To this end, rather than more border patrols, border walls, and punitive laws, we need more and better information about one another. Culture and education are at the core of the solution. We need to learn each others' languages, histories, art, and cultural traditions. We need to educate our children and teenagers about the dangers of racism and the complexities of living in a multiracial borderless society, the inevitable society of the next century.

AFTERWARDS

Vocabulary

*mestizo, scapegoating, nativism, dysfunctional, nostalgia, xenophobia, indige-
nous, Dantesque, paganism, paradigm shift, demographic, multilateral.* Look up
the vocabulary words in your dictionary and review how Gómez-Peña uses them

in his essay. Then, write a paragraph describing or explaining a situation in which you have been excluded or confronted with a barrier (literally or figuratively).

Content

1. Historically, what has determined the concept of American identity?

2. In your experience, how have Mexican/Latino communities been the scapegoats of society? How do you think Gómez-Peña would answer this question? Why?

3. Refer back to the definition of "xenophobia." In what way might xenophobia be the real cause behind anti-immigration feelings? Explain this answer in terms of your own personal experience.

Style and Structure

1. In what way do rhetorical questions such as "Why? What does this mean? What are we all losing?" (the last three sentences in paragraph 6) stimulate readers' imaginations and prepare them for the following paragraphs?

2. Gómez-Peña employs words with distinct connotations (associated meanings) from the beginning of the essay until its conclusion. Identify these words and their connotations. How, in the end, do they assist the author in achieving his goals?

3. How does Gómez-Peña immediately establish his ethos (credibility and authority) on the topic of immigration and borders?

Collaborative Explorations

Why do you imagine Gómez-Peña titled his essay "Beyond the Tortilla Curtain"? In what way might he be alluding to another barrier—one between the free world and communist-controlled countries in Europe during the Cold War? Jot down your personal responses to these questions; then get together with a few of your classmates and take turns rereading Gómez-Peña's essay out loud. How does the image of a curtain function as a symbol that addresses the larger concerns of his essay?

Writing Assignments

1. In a well-organized essay, argue whether or not Gómez-Peña is correct in his claim that "the Mexican/Latino immigrant community" has been

singled out as the scapegoat for America's turmoil by Republican and Democratic politicians. Do some limited research in the library to gather evidence to support your claims.

2. What are the advantages and disadvantages of a borderless society? You may want to begin this writing assignment by brainstorming, clustering, or using some other prewriting method. Freely associate, for example, key words like "border" or "boundary."

Thematic Reading Cross-Links: See Chapter 5, Media: Controversies and Celebrities, for insight into how the media promote (intentionally or otherwise) the restrictions placed on immigrants.

Movie Cross-Links: See *Do The Right Thing,* a movie about another city at "Ground Zero," listed in the Film Links at the end of this chapter.

On the Backs of Blacks

Toni Morrison

A celebrated poet, essayist, playwright, novelist, and editor, TONI MORRISON was born Chloe Anthony Wofford in Lorain, Ohio, and she received her college education at Cornell and Howard universities. Following her divorce from her Jamaican husband, Harold Morrison, she worked for Random House publishers, often editing books by other African Americans, including Muhammad Ali, Toni Cade Bambara, Angela Davis, Gayle Jones, and Andrew Young. Morrison fully embraces her role as one of the most influential African American women writers of the 20th century, and her works are filled with memorable female characters whose stories frequently deal with growing up in a predominantly white racist and sexist society. Some notable characteristics of her fiction include emotional intensity, human sensitivity, historical contexts for her plots, and a sparse use of poetic language. Morrison's works include *The Bluest Eye* (1970), *Sula* (1974), *Song of Solomon* (1977, winner of the National Book Award and the National Book Critics' Circle Award), *Tar Baby* (1981), *Beloved* (1987, winner of the Pulitzer Prize and the Robert F. Kennedy Book Award), and *Jazz* (1992). In 1992, Morrison also published a collection of essays: *Race-ing Justice, Re-Gendering Power.* In the following essay published in a special edition of *Time* magazine in the Fall of 1993, Morrison asserts that media sources throughout history have shaped American race talk, the "mindless linguistic and cultural symbols that demonize American Blacks."

ALLUSIONS

Most of Morrison's allusions are defined within the text of her essay. That is, when she mentions a name, she goes on to explain who or what we associate with the person. As you read through her essay, imagine what would have been lost without her brief explanations. You might also consider how a greater knowledge of the people she talks about might enrich your understanding of her points.

1   Fresh from Ellis Island, Stavros gets a job shining shoes at Grand Central Terminal. It is the last scene of Elia Kazan's film *America, America*, the story of a young Greek's fierce determination to immigrate to America. Quickly, but as casually as an afterthought, a young blackman, also a shoe shiner, enters and tries to solicit a customer. He is run off the screen—"Get out of here! We're doing business here!"— and silently disappears.

2   This interloper into Stavros' workplace is crucial in the mix of signs that make up the movie's happy-ending immigrant story: a job, a straw hat, an infectious smile—and a scorned black. It is the act of racial contempt that transforms this charming Greek into an entitled white. Without it, Stavros' future as an American is not at all assured.

3   This is race talk, the explicit insertion into everyday life of racial signs and symbols that have no meaning other than pressing African Americans to the lowest level of the racial hierarchy. Popular culture, shaped by film, theater, advertising, the press, television and literature, is heavily engaged in race talk. It participates freely in this most enduring and efficient rite of passage into American culture: negative appraisals of the native-born black population. Only when the lesson of racial estrangement is learned is assimilation complete. Whatever the lived experience of immigrants with African Americans—pleasant, beneficial or bruising—the rhetorical experience renders blacks as noncitizens, already discredited outlaws.

4   All immigrants fight for jobs and space, and who is there to fight but those who have both? As in the fishing ground struggle between Texas and Vietnamese shrimpers, they displace what and whom they can. Although U.S. history is awash in labor battles, political fights and property wars among all religious and ethnic groups, their struggles are persistently framed as struggles between recent arrivals and blacks. In race talk the move into mainstream America always means buying into the notion of American blacks as the real aliens. Whatever the ethnicity or nationality of the immigrant, his nemesis is understood to be African American.

5   Current attention to immigration has reached levels of panic not seen since the turn of the century. To whip up this panic, modern race talk must be revised downward into obscurity and nonsense if antiblack hostility is to remain the drug of choice, giving headlines their kick. PATTERNS OF IMMIGRATION FOLLOWED BY WHITE FLIGHT, screams the *Star-Ledger* in Newark. The message we are meant to get is that disorderly newcomers are dangerous to stable (white) residents. Stability is white. Disorder is black. Nowhere do we learn what stable middle-class

blacks think or do to cope with the "breaking waves of immigration." The overwhelming majority of African Americans, hardworking and stable, are out of the loop, disappeared except in their less than covert function of defining whites as the "true" Americans.

6   So addictive is this ploy that the fact of blackness has been abandoned for the theory of blackness. It doesn't matter anymore what shade the newcomer's skin is. A hostile posture toward resident blacks must be struck at the Americanizing door before it will open. The public is asked to accept American blacks as the common denominator in each conflict between an immigrant and a job or between a wannabe and status. It hardly matters what complexities, contexts and misinformation accompany these conflicts. They can all be subsumed as the equation of brand X vs. blacks.

7   But more than a job is at stake in this surrender to whiteness, more even than what the black intellectual W. E. B. Du Bois called the "psychological wage"—the bonus of whiteness. Racist strategies unify. Savvy politicians always include in the opening salvos of their campaigns a quick clarification of their position on race. It is a mistake to think that Bush's Willie Horton or Clinton's Sister Souljah was anything but a candidate's obligatory response to the demands of a contentious electorate unable to understand itself in any terms other than race. Warring interests, nationalities and classes can be merged with the greatest economy under that racial banner.

8   Race talk as bonding mechanism is powerfully on display in American literature. When Nick in F. Scott Fitzgerald's *The Great Gatsby* leaves West Egg to dine in fashionable East Egg, his host conducts a kind of class audition into WASP-dom by soliciting Nick's support for the "science" of racism. "If we don't look out the white race will be . . . utterly submerged," he says. "It's all scientific stuff; it's been proved." It makes Nick uneasy, but he does not question or refute his host's convictions.

9   The best clue to what the country might be like without race as the nail upon which American identity is hung comes from Pap, in Mark Twain's *Huckleberry Finn*, who upon learning a Negro could vote in Ohio, "drawed out. I says I'll never vote ag'in." Without his glowing white mask he is not American; he is Faulkner's character Wash, in *Absalom, Absalom!*, who, stripped of the mask and treated like a "nigger," drives a scythe into the heart of the rich white man he has loved and served so completely.

10   For Pap, for Wash, the possibility that race talk might signify nothing was frightening. Which may be why the harder it is to speak race talk convincingly, the more people seem to need it. As American blacks occupy more and more groups no longer formed along racial lines, the pressure accelerates to figure out what white interests really are. The enlisted military is almost one-quarter black; police forces are blackening in large urban areas. But welfare is nearly two-thirds white; affirmative-action beneficiaries are overwhelmingly white women; dysfunctional white families jam the talk shows and court TV.

11   The old stereotypes fail to connote, and race talk is forced to invent new, increasingly mindless ones. There is virtually no movement up—for blacks or whites, established classes or arrivistes—that is not accompanied by race talk.

Refusing, negotiating or fulfilling this demand is the real stuff, the organizing principle of becoming an American. Star spangled. Race strangled.

AFTERWARDS

Vocabulary

terminal, solicit, insertion, hierarchy, estrangement, rhetorical, persistently, nemesis, denominator, wannabe, savvy, obligatory, contentious, electorate, submerged, connote, interloper. After looking up the above vocabulary words in your dictionary, review how they are used in context in Morrison's essay, and note when and where people use such words in your own life.

Content

1. What is the controlling idea of Morrison's essay? What does she write about, and to whom is it addressed? Does she seem to have any audience in particular in mind? Explain.

2. Morrison claims that "Popular culture, shaped by film, theater, advertising, the press, television, and literature, is heavily engaged in race talk." What specifically is she referring to? Is this also your experience or perception of popular culture?

3. Why would African Americans look at media sources differently than most Caucasians? What could influence their attitudes one way or another?

Style and Structure

1. Explain the method Morrison uses to "lead in" to her essay.

2. How does Morrison explain that the experience of African Americans differs from that of other immigrants—both in the past and in the present?

3. Discuss the tone of voice Morrison assumes in her essay. How does it assist her to establish authority as an author and to appeal ethically to her reader?

Collaborative Explorations

Just as any given essay may include a variety of rhetorical modes (comparison and contrast, cause and effect, illustration and example, process analysis), it frequently contains a number of subthemes that overlap the main theme of the essay.

Gather in a group and review Morrison's essay, locating, discussing, and recording as many (1) methods of development and (2) themes and motifs in the essay as you can. Which rhetorical modes develop some thematic points better than others? What does this suggest about the nature of rhetorical methods of exposition?

Writing Assignments

1. Brainstorm or cluster the words "social barrier." What positive and/or negative associations do you make with them? Why? Write a brief composition explaining your surprise or complete understanding of your responses.

2. Write an essay explaining how you think the media promote good and bad attitudes towards immigrants, particularly people of color, and how it could and should change in the future. Be sure to establish clearly what you perceive is the media's present attitude toward immigration and people of color. (Only then will a need for change be clearly apparent to your readers.)

Thematic Reading Cross-Links: See Stanley Crouch's essay, "Modern Day Minstrel Shows," in Chapter 11, Movies to further study the portrayal of African Americans in film history.

Movie Cross-Links: The miniseries based on the book *Roots* and the movie based on the book *Amistad*—which deal, in part, with immigrants from Africa—offer great companion pieces to Morrison.

One of the Bad Guys?

Ray Hanania

RAY HANANIA, a Chicago journalist, is also author of the humor books, *I'm Glad I Look Like a Terrorist: Growing Up Arab in America* (1997), and *Strike Back: Lentil Soup for the Arab-American Soul* (1999). An advocate of the Middle East peace process and an Arab American activist, he also serves as a communications consultant, political strategist, and news and radio commentator. Hanania's writings also include weekly columns published in newspapers throughout the Middle East. The following essay appeared in *Newsweek,* November 11, 1998.

1   As a child in the 1960s, I thought my relatives were famous. It seemed like they were in many Hollywood movies, often playing similar roles. OK. They weren't the headliners, but they did appear alongside stars like Paul Newman (*Exodus*), Sophia Loren (*Judith*) and Kirk Douglas (*Cast a Giant Shadow*). My "relatives" always played the "terrorists."

2   As I grew older, though, I realized that those actors were not my relatives, at all. They looked like them. They have that "terrorist" look, and so do I. I can safely assure you, though, I don't have the mannerisms. I'm tired of seeing my likeness wielding an AK-47, murdering innocent women and children, getting stomped by Arnold Schwarzenegger (*True Lies*), or Harrison Ford (*Indiana Jones and the Temple of Doom*), or Kurt Russell (*Executive Decision*), and now Bruce Willis (*The Siege*). I'm Arab-American. And for some reason, Hollywood seems to think it's OK to portray all Arabs—and all Muslims, for that matter—as the bad guys. I don't mean just bad. I mean really bad. It makes me so angry I want to get in my half-track with my 50-caliber howitzer that's parked in my two-Hummer garage, drive to the center of town and start shooting! I mean, isn't that what you've come to expect Arabs to do?

3   After I was honorably discharged from the U.S. Air Force in 1975, the FBI opened a file on me. It began with the ominous suggestion that I might be involved in "suspected" terrorist organizations, but the investigation concluded two years and 23 pages later that I was concerned only about improving the condition of my community. The investigation seemed based on the assumption that because I was an Arab, I must also be a potential terrorist. Most of the juicy text was blocked out with heavy, black Magic Markered lines, so it's hard to know for sure.

4   Hollywood movies are founded on the same assumption, that the Arab is the terrorist. I once thought movies were just entertainment, but they're much more. It's at the movies that the public learns about people like me. And it's also where I compare myself to the characters on the screen and wonder if there really is something wrong with me. How did my look suddenly become something so sinister? My eyes become even darker and more deep set? My accent heavier? I begin to question myself. Why is this person who looks like me so angry he wants to murder and harm innocent people? What is it that makes him wreak havoc and wanton suffering upon an innocent world?

5   Occasionally, there is an upside to being pegged as a terrorist. Once at Miami International Airport, a gaggle of people all wearing the same light gray jackets were following me around the terminal. Finally, introducing themselves as airport security, they directed me to a room where they rifled through my bags and grilled me about my travel history. They held up the embarrassing evidence of my terrorism. Wood carved heads. Goofy-looking hats. And dirty clothes.

6   When they finally realized I was just a tourist-trap junkie, they excused themselves. Usually, it takes about 15 minutes before I am released from airport detention and I'm on my way. Meanwhile, the nonterrorist-looking commuters are left waiting in the long immigration lines, impatiently nudging luggage across the tile floor, complaining about the heat and delays. But the security officers always have a

reason to stop me. At Miami, they said I looked like the suspect they were pursuing. And, they just happened to have a Polaroid picture of the "suspect." He wore a double-breasted, polyester leisure suit, with a wide-brimmed Panama hat. And he had olive skin, dark eyes and those skinny little fingers that fit neatly around the trigger of a gun, like mine do. Naturally, I was very impressed. It must be difficult to get a terrorist to stop long enough to pose for a Polaroid picture.

7   Look, I'm realistic. I don't think we can erase all of Hollywood's stereotypes. But the movies seem fixated on the exaggerated bad side of Arabs. To Hollywood, the Arab is the wife-abuser who wants to buy Steve Martin's home in *Father of the Bride II*. Or the guy hanging from the missile in *True Lies* when Schwarzenegger pushes the launch button and says in his Austrian accent, "Yaw're fi-yard!" We Arabs murder innocent airline passengers in *Executive Decision* simply because it makes us feel good.

8   Even a company like Disney takes a shot at us, with these lyrics from the movie *Aladdin*: "Oh I come from a land, from a faraway place, where the caravan camels roam; Where they cut off your ear if they don't like your face; It's barbaric, but hey, it's home." (Disney responded to Arab-Americans' complaints by changing the last line for the video release.)

9   Must every Arab portrayed in the movies be the villain? Why can't we be the hero just once? There are plenty of overlooked role models to choose from. The first heart-transplant surgeon is an Arab-American, Michael DeBakey. Candy Lightner, who founded Mothers Against Drunk Drivers, is Arab, too. There were at least 74 Arab passengers aboard the *Titanic* when it sank. Half of them drowned. Director James Cameron had a good opportunity to highlight the human side of the Arab community. Instead, he chose to highlight a make-believe Irish wedding aboard the ship, rather than include one of the three Arab weddings that actually took place.

10   Arabs are everyday people. Doctors. Teachers. Football stars and team owners. Grocery-store clerks. Engineers. Elected officials. We're the mail carriers who deliver your mail. The nurses and emergency medical technicians who hold your hand through tragedy. The clerks who help you at the bank.

11   I'm not asking Hollywood to hate someone else. That would be wrong. But, I'm asking Hollywood to be fair. Don't just show the bad. Show our good side, too. But, if that can't be done, I do have one last question: are you still mad about the Crusades?

AFTERWARDS

Vocabulary

The vocabulary in Hanania's essay is rather straightforward and easy to follow. To gain a full appreciation of his allusion to Arabs and Muslims in Hollywood, however, you might look up some of the movies he mentions. Write a brief summary of at least two scenes from one of these films—paying particular attention to Arab stereotypes.

Content

1. What early memories does Hanania have of Arab or Middle Eastern role models?

2. Do you agree or disagree with Hanania's statement that "movies seem fixated on the exaggerated bad side of Arabs"?

3. How, according to Hanania, does Disney reinforce Arab/Muslim stereotypes in movies like *Aladdin*?

Style and Structure

1. How does Hanania structure his essay? In what way does he use rhetorical questions to stimulate interest and involve readers in his topic? Does the essay lead to a logical and ethical call to action?

2. Why would Hanania imply that a Hollywood that is reluctant to depict Arabs and Muslims in a positive light might still be "mad about the Crusades"? What were the Christian Crusades? What happened? You might want to do a bit of surfing on the net for some background information on European medieval history. How does knowing something about the Crusades help you understand what Hanania is talking about?

3. Hanania tends to use irony or humor when discussing very serious subjects. What might be his strategic purpose for doing this? How might an incongruity between what he states and what he really means highlight injustices and absurdities?

Collaborative Explorations

For a group project, research harassment of minority, religious, or gender groups. Are there double standards for conduct—depending on one's social/economical status? After your group has collected all its data, share it and analyze findings. Then, write them up in a concise report, along with any recommendations you have for reducing stereotypes. Consider your group a "task force" that has been created to look into gender/ethnicity/lifestyle stereotypes. As such, your audience would be the officials who set up the "task force."

Writing Assignments

1. Write an essay in which you illustrate the similarities or differences in your observations of Arabs/Muslims in American society and Hollywood's stereotypical depiction of them.

2. Write an essay entitled "One of the Good Guys?" in which you reveal the unethical or negative portrayal of a minority group, but write it from an ironic point of view.

Thematic Cross-Links: Compare the stereotyping of Arabs and Muslims in Hanania's essay to that of African Americans in Stanley Crouch's "Modern Day Minstrel Shows" in Chapter 11, Movies.

Movie Cross-Links: See *Die Hard* or one of the other movies mentioned by Hanania for typical portrayals of Muslims and Arabs in film.

Ground Zero

Ishmael Reed

Born in 1938, ISHMAEL REED is a native of Buffalo, New York. A prolific writer, Reed has explored his talents in many genres. He writes verse, songs, plays, essays, and novels. In addition, Reed produces television shows and works as a publisher and a magazine editor. Reed's fiction is often marked by surrealism, fantasy, and satire. His award-winning works include the novels *The Free Lance Pall Bearers* (1967), *Mumbo Jumbo* (1978), *The Terrible Twos* (1982), *Restless Eyeballing* (1986), and *Japanese by Spring* (1993); several volumes of verse like *Catechism of D Neoamerican Hoodoo* (1970) and *Conjure* (1972); and the essay collections, *Shrovetide in New Orleans* (1979), *Writin' Is Fightin'* (1988), and *Airing Dirty Laundry* (1993).

ALLUSIONS

Howdy Doody: A popular TV puppet during the 1950s.

Skid-row: Reference to a slum area.

Robin Hood: Legendary English outlaw who stole from the rich to give to the poor.

Mother Teresa: A Catholic nun and founder of the Order of the Missionaries of Charity who are dedicated to serving the homeless of India.

Felix Mitchell: A big-time drug dealer.

Caesars: Leaders of the Roman Empire.

Bill Lowe: Chair of the North Oakland District Community Council.

Paul Muni: An actor popular in the 1940s for such films as *The Good Earth* and *The Life of Emile Zola*.

Jonathan Kwitny: Author of *Crimes of Patriots: A True Tale of Dope, Dirty Money, and the CIA*, among other works.

Beirut: A city in Lebanon.

1   You discover that living in an area in which a crack den, smokehouse, or in the language of the police, problem house is in operation, is like living under military rule. Your neighborhood is invaded at all times of the day or night by armed men and women—death squads—who carry the kinds of weapons that are employed in small wars all over the world. People are trapped in their home, intimidated by rival drug armies who on more than one occasion have caused the murder of innocent men, women, and children as they fight over the spoils. A policeman's comment to the press that only if you live in this kind of area are you likely to become a statistic, is not reassuring. The couriers, usually teenagers, ride bicycles; the suppliers drive Japanese pickup trucks or unlicensed Broncos; and the assassins ease by in BMWs, or in noisy, dilapidated hotrods with two people riding shotgun in the back and two up front. When their menacing sentries stand about on the lookout for cops, people don't dare come out of the house.

2   The retired people, single-parent families, and widows who used to take so much pride in the neighborhood stay indoors. The lawns are still kept up and the repairs done, but the mood is one of trepidation. You dread coming home because you never know when a car full of unsavory characters might be parked in front of your house, or a drug dealer's pit bull, "a dangerous weapon," might be running up and down the street unleashed and terrorizing the neighborhood children. The streets are quiet during the day, an improvement over the situation in June, but at night it sounds like troop movements. You think of the song, "The Freaks Come Out At Night." This must be how it is in Haiti under the Duvaliers, which is the kind of regime that comes to mind when you see the hoodlums milling about on your street. They have all of the charm of the Tonton Macoutes and wear the same kind of sunglasses. Robberies occur; within one month, four auto break-ins and four burglaries, as The Living Dead attempt to steal radios or anything that will finance their habit.

3   The patrolman who arrives after the second break-in of your car within the month of October says that the Oakland police can't cover all of the posts, and that stopping the cocaine epidemic is like stopping sand; Chief Hart says that his forces are "stretched thin," and that there should be more concentration on education; the people you see involved in the drug trade have been out of school for a long time. You hear this from most of the people you interview: the drug war is over and the bad guys have won. The chief of police cites all of the arrests that he's made, only to conclude that "the problem is getting worse. It's horrible." He tells this to the newspaper, a remark that is in sharp contrast to the conclusion of howdy-doody optimism reached by the Oakland Interagency Council on Drugs, November 1986: "there is a 'sense of containment' of the problem, and a perceived response from a

previously protesting community of residents that progress is being made." On the other hand, Councilman Leo Brazile credits the agency with having successfully driven the street operations indoors where arrests are easier to make.

4   This crack stuff is cheap and highly addictive, and so some of the addicts come into your neighborhood three or four times during the night. They belong to the kind of armies that don't clean up after themselves, and so the morning after a night of cars arriving and departing every ten minutes or so, all of which seem to have bad engines and worse mufflers, your neighborhood sidewalks and streets are filled with the kind of dreck you find on the grounds of a drive-in theater the morning after a horror movie has played. The kind of people who seem to want to advertise the fact that they drink Wild Irish Rose and Night Train.

5   The horror-movie metaphor is apt because the customers for this brain-scrambling stuff resemble cadavers as they wander in zombielike, some barefoot and wearing pajamas under overcoats. Some are obviously into prostitution to support their habit, and you read that in Chicago a woman sold her child for cocaine. In Oakland, another woman hid in the closet so her mother wouldn't share her profits. She was making one hundred dollars per day. So that her child wouldn't cry and her position be given away, she smothered the child to death.

6   A next-door neighbor said that he complained to the police about "that house" but nothing was done. People say that they call the Oakland police and the police don't arrive, and when they do arrive they complain about how they're undermanned, and how budget cuts have harmed the force, and later you hear from Bill Lowe, a man who confronts drug dealers regularly with nonviolent techniques, that there have been no budget cuts.

7   The children are receiving an education about how low some adults can become. On the way to school they may have to step over some drug creep lying on their lawns, cracked into insensibility. You read about the effects of the drug operation on the psychological well-being of the children in Oakland. You really don't have to read; your daughter and the children on the block have nightmares about it. Drug dealers show up in their poetry.

8   No matter what you've done to maintain your house, your property value is reduced because who wants to buy a house in a neighborhood that has become a skid row, which is what can happen to a formerly decent neighborhood overnight, especially on the first and on the fifteenth when the welfare and Social Security checks are received.

9   This scene is spreading throughout Oakland. No matter what the people in the Junior League, the Lakeview Club, the ballet and symphony boosters may say about image, Oakland is in a state of war against drug fascists, and for the time being the drug fascists have gained the upper hand.

10   When you hear that the Oakland cocaine operation is a sort of take-out center for people in some of the more exclusive neighborhoods of Berkeley and Oakland, you wonder how many of the people in these exclusive neighborhoods have "Out of Nicaragua" bumper stickers on their Volvos, but are perfectly willing to tolerate drug fascists who prey upon the decent citizens of Oakland. You wonder how many agreed

with a reporter for an alternative East Bay newspaper who just about drooled on his copy as he recorded the lurid activities of a heroin street dealer, making out as though this man were Robin Hood, or with another talented writer who made Felix Mitchell appear to be some sort of Mother Teresa—a man who headed an operation that took $50 million per year out of poor neighborhoods, enough to employ thousands of teenagers during the summer. Anybody who praises a person who is trafficking in cocaine and heroin, when intravenous drug use may wipe out one third of the black population—something that even the segregated regimes of the South and all of American racists combined haven't been able to accomplish—must be sick, and the admiration that some blacks have for these people must be the kind of twisted, perverted affection that a dog feels toward a master who sadistically tortures him.

11   What's hip about somebody who does errands for multinational drug Caesars for the peanut end of the take? What's hip about somebody who puts blacks and Latinos in a position where they're spending billions of dollars on hard drugs, and in doing so financing the economics of Third World and Western countries; a sort of Marshall Plan whose bills are paid by the destitute? What's hip about somebody who doesn't have the sense to funnel his underground profits into community projects like the ethnic gangsters of the past, but sends money to the white suburbs because of his clownish, brazen lifestyle, which demands BMWs and gold-trimmed Rolls-Royces?

12   What's hip about drug dealers whose infamous activities attract bad media coverage and dissuade investors from coming into Oakland, therefore losing thousands of jobs for Oaklanders? George Williams tells you that some investors won't come into Oakland because they are afraid that their safety can't be guaranteed. What's so hip about crack merchants who, according to a theory proposed by Bill Lowe, chairperson of the North Oakland District Community Council, have joined with unscrupulous realtors to scare the black elderly out of town, and make room for regentrifiers? Books such as Jonathan Kwitny's *The Crimes of Patriots* claim that the contras are financing their despicable operations by dumping drugs into the poor neighborhoods of America, so what's hip about somebody who puts poor blacks and Latinos into a position where they're financing a foreign policy they might not approve of?

13   In Oakland, there are two governments, the legally elected representative government and the government of crackers who can make decisions about how your neighborhood should operate without calling public hearings, which is the way things are managed by their fellow fascist governments. As you think about all of this, you've worked yourself into a state of anger, and you feel like Paul Muni in *The Last Angry Man*. On July 1 you read that a sixty-year-old man living in what is described as a quiet black neighborhood near the Berkeley border is caught in crossfire between some drug fascists and is paralyzed from the neck down.

14   When you attend a meeting of the Oakland Arts Council the next day, you say that this place is becoming like Beirut, and a couple of women who look like the Piedmont types who seem to rule over Oakland society and culture look at you as though you're crazy. They don't live at Ground Zero.

AFTERWARDS

Vocabulary

crack den, smoke house, intimidated, trepidation, couriers, dilapidated, hoodlums, sentries, unsavory, regime, containment, cadavers, fascists, zombie, epidemic. The vocabulary words in Reed's essay tend to carry negative connotations. Look each word up in (1) your dictionary and (2) your thesaurus to discover both their direct and implied meanings. How might words with negative connotations—or positive connotations, as the case may be—assist you in establishing and maintaining a consistent tone in a composition? Offer some specific examples to support your beliefs.

Content

1. To what does Reed compare his living area and why?

2. What specific representative examples demonstrate the horrors of Reed's immediate living environment? How do Oakland citizens themselves contribute to the creation of city barriers?

3. According to Reed, the Oakland Police say they have good reasons for not effectively responding to the city's drug problem. What are some of the stock phrases or explanations the police offer concerned citizens to excuse themselves? How reasonable are their excuses? In Reed's position, would you have been satisfied with a police officer saying, "Our budget has been cut, so we really can't help you at this time?" If the same citizens were rich, do you think the police would be more responsive to them?

Style and Structure

1. Analyze how Reed effectively structures and convincingly argues his thesis. How and why does his perception appear justified?

2. In what way is it quite obvious that Reed does not intend to "preach to the choir" but, rather, to inform those who are not aware of Oakland's severe drug—especially crack—problem? What exactly is the tone of his essay?

3. Why does Reed use a series of rhetorical questions (questions directed at readers or listeners to think about but not to answer), beginning with the words, "What's hip . . ." in the latter part of his essay? How do

such questions encourage active reader participation in Reed's discussion?

Collaborative Explorations

Come together in groups and compare and contrast your responses to Content and Style and Structure questions, as well as your definitions of the vocabulary words. Then, brainstorm the phrases "Ground Zero" and "living environment" as a group. How are they significantly different, and in what way do they have similar qualities? Finally, analyze your own city, or a city all group members know something about, and write a collaborative essay arguing that where you live is or could easily (or never) be at "Ground Zero" because of its social or physical barriers.

Writing Assignments

1. Brainstorm the words *fear, anger, resentment, confinement*, or *prejudice*, and determine which you feel strongly about one way or another. How does each word create psychological barriers restricting your freedom to experiment or preventing you from attempting something new? How do stereotypes or barriers place people in a rut? Devise a thesis statement based on your brainstorming activity, and write an essay arguing and defending your position.

2. Write an argument of fact, persuading your readers that while one's living environment alone does not "make the person" (e.g., a person raised in the country will not necessarily become a rancher), it greatly influences one's possibilities of success, one way or another. You might want to consider some recent individuals in the news who, though well-off financially, were guilty of hideous crimes, as well as poor people who were able to lead good, moral lives.

The Visual Connection: Photograph Writing Activity

1. Whereas we talk about how ethnic diversity and equality constitute a major strength of the United States, often, individuals still become the targets of bigotry and stereotypes. As you look over the following photographs, can you identify the ethnicities of each person? Did you rely on a stereotype to form conclusions about a person's identity? Check your answers against how the people in the following photographs identify themselves, using the chart at the bottom right-hand corner of this picture.

1. Richard Ly   2. Tiffany Gore   3. David Hyde   4. Ginele Marquez

5. Robert Williams   6. Deann Stevens   7. Troy Wailehua   8. John Tiger

9. Sam Levine   10. Naziroh Ahmath   11. Brenda Boos   12. Victoria Jones

13. Aaron Miles

Ethnicity:

1. Filipino-Chinese
2. Portuguese
3. Caucasian
4. Hispanic-Latino
5. African American-Korean
6. German-Dutch
7. Hawaiian-Filipino
8. Delaware-Euchee Tribes
9. Austrian-Jewish
10. Cham
11. Korean
12. Black-Asian
13. Asian American

Faces

2. The following photograph captures the Statue of Liberty as the photographer looks up at it. What are its most dominant features? What does the statue symbolize? How might it mislead some with false promise? Does it assure anyone of freedom from stereotyping or other social barriers? Are you familiar with the inscription at its base? How does it greet new immigrants to America? Finally, how does the feeling of the above photo compare with other pictures you have seen of the statue?

The Statue of Liberty

Film Links: Stereotypes and Social Barriers

1. Do you think gender images in recent films reinforce negative stereotypes? Rather than simply mentioning a film title from the list below, watch a couple of the movies, draw examples from them, and use these examples, followed by explanations, to illustrate and justify the controlling idea or thesis in your paper.

2. Choose any combination of films below and write an essay that examines the problem of racial perception. How is race related to personal identity, male/female relations, family structure, social status, employment, and political conflict in any of these films. Choose a film and explain how racial stereotypes cause conflicts within these films.

Alamo Bay (USA, Louis Malle, 1985). Vietnamese fishermen living on the Gulf Coast of Texas encounter the contemporary version of the Ku Klux Klan.

Do The Right Thing (USA, Spike Lee, 1989). A day in the life of a neighborhood in Bedford-Stuyvesant, Brooklyn, New York City. A dispute in a pizza parlor touches off racial conflict.

Mississippi Masala (USA, Mira Nair, 1991). Hindu Ugandans, forced into exile, go into the motel business in Mississippi. Their Americanized daughter seeks a life of her own.

Boyz N the Hood (USA, John Singleton, 1991). Three friends who grow up together in South Central L.A. seek to find a direction in life to take them beyond a neighborhood dominated by violence, alcohol, and crime.

Hollywood Shuffle (USA, Robert Townsend, 1984). An African American actor finds it hard to get roles that are not stereotypes and fantasizes about the role he would like to play.

Picture Bride (USA, Kayo Mata, 1995). Japanese immigrants struggle to adjust to life on a Hawaiian sugar cane plantation in the early 20th century.

Higher Learning (USA, John Singleton, 1995). Freshman year at fictional Columbus University brings together students who have a hard time adjusting to the pressures and ethnic diversity on a large college campus.

American History X (USA, Tony Kaye, 1998). A neo-Nazi skinhead commits a murder and while in prison begins to rethink his attitudes toward race and violence.

Rush Hour (USA, Brett Ratner, 1998). A slapstick action comedy in which two detectives, one an African American, the other from Hong Kong, try to work together even though neither wants to be the "sidekick."

Smoke Signals (USA, Chris Eyre, 1998). Two young Native Americans leave "the rez" in Idaho and go on the road in search of a lost father.

Bamboozled (USA, Spike Lee, 2000). An African American television producer decides to bring back the minstrel show on prime-time TV and has a huge hit on his hands.

Snow Falling on Cedars (USA, Scott Hicks, 2000). An interracial romance and a murder become entangling events in Washington State in the early days of World War II.

Additional Writing Assignments

1. What do you associate with the word "stereotype"? Use prewriting (for example, clustering, brainstorming, freewriting) to examine some of your ideas about it. Then, write an expository entry explaining how and why you arrived at your present awareness of social, ethnic, gender, and religious stereotypes. Does an awareness of them affect your own tendency to think in stereotypes? For instance, do you stereotype due to gender?

2. Analyze how modifying words such as "legitimate" and "illegitimate" can affect one's attitude toward other people's occupations, places, activities, and so on. Select several representative examples to illustrate and explain each of your discussion points.

3. Explain how the media have influenced your attitude toward other people and places in the United States and beyond? Take regions of the United States like the South, Southern California, New England, the Midwest, and Texas and describe your impressions of these regions and the people who live there. If you have lived in any of these regions, discuss the difference between your perception of these places and the way they are represented in media.

4. Think about recent immigrant groups who have come to the United States: Haitians, Cubans, Vietnamese, Cambodians, and Russians. What stereotypes have been used to portray them in the media? What impressions do you have of each of these groups? What positive and negative expectations have these images created?

5. How do institutions (churches, political parties, government agencies, colleges) create and utilize stereotypes? Interview some people on your campus: peers, instructors, administrators, counselors, and so on. Ask them how stereotypes can become *institutionalized* by colleges. How does your college strive to overcome the negative effects of stereotyping?

Chapter Five

Media: Controversies and Celebrities

Observations and Opinions

We are living in an age of publicity. It used to be only saloons and circuses that wanted their name in the paper, but now it's corporations, churches, preachers, scientists, colleges, and cemeteries.

—WILL ROGERS FROM *DAILY TELEGRAM*

If the myth gets bigger than the man, print the myth.

—DOROTHY JOHNSON FROM *THE MAN WHO SHOT LIBERTY VALANCE*

The medium is the message.

—MARSHALL MCLUHAN FROM *THE MEDIUM IS THE MESSAGE*

The deeper problems connected with advertising come less from the unscrupulousness of our "deceivers" than from our pleasure in being deceived, less from the desire to seduce than from the desire to be seduced.

—DANIEL BOORSTIN FROM *THE IMAGE*

Sex as communication can send messages as different as life and death: even the origins of "erotica" and "pornography" reflect that fact. After all, "erotica" is rooted in eros or passionate love and thus in the idea of positive choice, free will, the yearning for a particular person. (Interestingly, the definition of erotica leaves open the question of gender.) "Pornography" begins with a root

meaning "prostitution" or "female captives," thus letting us know
that the subject is not mutual love, or love at all, but domination and
violence against women.

—GLORIA STEINEM FROM "EROTICA AND PORNOGRAPHY"

Observations and Opinions:
Reading/Writing Activities

1. To what extent do you agree with what Will Rogers says about publicity in his quote from the *Daily Telegram* and with what Dorothy Johnson states in her quote from *The Man Who Shot Liberty Valance*?

2. In your own words, explain Daniel Boorstin's perception of advertising media in *The Image*. What position would Boorstin take on the concept "The medium is the message," a phrase coined by Marshall McLuhan? Do you think Boorstin would share Steinem's attitude toward "Erotica and Pornography"? To what extent do the advertising media use sex to sell products? Offer a few examples.

3. Describe or explain how and why various forms of media affect your life. Start by asking yourself a series of questions. What sorts of media appeal to you or annoy you? When? Where? Why? How? The answers to your questions will provide you with details and examples to illustrate what you write.

Introduction

This chapter could also have been titled "Fame and Infamy: How the Media Use People and How People Use the Media." The media seek to communicate information by spoken words, images, and print. The media are an important tool used in everything from commercial advertising to the electronic posting of incoming and outgoing airline flights. Media package information; media inform. They sometimes take liberties with their subject matter by manipulating information and exaggerating the significance of the events they cover. Other times, the media withhold information. For example, a recent book, *In Retrospect*, by Robert McNamara, Secretary of Defense during the Vietnam War, reported that in 1965 the National Security Council concluded from intelligence reports that the Vietnam War was not winnable. However, the United States not only continued the war but escalated it until 1972, before it began to negotiate peace terms in earnest. Tens of thousands of people lost their lives because of information withheld from the media. On the other hand, it could be argued that the media were a strong force in persuading the public that the war policy was a mistake. The media both conceal some information and reveal the unpleasant truth.

Media are the spotlight on the world stage of current events. They create celebrities by exposing them to millions of consumers via television, radio, magazines, and newspapers. The word "media" refers to the many kinds of mass communication. All the forms of media compete with one another for audiences and money. They provide the publicity that can create fame instantly. Try to see what you can remember about Fawn Hall, Mark Fuhrman, Tonya Harding, Mary Kay Letourneau, Rodney King, Richard Jewel, Gary Condit, Willie Horton, or Jeff Bezos. All these people were catapulted from obscurity to fame in a matter of days, then forgotten when a new wave of news and publicity replaced them.

Some shrewd publicity seekers have the skill to create publicity and notoriety for themselves. Madonna, Howard Stern, Muhammad Ali, Richard Simmons, Oprah Winfrey, Jerry Springer, Geraldo Rivera, Roseanne, P. Diddy, Jennifer Lopez, Kathie Lee Gifford, Regis Philbin, Tom Green, and Julia Roberts are among those who seem to be able to keep their names and faces before the public. They seem to exist solely to promote themselves by every known form of media. Anyone who can gain access to the mass media has an opportunity to influence the world.

The following essays take a look at both the media and people in the media, using a variety of rhetorical modes—satire, exposition, argumentation. In "Boycott America's Media," Rose Anna Higashi sets the chapter's tone as she critiques the mass media, noting how advertising and "Hollywood hype" manipulate us, how people spend their money on "empty entertainment," and how the mass media have distorted the "average person's sense of identity." Indeed, she contends that the "cult of popularity" is outrageous because it elevates sports figures, movie stars, and singers to the level of celebrity just because they break laws or are involved in a scandal.

The very meaning of exposition—to expose—runs throughout Victor Martinez's essay "Chicanos, the Media, and Vietnam." There, Martinez blends expository strategies (cause and effect, description, illustration, and example) with argumentation to develop his topic. Combined, all of these strategies work to explain effectively how and why the media overlooked Chicanos and the role they played during the Vietnam War.

In "Diana and the Paparazzi," Carol Squiers points out that because Princess Diana and Emad Mohamed "Dodi" al-Fayed were being pursued by photographers at the time of the accident that killed both of them, it is as if Diana died for the sake of some "quick snaps." However, Squiers also argues that "if all of photography is to be indicted, it is only right that the entire enterprise of celebrity journalism be examined," thereby questioning the popular antipaparazzi publicity surrounding the incident. Her essay combines exposition and deductive reasoning.

Dr. Jack Kevorkian's essay, "A Modern Inquisition," is an excerpt from a speech he made to the American Humanist Association. Like Squiers's essay, Kevorkian's speech makes use of logic and reasoning to explain why he is justified in "hastening death with dignity"—that is, assisted suicide—and does not deserve to be indicted for murder. He has skillfully used the media to publicize his belief that individuals have the right to choose when they die. As many people criticize as applaud Kevorkian's ethics, but one thing is certain: He has succeeded in using controversy to achieve fame via the media. In 1999, a jury found him guilty of second degree murder: the 1998 injection death of Thomas Youk, a man who had Lou Gehrig's disease. Although he continues to appeal the court's conviction, Kevorkian is presently in prison, serving a 10- to 25-year sentence.

Regardless of whether celebrities create controversies or controversies produce celebrities, one thing is definite: The media frequently blow up small situations into prime-time events. After you consider the Prereading Inquiries for this chapter, ask yourself, "Do the media seek to inform me, entertain me, or persuade me?" How might the media's objectives determine their attitude toward and treatment of controversial issues and celebrities?

Gathering Thoughts: Prereading Inquiries

1. How often do you accept the media's portrayal of an event or a person's life as truth?

2. What is the difference between a photo op (photo opportunity for publicity) and tabloid photographs?

3. Make a list of as many media sources as you can. How can or do they affect human behavior or beliefs?

4. What is the balance between general statements and specific details and examples in each of the following essays? Why are the details so important? With what do they provide you?

5. Are there other methods of communication besides reading, writing, signing (sign language), and viewing? Which method of communication do you use the most, and which sort of communication would you like to experience?

Continued

6. What is political correctness? Describe its place in popular culture and the media. How might efforts to be politically correct improve or confuse clear communication?

7. What is the relationship between advertising or publicity and the media?

8. Ask yourself what sort of things are not, to your knowledge, ever mentioned by journalists or newscasters? What might be the media's reason for withholding information?

9. Can a person ever be totally impartial? How? Why? By the same token, can the media ever portray a person impartially? What do you consider the difference between impartiality and coldhearted indifference?

10. How do the media use euphemisms and doublespeak to conceal the real nature of a person, place, or thing? When might even a direct, concrete reference be misleading?

Boycott America's Media: Take Back Your Thinking Skills

Rose Anna Higashi

A professor of English, ROSE ANNA HIGASHI specializes in Japanese, English, and Asian literature, as well as composition. Her poems frequently appear in magazines, textbooks, and professional journals. After the publication of her personal journal and poetry collection, *Blue Wings* (1995), she wrote the scholarly text, *Finding the Poet* (1996), a book on writing poetry and about self-discovery. In addition, she has written several novels such as *Waiting for Rain* and *The Learning Wars* (2000), *Keeping Secrets* (2001), and *To the Rescue* (2002). Over the years, many people, places, and things have helped shape Higashi's prose and piety: her hometown, Joplin, Missouri; authors Matsuo Basho, Gerard Manley Hopkins, and Robert Browning; and mysticism and spirituality. In the following essay, Higashi takes a critical look at the influence of the mass media in American culture, arguing for renewed personal awareness in order to take charge of critical thinking skills—skills too often manipulated by the media.

ALLUSIONS

Although Higashi does mention a few movies and celebrities by name, she more frequently alludes to them as a group. By so doing, how does Higashi invite readers to relate specific circumstances to scandals or other forms of media outrage to their own experiences?

1   For the past thirty years, I've been boycotting America's mass media, particularly the advertising industry. My personal boycott has included never wearing an item of clothing that displays a logo or a brand name, never watching a Disney animated film, never purchasing or eating nationally advertised fast food, never reading a fashion magazine and never watching a televised soap opera, beauty contest, "reality drama" or talk show. Do I live a life of cultural deprivation? Certainly not. Am I a lunatic, a fashion frump, a social misfit or an anti-American? I don't believe I am any of these. Then what are my reasons for avoiding so much of what comprises the core of America's lifestyle today? One motive is my profound aversion to mediocrity and my belief that Americans can do better than the drivel dished up to us routinely on daytime T.V. and passed off as food and fashion. Indeed, I contend that the mass media have corrupted American culture by robbing us of our ability to discern excellence, to make moral judgments and to appreciate our own self-worth.

2   Let's start with excellence. Tragically, Americans are so easily manipulated by advertising and Hollywood hype that we have lost the critical thinking skills to establish our own criteria for excellence. When watching a film, for example, how many Americans have trained themselves to evaluate acting techniques, character development, theme, cinematography, directing, writing, creativity and all of the other elements that make a movie good, bad or mediocre? How else can we explain the fact that Julia Roberts won the Academy Award for best actress in 2001 for a mediocre performance in a mediocre film, *Erin Brockovich*? Sadly, the popularity of the leading actors (artificially created through advertising, popular magazines and inane television talk shows), sensationalism, violence, sexuality or visual tricks and special effects are what sell films today. And viewers seem to have abandoned their responsibility to demand excellence. As long as we are willing to be brain washed by advertising to pay for bad movies, Hollywood will have no motivation to make good ones. For a weekend in July of 2001, for example, the top money making movie was *Jurassic Park III*, which earned $50.3 million. *America's Sweethearts* came in second with $31 million. Why did people rush out to spend their money on these unoriginal, third-rate and soon to be forgotten productions? Advertising.

3   It is one thing to throw our money away on empty entertainment, but even more disturbing is the fact that the mass media have warped our ethical standards. In a recent two-page advertisement in *Gourmet* magazine, I observed a full-page photograph of two smiling female chefs with the headline, "Want to change your life? Step into our kitchen." The text went on to say, "In this kitchen, chefs Linda Vogler and Sibyl Durant make a difference in the fight against hunger." At the bottom of the second page appeared the following five words: "Supported by the Philip Morris companies." I was

astounded that the Philip Morris Company, producer of cigarettes, would feel so confident of Americans' inability to evaluate ethical issues that they would actually attempt to present themselves as humanitarians and philanthropists. This advertisement clearly assumed that the readers were so gullible that they could actually be convinced that a company that has killed millions of our citizens at an enormous profit to themselves, is seriously committed to helping the hungry and homeless. A host of other ethical standards have been blurred by advertisers' relentless assault on our savings by trying to get us to purchase products that we may not need, that may be harmful to the environment and that certainly squander our natural resources.

4   In addition, the cult of popularity, particularly the media's obsession with movie actors, sports figures and politicians, has poisoned our understanding of acceptable civilized behavior. Breaking solemn vows, lying, deceit, physical violence (especially wife beating), ignoring parental responsibilities and drug and alcohol abuse are now acceptable behaviors. Every day television programs, movies and magazines make it abundantly clear: if actors and athletes can behave in this fashion and continue to earn millions of dollars, why should the average American hold himself or herself to a higher moral standard?

5   Finally, I am deeply saddened by the effect that the mass media's shoddy values have had on the average person's sense of identity. Before television came to rule our lives, anorexia and bulimia were not serious health problems. And the advertising industry has created anxieties that did not exist for previous generations. Fear of gray hair, wrinkles, cellulite, balding, sexual dysfunction, or driving the wrong car were simply not issues for our grandparents. My own mother, who is now in her eighties, had the good fortune to grow up before television was invented, and she has never been dependent on movies or magazines for her sense of self. On our frequent luncheon outings, she often wears a twenty-year-old pink suit, which was not expensive when she first bought it. Nevertheless, invariably complete strangers come up to her and tell her how nice she looks. This happens because my mother's sense of personal worth and confidence comes from knowing herself, knowing what looks good on her and feeling comfortable with who she is. On the other hand, looking at the young women in my classes, I frequently observe insecure creatures who have wasted their hard-earned money on over-priced brand names and dreary looking trendy fashions that do not enhance their natural beauty in any way.

6   What can we do to reclaim our right to like ourselves for who we are? How can we once again live our lives with dignity according to carefully developed standards of ethical conduct? And how can we experience the joy of living with excellence, even in the small ordinary things such as food and entertainment? We must put out the effort to think clearly. We must recognize the fact that the world of movies, television, magazines, and newspapers is an artificial reality that has nothing to do with the lives we are actually living. We must stop being lazy and find our role models in real people who truly deserve to be admired, rather than celebrities and social icons. And finally, we must access our own inner creativity to discover what excellence really means for us. Trust me when I tell you that boycotting America's mass media can begin your journey of liberation.

AFTERWARDS

Vocabulary

deprivation, frump, humanitarians, philanthropists, anorexia, bulimia, dysfunction. Review the denotative and connotative means of each of these vocabulary words, and then write three original sentences using a different pair of vocabulary words in each.

Content

1. Identify the thesis of Higashi's essay; how does it frame her argument? To what extent does the thesis prepare readers for the four major discussion points in her composition?

2. According to Higashi, how has excellence in critical thinking skills diminished due to the influence of America's media? Explain how she argues her position. Do you agree with her argument? Why or why not? (Support your position with specific reasoning.)

3. Explain what Higashi refers to as the "cult of popularity." Why should she or anyone else be concerned that, with the exception of the sort of criticism that sparks public interest in a news item and "sells" a story, the media too often end up glamorizing, romanticizing, or condoning the socially unacceptable behavior of its celebrities?

Style and Structure

1. How do the sentences in Higashi's initial paragraph "lead into" her thesis statement? In what way does she provide readers with sufficient background information to appreciate the author's point of view—even if you disagree with it?

2. In general, transitions and linking devices assist writers to establish clear relationships between words, clauses, sentences, and entire paragraphs. How well did Higashi connect ideas with transitions? Underline all the transitions and linking devices you can find in this essay and reread at least a paragraph or so aloud WITHOUT them.

3. What call to action does Higashi make in "Boycott America's Media: Take Back Your Thinking Skills"? How do all four parts of her essay lead logically and convincingly to her final paragraph?

Collaborative Explorations

There are many forms of journalism—a part of the media. Photo journalism is particularly compelling for many people because "what they see they believe." However, pictures can also be misleading. What pictures or photographs come to your mind when someone mentions a historical character or event related to the theme Media: Controversies and Celebrities? Find at least two photographs you feel are particularly powerful and memorable, and, along with four or five of your peers, assemble a group portfolio of photographs (each individual should contribute two photographs to the portfolio). Beneath each photograph write a one-sentence caption explaining what it displays. Finally, exchange portfolios with another group and draw some conclusions about information being passed on visually or in the written word. Which impresses or stays with you longer and why?

Writing Assignments

1. Write an essay in which you agree or disagree with Higashi's contention that "We must recognize the fact that the world of movies, television, magazines, and newspapers is an artificial reality that has nothing to do with the lives we are actually living." Make sure you provide sentences leading into a clearly defined thesis. Then, as you develop your paper, illustrate your discussion points with specific, representative examples—not generalities—to justify your argument.

2. Write a paper fully illustrating how through clever advertising the media manipulates audiences, creating needs where none exist, and persuades people to invest time and money on such things as questionable *quality* entertainment (movies) instead of luxury ocean liner cruises.

Thematic Cross-Links: For another discussion on how the mass media seem to pervade American culture, influencing our decisions and affecting our attitudes, see the introductions to Chapter 8, Popular Culture, and Chapter 12, The Body: Language, Ritual, Wellness—A Casebook.

Movie Cross-Links: See *Network*, a movie mentioned in the Film Links in Chapter 9, Television for a bird's-eye view of television media dynamics. You might also check out *Holy Man* (noted in the same Film Links), an Eddie Murphy movie satirizing television's "shop around the clock" consumer mentality.

Chicanos, the Media, and the Vietnam War

Victor Martinez

A poet and a writer, **VICTOR MARTINEZ** lives in San Francisco. The following article, "Chicanos, the Media, and the Vietnam War," was originally printed as the preface to Charley Trujillo's narratives of the Vietnam War: *Soldados: Chicanos in Viet Nam* (1990). Here Martinez details how inaccurately the 1960s news media reported the role of Chicano soldiers during the war.

ALLUSIONS

Publius Cornelius Scipio: A Roman general (d. 211 B.C.E. who fought against the Carthaginian general Hannibal for seven years in Spain.

Second Punic War: War between Rome and Carthage from 218 to 201 B.C.E.

agent orange: A toxic herbicide/defoliant containing dioxin and used in the Vietnam War.

Hiroshima: A city in Japan where the United States dropped the first atomic bomb used in war.

Odyssey: An epic tale by Homer that details the adventures of the Greek Hero Odysseus on his return home after the Trojan War.

1   When a reluctant group of wealthy aristocratic volunteers offered their services to the Roman general Publius Cornelius Scipio (later to become Scipio Africanus) before his invasion of Africa during the Second Punic War, he thanked them but suggested that perhaps they were averse to his military enterprise. He proceeded then to strip them of their expensively embellished armor and horses, and assigned the equipment to more deserving men, many of whom were conscripts from the more wretched slums of Rome who ranked the legions of Rome's Imperial Army. The adage that the poor make more resolute and compliable [*sic*] soldiers is verified when applied to Chicanos. As the personal accounts in *Soldados: Chicanos in Viet Nam* attest, Chicanos were often the easiest and most malleable resource the U.S. had for achieving its quota for combat soldiers. And to those ends, they were used generously.

2   The personal accounts of these veterans, many of whom experienced the war viscerally and whose private reasons were myriad and expressed in this book with a severe authenticity, can be of service to all. They fought for reasons that were ill-defined, often confusing, but for the most part devoid of any cogent understanding of the political and economic forces at play which took them from labor fields in Corcoran, California, to rice paddies in Indochina. From their odyssey a great house of knowledge can be gained, a knowledge that was, unfortunately, purchased with blood.

3   Viet Nam, to Chicanos, was the most questionable and dangerous undertaking of their lives. When drafted, they served, when "volunteered," they did so because of the scarcity of jobs and unequal opportunity of hope. Once there, they populated for the most part the trenches, and they were often maimed and killed. Many, incredibly enough, genuinely believed the propaganda of being "defenders of freedom" and went willingly. But most were victims of an economic exploitation and pernicious cultural suppression at home that made the military a step up in stature, and the need to "prove" oneself, a disturbing and misplaced search for self-esteem and acceptance as legitimate citizens. Of those who lived to return home, some were given medals to garnish the plate of their heroism, some were handed honorable discharges and the small gratuities of veteran's benefits. Others left Viet Nam with hidden deposits of agent orange waiting to erupt on the surface of their skin, and the ticking time bomb of post-traumatic stress disorder (PTSD). None left Viet Nam the same as when they entered.

4   But many questions continue to remain hidden and unexplored, and these hover ominously in the background of this book. How many Chicanos, for example, had the privilege of being exempt from service as opposed to the more prominent sectors of society? How many actually died or served closest to the more dangerous theaters of action? How many were predominantly poor and working-class? These are questions that are just now being looked into, but most statistics are unavailable and when available, incomplete and, at times, anything but impartial. One study, for example, after concluding that of the 470,000 who suffer from PTSD, 27 percent are Latino, suggested that the reasons for so swollen a figure was because many were raised in "unstable" families.

5   This poverty of information and its consequences, of course, underscore the need for Chicano and Latino youth to attain a perspective as to where exactly they stand in relation to a society of which they are paradoxically both citizens and aliens. As a people grossly manipulated by factors over which they have little or no control, brutalized as a class and culture, Chicanos and Latinos must realize how pivotal and vitally significant their own attitudes and cultural allegiances are, and how important it is to their communities and to the country to be vocal about them. For them, Viet Nam is by no means over, and that is why the Chicano Moratorium continues every year in cities throughout the U.S. Chicano families, however "unstable," should be wary about again placing their youth in the line of sight of a gun barrel.

6   The accounts in this book also serve as a corrective reminder to many white North-Americans who are, for the most part, kept in a tragic state of unawareness as to how many Chicanos fought in the war, especially considering the almost total absence of Chicano soldiers in films, newspaper stories, television programs, and even war footage. That this book is the first of its kind, and issued so long after the fact speaks much about the erasure of any conscious understanding of the war other than patriotic flag-waving. It is an erasure which persists despite our vaunted educational system and the impressive applause tracks of our new Information Age.

7   In truth, the majority of people living in the U.S. know almost nothing about how our leaders perpetuated and instigated the Viet Nam war. Like Hiroshima,

Viet Nam exhibited with scorching clarity the levels of arrogance and cruelty that the U.S. government can exert on any nation, anywhere in the world. Anything but a mistake, Viet Nam was a premeditated slaughter, and so it measured how much punishment we are willing to inflict on a people we held in contempt simply because they refused to benignly accept our superior dictates over their affairs. But in the absence of this assessment, Viet Nam to many, has become a long list of bogus rationales and self-serving justifications for spreading our own investments of state terrorism and death. The list runs so long that we grow tired of reading and close our eyes.

8   If there has been a prevalent notion promulgated by most major media sources and eloquent pundits on talk shows and lecture circuits, it is that Viet Nam was a "lesson," and this lesson is that "we" as a nation, should never again enter into a war unless "we" as a people are in consensus as to its objectives and are resolved to "win" it. There is also the popularly exchanged currency that our intentions were noble, our motives misguided but pure. History has shown these two astonishingly fashionable digressions to be somewhat effective but fraudulent placebos for recovering from what many national leaders diagnose as "The Vietnam Syndrome." Until the absurdity of Viet Nam became glaringly apparent, the U.S. public, whether outward proponents, or liberal columnists whose most pronounced criticism was a long and ineffectual whine, by and large supported the war by mass abstention.

9   Another misconception heard in the most acoustically resonant halls of free-market forums, is that Kennedy, Johnson, and later Nixon and Kissinger, skillfully "misled" the people of the U.S. through the media. This is not only unconscionably naive, but a slickly routed avoidance to divert culpability. The realities of Viet Nam were evident, and they should have seared a wound so deep into the body of America that a great and permanent scar would forever remind us of the crimes of which a materially gluttonous society such as ours is capable. A public that allows itself to be lied to by its leaders and misinformed by the institutions which should be providing it with honest information are not participants in a well-functioning democracy; they are conspirators, a curious ostrich of conspirators who think that if the knowledge of their acquiescence remains hidden, then they are innocent. Ignorance of this type ultimately creates a willful, self-induced amnesia couched in middle-class luxury which says much worse about us as a people than if we had accepted the ugly face of our belligerence from the beginning.

10   In the aftermath of Viet Nam, we in the U.S. need to quit making excuses and understand that it was our compliance, not solely the lies of our elected officials and not solely the complicit Fourth Estate, but our compliance, often mistaken for apathy, that helped perpetuate the ruthless, criminal lawlessness that went on in Viet Nam, and continues to go on in countries like El Salvador, Guatemala, Palestine, Haiti, Chile and South Africa. It is we who, in the end, brought a stop to the calculated ferocity called Viet Nam, and it is only we who can stop the others. That no excuses are justifiable and that perhaps no amount of atonement is possible should be prerequisite to this understanding. Until we recognize this, Viet Nam has not ended, no "lesson" has been learned, and we, as well as those we victimize at home and abroad, will always be susceptible to other and perhaps more deadly wars.

AFTERWARDS

Vocabulary

reluctant, aristocratic, averse, embellished, adage, resolute, compliable, conscripts, myriad, malleable, devoid, cogent, propaganda, pernicious, suppression, garnish, paradoxically, pivotal, moratorium, perpetuated, instigated, arrogance, exert, premeditated, benignly, bogus, rationales, promulgated, eloquent, pundits, consensus, digressions, fraudulent, placebos, proponents, abstention, misconception, acoustically, resonant, culpability, acquiescence, amnesia, belligerence, compliance, complicit, apathy, ferocity, atonement. Look up the above words in your dictionary. Then, write a brief paragraph in which you discuss the atmosphere where you work, live, or study using at least ten of the vocabulary words.

Content

1. Why were Chicanos drafted in disproportionate numbers during the Vietnam War? Why did they often volunteer for the armed forces?

2. Explain what Martinez means by the statement, "History has shown these two astonishingly fashionable digressions to be somewhat effective but fraudulent placebos for recovering from what many national leaders diagnose as 'The Vietnam Syndrome.'"

3. What did you know about the role of Chicanos in Vietnam prior to reading Martinez's introduction to *Soldados: Chicanos in Viet Nam*? What facts in his article impressed you the most and why?

Style and Structure

1. Identify how Martinez indicates his attitude toward his subject matter. To what extent is diction (specific word choice) essential in conveying his point of view?

2. How does Martinez organize his material? How do the various parts of his essay lead up to his conclusion?

3. At the end of his essay, Martinez makes a "call to action." How does this place the material he has discussed into a "constructive" perspective? Refer to specific details in your answer.

Collaborative Explorations

In small groups, go to your college's library and look up the topic "Chicanos in Vietnam." How much information did you find? Make a list of your findings.

Then go online and search for similar information. You may want to enter a number of different terms when you do your "key word" search. Finally, print out or type all of the books, articles, and newspaper clippings your group located and bring them to class with you. You will compare and contrast your findings with those of your peers—and possibly draw some conclusions about the importance of Martinez's introductory essay to Charley Trujillo's narratives of the Vietnam War, *Soldados: Chicanos in Viet Nam*, prior to submitting them to your instructor.

Writing Assignments

1. Write an essay in which you express your reasonable anger on an issue involving an injustice to a group you identify with.

2. Compare and contrast the way the media portray two ethnic groups, two people of different gender or sexual preferences, or two individuals who come from different social or economic backgrounds.

Thematic Reading Cross-Links: Consult Chapter 4, Stereotypes and Social Barriers, to read about other situations in which people of color didn't receive due recognition for their work or opportunities for advancement.

Movie Cross-Links: For a look at popular Hollywood films about American soldiers in the Vietnam War, see *Apocalypse Now, Platoon*, and *Coming Home*. Does the role of Chicanos in the war seem to have been overlooked in these films?

Diana and the Paparazzi

Carol Squiers

CAROL SQUIERS is a writer for *American Photo* magazine, and her work has appeared in many other publications, including the *New York Times*. She wrote the following article for the November/December 1997 edition of *American Photo*. Therein she offers a retrospective look at Diana, the Paris car crash that ended her life, and the "indiscriminate condemnation of photographers who cover celebrities"—the paparazzi.

ALLUSIONS

Rwanda: A country in Central Africa, torn by ethnic violence between tribes.

Bosnia: A recently created state formed after the breakup of Yugoslavia.

1   The death of Diana, Princess of Wales, in a Paris car crash last August was a profoundly sad event. That she was being followed by photographers at the time of the accident made it feel even more appalling, as if she had died for the sake of some quick snaps. That perception—that photography was the cause of her death—brought the medium unprecedented public scrutiny. Indeed, the profession of photo-journalism came under attack for a variety of sins, ranging from craven callousness to deadly pursuit. The public scrutiny has caused photography professionals around the world to scrutinize themselves—at least that's the impression we got in conversations with several celebrity photographers and photo-agency editors in the week after the tragedy. Such soul-searching is commendable. And if nothing else, the awful death of Diana has forced all the media (as well as media consumers) to question the mass appeal of celebrity news.

2   Unfortunately, the incident provoked a good deal of indiscriminate condemnation of photographers who cover celebrities—whether these photographers call themselves paparazzi or not. From our perspective, much of the criticism was hasty—and sometimes shamelessly self-serving. Worse, it often betrayed a lack of understanding about what photojournalists do, and how they do it.

3   Even before the facts about the crash were made known by French authorities, the media had pinpointed the culprits: They were the photographers, uniformly referred to as paparazzi, who had caused the death of Diana, her companion Emad Mohamed "Dodi" al-Fayed, and their driver, Henri Paul. French police arrested six photographers and one motorcycle driver at the scene; three photographers later turned themselves in. Authorities began an investigation into their culpability.

4   The revelation that the driver was extremely intoxicated and speeding that night in the Paris tunnel did not take the heat off the photographers. There was no real public outcry over reckless and drunk driving. Nor did it seem to matter that many of the photographers arrested, including famed Sygma photojournalist Jacques Langevin, denied having chased Diana's car. Instead, there was disgust over the behavior of some photographers who took pictures immediately after the accident.

5   This sense of disgust was sharpened by media commentators eager to distance themselves from the "unsavory" people in their own profession. Often they did so in inflammatory language. *New York Times* columnist A. M. Rosenthal referred to the "gang" of photographers who had chased the princess to her death.

6   Likewise, celebrity publicist Michael Levine went on television and equated the paparazzi with criminals. He was joined by a chorus of celebrities—Tom Cruise, George Clooney, Fran Drescher, and Tom Selleck, among others—who saw Diana's death as a chance to talk about their own problems with celebrity photographers. Some stars apparently viewed the episode as a unique public relations opportunity: Gossip

columnist Liz Smith disclosed a "somewhat bizarre endeavor" in which irate celebrities were reportedly planning to hire private investigators to poke into the private lives of the top tabloid newspaper editors and their families as well as American paparazzi such as Phil Ramey, Russell Turiak, Vinnie Zuffante, and Alan Zanger.

7   Fueled by such criticism, the public began indiscriminately venting its anger. A shouting mob in London set upon a photographer working for the Saba Photos agency as he photographed people laying flowers in Diana's memory. In New Zealand, construction workers beat a female photographer while she was on assignment to document the site of an industrial accident.

8   Such wholesale attention and denunciation of photographers is not only unwelcome, but unjust.

9   "There is something very disturbing about the finger-pointing toward photographers," says Robert Pledge, president of Contact Press Images. "Some photographers may have acted badly, but that doesn't give the media the right to allow this flow of hatred to go toward an entire professional community. It's outrageous."

10   "There is too much hypocrisy," says Jean-Francois Leroy, director of the Visa Pour L'Image photojournalism festival in Perpignan, France, which, ironically, had opened the day after Diana's death. "Those who denounce the paparazzi today will be the first to buy the photos of the young princes crying at [Diana's] funeral. The paparazzi respond to the photo agencies, which respond to the newspapers and magazines, which respond to the public."

11   Leroy is correct in his assertion, with one caveat. Commentators from across the spectrum say that the media is filling the appetite of a seemingly insatiable public. But the media has lustily stoked the popular passion for celebrity and cannot so easily escape responsibility. Nor can celebrities who court publicity. This much is certain: To simply blame photographers is to ignore important realities. The demand for celebrity pictures and news has largely reshaped the profession of photojournalism; with more space available for star shots and less space available for coverage of war, politics, and social problems, some photographers and photo agencies have followed the market—often against their own wishes. "We estimate that 65 to 75 percent of publications worldwide are doing celebrity coverage now," says Marcel Saba of the Saba agency, which doesn't do celebrity coverage. "It's frustrating. We do a documentation on Rwanda, and our agent will say, sorry, we're selling Madonna today."

12   Even critics who understand the financial realities of photojournalism often have a hard time understanding how photojournalists work. Photographers are paid to make pictures, and to do so they must be where the story is happening, directly confronting the event or the person they are covering. Unlike reporters and editors, they do not have the luxury of sitting in a hotel room or behind an office desk "working the phone." When many photographers are sent to cover the same story, the scene can be chaotic and off-putting—especially in the context of a story like Diana's death. "People don't understand what photographers do," says Saba. "The news media is quoting tourists as saying the photographers [around Diana's car] were swarming like sharks, when what they were doing was taking pictures. They do the

same thing when they document a massacre in Bosnia, and no one calls them sharks then."

13   Photographic coverage of celebrities has grown more aggressive in the recent past. This is a result of greater competition among a growing number of celebrity photographers and the possibility of greater rewards for snapping a sellable picture. But it also comes from the increasing clout of celebrities themselves who want publicity—but only on their terms. The recent campaign against paparazzi by Hollywood stars, while played out in response to Diana's death, is part of a much older power struggle. Celebrities want control of their image—their image being as important to them as a camera is to a photographer. And to a large degree they get that control: Powerful press agents working for stars often dictate to magazines which photographers can shoot them, and they demand approval over which images are published. Magazines agree for the simple reason that they need celebrities on their covers to sell copies on the newsstand.

14   Within this rigid system, the paparazzo is the wild card. Amid all the bashing of paparazzi, it should be noted that they are sometimes—even often—the only journalists who cover celebrities outside the control of publicity agents, showing the celebrities as real people in the real world.

15   As publicity agents have exerted greater control over the press, and as competition increased when television moved into tabloid journalism, the ever-increasing legion of paparazzi have taken their aggressive approach to new levels. "This hounding of the celebrity is the result of that control by publicists and others," says Pledge. "There should be more openness on the part of the celebrities, who surround themselves with often imbecilic publicity people."

16   During the turbulent week after the accident, the paparazzi were repeatedly excoriated for the way they hunted Diana, as if she were a bird of prey. However, soon after she was married she had begun to master the art of turning the hunt to her own advantage. "Being permanently in the public eye gives me a special responsibility," she told one interviewer. "Notably that of using the impact of photographs to get a message across, a message about an important cause or certain values." Her trade-off was to use her enormous publicity value to further her own charitable ends rather than simply be victimized by the mercenary gamesmanship of the tabloid press.

17   The presence of photographers and possible culpability of some of them in the accident means that photography could not escape some measure of blame for a seemingly senseless and horrific event. But if all of photography is to be indicted, it is only right that the entire enterprise of celebrity journalism be examined.

AFTERWARDS

Vocabulary

craven, scrutiny, commendable, indiscriminate, culprits, culpability, unsavory, bizarre, tabloid, caveat, massacre, clout, turbulent, excoriated, mercenary. The connotative (see entry for connotation in Glossary) meaning of words contributes to a writer's style. First, look up the above words in your dictionary, noting both the denotative (see denotation) and connotative associations. Then, go back through Squiers's essay and gloss wherever the vocabulary words appear. Finally, make a list of words that could have been used in place of the vocabulary words, but indicate what "suggestive meanings" would have been lost in the process.

Content

1. What is the controlling idea or thesis of Squiers's essay? Where does it appear?

2. With whom did "celebrity publicist" Michael Levine equate the paparazzi? Who were some of the celebrities who used Diana's death to talk about their own problems?

3. Why were people so outraged with the paparazzi? Were the photographers doing anything they were not supposed to be doing? Explain.

Style and Structure

1. How does Squiers explain the way celebrities gain control of their image? Why is this control so important to them? What examples and reasoning does she offer?

2. Analyze the tone and content of Squiers's opening paragraph. How does it address readers who might have responded negatively to her article if she had led into it without some sort of reverent note about Diana's passing?

3. In what way does the conclusion of Squiers's essay look back to her introductory paragraphs? That is, how does her concluding paragraph create a sense of completion for her composition as a whole?

Collaborative Explorations

In groups of two or three, gather some afternoon with cameras and spend a few hours driving or walking around town taking pictures of people. How do those you photograph respond to your presence? Do they pose? Do they cover their faces?

If you have a television station in your city or town, go there and photograph employees. Do they appreciate your attention? When you develop your pictures, try to locate some of the people you photographed, and ask them if they would like to buy your pictures. Overall, evaluate how your brief experience as a paparazzi reinforces the attitude you already held toward them or gives you a new perspective on what it would be like to make your living photographing people.

Writing Assignments

1. Compare and contrast the coverage of the same event by two different writers in two different newspapers or two magazines. How are they similar? In what significant ways do they differ—if any? Be specific, and make sure to "show" what you mean. Did they use photographs to help tell their story? If so, explain their effect.

2. Write an essay in which you either support or disprove Squiers's claim that "Celebrities want control of their image—their image being as important to them as a camera is to a photographer." Provide specific evidence to demonstrate how and why you arrived at your conclusion.

Thematic Reading Cross-Links: See the introduction to Chapter 8, Popular Culture, to gain an insight into Princess Diana as a cultural icon.

Movie Cross-Links: For a different look at a person who has little privacy from media or government agencies, see *Brazil*, listed in the film links at the end of this chapter.

A Modern Inquisition

Jack Kevorkian

DR. JACK KEVORKIAN is a proponent of physician-assisted voluntary euthanasia (mercy killing). He has been present at the deaths of more than 40 people since 1990, and he makes his assistance public knowledge as part of his determined campaign to change attitudes and laws on physician-assisted suicide. According to one Web site (http://www.efn.org/~ergo/kevorkian.html), Dr. Kevorkian has helped more than 76 patients die. At 72 years of age, Kevorkian was convicted for the 1998 injection death of Thomas Youk, a man who had Lou Gehrig's disease. The death was videotaped by Kevorkian, and part of it was played on the CBS newsmagazine *60 Minutes*. Currently confined at the Egeler Correctional Facility in Michigan, Kevorkian is serving a 10- to 25-year sentence for assisted suicide; his earliest parole date is May 2007.

Kevorkian's books include *Medical Research and the Death Penalty: A Dialogue* (1983) and *Prescription Medicide: The Goodness of Planned Death.* In 1994, he won the Humanist Hero Award from the American Humanist Association. The following is an excerpt from his speech to the association, and it initially appeared in the November/December 1994 edition of *The Humanist.*

ALLUSIONS

Inquisition: A religious tribunal used by the Catholic Church during the Counter-Reformation to identify and punish heretics.

Pythagoreans: A philosophical/religious group founded upon the ideas propounded by the Greek mathematician and mystic Pythagoras in the sixth century B.C.E.

Hippocratic oath: A solemn promise made by physicians to "do no harm." It derives from the teachings of the Greek physician Hippocrates.

1   This is probably the first time that this august body [the American Humanist Association] has been addressed by someone under indictment on two counts of first-degree murder.

2   The Inquisition is still alive and well. The only difference is that today it's much more dangerous and subtle. The inquisitors don't burn you at the stake anymore; they slowly sizzle you. They make sure you pay dearly for what you do. In fact, they kill you often in a subtle way. My situation is a perfect example of it.

3   This is not self-pity, understand. I don't regret the position I'm in. I'm not a hero, either—by my definition, anyway. To me, anyone who does what should be done is not a hero. And I still feel that I'm only doing what I, as a physician, should do. A license has nothing to do with it; I am a physician and therefore I will act like a physician whenever I can. That doesn't mean that I'm more compassionate than anyone else, but there is one thing I am that many aren't and that's honest.

4   The biggest deficiency today and the biggest problem with society is dishonesty. It underlies almost every crisis and every problem you can name. It's almost inevitable; in fact, it's unavoidable as you mature. We feel that a little dishonesty greases the wheels of society, that it makes things easier for everybody if we lie a little to each other. But all this dishonesty becomes cumulative after a while. If everyone were perfectly honest at all times, if human nature could stand that, you would find many fewer problems in the world.

5   When we (my lawyers, sisters, medical technologist, and myself) first started this work [physician-assisted voluntary euthanasia], we didn't expect the explosion of publicity that followed. The mainstream media tried to make my work look very negative—they tried to make me look negative—so that they could denigrate the concept we're working on. They said I should not be identified with the concept, yet

they strived to do just that. They insulted and denigrated me and then hoped that it would spill over onto the concept. It didn't work, however; according to the polls, people may be split 50–50 on what they think of me, but they are three-to-one in favor of the concept, and that's never changed.

6   Now isn't it strange that on a controversial subject of this magnitude—one that cuts across many disciplines—the entire editorial policy of the country is on one side? Even on a contentious issue like abortion, there is editorial support for both sides. And our issue—death with dignity—as far as we're concerned, is simpler than abortion. So why is every mainstream editorial writer and newspaper in the country against us on this? Not one has come out in wholehearted support of us, even though public opinion is on our side.

7   As I surmise it, they're in a conspiracy, which is not a revelation to many people. But with whom? Well, let's take a look at who's against this: organized religion, organized medicine, and organized big money. That's a lot of power.

8   Why is organized medicine against this? For a couple of reasons, I think. First, because the so-called profession—which is no longer a profession; it's really a commercial enterprise and has been for a long time—is permeated with religious overtones. The basis of so-called medical ethics is religious ethics. The Hippocratic oath is a religious manifesto. It is not medical. Hippocrates didn't write it; we don't know who did, but we think it's from the Pythagoreans. So if you meet a physician who says "Life is sacred," be careful. We didn't study sanctity in medical school. You are talking to a theologian first, probably a businessperson second, and a physician third.

9   The second reason that organized medicine is against physician-assisted voluntary euthanasia is the money involved. If a patient's suffering is curtailed by three weeks, can you imagine how much that adds up to in medical care? And a lot of drugs are used in the last several months and years of life, which add up to billions of dollars for the pharmaceutical industry. This is what is so dismaying to me, what makes me cynical. You have to be cynical in life when you read about a situation that's so terrible and so incorrigible. There are certain ways to deal with it: you can go along with it, which is hard to do; you can go insane, which is a refuge (and some do that); or you can face it with deep cynicism. I've opted for cynicism. In responding to the religious issues, I ask this: Why not let all the religious underpinnings of medicine apply only to the ethics of religious hospitals and leave the secular hospitals alone? The doctors who work in religious hospitals can refuse to do abortions, they can refuse assisted suicide or euthanasia, they can do anything they want. But they have no right to impose what they call a universal medical ethic on secular institutions.

10   Besides, what is ethics? Can you define it? My definition is simple: Ethics is saying and doing what is right, at the time. And that changes. Seventy-five years ago, if I told you that for Christmas I was going to have a truck deliver 10 tons of coal to your house, you would have been delighted. If I told you that today, you would be insulted. Doing the right thing changes with time.

11   That's true of human society also. There is a primitive society—I don't know which one exactly—whose members were shocked to learn that we embalm our

dead, place them in boxes, and then bury them in the ground. Do you know what they do? They eat them. To them, it's ethical and moral and honorable to devour the corpse of your loved one. We're shocked at that, right? It's all a matter of acculturation, time, where you are, and who you are. If I visited this primitive society and I was a real humanist, I'd say, "Oh, that's interesting." And if the so-called savage in turn said "Gee, that's interesting what you do," then he or she would be a humanist. I used to define maturity as the inability to be shocked. So I guess in some ways we're still immature. But if you're truly mature, and a true humanist, you can never be shocked. If they eat their dead, so be it—that's their culture. But you know what our missionaries did, don't you? That's immoral action.

12   I think you get the gist of my position.

AFTERWARDS

Vocabulary

deficiency, inevitable, cumulative, euthanasia, magnitude, denigrate, contentious, surmise, manifesto, sanctity, acculturation, curtail, incorrigible, embalm. Analyze the appropriateness of Kevorkian's word choice for discussing his subject.

Content

1. Summarize the content of this speech excerpt.

2. Why does Kevorkian refer to his present situation (accused of two murders) as an "Inquisition," not unlike the persecutions of the Counter-Reformation?

3. What is the tone of Kevorkian's speech?

Style and Structure

1. How does Kevorkian use ethical and logical appeals to the people he addresses? What logical fallacies can you detect in his argument?

2. How well does Kevorkian explain himself? What issue is he attempting to address?

3. In what way is Kevorkian's speech organized? How does it provide a definite beginning, middle, and conclusion?

Collaborative Explorations

In groups of two or three, visit convalescent homes and the people in them. Talk awhile. After doing so, reflect on the living conditions and desires of those in the home. Then write a collaborative essay arguing that people in convalescent homes should have a choice: to live or to die with dignity.

Writing Assignments

1. Kevorkian describes his actions as anything but immoral. He says negative reaction to his aiding people to end life with dignity is a matter of "acculturation." In a well-developed, argumentative paper, demonstrate how and why you disagree with his premise. Develop your paper using logic and ethics rather than emotions.

2. In a short composition, evaluate the concept of euthanasia. How could it be abused?

Thematic Reading Cross-Links: Look back and review Rose Anna Higashi's essay, "Boycott America's Media." Compare the way Kevorkian achieves celebrity status as a proponent of patient-assisted suicide for the terminally ill to the notoriety movie stars receive through the "cult of popularity."

Movie Cross-Links: See *Extreme Measures*, a film about a neurosurgeon who believes it is necessary and therefore ethical to conduct research on human beings. How is he both alike and different in spirit and practice from Dr. Kevorkian?

The Visual Connection: Photograph Writing Activities

1. Journalists who reported on the Vietnam War are often credited with exposing the horrors of modern warfare on film and in photographs, as well as in frontline news accounts. Since the United States pulled out of Vietnam in 1975, numerous memorials have been erected. Go online and type in "The National Vietnam Memorial," and see how many items appear. Then select those entries with photographs that are different from, yet similar to, the following photo (top right) and either download them or print them. Assess the memorial. How appropriate do you find the tribute to Vietnam veterans? Why?

The National Vietnam War Memorial

Patty "Tania" Hearst

2. In 1972, Patty Hearst (bottom, p. 163), the daughter of Randolph Hearst, the owner of a newspaper chain, was kidnapped by, but then appeared to have joined, the Symbionese Liberation Army (SLA), an obscure revolutionary group that claimed to be at war with the "fascist state of Amerikkka." Later, when she stood trial for bank robbery, she claimed that her revolutionary beliefs and "urban guerrilla" status were faked. She further claimed she had been a "prisoner of war." Many people—especially media commentators—did not seem to believe in her innocence. Why would the Symbionese Liberation Army, a handful of unknown political zealots, plan and stage such an event? How did they use the very media that the Hearst family owned in order to gain publicity for themselves and their cause? How were they using the media to attack the media? What does the following image of Patty Hearst holding an automatic weapon communicate? What effect do images like this have on the producers of media? Think of other famous images—the JFK assassination, the Rodney King video—and how they took on a life of their own in the media. What does the case of Patty Hearst tell us about the power of media images?

Cosmopolitan

3. Observe the personal identity collage (p. 164)—a basic exercise in a college photography class. What might you infer about the student's (center photo) relationship with *Cosmopolitan*, a woman's magazine? To what extent do you imagine that her sense of self has or has not been shaped by the media? Make your own identity collage and photograph it. Were any of your values expressed in the photograph influenced by the media? (The media include the printed word, the cyber world, television, and movies.)

Film Links: The Media: Controversies and Celebrities

1. What does the public have a right to know, and what information should remain private? How do films like *Absence of Malice* reveal the often difficult decisions made by people in the media? Who should the media trust for their sources, and what information should not be published—if any?

2. Write an essay analyzing how people's personal lives are affected by the media (e.g., advice from psychics or advice columnists, suggestions made by talk-show hosts, and so on). How do movies such as *My Life as a Dog* or *Choose Me* show how radio can become an important part of listeners' lives? Think about how you relate to newspapers and radio stations. What sort of information do you get from them? What influence do they have on your daily life? Do they make a personal connection? Write an essay in which you describe and reflect upon your relationship to these two forms of media.

3. After watching a movie like *All the President's Men*, *Citizen Kane*, or *The Killing Fields* (select one of these or another movie from the list below), assess how well films reflect the problems that arise for journalists and other media representatives. After all, radios and news programs do more than report the news; they create the news. They reveal secrets and spread gossip and scandal via their reporting. How did the films you watched give you insight into the nature of journalism?

Citizen Kane (USA, Orson Welles, 1940). Life of a newspaper mogul seen from several perspectives. Contains many cinematic innovations.

All the President's Men (USA, Alan J. Pakula, 1976). Story of Bob Woodward and Carl Bernstein's successful effort to investigate the Watergate scandal that ultimately ended the presidency of Richard Nixon.

Network (USA, Sidney Lumet, 1976). Network anchorman behaves irrationally on the air and becomes a media cult hero.

Absence of Malice (USA, Sidney Pollack, 1981). Zealous reporter causes havoc for falsely accused businessman.

The Year of Living Dangerously (Australia, Peter Weir, 1982). Australian reporter attempts to understand the forces that bring about a military coup in Indonesia.

The Killing Fields (USA, Roland Joffe, 1984). *New York Times* reporter and Cambodian interpreter endure the chaos and bloodshed of the Khmer Rouge revolution.

Choose Me (USA, Allen Rudolph, 1984). Female radio talk-show host dispenses sex therapy over the air while her personal life gets crazy.

Brazil (Great Britain, Terry Gilliam, 1985). Futuristic vision of a nightmare world of bureaucracy and media control.

Talk Radio (USA, Oliver Stone, 1988). Late night talk-show DJ taunts his listeners with disastrous results.

The Paper (USA, Ron Howard, 1994). Ethical dilemmas and personal conflicts rage behind the scenes of a big-city newspaper.

Wag the Dog (USA, Barry Levinson, 1998). A movie producer creates a fake international incident to divert attention from the president.

Bulworth (USA, Warren Beatty, 1998). U.S. senator adopts rap singing as a mode of communication and causes public relations and media confusion.

Additional Writing Assignments

1. Write an essay in which you recommend a television show, radio station, or movie to a friend. Point out the merits of this form of media. What do you enjoy about it? What does it add to your daily life? What does it communicate? How? Be persuasive. Use specific details to show what you mean.

2. Compare and contrast what you consider the tasteful and tasteless humor advertisers use to sell their products. To whom or what does tasteful comedy appeal? What makes a particular type of humor tasteless? Which kind of humor found in commercials leaves a lasting impression on you and why?

3. Write an essay about a television program using a friendly, conversational tone of language, freely using words, phrases, and allusions from popular culture. How might allusions to specific people, places, and events in popular culture create connections with your readers?

4. Critique the appeal of a commercial, a popular situation comedy, a movie, and so on. You might begin by asking yourself a series of questions: What makes the people, places, and things in the media "sexy," "intriguing," or "thought provoking"? Answers to your questions will provide you with major discussion points to analyze and illustrate with specific examples in your critique.

5. Write your own satirical essay on some aspect of the media that you think is given importance beyond its true value. Satirists often make use of irony by saying the opposite of what they mean. They also use exaggeration, parody, and caricature to make their points. Try to use some of these techniques to make your satiric observations.

Chapter Six

Environments

Observations and Opinions

The "control" of nature is a phrase conceived in arrogance, born of the Neanderthal age of biology and the convenience of man.

—RACHAEL CARSON FROM *THE SILENT SPRING*

April is the cruelest month, breeding
Lilacs out of the dead land, mixing
Memory and desire, stirring
Dull roots with spring rain.

—T. S. ELIOT FROM *THE WASTELAND* (1922)

I was lucky to be brought up in Nature. There, lightning strikes taught me about sudden death and the evanescence of life. Mice litters showed that the death was softened by new life. When I unearthed "Indian beads," trilobites from the loam, I understood that humans have been here a long, long time. I learned about the sacred art of self-decoration with monarch butterflies perched atop my head, lightning bugs as my night jewelry, and emerald green frogs as bracelets.

—CLARISSA PINKOLA ESTÉS FROM *WOMEN WHO RUN WITH THE WOLVES*

We can be thankful that carbon dioxide is keeping us comfortably warm, but the concentration of carbon dioxide in the atmosphere is going up steadily and that is where the villainy comes in. In 1958, when carbon dioxide of the atmosphere first began to be measured carefully, it made up only 0.0316 percent of the atmosphere. Each

year since, the concentration has crept upward and it now stands at
0.340 percent. It is estimated that by 2020 the concentration will be
about 0.660 percent, or nearly twice what it is now.
—ISAAC ASIMOV FROM "THE VILLAIN IN THE ATMOSPHERE"

Observations and Opinions: Reading/Writing Activities

1. Discuss the extent to which you agree with Rachael Carson's quote from *Silent Spring*. What does the title, *Silent Spring*, imply? How might Isaac Asimov's excerpt from "The Villain in the Atmosphere" demonstrate the results of arrogant humans who think they can control nature?

2. Select a month of the year, make a statement about it (e.g., July is the happiest month of all, December is the coldest month of all, and so on), and then illustrate your point using concrete nouns and active verbs. You may write in either prose or verse like T. S. Eliot did in his excerpt from *The Wasteland*.

3. What relationship exists between the speaker and nature in Clarissa Pinkola Estés's quote from *Women Who Run with the Wolves*? Rewrite what she says about her good fortune (to be "brought up in Nature") by replacing the focus of her good luck with your own in your journal. Then, like Estés, illustrate how and why you were lucky. Feel free to substitute the key word "lucky" with "unlucky" if it more accurately conveys your fortune as a youth. You might want to distinguish between the natural environment and human-made environments.

Introduction

Most people think they know what nature is. If asked, they will say, "It's the trees and flowers, all the stuff that is not man-made." This makes sense. The word itself comes from the Latin *natus*, which means "born," and is related to other words like *native*, *nativity*, and *natal*, all of which have to do with birth. So anything that is born must be part of nature, but what about stones, water, molecules, and crystals? They would seem to be a part of nature too. Also, if you say that human-made things like apartment buildings and dams are not parts of nature, then what about beehives and beaver dams? These are constructed by other species and are usually quite well made. Are they not part of nature, or are only human-made structures excluded? Why should they be? What is it about human intervention that somehow makes "human-made things" separate? Perhaps everything is a part of nature. This leads to a whole series of other thoughts and questions. Human beings are born, and they seem to have a human nature. Should we then conclude that human beings and everything human beings do is just as much a part of nature as the rest of the plant and animal world?

Shopping for a new shirt or a new outfit doesn't usually provoke reflection on nature, yet in her essay, "Clothing Arguments," Leora Broydo suggests we ought to have an "eco-conscience" that affects our choices about what we wear every day. How natural are natural fibers? What happens to materials, like polyester, that are synthetic and not biodegradable? Broydo helps us to see how all commodities have a connection to the environment through the various stages required by manufacturing processes. Even our most routine acts are part of a much larger process that transforms "natural resources" into "products." Broydo reminds us that these products also have to go somewhere when we are finished with them. How far can we go with recycling? What lifestyle choices are we willing to change? Where did the clothes you are wearing come from, and where will they end up?

A similar feeling of making connections comes from Gary Snyder's essay "Back to Nature." Here he encourages his readers to get to know their "natural neighborhood" because no matter where you are on the planet—standing in the Sierra Nevadas or on a street corner in New York City—you are still part of an ecosystem. Snyder thinks we need to check out our neighborhoods a little more closely in order to see and understand all the connections that are necessary to sustain life. He reminds us that "eco" is derived from the Greek word for "home" and that we ought to have concern for our whole territory, our "bio-region." That is what our ancestors did to survive. Perhaps we should do the same.

The human connection to nature is also reflected in stories. Jeanne Wakatsuki Houston's story of an old woman's memories of life in Japan and in a Japanese-American internment camp in World War II are also full of the delicate sensory experiences that the natural world places in our minds. Snowflakes drifting through a night sky beneath a full moon can leave an impression undiminished by time and the passing of years. Indeed, simply soaking in a hot tub can evoke feelings and memories that make a person feel whole.

People and the natural environment suffer if and when they stand in the way of what some hail as human progress. Andrew Lam cites one such example of this in "A Fate Worse Than War." No stranger to the devastation inflicted upon people and the ecosystem in times of warfare, he explains how the Mekong Delta Plan to build a series of six dams on the river would displace at least 60,000 people, eliminate vast acreage of forest lands affecting "one out of three Vietnamese" who depends on "forestry and forest products for a livelihood," and impact the

Mekong River Delta fisheries that produce the main source of protein for millions living in the river basin.

In "Minnesota's Sensible Plan," Garrison Keillor presents a tongue-in-cheek proposition for using Minnesota's best known natural resource—water from the land of "ten thousand lakes." His plan suggests exploiting the environment for personal gain by selling water, literally changing Lake Superior into a "superior canyon"—the latter being a great tourist attraction. Ironically, Keillor states that "the Superior Canyon project can help bring the country to its senses, putting a big chunk of the economy into the hands of modest and sensible people, people who have been through some hard winters and are the better for it." What is missing here, of course, is a responsible human connection to nature and the fragile ecosystem.

Each of the essays in this chapter introduces us to the complex relationship between human beings and the environment that surrounds what we call nature. You might think about the connections between these writings as you read them. They may grow together in your mind, forming a small garden of ideas that grow, develop, and take on lives of their own.

Gathering Thoughts: Prereading Inquiries

1. What attitude do you have toward the past and the future? Are human beings making progress, socially and environmentally?

2. The Greeks used the word "cosmos," meaning "order," to describe the universe. What is your picture of the cosmos?

3. How would you define nature?

4. Define ecology in your own words. Why has there been such an emphasis on ecology in the last thirty years? Are ecologists troublemakers, professional activists, or simply concerned individuals? Explain.

5. What is the relationship between nature and your living environment? Does one affect the other? How? Why? What should the relationship be like?

6. Are human beings separate from nature, above nature (better or more important), or at one with nature?

Continued

7. Should human beings try to obey nature's laws or strive to manipulate them for human purposes?

8. Why do human beings commit crimes against nature? Why do human beings commit crimes against each other? Is there a difference?

9. Does life change for a person who moves from one environment to another? What exactly is a "social environment"? How does it differ from a "natural environment"?

10. What sacrifices are you willing to make to preserve the natural environment around us? What do you imagine will be left of our natural environment when your grandchildren are grown?

Clothing Arguments

Leora Broydo

LEORA BROYDO is a staff writer for *Mother Jones* magazine. Her articles deal with a range of issues from health and wellness to environmental concerns. In the following essay, initially published in the July/August 1997 issue of *Mother Jones,* Broydo argues that for duds that don't wear on the planet, the best bet is to buy used.

ALLUSIONS

Isaac Mizrahi: A fashion designer.

Giorgio Armani: An Italian clothes designer.

Woody Harrelson: An actor and social activist for environmental causes.

Patagonia: A fabric company.

Sally Fox: An entomologist who grew colored cotton for her own company, National Cotton Colours, Inc.

green: An allusion to manufactured products—and lifestyles—compatible with nature.

EPA: An acronym for the Environmental Protection Agency.

1   Can the fashion-conscious have an ecoconscience? Designer Isaac Mizrahi would probably say yes, given that the dresses in his fall collection are accented with

recycled furs. So would Giorgio Armani—he created the hemp tux Woody Harrelson wore to this year's [1997, actually] Oscars.

2   But pose the question to environmental purists and they'll tell you that, for the most part, the catwalk is a real dog when it comes to ecofriendliness, and if you truly want an outfit that matches your green sensibilities, buy used.

3   Clothes manufacturing wears on the planet. Twenty-five percent of the insecticides used globally go on cotton plants, grown for the world's most popular fabric. Synthetics, like polyester, are made from petroleum products and are nonbiodegradable. And fabric-finishing processes such as dyeing are highly toxic and polluting.

4   So, if the creation of clothing has a negative impact on the environment, what then is behind all the green-labeled clothing on the market? Let's take a look at the cloths many of these clothes are cut from:

5   ***Organic Cotton.***   Organic cotton is grown using chemical-free, soil-enriching methods, but its use in manufacturing doesn't guarantee ecofriendliness. Even companies, such as Patagonia, that exclusively use organic cotton still use color dyes. "Dyes are as bad, if not worse, than the agricultural chemicals," says Sally Fox, an entomologist who grows colored organic cotton for her company, Natural Cotton Colours Inc.

6   Patagonia is well aware of this criticism, but responds that it's promoting the first steps of change. "If no one buys the product," explains Lu Setnicka of Patagonia, "you're not going to build an organic cotton market."

7   ***Hemp.***   Durable and versatile, hemp can be grown without chemicals and does not deplete soil. And consumers have been snapping up hemp fashions. However, industry experts say those hemp jeans you paid so much for may have been "green-washed." Since it's illegal to grow hemp in the U.S., it's imported, primarily from China, Hungary, Romania, and Russia—which aren't exactly ecopioneers.

8   According to Owen Sercus, a textile professor at New York's Fashion Institute of Technology, hemp producers in these countries are using harsh chemicals to speed up the growing process. "If hemp is properly grown by nature," he says, "it takes a long time."

9   ***Tencel.***   Tencel is a natural fiber created from wood pulp using a nontoxic, "closed loop" process that recycles solvents. Additionally, the pulp is only taken from trees grown on managed tree farms.

10   Unfortunately, the EPA lists Courtaulds Fibers, the manufacturer of Tencel and other fiber products, as the sixth-largest polluter in the country, having released 34.5 million pounds of toxins into the environment in 1994. (Guess some things escaped "the loop.")

11   ***Recycled Polyester.***   Fortrel EcoSpun is a polyester made from recycled plastic containers. Its manufacturer, Wellman Inc., says the production of EcoSpun saves 650,000 barrels of oil annually, while eliminating 375,000 tons of toxic air emissions. The material is made into jeans and Polar Fleece (which are, of course, dyed).

12   Clearly, all fabrics have a downside. But remember, the fabrics and finishes are there because consumers want cheap, easy-to-care-for clothing. Oh, and we also want to express ourselves. "Do we want to end up like Maoist China, where everybody wore the same garment?" Sercus asks. "We in the fashion industry do what the consumer demands of us."

13   So, if you want your clothes to be green, demand it. If you want to know why a company has slapped an "ecolabel" on a garment, ask. And, if all else fails, there's one surefire way to style yourself while minimizing environmental harm: Head to the secondhand store and grab that polyester leisure suit off the rack.

AFTERWARDS

Vocabulary

clothes, ecofriendliness, nonbiodegradable, versatile, hemp, ecopioneers, polyester. Locate as many of the words as you can in your dictionary. To arrive at definitions for the remaining words, consider the meaning of prefixes and suffixes attached to "standard word roots."

Content

1. What does Broydo claim is the best clothing for an ecology-conscious person to buy? Why?

2. Why do you think Broydo mentions manufacturers by name?

3. In what way does Broydo immediately capture her readers' attention?

Style and Structure

1. How does dividing and classifying so-called green manufacturers assist Broydo in the development of her essay?

2. Explain how Broydo's "matter-of-fact" tone works as a persuasive device in her argument.

3. How does Broydo's concluding paragraph look back to her thesis? In what way does it function as a "question" and an "answer," providing a framing device for the entire essay?

Collaborative Explorations

Place yourselves in one large circle (the entire class), take out a piece of paper, divide it into two columns, and in the first column, jot down reasons to wear "green clothing." In the second column, outline why it is or is not important to wear fashionable clothing. Which type of clothing—if either—makes you feel good about yourself when you wear it? Finally, go all the way around the room either reading or discussing your impressions about clothes. (*Suggestion*: Constantly be taking notes on new thoughts that come to mind as peers present their material; that way, you'll be sure to have something to say when it is your turn to discuss the topic of "green" and fashionable—though not ecologically friendly—clothes and their producers.)

Writing Assignments

1. Construct an argument refuting Broydo's belief that the only way to be certain that the clothes you buy are ecofriendly is to purchase used clothing. As a starting point, you might want to consider the fact that even secondhand clothes were made or manufactured by someone who was possibly "ecounfriendly."

2. Do a bit of research and evaluate the most recent arguments revolving around growing hemp as a source of clothing fiber, paper, and so on. Acknowledge early in your paper that you are aware that growing hemp currently is not legal, but then persuade your readers that perhaps we should reconsider the ecological value of fast-growing hemp plants.

Thematic Reading Cross-Links: Compare the attitude toward clothing in this essay to that in one of the essays such as "Striving to Be a *Baywatch* Barbie" from Chapter 12, The Body: Language, Ritual, and Wellness—A Casebook. To what extent would a "material" world always deny Broydo's argument?

Movie Cross-Links: See the film *Norma Rae* for a picture of labor/ management disputes in a textile mill.

Back to Nature

Gary Snyder

GARY SNYDER, a poet, essayist, translator, and mountaineer, first emerged as a writer in the 1950s when he was identified with the Beat writers in San Francisco, including Jack Kerouac, Allen Ginsberg, and Lawrence Ferlinghetti. He subsequently spent three years studying and practicing Zen Buddhism in

Japan. After his return to the United States and the publication of his *Earth Household* (1969), he also became strongly identified with the ecology movement, especially ecologists who argue for a more biocentric view. Snyder believes that the preservation of wilderness is essential to human survival and that human communities can imitate ecosystems by diversity, by flexible adaptation to change, and by wisdom that comes from knowing as much as you can about the place where you live. His works include *A Range of Poems* (1966), *The Back Country* (1968), *Regarding Wave* (1970), *Manzanita* (1972), *Turtle Island* (1974, Pulitzer Prize winner), and *Mountains and Rivers Without End* (1996); his essay collections include *The Old Ways* (1977), *The Real Work* (1982), and *The Practice of the Wild* (1989). Snyder teaches at the University of California at Davis. The following article was written in response to "There Is No Going Back to Nature" by Walter Truett Anderson (*Mother Jones,* Sep/Oct 96, vol. 21); according to Anderson, the idea of returning to nature is unrealistic because "bad money drives out good, and muzzy slogans drown out serious thinking."

ALLUSIONS

Blade Runner: A futuristic film starring Harrison Ford as a man charged with locating and eliminating cyborgs (human-like robots).

New Agers: A broad category for writers interested in non-Western, holistic ways of thinking. It would include Fritjof Capra, Charlene Spretnak, and William Irwin Thompson.

Norwegian philosophers: The phrase "deep ecology" was coined by Arne Naess, author of *Ecology, Community and Lifestyle* (1989), who taught philosophy at the University of Oslo for many years.

1   If societies were incapable of surprising shifts and turns, if religions and philosophies, languages, and clothing never changed, we'd surely have to grimly crunch away in the same old story and eventually drown in some sort of Blade Runner–type movie. Walter Truett Anderson ("There's No Going Back to Nature," September/October) seems to assume that the track we're on will go forever and nobody will learn much. He provides some excellent information, he is clearly sincere, but it's basically the same old engineering, business, and bureaucracy message with its lank rhetoric of data and management.

2   The oh-so-foolish deep ecologists, greens, ecofeminists, etc., are out there—at almost no cost to the system—providing imagination, vision, passion, a deeply felt ethical stance, and in many cases some living examples of practice. The ethical position that would accord intrinsic value to non-human nature, and would see human beings as involved in moral as well as practical choices in regard to the natural world, makes all the difference.

3   I have no quarrel with restoring creeks, crunching understory fuel load, logging out genuinely sick trees, hanging out counting the frogs in the creek, taping owl calls, piling up data in the workstation, and all that. I do it myself. If it's done with the commodity mind, you might as well be managing a concentration camp. If it's done with the mind of the natural neighborhood, with the intimacy that comes with knowing yourself as a member of the ecosystem, then those very same chores are a matter of working with and learning from the non-human critters in the 'hood. It becomes a collaboration, a feast, a memorial gathering, a ceremony. This is what deep ecology is about. The ethic of concern for all beings including the non-human, incidentally, is not just some invention of New Agers, Norwegian philosophers, or Native American academicians, but is anciently and deeply rooted worldwide, going back for millennia. Buddhism and much of Hinduism put this ethic at the top of their list of precepts.

4   I think it's clear, in this election campaign year, we can't afford to trash any values. They'll all come in handy.

5   Mr. Anderson quotes me correctly—from a mid-'80s issue of *Sierra* magazine where I spoke on bioregions and place. And indeed I do believe that more people staying put, learning their place, and taking on some active role, would improve our social and ecological life. I said people should try to become "paysans, paisanos, peones," meaning people of the land, people of the place. But note: I didn't specify how big the place can be. The size of place one becomes a member of is limited only by the size of one's heart. We speak of watershed consciousness, and the great water cycle of the planet makes it all one watershed. We are all natives to this earth. Yet one has to start where one is and become nature-literate to the scale of the immediate home place. With home-based knowledge, it is then within our power to get a glimpse of the planet as home. As a rule though, local knowledge (combined with an understanding of the dynamics of systems) remains the most useful, and the most delicious.

6   No one ever said that "don't move" means you can't go on trips—peasants of Japan, religious devotees of India have always gone on long pilgrimages to the mountains after harvest was over. The thing is, even when on a trip, you are always clear as to where you came from. We can be thankful that bioregional practice is more sophisticated than some replay of the medieval village. Since it is a line of thought for the future, it calls us to be ecologically and culturally cosmopolitan, hip to the plant and weather zones of the whole world, as well as to the cuisine and architecture.

7   As for technology: Smarter bombs, faster computers, and quieter chainsaws certainly have their place. The struggle for the integrity of the environment will need good tools—the good guys want their computers to be as big and fast as those of the bad guys. Understandably. But though weapons win battles, they don't win the peace. Peace is won by winning hearts and minds. Watershed imagining, bioregional ideas of governance, the actual existence of communities that include the non-human in their embrace, myths of ecological justice, the thought of enlightenment—all this nutty ancient stuff is a matter of engaging hearts and minds.

AFTERWARDS

Vocabulary

intrinsic, commodity, millennia, bioregions, watershed, ecosystem, incidentally, cosmopolitan, cuisine. Select prefixes or suffixes from the vocabulary list, and then write out their definitions. How do both help readers determine the meaning of unfamiliar words?

Content

1. What is the picture of the future that is promised by "engineering, business, and bureaucracy"? With their embrace of technology, growth, and management, how do they envision the relationship between human beings and the environment?

2. What are some of the basic precepts of Buddhism and Hinduism that are relevant to thinking about nature?

3. What do you think Snyder means by "home-based knowledge"? (Keep in mind that the prefix "eco" derives from the Greek for "home.")

Style and Structure

1. Although Snyder states his views in a straightforward manner, he adopts a nonconfrontational tone. What words or phrases give this sense of good-humored, challenging disagreement?

2. How does Snyder make his points? What is his strategy for convincing his readers that deep ecology is not just some passing fad?

3. How would you apply the phrase "intrinsic value" to places in nature? What does this imply about the way human beings should relate to their natural surroundings?

Collaborative Explorations

As a group, list as many characteristics of the bioregion you live in as you can. How many ecosystems are parts of the world you inhabit? How many plant and animal species can you name that are part of the living community of which you are a part?

Writing Assignments

1. Write an essay persuading readers that there are or are not precepts in the Judeo-Christian or Islamic traditions that could serve as the basis for an ecological ethic.

2. In a logical, well-supported essay, argue that we can return to nature as Snyder says or that such a return is impossible because society values immediate financial and personal gains over a logical, ecologically responsible style of living (Walter Truett Anderson's position on the realistic return to nature, mentioned in more detail in Snyder's biographical notes prior to his article). Make sure to offer arguments and examples drawn from your own experience, observations, and readings rather than restating what Snyder has already said.

Thematic Reading Cross-Links: Take a look at a couple of the readings in Chapter 7, Cyberspace and Technology, to get a perspective on progress and need, as well as the importance of ecological integrity in the midst of a modern society.

Movie Cross-Links: See *Never Cry Wolf* or *The Bear* from the Film Links for this chapter in order to better understand the "biocentric" view Snyder expresses.

O Furo (The Bath)

Jeanne Wakatsuki Houston

Born in Inglewood, California, **JEANNE WAKATSUKI HOUSTON** has spent most of her life on the Pacific Coast. During World War II, her family was moved to the Japanese-American internment camp in Manzanar, California, for four years. Ms. Wakatsuki Houston was only seven years old at the time, and the memories of her years there are recorded in *Farewell to Manzanar* (1973), now in its thirtieth Bantam printing, which she co-wrote with her husband, James D. Houston, a well-known novelist. In 1988, they collaborated again in *One Can Think about Life After the Fish Is in the Canoe: Beyond Manzanar*. The Houstons also worked on film projects together such as *Barrio* (1978) and *The Melting Pot* (1980). Ms. Wakatsuki Houston's essays, articles, and reviews have appeared in numerous magazines and periodicals such as *Mother Jones,*

California Living, West Magazine, New England Review, The Reader's Digest (Japanese edition), *Dialogue* (international edition), and the *Los Angeles Times*, as well as in several anthologies. Other works include *Don't Cry, It's Only Thunder*, co-authored with Paul Hensler (1984), and *Beyond Manzanar: Views of Asian American Womanhood* (1985). She has just completed *Fire Horse Woman*, a novel. Among the many awards and accolades Ms. Wakatsuki Houston has received is the prestigious Wonder Women Award (1984), an award honoring women over forty who have made outstanding achievements in the pursuit of positive social change.

ALLUSIONS

Furo: Japanese for "bath."

Karma: A Hindu and Buddhist belief than one's conduct defines one's fate through successive lifetimes; this concept or quality is sometimes summarized by the saying "what goes around comes around."

Shamisen: A Japanese stringed instrument.

Andrews Sisters: A vocal group popular in the 1940s, well known for their harmonies.

Kimonos: Loose-fitting robes, usually silk and often decorated, that are tied at the waist.

1   Snow fell in sheets of lace, a translucent curtain swirling and fluttering with the wind. Through the barracks window, Yuki watched in wonderment. She had not seen snow for forty years, not since leaving Japan. Unused to the glare, she blinked, hoping it was not cataracts that caused her eyes to sting. Many elders in camp had developed cataracts, invisible films that grew over the dark part of the eye. She didn't want any veil to soften her view of the desert's harsh landscape.

2   The room felt cold. She turned up the oil heater and set a pan of water on top. It was still too early to retire. The thought of bundling up in blankets and sleeping the day away was tempting. But Dixon would soon be bringing dinner. She sat down and rubbed her cold stockinged feet. Should she worry about frostbite?

3   How good a furo would feel. She had not taken a hot bath since coming to internment camp a year ago. The communal showers and toilets were one of the more distasteful necessities she had to endure in this crowded settlement of strangers. When she first arrived, she had refused to shower in the dark cement room where a dozen metal nozzles sprayed water over huddled figures, who covered their privates with a towel in one hand, and with the other—and another towel—washed themselves. Such humiliation! Wasn't it bad enough for one family to live all in one small room! But to bathe with strangers—and not even in a tub—was too much to expect. Now she showered in the middle of the night when others slept.

4   Yuki was seventy-three. She was proud of her youthful looks. Most people were surprised she was over sixty and often asked what she did to stay so young. "Dance and sing a lot," she'd say, "and take o furo every night." She would like to say, "and please yourself as much as you can." But that sounded selfish, especially from an elder, a grandmother who should reflect ideals of martyrdom and self-sacrifice.

5   Remembering her warm apartment in East Los Angeles, the large three rooms above Nishio's Shoe Store, Yuki often wondered what bad karma she had earned to end up in such a place. Dust, tumbleweeds, wind and heat! She welcomed the snow, how it blanketed the bleakness with white, giving an illusion of space, so that when she looked out, she could imagine herself back in Japan, back in the farmhouse surrounded by fields, large fields that spread up to pine forests bordering the land. She didn't think of Japan often. There were years when it seemed she never had lived there. She did play the shamisen and also taught dancing and singing. But sometimes it seemed she had created the art herself in America.

6   Yuki contemplated the snow. Did it have meaning? Her first thought was its purity. Its cleansing and purifying powers. But she also could look at the truth. She could accept the fact that winter had arrived, and she was now in the winter of her life, the time when tree limbs turned barren, just as her own limbs felt stripped of flesh. She had not seen snow for so many years. Was this a sign? An omen? Was she to die in this camp? What calamity! To die in an infertile desert, where she had not seen one bright flower! Even the rocks looked tired and jagged, chipped away by tumbleweeds smashing against them. No, she would not die here. Instead, she read it to be a gift from the snow-god, a gentle covering of ugliness, a reminder of beauty and innocence.

7   As the snow had transformed the desert, Yuki realized she too must transform her spirit. With this illumination, she felt a lightness in her heart she had not felt since the war began. It somehow gave meaning to the true purpose of her imprisonment. She now had a goal, a reason to create new rituals and ceremonies. Singing and playing the shamisen were not enough.

8   When Dixon brought dinner from the messhall, she ate with rare gusto. Even the dry rice and rubbery Vienna sausages seemed tasty. Noticing his grandmother's new zest, Dixon asked, "What's up, Ba-chan?"

9   The chopsticks gently gripping a sausage stopped midair. Yuki looked at him with mock startled eyes. "What you mean?"

10   "Come on, Ba-chan, I know you. What's cooking?"

11   She studied his face before biting the sausage. She liked the square jawline and swarthy complexion, double-lidded eyes beneath feathery eyebrows that lifted at the outer corners like eagle wings. Her own complexion was pale, with pink-tinged cheeks, a complexion coveted by both men and women in Japan. Lucky she was born into a family of Niigata, a Japanese province known for its ivory-skinned women. Dixon had inherited dark skin from his mother whose parents came from Kagoshima, the southernmost part of Kyushu. Yuki knew her grandson was intelligent, a fact revealed by his high forehead and steady gaze. He sensed things, felt thoughts . . . especially hers.

12   Yuki wisely had chosen him early, the middle son, a quiet, gentle child lost in the shuffle of a hectic brood. A widow such as herself would need a devoted grandchild to champion her causes, a defender and willing helper to depend upon in old age. She had raised Dixon to fit that role. He was her favorite and, even though the special treatment brought cruel teasing from his siblings and a coolness from his mother, he seemed to love obachan despite it all.

13   Yuki and Dixon now lived by themselves away from the family. It had been hard living with noisy teenagers, and she never had approved of her daughter-in-law, Rosie, either. Too much like the hakujin, not teaching the children Japanese ways and letting them run wild like coyotes.

14   A few months earlier, Yuki's senses had been bombarded to the flash point. Clifford's clarinet whined in concert with the grating voices of Dolly, Frances and Mary as they attempted to imitate a singing trio called The Andrews Sisters. She had crawled under one of the iron cots, refusing to talk to anyone—even Dixon, who tried coaxing her with food and promises of walks by the creek outside the barbed wire. But she remained silent, curled like an old cat taking refuge from a pack of savage dogs.

15   After three days, her son and Rosie became concerned, worried they might have to report this strange behavior. What would the authorities do to someone gone crazy? The whole family tried to cajole her, lying on their stomachs, baby-talking and patting her like she was a petulant pet. But she withdrew further, hiding her head under the army blanket Dixon draped over her.

16   On the fourth day, when Dixon brought food, she accepted it.

17   "Why are you doing this?" he whispered as he shoved the tray of rice and stew toward her.

18   "So we have place alone," she whispered back.

19   "Oh . . . ," his eyes round, finally understanding her antics. "But there aren't any empties on the block. They're all full, Grandma."

20   She smiled, eyes crinkling into slits of light beaming from the dark lair. "Go to other block! Think big, Dixie-chan." Her voice was strong. "Tell papa ba-chan crazy because too much people. You me live someplace away. Okay?"

21   "Obachan is not used to so much noise, Pop," Dixon said. "Shouldn't we find another place for her?"

22   "Is that what she wants?" His father was surprised. Why hadn't she just asked? he thought. "But there aren't any empty rooms in this block."

23   Dixon answered quickly . . . too quickly. "There's one small room in the next block . . . block 30. I can stay with her."

24   "Oh, you've already checked?"

25   "No . . . I didn't check with anyone. I just noticed one of the end compartments was empty. When I was over at Lincoln Takata's place."

26   His father mulled the situation. Dixon had spent most of his life at his mother's apartment in Japantown. It would not seem odd for the two to stay together in the next block. In fact, it was logical, he rationalized.

27   Feeling a tinge of guilt for the relief he knew his wife and other children would savor with his mother's departure, he, nevertheless, agreed to talk to the next block's manager and request the empty room for medical reasons.

28   The new cubicle was located at the end of a barrack, smaller than others, but with the advantage of double doors. They could be swung open, allowing air and light into the dark interior of rough-hewn boards, shaggy and knot-holed and smelling of tar.

29   Yuki had kept the room stark and sparsely furnished. Even the iron cots were missing. With extra army blankets procured by Dixon, she had fashioned some thick futons upon which they slept at night and rolled up during the day. She stored her clothes—mostly kimonos—folded in the wicker trunk she had brought from home. Dixon's were stacked in an upended wooden box that served as a closet, its opening covered by a maroon curtain splashed with pink and white flowers. A shrine rested on a low shelf along with a picture of her deceased husband, Jun, and an incense burner and small plate for food.

30   Dixon asked his grandmother again, "Ba-chan what are you thinking about?"

31   "No know yet, Dixie. I thinking too much. But, no worry. I not going to die this place."

32   "Ba-chan! What are you doing thinking about dying!" Wasn't her act about going crazy enough? What was this about dying!

33   "The snow, Dixie-chan. The snow. Something tells me: Soon I know."

34   Dixon gathered up the dishes to return to the messhall. It sobered him to think of Obachan dying. He knew it would happen someday, but he pushed those thoughts away, clinging to the hope that when that time came, he would be a grown man and blessed with the love of another woman.

35   That night Yuki meditated and chanted before the picture of her long-deceased husband. She lit the last of the incense she had brought from Los Angeles. She prayed to the kamisama of the desert, of the rocks, of the mountains, and even of the tumbleweeds. When she finally lay down to sleep, her last conscious image was herself as a child in Japan, walking in snow, her bare feet elevated by tall getas (wooden clogs). Gliding like a skater on ice, she seemed to float skimming the snow to a destination she did not yet know.

36   She awoke at dawn. Her last thoughts before sleep had continued into a dream she remembered in clear detail. Instead of being a child, she was a young girl of fifteen. Dressed in a cotton yukata (kimono) and no longer wearing getas, she trudged up a narrow rocky path on the side of a mountain. It was winter, cold and windy, and her bare feet ached against the steely granite. Still she persevered,

knowing there was a purposeful end to her journey. She rounded a bend. On the side of the mountain, a grotto appeared. It seemed carved into the rocks. Inside, steam hissed over a bubbling pool. It was a hot spring.

37   She knew the dream's meaning. Gratefully, she prayed an extra strong mantra and left more food than usual before the shrine.

38   "Dixie! Dixie-chan, get up." She shook her sleeping grandson.

39   His eyes snapped open. He was beginning to wonder if Ba-chan really had suffered a nervous breakdown or stroke. Her actions were so strange lately.

40   "We make o furo. Real kind. Japan style."

41   "O furo? What's that?"

42   "Bath . . . bath. Lots hot water."

43   "What's the matter with the showers?"

44   "Not same same, Dixie. Ba-chan have to clean heart, spirit." She pointed to her chest. "Just like snow. That's why we have snow in desert."

45   "Can't you take a pail or bucket into the latrines? I see other ladies doing that."

46   She was filled with a sense of urgency and felt impatient with Dixon's lack of enthusiasm.

47   "No." She almost shouted. "I teach you make furo. Help Ba-chan, OK?"

48   Dixon sat up and yawned. He saw his grandmother wrinkle her nose and wave a hand in front of her face.

49   "Phew . . . bad smell, Dixie. You need clean soul, too."

50   The first thing to decide was where to put it. The space between barracks was too public, so the only choice was in front of their apartment, beyond the double doors. It meant they would have to extend a fenced-in area that would jut out past the other barracks. Yuki disregarded what the neighbors might think of this. She was tired of thinking of others. After all, her age entitled her to some self-indulgence.

51   Dixon scavenged some posts and plywood boards from the edge of camp where new barracks were under construction. He built a square fence about six feet high. Inside the enclosure, Yuki shoveled snow away and raked the sand underneath. She instructed Dixon to dig a shallow hole and place around it large flat boulders he had retrieved from the creek. But the most important item was missing. The tub. It was impossible to build a watertight tub of wood. And no metal could be found for flooring, which had to withstand the heat of a fire underneath.

52   For several days, Yuki was depressed. Like her mood, the weather became ominously darker. The wind howled, tearing at the new fence and rattling windows. It was a blizzard, a fierce storm that brought cold she could not remember, even in the long winters of her childhood in northern Japan.

53   She knelt beside the oil stove, playing shamisen and singing old love ballads. Perhaps the gods heard and enjoyed her plaintive songs, for it was during

an especially intense rendition that she thought of the solution. Or maybe it was the smell of burning oil. Suddenly she saw her o furo . . . an oil drum! The perfect tub!

54   "Dixie!" she shouted. "Tomorrow we go find empty drum! We make o furo from oil drum!"

55   Fortunately the storm passed enabling Yuki and Dixon to search the maintenance area, where stacks of grey barrels, some streaked with tar, were mounded behind a large warehouse. Brushing away snow, he searched the pile until he found one that had contained laundry detergent. About the size of a large wine cask, it was shiny and clean and smelled sweetly of pine. A perfect tub, too narrow for one to recline in, but wide enough for someone Yuki's size to comfortably sit on a stool.

56   They waited until dusk to build a fire. Yuki estimated the water would be hot enough by nightfall and hoped darkness would discourage nosey neighbors from peering into the yard. Already gossipy Ikeda and self-appointed block security officer Goto had paid uninvited visits, bringing omiyage (gifts) of old Japanese magazines and raisins. She knew they only wanted to see what she was up to and was smugly amused at their questioning eyes scanning the stark space cleared of snow with only a shallow pit surrounded by rocks.

57   "Dixie-chan and I are making a wishing pool," she had said in Japanese.

58   Their faces stony, they bowed stiffly, uncertain how they should assess the situation. Yuki knew they thought her strange. She had heard gossip she "wasn't all there," that the camp had driven her mad.

59   "Gentlemen! Tell me your wishes and I will ask the watergod for you when our pool is finished!" she shouted as they left the yard.

60   Dixon had fashioned a wooden stool from scrap lumber and also had made a platform of slatted wood to set on the metal bottom for protection from the heat. He put them in the tub, raising the water level up to three-fourths full. Outside, he had piled three boxes—like stairs—so Yuki could climb in. He was anxious, worried she might fall or even be boiled. The tub looked like a witch's cauldron to him. But his grandmother was shuffling around the yard, a busy pigeon checking the temperature and stoking the fire. He knew she, more than anybody, could take care of herself.

61   "O furo ready, Dixie-chan. Go now. I take bath."

62   Yuki took off the yukata and hung it on a peg attached to the fence. The air cut into her naked body. Sucking in her breath, she quickly discarded the getas and stepped up on the boxes, grasping the tub's metal edge. She swung one leg over the rim and felt for the stool with her foot. Finding it stable, she stepped down and brought the other leg into the tub, raising the water level to her breasts, barely reaching the nipples. Gingerly she seated herself on the stool and slid her feet across the slatted raft. The water was hot, very hot and in the seated position reached up to her neck. Already she felt pimples of perspiration erupting on her forehead and upper lip.

63   Her head rested below the rim. She was encased in blackness and savored the solitude, a canopy of blinking diamonds overhead the only source of light. The stars seemed to hang so close, she felt she could pluck them like cherries from a tree. Not even the steamy wooden o furo of her childhood in Japan could match this.

64   Yuki stroked her arms under water, softly massaging her bony elbows and hairless armpits. She rolled the flesh of her narrow haunches and thighs, noticing how easily she could grasp a handful of skin. Even the flat breasts, once taut and round with desire and then milk, felt like deflated balloons. Heart twinging at the remembrance of her sensuality, the succulence of youth, she closed her eyes.

65   Her first bath in America came to mind. It was her wedding night, the first night she would sleep with her husband, a stranger she had met only a few days before. She had been a picture bride, married by proxy to Shimizu Jun, youngest son of a stone cutter from a neighboring village. Already immigrated to America seven years earlier, he had earned enough money to pay for a bride's passage.

66   He had met her at the dock in San Francisco, and after a day of travel by wagon, they finally had arrived at the compound of bachelors in San Jose where he had been living. She had worn a kimono for the entire trip, arriving grimy and exhausted and grateful for the o furo the bachelors had fired up. They had anticipated the newlyweds would appreciate a hot soak.

67   Yuki recalled the bath ritual. While Jun poured buckets of boiling water into a large wooden tub partially filled with cold water, she washed her face, scrubbing away white rice powder. He removed his cotton yukata and began soaping himself. She had kept eyes downcast, trying not to look directly at him. He was her husband but still a stranger. She had scarcely seen his face, and now she would be sharing o furo with him.

68   Steam and smoke clouded the night air. He sat down on a small wooden stool to wash his feet. Hesitantly, she had moved next to him and washed his back with a cotton cloth. His muscled, yet smooth back, felt hard. With a small basin, she scooped water from the tub and poured it over him, rinsing away the soap.

69   They didn't speak. He stood up and stepped into the tub, his cool body sending hisses of steam as he sat down in the hot water. He beckoned for Yuki to join him. She took off her yukata and sat on the stool he had just left and scrubbed herself with a strong smelling yellow soap and cloth. She was shivering.

70   Water spilled over the sides and onto pebbles covering the ground as she slipped into the tub. She sat down, facing him with legs bent. Their legs pressed against each other, and she could feel his taut calves and hairless skin. Through the mist, she saw sweat roll down his cheeks and drip into the water. Her own sweat slipped down her forehead and stung her eyes. Afraid and excited, she felt her heart thumping. She wondered if Jun could feel its throb through the water.

71   A cool wind whistled into the drum. Her eyes snapped open. Slightly embarrassed by the sensual reminiscence, she stood up and peered over the edge into the yard. Where was Dixon? Another gust forced her to sit down again. Gathering clouds had not yet covered the moon, but the stars had lost their brilliance. She stared at the milky disc, imagining its rays stroking her body like a masseuse's hand. The

light engulfed her whole body . . . the tub . . . then the yard and barracks. She saw it envelop the block, the fire-break, the camp . . . the country . . . even the world!

72   Softly and quietly, snow began falling. Delicate flakes floated from the now dark sky. Yuki studied an intricate flake as it descended, following the wafer of ice—so full of its own life and beauty, so unaware of the imminent end when its free-falling journey from heaven would finish in a metal drum filled with hot water. She watched the flake flutter close to her face. It seemed to dance and jump, almost mischievously. Then it fell into the water near her breasts.

73   "Obachan!" Dixon shouted through the open door. "Are you Okay?"

74   "Me Okay," she shouted back. "I get out. Your turn o furo. This bath number one bath, Dixie-chan. Best o furo in camp."

75   Dixon closed the door, allowing privacy for his tiny grandmother, who was rising up through the steam.

AFTERWARDS

Vocabulary

internment, translucent, communal, martyrdom, inherited, cajole, tinge, futon, mantra, enclosure, plaintive, cauldron, succulence, masseuse. Add all of the above words to your vocabulary log, and then look up antonyms and synonyms for as many words as you can. (You will be using this list later on in a group activity, so be as thorough as possible.)

Content

1. Where does Wakatsuki Houston's story take place? What effect does Yuki's living environment have on her?

2. What was the significance of Yuki's dream? What did she dream about?

3. Why does Yuki desperately want a furo (a bath)? Explain your perception of the symbolic and literal use of water in the story. What does Yuki recall as she bathes?

Style and Structure

1. How does Wakatsuki Houston structure her narrative story? What does it reveal and when?

2. Explain the effect of Wakatsuki Houston's use of occasional Japanese words in the story. How does she tend to define them? When she does not define Japanese words, how does she keep from confusing her readers?

3. Illustrate how vividly and strategically Wakatsuki Houston develops Yuki's character in this story. How do descriptive sentences along with the tone create a delicate, sensual, overall picture of Yuki?

Collaborative Explorations

For a collaborative project, do some research about internment camps, paying particular attention to (1) where they were located, (2) what the physical characteristics of the camps were like, (3) and how the natural environment (e.g., climate) made internment more than just relocation camps, which the government justified in the name of national security. Write up your findings in the form of a collaborative report. Have each member of the group responsible for a particular area of research so that everyone contributes equally to the project. Finally, as a group, revise and edit your report.

Writing Assignments

1. Write a narrative story about something your own grandmother, great-aunt, or a female "elder" in your family did, thereby demonstrating her power, determination, and resourcefulness in a bleak situation.

2. Prepare a paper discussing the process you or someone you know used to build (a fence, shack, bathroom, house) or to create (a scythe, a skateboard) out of objects that were either thrown away by others or else found in nature. Use transitions and linking devices to indicate clearly the procedure for completing your project.

Thematic Reading Cross-Links: Compare and contrast social environments as discussed in Wakatsuki Houston's essay and Ishmael Reed's essay, "Ground Zero" from Chapter 4, Stereotypes and Social Barriers.

Movie Cross-Links: See *Woman in the Dunes* in the Film Links for this chapter for a vision of village life in rural Japan.

A Fate Worse Than War

Andrew Lam

ANDREW LAM is an associate editor with the Pacific News Service, a short story writer, and a regular commentator on National Public Radio (NPR). He was born in Saigon, Vietnam, and came to the United States when he was eleven years old. His awards include the Society of Professional Journalist Outstanding Young Journalist Award (1993), the Media Alliance Meritorious Award, the World Affairs Council's Excellence in International Journalism Award (1992), the Rockefeller Fellowship in UCLA (1992), and the Asian American Journalist Association National Award (1993; 1995). He was honored and profiled on KQED television in May 1996 during Asian American heritage month. Lam is currently working on his first short story collection. He has also co-edited *Once Upon a Dream . . . : The Vietnamese American Experience*. In "A Fate Worse Than War," Lam examines the Mekong Delta Plan for a series of dams in Vietnam. He dubs the plan "a disaster in the making," with consequences more devastating to the Vietnamese people and their natural environment than the Vietnam War.

ALLUSIONS

Huyen Thanh Quang: Vietnam's most celebrated female poet.

1   DANANG—From where Vietnam's most celebrated woman poet, Huyen Thanh Quang, once stood overlooking the Hai Van pass, there are now burned patches of forest. Where rocks, clouds, leaves, flowers and trees once filled the poet's eyes, today rickety American-made army trucks, loaded with freshly cut timber, head toward the port of Danang.

2   Signs posted along the fringe of Vietnam's dwindling jungles and woodlands threaten jail sentences and fines for any act of deforestation. But the Vietnamese Communist regime, long weakened by regionalism and corruption, can barely control the relentless destruction of the country's forests, which are home to some of the most spectacular wild species in Asia, including the Java rhinoceros, dagger-horned goat, as well as newly discovered animals previously unknown to Western science.

3   Since the country's reunification 20 years ago, Vietnam's population has nearly doubled to 72 million and is expected to reach 82 million by the end of this century. One out of three Vietnamese depends on forestry and forest products for a livelihood. Each year, an estimated 500,000 acres of forest are destroyed. At this rate, Vietnam will have no forest left by the early part of the 21st century. "Economic survival overwhelms any long-term views of environmental preservation," said Le Doan of the Ministry of Construction. "Besides, environmentalism (moi truong) is not a household word in Vietnam."

4   "In the last two decades, Vietnam's forest has shrunk from 51 million acres to 22 million acres," said Michel Gautier, a United Nations Development Program official in Hanoi. Less than one million acres were destroyed during the war with America, while 13 million have been destroyed as a result of population pressures.

5   "If people continue to cut down more forest . . . it will be a catastrophe for this country," said Francis Rinville of the UN Food and Agricultural Organization. As Vietnam's forests shrink, he warned, soil erosion, dwindling mangrove forests, mudslides and weakening harvests, combined with heavy monsoons, will prove an ecological disaster worse than the war.

6   Nonetheless, the government has a laissez-faire attitude toward environmental protection. In 1993, city officials in Ho Chi Minh City transformed a woodland area near the city into a resort development with a 300-room luxury hotel and two 18-hole golf courses.

7   Occasionally loggers are severely beaten and sent to re-education camps for "crimes against the state," but, as Dang Nguyen, a Danang taxi driver, argued, "They should arrest government officials who sell tons of wood to the Japanese, Taiwanese and Thais, not the people who collect wood to build their beds and cook their rice."

8   French businessman Michon Christian fears the social contract between the state and its people has broken down in Vietnam. "Unless Vietnam's economy develops with the welfare of the people in mind," he warned, "any effort to protect environmental resources won't work in the long run."

9   "People no longer listen to the government," Nguyen said, explaining the failure of the state's population-control plan. "For the poor, having children is the only luxury we will ever have."

10   Along the once tree-lined road leading from the mountain city of Dalat, Nga Le, a widowed mother of three, collects firewood to sell. "We never waste anything," she said. "My children collect paper, plastic, metal and glass to recycle—but we are still committing crimes against the state." Le must walk further now to collect wood, although she recalls a time when the hills were beautiful instead of "bald and muddy."

11   "I remember when I was young," Le said wistfully, "there were lots of trees and tigers. Now there's just a lot of people in there, talking and cutting down trees."

AFTERWARDS

Vocabulary

deforestation, laissez-faire. After reviewing the use of these vocabulary words in context, write two original sentences using each.

Content

   1. What has been the Vietnamese government's main focus since the reunification of North and South Vietnam? Why does Lam assert that it's a disaster in the making?

2. How many Vietnamese workers depend on the forestry industry for employment? Why, in the long run, might this be a problem?

3. Lam quotes a poet, government officials, UN administrators, a taxi driver, a French businessman, and a widow. Why do you think he includes such a range of testimonies?

Style and Structure

1. How does Lam's essay title, "A Fate Worse Than War," emphasize the gravity of his topic? What could be worse than the death, destruction, and desecration of war?

2. In what way do facts and statistics—as well as future projections—assist the author in arguing his case?

3. Lam originally wrote this article for *Earth Island Journal*. How do his shorter paragraphs reflect a journalistic style? Regardless of style, in what ways does he remain committed to the principles of exposition?

Collaborative Activities

Examine Lam's article and, as a group, assess it in terms of (1) purpose, (2) occasion, (3) likely audience, and (4) evidence. Next, discuss how situations different from and yet similar to the exploitation or destruction of natural resources in Vietnam are affecting human lives and a balanced ecosystem in other parts of the world. Finally, share your group's insights with the rest of the class in a five-minute presentation.

Writing Activities

1. In many respects, Lam's essay foresaw an ecological disaster in the making. Go to the Internet and look up articles written since 1995 on the Mekong Delta Plan. Next, write an essay comparing and contrasting Lam's predictions to what has happened since he initially published this essay. Were critics justified when they accused him of being an alarmist?

2. Write a paper where you argue that one fate would be worse than another horrible situation. You may want to model your title after Lam's (e.g., "A Fate Worse Than . . ."). Illustrate how and why you arrived at ethical, reasonable conclusions about each fate with evidence gained through personal experience, observations of others, and readings.

Thematic Cross-Links: Read "Minnesota's Sensible Plan," a satire by Garrison Keillor, the next essay in this chapter, for an appreciation of the irony behind the rhetoric of progress.

Movie Cross-Links: See *Clear Cut* and *The Burning Season*—listed in the Film Links at the end of this chapter—for movies dealing with destructive logging and individuals trying to stop it.

Minnesota's Sensible Plan

Garrison Keillor

Born in 1942, author-humorist **GARRISON KEILLOR** began his successful writing and broadcasting career after graduating from the University of Minnesota. Keillor received nationwide attention for his radio program, *A Prairie Home Companion*, broadcast every Saturday evening on NPR. His printed works include *Happy to Be Here* (1982), *Lake Wobegon Days* (1985), *Leaving Home: A Collection of Lake Wobegon Stories* (1987), *We Are Still Married* (1989), *WLT: A Radio Romance* (1992), *The Book of Guys* (1993), *Wobegon Boy* (1998), and *Me: By Jimmy (Big Boy) Valente* (1999). Keillor offers audiences a rarefied style of homespun humor, frequently distinguished by tongue-in-cheek remarks, understatement, and irony. In the following essay initially published in the September 11, 1995, edition of *Time*, Keillor expresses his belief that the "water resource management team" is anything but sensible. Therefore, he uses satire and irony to point out the folly of the water diversion project. By approaching the issue from the standpoint of a supporter, he disarms his real opponent. Then, Keillor offers an extreme case scenario to demonstrate the destructive horrors such a project would have on the environment, now and in the future.

ALLUSIONS

Cortés: A reference to Hernando Cortés, a 16th-century Spanish conquistador (a conqueror), who was responsible for overthrowing the Aztec rulers of Mexico, claiming the land for Spain.

Aztecs: Native American people who lived in present-day Mexico and Central America; their highly advanced culture was overthrown by Hernando Cortés.

Suez Canal: A canal in the Middle East that separates Egypt from the Sinai Peninsula. The canal reduces the "sea distance" between Western Europe and India by 5,000 miles.

Lake Superior: The largest freshwater lake in the world, located in the Great Lakes region in North America.

1   This fall, in an unmarked office in the subbasement of the Minnesota state capitol, a team of resource-management planners is fine-tuning the biggest water-diversion project in the history of mankind and the largest transfer of wealth since Cortés acquired the Aztec empire.

2   Its code name is Excelsior, and the preliminary plan alone fills a portfolio the size of a breadbox. If all goes according to plan, on Nov. 4, 1999, the Governor of Minnesota will stand on a platform in Duluth and pull a golden lanyard, opening the gates of the Superior Diversion Canal, a concrete waterway the size of the Suez. Water from Lake Superior will flood into the canal at a rate of 50 billion gal. per hour and go south.

3   It will flow into the St. Croix River, to the Mississippi, south to an aqueduct at Keokuk, Iowa, and from there west to the Colorado River and into the Grand Canyon and many other southwestern canyons, filling them up to the rims—enough water to supply the parched Southwest from Los Angeles to Santa Fe for more than 50 years.

4   In the past, Lake Superior, which represents one-tenth of the world's supply of freshwater, was considered "inviolable," but with environmental groups in retreat and a Republican Congress favoring "wise use" of natural resources, the Excelsior project is moving full tilt toward opening day.

5   What will Excelsior mean? It means that America's Sunbelt retirees will be able to shower, flush toilets and have lush, green lawns for decades to come. And it means that Minnesota will earn pots of money. Typically, residents of the Southwest today pay up to $45 per 1,000 cu. ft. of water. That price may rise as the aquifers of the Western plains recede and more rivers are diverted to irrigation. But assuming the price remains at $45 per 1,000 cu. ft., the value of Lake Superior would be an astounding $20 trillion. In addition, Minnesota would receive current market prices for the fish.

6   After deducting the cost of canal and aqueduct construction, the net profit for Minnesota will be $17.5 trillion, or $3.8 million per person. Placed in a trust fund earning 6% interest, divided fifty–fifty between individual citizen and state treasury, the sale of Lake Superior would provide an annual sum of more than $100,000 to every Minnesota resident.

7   To many Americans, whose only knowledge of the North Star State is that it gets cold in the winter and produces cheese, it will come as a surprise to wake up one morning in 2004 and read in the newspaper, HALF OF U.S. ECONOMY NOW IN HANDS OF MINNESOTA. But there is something inevitable about economics, and $17.5 trillion talks in a loud, clear voice.

8   Overnight Minnesota will be transformed from corn belt to money belt. Gigantic glass skyscrapers will rise in downtown St. Paul, home of the nation's wealthiest state legislature, and as the money floods in, Minnesotans will look for acquisitions: IBM,

UPS, USX, GTE, Time Warner, Minnecorp, J.P. Olson, Chase Minnesota. Presidential candidates will hold their big, $100,000-a-plate fund raisers in Minneapolis, will pledge their support for water diversification and mention that, conservative though they be, they've always had a soft spot in their hearts for Hubert Humphrey.

9   The term "Wall Street" will become archaic slang, like Route 66—instead we'll refer to "Marquette Avenue," home of the Minnesota Stock Exchange. The big entrepreneurs—the Buffetts, the Eisners, the Gateses—will jet off to Minnesota to line up financing for their future moves. And one day Donald Trump will discover that he is owned—lock, stock and roulette wheel—by Lutheran Brotherhood and must renegotiate his debt load with a committee of silent Norwegians who don't understand why anyone would pay more than $120 for a suit.

10   Most Americans have never imagined such a project, and that's why they have so many questions about it.

> **Q**: Will Excelsior require state or local tax abatements, so the taxpayers wind up subsidizing the whole thing?
>
> **A**: No way.
>
> **Q**: Isn't there a danger of environmentalists blocking the project with a bunch of nuisance lawsuits?
>
> **A**: $17.5 trillion buys some powerful legal talent.
>
> **Q**: Won't Minnesota be forced to share this windfall with its neighbors, such as Wisconsin, Michigan and Ontario?
>
> **A**: See answer above.
>
> **Q**: Whatever is Minnesota going to do with all that money?
>
> **A**: Create a social utopia, of course: a state with vast libraries, sports centers, every home wired for interactive television, cradle-to-coffin health care and unemployment benefits equal to your previous year's salary paid until you're 68.
>
> **Q**: What will you do when the money runs out?
>
> **A**: It won't. Minnesota is sitting on a lot of water. It has more lakes than there are names to call them—for example, there are 40 Round Lakes, 33 Big Lakes, 19 Sandy Lakes and 14 Green Lakes—so Minnesota can earn billions more by selling off these duplicates.
>
> **Q**: How can I become a Minnesota resident?
>
> **A**: Thirty days is all it takes. That and four recommendations from current residents.

11   Lake Superior is a valuable asset, but the Superior Canyon will prove to be even more valuable than the lake was, according to people familiar with the situation.

12   "Look," says one of the resource-management planners, jabbing his finger at a graph. "Lake Superior isn't much of a tourist attraction. Who wants to come and look at 31,820 sq. mi. of water? Nobody. The water's too cold for swimming, and frankly, lakes don't draw like canyons do. Ask Lake Mead. Lakes only draw fishermen, a bunch of lowly guys who drive in, buy a six-pack of beer and a bologna sandwich. Canyons draw families. And the Superior Canyon, without a doubt, will outdraw

the Grand. It's bigger, for one thing, plus it has islands and sites of famous shipwrecks. You'll have a monorail tour of the sites with crumpled hulls of ships. Very respectful. But a major draw."

13   By 2006, Lake Superior will be gone, and its islands will be wooded buttes rising above the fertile coulees of the basin. A river will run through it, the Riviera River, and great glittering casinos like the Corn Palace, the Voyageur, the Big Kawishiwi, the Tamarack Sands, the Clair de Loon, the Sileaux, the Garage Mahal, the Glacial Sands, the Temple of Denture, the Golden Mukooda will lie across the basin like diamonds in a dish. Family-style casinos, with theme parks and sensational water rides on the rivers cascading over the north rim, plus high-rise hotels and time-share condominiums. Currently there are no building restrictions in Lake Superior; developers will be free to create high-rises in the shape of grain elevators, casinos shaped like casserole dishes, accordions, automatic washers. Celebrities will flock to the canyon. You'll see guys on the Letterman show who, when Dave asks, "Where you going next month, pal?" will say, "I'll be in Minnesota, Dave, playing four weeks at the Pokegama." Tourism will jump 1,000%. Guys on the red-eye from L.A. to New York will look out and see a blaze of light off the left wing and ask the flight attendant, "What's that?" And she'll say, "Minnesota, of course."

14   What will Minnesota's vast wealth and pre-eminence mean for the rest of the country?

15   Almost nothing but good. Minnesota is a state of public-spirited and polite people, where you can find excellent cappuccino and Thai food and great bookstores yet live on a quiet, treelined street and send your kids to public school. When a state this good hits the jackpot, it can only be an inspiration to everybody. Of course, there is bound to be resentment. But in the end, our prosperity will benefit everyone.

16   The media will be transformed as Minnesota buys up networks and cable companies. News will be less about politics and more about civilization—history, art, literature and sweet corn. And creamed onions. The movie business, as Minnesota buys major studios, will start to make pictures in which snow occurs as a normal part of life. Movies in which there is less machine gunning and car bombing and more scenes in which people enjoy a good meal and tell jokes.

17   The Superior Canyon project can help bring the country to its senses, putting a big chunk of the economy into the hands of modest and sensible people, people who have been through some hard winters and are the better for it. But winter isn't the only reason Minnesotans are as good as they are; it's also because of something in the drinking water. Try some and you'll see. That's why the lake was named Superior.

AFTERWARDS

Vocabulary

lanyard, aqueduct, inviolable, aquifers, recede, entrepreneurs, renegotiate, roulette wheel, abatements, subsidizing, Utopia, interactive, monorail, pre-eminence, cappuccino, condominiums. Write a short composition about "opportunity" using at least seven of today's vocabulary words. When you review your composition, supply an appositive phrase (a noun or noun phrase used to rename another noun) with at least five of the new words in your piece.

Content

1. What is the essence of "Minnesota's Sensible Plan"? What are its various parts, and who will be affected by it?

2. When and where does Keillor's attitude toward Minnesota's "sensible plan" become clear to you?

3. Explain the question/answer format of paragraph 11. What purpose does it serve? What does it reveal to Keillor's readers?

Style and Structure

1. How does Keillor anticipate reader questions and respond to them as he discusses Minnesota's "sensible plan"?

2. In what way does Keillor blend understatement, hyperbole, and irony in his essay in order to create a distinct "style"?

3. Identify some specific instances in which Keillor appeals to his reader's sense of ethics and logic. How does he poke fun at "emotionally appealing" information?

Collaborative Explorations

"What is significant about the environmental impact of large corporations—like IBM, UPS or AOL Time/Warner—on American culture? Assemble in small groups and do some collaborative research by having each member look up information on a nationally known corporation. Then get together, share your findings, and have the group recorder make a master list of environmental impacts to submit to your instructor and/or to present to class."

Writing Assignments

1. Select a social issue needing public attention or a call to action (e.g., more freeways, larger parking lots, fewer—or more—benefits for millionaires, faster cars, lower taxes, more social programs, and so on). Then outline a proposal that modestly proposes a method for informing people about a social "need" as well as a way of addressing it (the call to action). Before you begin, reread Keillor's essay, noting how what he says and how he expresses himself both work to achieve his goal as a writer.

2. Using satire and humor to your best advantage, write an essay exposing how an unfortunate incident is anything but unfortunate or how a "sensible plan" is just about everything but "sensible."

Thematic Reading Cross-Links: Compare Keillor's satiric essay to Dave Barry's "Why Sports Is a Drag" in Chapter 8, Popular Culture.

Movie Cross-Links: For another example of how irony and satire illustrate human folly and even lead to a renewed outlook on environmental issues, see *Local Hero* in the Film Links at the end of this chapter.

The Visual Connection: Cartoon/Photograph Writing Activities

1. Describe both of the following pictures: Footprints in the Sand and View of the Washington State Coast. What mood does each picture convey? What details in each photograph suggest a story about something that happened? Finally, compare and contrast both photos, explaining which one you like better and why.

Footprints in the Sand

View of the Washington State Coast

2. Compare Rachel Carson's remark (see Observations and Opinions) about human arrogance in thinking humans can control nature and their environment to the cartoon below by Gary Larson, Animal Waste Management. How does the cartoon place human waste management in another light?

Animal Waste Management

Film Links: Environments

1. Choose any two films from the following list and explain how they communicate a certain conception of the nature of nature. Do the movies communicate a common mood, tone, or point of view? Are these environmentalist films? To what extent were you able to make a connection to your own experience?

2. Pick one or more of the films and analyze how it portrays the nonhuman world. Use a combination of expository and argumentative techniques to develop your composition. (*Hint*: You should attempt to use as many concrete nouns and verbs as you can to bring a sense of life to your discussion.)

3. Refer to Writing About Film in the Appendix in order to approach the topic "nature and the environment." As a result of using the starter questions in the Appendix, what do you have to say about nature and film? Do directors highly stylize or romanticize the grace and goodness of nature, or do they present nature as cold, heartless, and unforgiving? Write an essay explaining your thoughts, illustrating your insights with specific references to one or more of the following films.

Woman in the Dunes (Japan, Hiroshi Teshigahara, 1964). A scientist finds himself trapped in a village surrounded by sand dunes.

Never Cry Wolf (Canada/USA, Carroll Ballard, 1983). A young biologist studies wolves and himself in the mountains of Alaska.

Where the Green Ants Dream (Germany/Australia, Werner Herzog, 1984). An Australian geologist strives to understand the aboriginal view of time, space, and nature.

Local Hero (Scotland, Bill Forsyth, 1984). A Houston yuppie attempts to purchase a Scottish coastal village for an oil refinery and discovers a way of life beyond price.

The Emerald Forest (USA, John Boorman, 1985). A young boy is kidnapped by a tribe in the Amazon jungle.

Gorillas in the Mist (USA, Michael Apted, 1988). Based on the life of Dian Fossey and her study of gorillas in East Africa.

The Bear (France, Jean-Jacques Annaud, 1989). The life of a young bear filmed from the bear's point of view.

Mindwalk (USA, Bernt Capra, 1991). A scientist, politician, and poet debate the nature of nature.

Baraka (USA, Ron Fricke, 1992). An experimental documentary that uses cinematography and music to create a global vision, and represents the incalculable variety of events going on simultaneously around the world at all times.

Clearcut (Canada, Richard Bugajski, 1992). A Canadian Indian resorts to torture to save his land from logging.

A River Runs Through It (USA, Robert Redford, 1992). Montana, fly-fishing, and family life are examined at the turn of the 20th century.

The Burning Season (USA, John Frankenheimer, 1994). Chico Mendes tries to organize Brazilian peasants to save the rain forest.

The Beach (USA, Danny Boyle, 2000). A young American traveling in Asia seeks a new life on an island that promises to be a utopian community living close to nature, but finds that things are not what they seem.

Additional Writing Assignments

1. Write an essay in which you defend the preservation of wilderness. What opposing arguments would you have to answer?

2. What do you imagine people seem like to an animal? Write an essay describing what people refer to as progress (e.g., building a bridge, damming up a natural lake, leveling an orchard to build a housing tract, and so on) from an animal's point of view.

3. Compare and contrast two nature shows on television. Do they tend to follow a similar format? How did the shows begin and end? What conclusion(s) might you be able to reach as a result of your comparative study of the two nature shows?

4. Construct an essay in which you compare and contrast a natural disaster to a human-initiated disaster. Are natural disasters really "acts of God," as insurance agents so fondly refer to them?

5. Write an essay explaining what would be needed to construct and maintain an ideal living environment at one with the laws of nature? How and why will people buy into your society? How would you address people who claim, "I have the right to do whatever I want," when such an attitude might destroy the moral or ethical foundation of your society?

Cyberspace and Technology

Observations and Opinions

Despite claims by digital utopians that the internet is an ideally democratic, discrimination free space, a space without gender, race, age, disability and so on, a quick visit to both textual and graphical chatspaces such as Lambda Moo and Club Connect will reveal these identity positions are still very much in evidence.

—LISA NAKAMURA, FROM "HEAD HUNTING IN CYBERSPACE"

Beware of the technological juggernaut, reckon the terrible costs, understand the worlds being lost in the world being gained, reflect on the price of the machine and its systems in your life, pay attention to the natural world and its increasing destruction, resist the seductive catastrophe of industrialism.

—KIRKPATRICK SALE FROM *REBELS AGAINST THE FUTURE: LESSONS FOR THE COMPUTER AGE*

The word "robot," first introduced by the Czech writer Karel Capek, is derived from the Slavic root for "worker." But it signifies a machine rather than a human worker. Robots, especially robots in space, have often received derogatory notices in the press.

—CARL SAGAN FROM "IN DEFENSE OF ROBOTS"

It was on a dreary night of November that I beheld the accomplishment of my toils. With an anxiety that almost amounted to agony, I collected the instruments of life around me, that I might infuse a spark of being into the lifeless thing that lay at my feet. It was already one in the morning; the rain pattered dismally against the panes, and my candle was nearly burnt out, when, by the glimmer of the half-extinguished light, I saw the dull yellow eye of the creature open; it breathed hard, and a convulsive motion agitated its limbs.

—MARY SHELLEY FROM *FRANKENSTEIN*

Once met by the public with wild enthusiasm for their potential benefits to humanity, X-rays, radium, nuclear energy, and nuclear arms now generate fear and foreboding as their unforeseen side effects became known.

—KORI QUINTANA FROM "THE PRICE OF POWER: LIVING IN THE NUCLEAR AGE"

Observations and Opinions: Reading/Writing Activities

1. After considering what Lisa Nakamura says about the reality of online chat rooms (their claims and what they actually value and provide), explain why you agree or disagree that computers represent the great social equalizer.

2. Compare and contrast Kirkpatrick Sale and Kori Quintana's technology quotations. Then, assess the reasoning behind each author's point of view. Finally, demonstrate how Kori Quintana's quotation from "The Price of Power: Living in the Nuclear Age" affirms Sale's citation from "Rebels Against the Future: Lessons for the Computer Age."

3. Carl Sagan contends that robots in outer space have received negative comments and undue criticism from the press. Why might you agree or disagree with him? Have you read any articles that criticize the use of robots lately? How might Hollywood's depiction of robots affect people's opinion of them? Cite a few representative examples to support your position.

4. Write a detailed journal entry in which you explore the positive and the negative aspects of technological advancements in the computer age. What are the benefits of cyberspace and computers over pens and typewriters for the composition student? How has technology improved or interfered with your healthy growth and development? (You might want to consider how Mary Shelley's quote from *Frankenstein*, arguably the first science fiction novel ever written, reflects both the fascination and horror at the potential progress in technology.)

Introduction

Cyberspace, the realm of the Internet, is the most recent frontier for technology. Cyber comes from the Greek prefix *kuber*, meaning "govern." Today, cyber is defined as "governing with technology or mechanics," and it has become a common prefix for pop-culture jargon such as "cybernetics" (the communication and control processes—the governing principles—in biology, mechanics, and electronics), "cyberpunk" (a type of science fiction in which computers rule; also, reference to a hacker or computer privacy freak), "cybersex" (interactive computer-enhanced sex often related to specific online magazines or chat rooms), and "cybercafés" (coffeehouses that serve high-end java and feature computers hooked up with the Internet so patrons can surf the Net while drinking coffee).

Before the world of the Internet and cyberspace arose, technology—the art or craft of inventing devices for human comfort or increasing the productivity of machines—had both inflamed and excited minds for centuries. Steam engines, telegraphs, clocks, watches, cannons, siege towers, photographs, even basic locks, are the results of some sort of technology. As we move into the 21st century, the words "cyberspace" and "technology" are frequently spoken about as if they were one and the same. To be sure, "cyberspace" has evolved out of modern technology, but so have many other conveniences and necessities such as automobiles, television sets, cameras, electronic tools, and so on. Cyberspace and technology have been intimately tied to popular culture. From bicycles to airplanes, steam engines to solar-powered vehicles and heating systems, radar units to communications satellites, the objects of technological advancement are so integrated in most lifestyles that they are frequently taken for granted.

Just how dependent are you on cyberspace and technology for work, entertainment, and travel? Imagine living with no electrical power for two weeks, during which time solar batteries did not work and gasoline, diesel fuel, and natural gas used to fuel vehicles and operate generators were unavailable. Would you feel helpless or inconvenienced? How would you adapt to the situation? Then, take this situation a step further by imagining that, in addition to everything else, anything mechanical such as a watch, a telephone, a conveyer belt, or a lock did not work. How would commerce and trade proceed? How could security systems be enforced?

The question "What if . . . ?" has plagued technological advances, but not without reason. The fear of technological advances such as cloning cells—genetically engineering livestock for human consumption—for instance, worries many people because its long-term effects are either unknown or ignored. Granted, some people simply dislike change. Others, however, justify their rejection of some technology today on moral and ethical grounds (e.g., efficient killing machines like nuclear bombs, laser "death-ray" space satellites that destroy rather than advance "civilized" cultures). In another instance, electricity, the technology that brought the Frankenstein monster to life, was relatively new when Mary Shelley wrote her famous Gothic novel in 1815; although she may not condemn the possibilities of electricity as a new source of energy, she does point to its possible misuse.

The following readings observe cyberspace and technology from several viewpoints, some raising questions such as "What if . . . ?" or "What has happened?" and others simply informing or arguing the pros and cons of cyberspace and technological "advance" to readers. While Kurt Vonnegut does not really propose a cautious approach toward embracing technological conveniences in "Technology and Me," his brief, amusing composition demonstrates that he has no real need for them either. As far as Vonnegut is concerned, "We are on earth to fart around, and don't let anybody tell you any different."

"The Robotniks," Vladlen Bakhnov's short story, on the other hand, places technological advances and human beings in the future, a setting where robots are imitated and revered by the young. Robotniks, like the beatniks of the 1950s, are "hip," but there is something wrong or menacing about a society that downplays the importance of human relationships. Students in the story "learned to imitate the gait and angular movements of robots and to stare blankly without blinking: their faces became as expressionless and impassive as the flat, vacant faces of robots."

Grace Mateo acknowledges the essential role of cyberspace in our modern society, for it "has made a global village for us all." Still, as she appraises cyberspace and technology, Mateo realizes a downside to "real-time" progress. For instance, sometimes we become "closer to our e-mail friend in Australia than our neighbor down the street." Moreover, on the Net where faces become unimportant, true identity often becomes buried beneath an alias or a role (e.g., 70-year-old men and women who play the part of teenagers in chat rooms). "At best, such deception is used for the entertainment of harmless individuals. At worst, it is the tool of sexual predators seeking young victims."

In "Life and Death on the Web" by Joshua Quittner, the fear the Director suggested in "Robotniks" about the power of machines over the human mind resurfaces as Quittner discusses how "Every time this country extrudes any significant bit of evil at its fringes," his editors send him to the Internet to locate its source. Ironically, in the case of the Heaven's Gate Cult, some people (not Quittner) hold the Internet responsible for assembling people into a "suicide cult." Thus, the tool of ultimate information becomes the instrument of destruction.

No matter what position you take on cyberspace and technology, the fact remains: Both are here to stay. Just how we respond to innovations in the future, however, remains to be seen. Carefully go through "Gathering Thoughts: Prereading Inquiries" to take an inventory on where you presently stand on cyberspace and technological advances of all kinds. You might review your list from time to time, and, at the conclusion of the chapter, go over your initial inventory, noting any additional perception on a topic or issue you gleaned from your reading.

Gathering Thoughts: Prereading Inquiries

1. Can you ever have more of one thing without less of another? When we add a new form of technology to our lives—like television—we gain something, but we give up other things. Apply your answer to other technological advancements.

2. To what extent do computers and the Internet play an important role in your life?

3. What is the difference between a robot and a human being? Offer specific, representative examples to illustrate your position. (See *2001: A Space Odyssey*, in Film Links at the end of the chapter.)

4. Do you ever explore cyberspace? If so, where do you go? With whom do you communicate? If you do not explore cyberspace, then make a point of logging onto the Internet at your college technology center or library and "surf the Net."

5. Advocates for the use of the Internet like to say, "Information wants to be free," implying that there should be no restrictions at all on what is available online. Do you agree that freedom of speech means that no form of censorship on the Internet is acceptable?

6. How have machines and computers desensitized people toward each other—or have they? Explain how you arrived at your present attitude toward machines and computers.

7. Do you agree with those who claim that the place to get information in the future will be the Internet? What are the potential strengths of the Internet as a source of information? Do the strengths outweigh the weaknesses? How or why?

8. How might you or someone you know be affected as computers, cyberspace, and databases open up new possibilities for businesses and the government? How will automated efficiency lead to job reduction or downsizing?

9. Make a list of all the instruments of technology you take for granted that require power (e.g., toaster, hair dryer, CD player, cell phone, television, and so on). Then circle all the items you consider "necessities" for living and underline all luxuries.

10. Who benefits most from technological advancements and cyberspace, and who profits least?

Technology and Me

Kurt Vonnegut, Jr.

KURT VONNEGUT, JR., was born in Indianapolis in 1922, and prior to getting drafted in World War II, he studied biochemistry at Cornell. During the war, Vonnegut was captured by the Germans and held prisoner in an underground slaughterhouse in Dresden. He would later draw on his Dresden experience when he wrote the surrealistic dark comedy *Slaughterhouse Five* (1969). Vonnegut's works frequently blend science fiction concepts and satire to comment on the human race and the tyrannies of automation. His numerous novels include: *Player Piano* (1952), *The Sirens of Titan* (1959), *Mother Night* (1961), *Cat's Cradle* (1963), *God Bless You, Mr. Rosewater* (1965), *Breakfast of Champions* (1973), *Slapstick* (1976), *Jailbird* (1979), *Deadeye Dick* (1982), *Hocus Pocus* (1990), and *Timequake* (1997). Vonnegut's collections of short stories and essays include *Welcome to the Monkey House* (1968), *Wampeters, Foma and Granfalloons* (1974), *Palm Sunday* (1981), *Fates Worse Than Death: An Autobiographical Collage of the 1980s* (1991), and *God Bless You, Dr. Kevorkian* (1999). He has also written a play, *Happy Birthday Wanda June* (1970), as well as television scripts. The following excerpt was taken from "Technology and Me," which originally appeared in *Technology Inc.* (November 1995).

1   I work at home, and if I wanted to, I could have a computer right by my bed, and I'd never have to leave it. But I use a typewriter, and afterward I mark up the pages with a pencil. Then I call up this woman named Carol out in Woodstock and say, "Are you still doing typing?" Sure she is, and her husband is trying to track bluebirds out there and not having much luck, and we chitchat back and forth, and I say, "Okay, I'll send you the pages," then I go down the steps and my wife calls, "Where are you going?" "Well," I say, "I'm going to buy an envelope." And she says, "You're not a poor man. Why don't you buy a thousand envelopes! They'll deliver them, and you can put them in the closet." And I say, "Hush." So I go to this newsstand across the street where they sell magazines and lottery tickets and stationery. I have to get in line because there are people buying candy and all that sort of thing, and I talk to them. The woman behind the counter has a jewel between her eyes, and when it's my turn, I ask her if there have been any big winners lately. I get my envelope and seal it up and go to the postal convenience center down the block at the corner of Forty-seventh Street and Second Avenue, where I'm secretly in love with the woman behind the counter. I keep absolutely poker-faced; I never let her know how I feel about her. One time I had my pocket picked in there and got to meet a cop and tell him about it. Anyway, I address the envelope to Carol in Woodstock. I stamp the envelope and

mail it in a mailbox in front of the post office, and I go home. I tell you, we are on earth to fart around, and don't let anybody tell you any different.

AFTERWARDS

Vocabulary

The relatively simple diction in Vonnegut's essay makes it an ideal essay to review sentence variety. Write a journal entry explaining how something is done, using a variety of sentence patterns and transitional devices.

Content

1. What relationship exists between Vonnegut and technology? What does the author find "meaningful"?

2. Does Vonnegut, the author, seem to be the sort of person who is open to change? By his own admission, how does he tend to respond to technological breakthroughs?

3. Summarize Vonnegut's brief composition. Then, to practice sentence variety and draw on your growing vocabulary, paraphrase your summary (write it using different words).

Style and Structure

1. How does the use of a narrative structure and his day's outing enable Vonnegut to comment on the essential role of technology in his life?

2. How might the use of dialogue with various individuals throughout this composition reflect the author's values and interests? Jot down a few lines of additional dialogue that might have been used to develop characters in the story.

3. Characterize Kurt Vonnegut's style of writing. How is it memorable or effective?

Collaborative Explorations

After breaking up into groups of four, pair off with one of the people in your group. Then, together, prepare a team debate—one taking the pro and the other taking the con side of some technological issue. (All four group members will first have to work together to narrow the focus of their common theme.) When your group begins to debate in front of the class, alternate speakers on each side of the debate team (e.g., pro speaker number 1 and pro speaker number 2; con speaker number 1 and con speaker number 2).

Writing Assignments

1. Write an essay detailing a habit you have developed as a result of the availability and addictive nature of a technological gadget (e.g., electronic games—many on-line—computer chat rooms, television, and so on). If possible, begin your essay by explaining why you may have originally been "against" indulging in your topic. Then, show what occurred to make you reevaluate your initial impression, concluding your composition with how you feel about it now.

2. Write an informative process essay explaining how you came to terms or learned to get along with a technological annoyance. Make sure to use plenty of time transitions to lead readers clearly through the sequence of steps you took to reach your objective.

Thematic Reading Cross-Links: Relate Vonnegut's attitude toward progress to Gary Snyder's feelings as expressed in "Back to Nature," in Chapter 6, Environments.

Movie Cross-Links: In this short piece, Vonnegut simply seems to want to enjoy life without all of its technological "conveniences." For a darker view of Vonnegut's outlook toward technology in the 20th century, see *Slaughterhouse Five*, a movie version of his novel by the same name.

Cyberspace Dance Cards and Heartless Modems

Grace Mateo

Although **GRACE MATEO** says her career objective is to obtain practical working experience in the field of Information Technology, her perceptions and skill in the areas of critical thinking, literature, and social sciences give a broad view of life and sensitivity to all aspects of human needs and conveniences. A former Humanities major, Mateo cultivates a wide variety of interests. However, her children, Geoffrey and David, play a major part in her life and strongly influence her concerns about the world in which they live. In the following essay, for instance, she explains how cyberspace has opened doors to the information age, yet cautions that cyberspace in itself is not the final frontier.

1   Technology is a many-splendored thing. Of its many innovations that have affected our lives, the development of cyberspace is arguably the most far-reaching. Business can now be conducted worldwide, 24 hours a day, 7 days a week. News events can be reported from across the continents in a matter of seconds. Yes, cyberspace has made a global village for us all. Or has it, instead, made our village so global that we are closer to our e-mail friend in Australia than our neighbor down the street?

2   Electronic commerce has been recognized by many as a golden opportunity to reach a worldwide market. The advent of the Internet has enabled international trade to occur continuously as never before. Like the California gold rush, however, the majority of entrepreneurs have found cyberspace to be less than the stuff of which dreams are made. The disastrous failure of so many dot com companies and the financial ruin of their respective investors occurred not because of the medium of business itself, but because so many failed to understand how to truly utilize the Internet to its fullest advantage. We are no longer in the industrial age—we are in the information age. Why, then, do these so-called business experts continue to apply the rules of an industrial economy?

3   The ability of cyberspace to convey information in "real-time" has become both a boon and a curse. Fiction and fact alike are transmitted to voracious recipients all over the world. People compete for the distinction of having the latest information on any given topic. Unfortunately, due to the speed in which the information spreads, there often isn't enough time for its actual validity to be verified. In March 2000, 43-year-old Fred Moldofsky caused communications giant Lucent Technologies to lose 7.1 billion dollars off its market cap by posting a fake story on Yahoo! that Lucent's profits were down. Within hours of the fraudulent newsflash, Lucent's stock fell by 3.6% (Cohen). Five months later, a 23-year-old student, Mark Jakob, made $250,000.00 from the stock price drop of Emulex Corporation, a California-based hardware manufacturer. Jakob instigated a 62% drop on Wall Street by posting a press release that Emulex's CEO was going to resign. His hoax caused investors to lose approximately 100 million dollars, but Jakob has since been charged and is now serving time behind bars (Cohen). It's clear that by the time harmful rumors can be quashed, worldwide damage has already been done. It is naïve to believe that all of it can be as easily repaired. For celebrities, it may mean having tarnished reputations, but for hapless, impulsive investors, it could mean financial ruin.

4   One of the most beguiling aspects of cyberspace is that it offers the ability to connect with others in foreign countries while also providing anonymity. The ability for people to communicate with each other across geographical borders is certainly a wondrous thing. Grade schools often encourage students to maintain e-mail friendships with schoolchildren from other countries in order to gain a better understanding of each other's culture. Chat rooms and message boards alike enable people from all over the world to congregate and wax philosophical over every conceivable topic under the sun.

5   The anonymity of the Internet that enables otherwise silent introverts an outlet for communication also enables less scrupulous individuals to assume false

personalities. Plainly said, it would be far more difficult to lie to a person face-to-face than it would be to make "inaccurate" claims online. Think of how hard it is to gauge a person's age strictly through his or her written communication skills. Think of how easy it would be to manipulate vocabulary and style to make one seem years older or younger. At best, such deception is used for the entertainment of harmless individuals. At worst, it is the tool of sexual predators seeking young victims. Former Disney executive Patrick Naughton was arrested for arranging to have sex with a 13-year-old girl he met online, but pleaded not guilty because his actions were grounded in an online fantasy world (Yang). Because of the prevalence of such similar actions, law enforcement individuals have learned to play the same game to trap these criminals. Is the charming teen from London that you chat with every night truly who she says she is, or could she actually be a demented, middle-aged man? She may just be your friendly neighborhood police detective. Internet Romeos beware!

6   Cyberspace offers a unique venue for escapism. As Naughton noted previously, it offers a fantasy world that many find irresistible. Unlike television, Internet access is interactive. According to Kimberly Young, psychologist and author of *Caught in the Net* (the first book on Internet addiction), "Online content is immediate, constant, uncensored, and unregulated" (Yang). Users have control over who they will communicate with, what topics of interest to address, and what countries in the world they want to explore, often without guidance or leaving the comfort and safety of their own homes. Companies lose thousands of dollars in lost productivity because of time employees spend online. Psychologist David Greenfield conducted a study of 1500 companies asking about Internet abuse in the workplace. Companies such as the New York Times Co. and Xerox have dismissed employees for inappropriate e-mails and for accessing offensive websites (Williams). Workers in many other companies have been fired because of excessive time spent on Internet gambling, pornography, and shopping (Yang).

7   Marriages have been destroyed because spouses spend more time with e-mail friends and in chat rooms rather than with each other. There is growing documentation on cases of Internet addiction. Although people become Internet-dependent for different reasons, there are some common underlying factors. Maressa Orzack, a clinical psychologist at Harvard Medical School, found that people start using the Internet extensively for reasons such as excitement, a new sense of identity, or companionship (Mitchell). Although a correlation has been found between Internet addicts and conditions such as social phobia, impulse control disorder, and attention deficit disorder, a cause-and-effect relationship has not yet been firmly established. Interestingly, it has been found that those who spend an inordinate amount of time in cyberspace (usually defined as more than two hours per day) often suffer from severe depression despite their constant communication with others online. The reason? These online friendships lack the quality of personal, face-to-face interaction. People are social animals that still need an occasional hug or some form of physical affection. The cold glare of a monitor simply won't do.

8   Although technology has raised our standard of living and made many aspects of our lives much easier, cyberspace should not be the final frontier. Eventually, businesses will learn how to truly profit from the Internet and none will be able to

survive without it. On a personal level, however, it is essential that online friendships do not replace day-to-day, face-to-face interaction with others. Online writing skills should supplement, not replace, verbal and social communication skills. So say goodbye for now to Joe from Australia, go outside, explore your *local* environment, and say hello to your neighbors.

WORKS CITED

Cohen, David. "Keeping on Top of Your Press." *New Media Age.* 25 Jan. 2001. Online.

Mitchell, Peter. "Internet Addiction: Genuine Diagnosis or Not?" *The Lancet.* 19 Feb. 2000. p. 632. Online.

Williams, Kathy. "Corporate E-mail Monitoring on the Rise." *Strategic Finance.* Jan. 2000. 19. Online.

Yang, Dori Jones. "Craving Your Next Web Fix." *U.S. News & World Report.* 17 Jan. 2000. 41. Online.

AFTERWARDS

Vocabulary

commerce, beguiling, voracious, venue. Look up the vocabulary words and jot down their definitions in your writing log. Then write eight original sentences, using each word twice, on the topic of computers, cyberspace, or chat rooms.

Content

1. What are some of the technological innovations that have changed our lives? Which, according to Mateo, is the most far reaching and why?

2. In paragraph 4, Mateo states that "One of the most beguiling aspects of cyberspace is that it offers the ability to connect with others in foreign countries while also providing anonymity." Why is this "beguiling"?

3. What does Mateo identify as the relationship between "the medium of business" and the "ability of cyberspace to deliver information"?

Style and Structure

1. How would you describe the tone of Mateo's essay? In what way does it lend itself to the serious nature of her discussion?

2. In the thesis paragraph, Mateo questions whether cyberspace has strengthened or weakened communication between neighbors. In what

way do her concluding remarks refer back to her thesis and frame her broader discussion about the pros and cons of cyberspace development?

3. In what way does Mateo appeal to you ethically (ethos), emotionally (pathos), and logically (logos)? Is her discussion about cyberspace and technology satisfying and thought-provoking? Explain your position—based on personal experiences, readings, and observations.

Collaborative Explorations

As a group, prepare a list of questions that each member will use to survey part of your campus population about their use of chat rooms and communication with e-mail friends. Though it may seem like an obvious question, ask each person polled why he or she finds chat rooms practical, intriguing, or useful. To get a good sampling of the student body at your college, have some members survey other students during different times of the day—morning, afternoon, and evening. Tabulate the results of the individual surveys, placing everyone's findings on a master list. Finally, assemble the results of your group's survey in an analytical composition that draws some conclusions about the role chat rooms play in establishing or destroying enduring human relationships.

Writing Assignments

1. Write an essay arguing that Internet addiction is either healthy or harmless. Make sure to clarify your position on this issue in a sharply focused thesis statement, and support your claims with concrete, representative examples.

2. Write an essay where you offer insight into some aspect of technology such as laptop or palm computers, cell phones, or pagers by using an analogy. What makes one analogy more appropriate than another? Your analogy should conclude with a particular insight into your topic—not just a comparison for its own sake.

Thematic Reading Cross-Links: See John Leo's essay, "Who's for a Little Tongue Violence? Euphemism and Doublespeak," at the end of Chapter 2, The Writing Process: An Overview, to gain a perspective on the relationship between words and communication.

Movie Cross-Links: View *Hackers* from the Film Links at the end of the chapter. Make a list of the ways the students in that film represent rebellion from authority. How do they challenge the way computers have been used responsibly in order to achieve power for small, secretive groups?

The Robotniks
Vladlen Bakhnov

When *Russian Science Fiction: 1968*, an anthology of short stories compiled and edited by Robert Magidoff and translated by Helen Jacobson, was published, **VLADLEN BAKHNOV** was one of the few science fiction authors within the Soviet Union who had elected to write for a career. An author of three volumes of satiric verse and essays, along with several film scenarios, Bakhnov also wrote *How the Sun Was Extinguished*, a satiric science fiction novel. Helen Jacobson, the literary translator of "The Robotniks," has been a major translator of Russian science fiction since the late 1960s. Among her most important translations is *The Diary of a Russian Censor—1826–1877*. In addition, she has been a lecturer in the Russian Department of the State University of New York at Stony Brook.

1   It was late when the Scientific Council adjourned, and the old Professor walked slowly along the Institute's quiet corridors. Here and there lights still burned in the laboratories, and the shadows of students and robots flashed through the frosted glass windows.

2   The Professor had spent almost his whole life in the Institute—as a student, teacher, and now as its Director. . . . Some day it would probably bear his name, but the Professor hoped this day would not come soon. . . .

3   As he walked he thought about the debate which had again flared up at the meeting of the Scientific Council. It was not the first time the question had come up, and, most likely, time alone would tell who was right and whether what was now happening among students was merely a passing fad or something more serious. The Professor dearly hoped it was nothing more than the latest student craze.

4   It is difficult to say when and how it all began. . . . About five years ago. . . . At first, the ridiculous efforts of the students to emulate robots were merely amusing and perhaps a little irritating. Young people, calling themselves "robotniks," began to talk about themselves as they would normally talk about cybernetic systems: "This book fed me approximately so many units of new information. . . ."

5   Later on they learned to imitate the gait and angular movements of robots and to stare blankly without blinking: their faces became as expressionless and impassive as the flat, vacant faces of robots.

6   Naturally, there is always someone who is irritated by the latest fads. The Professor well remembered how, some fifty years ago, young fellows, himself included, began to sport beards and goatees in imitation of the beatniks. And before that . . . hairdos similar to Tarzan's were the rage. And now the latest craze was to shave your face and head clean, because robots, after all, were completely hairless.

7   But it wasn't this that worried the Professor.

8   Now it was considered, at the least, old fashioned to be happy or sad, to laugh or cry; real robotniks deplored the display of any emotion whatsoever. "Bad form," they said.

9   "In this day and age," they asserted, "when we can synthesize any emotion and break down any feeling into its component parts in the laboratory, sentiment is obsolete and irrational to the point of absurdity."

10   No bona fide robotnik would ever dare risk being called old fashioned and irrational. Pure, cold reason was their guide in everything they did. Robotniks studied conscientiously because it was the rational thing to do. Robotniks didn't cut classes because that would be irrational behavior.

11   On alternate Saturdays, the robotniks threw parties, drank, danced, and then, pairing off, went their separate ways. Their brains, those imperfect machines, demanded relaxation.

12   The robotniks were interested only in Science, because it was modern, cold, and rational. They worshipped Logic and Mathematics; "We shall be as robots" was their slogan.

13   Was this a fad or something far more serious? Literally all the young folk of today had become robotniks. And if it was only a passing craze, why did it persist so long. . . ?

14   "I can't bear to be without you, don't you understand? I can't!" the Professor suddenly heard someone say excitedly. "When you're not with me, I think about you, and as soon as I know that we're going to see each other in a short while I feel as if I'm dancing on air. Honestly, I don't know what to call the state I'm in. Do you understand what I'm trying to tell you?"

15   "Of course, darling . . ."

16   "How wonderful," thought the Professor, elated, "so there still are real feelings and real people! All is not lost."

17   And he was overwhelmed with such a feeling of gratitude toward those whose conversation he had accidentally overheard that he could not restrain himself from taking one quick look into the laboratory from which the voices were coming. There was no one in the laboratory except two robots. The old Professor shook his head sadly and closed the door.

18   He had completely forgotten about the latest silly fad among robots: robots were now trying to imitate human weaknesses.

AFTERWARDS

Vocabulary

adjourned, cybernetic, emulate. Write a paragraph that says something about robots (e.g., robots in science, robots from Hollywood, robots in fiction and nonfiction), using the above vocabulary words and at least five other words from your vocabulary log.

Content

1. What do the students who called themselves robotniks begin doing five years prior to the story?

2. Why is the Professor concerned by the "new fad"? Did it go too far? Explain.

3. List some behavior traits of robotniks. Why might these behavior traits be a cause for alarm?

Style and Structure

1. Explain the effect of the short paragraphs in Bakhnov's story. How might they reinforce the subject matter?

2. How does Bakhnov immediately create tension in "The Robotniks"?

3. Rather than resolving his story by having people resume their behavior prior to becoming robotniks, Bakhnov presents the sort of things that he wishes humans would say to each other (e.g., "I can't bear to be without you. . . .") from the real robots! How and why is Bakhnov's conclusion powerful and appropriate? What unpleasant point does it "drive home"?

Collaborative Explorations

In groups of three or four, brainstorm some of the causes and long-term effects associated with a fad or a phenomenon, narrow your focus on the topic, and then write a collaborative essay, defending your paper with several examples and—like a robotnik—reasoning. As you write various drafts of your paper, take turns revising and editing your group effort.

Writing Assignments

1. Write an essay commenting on recent discoveries in space exploration or oceanography (the study of the ocean) from the point of view of a robotnik. What particular characteristics would you attribute to a robotnik? What would make the voice of a robotnik unmistakable? Pay special attention to diction (word choice) and sentence structures you think a robotnik might use.

2. While written over twenty years ago, this story is just as relevant today, since people romanticize technology and cyberspace. Write an argumentative paper persuading your readers to give up their present behavior in class, at home, in the streets, or on the job, in favor of a fad that emphasizes rational, "robotic" reactions and verbal responses to people, places, and things. What would be the benefits and the limitations of the "robotic" behavior you champion?

Thematic Reading Cross-Links: Consider the quotations from *Frankenstein* by Mary Shelley and "Head Hunting in Cyberspace" by Lisa Nakamura at the beginning of this chapter. What potential horrors—or prices—for scientific advancement do human beings seem willing to pay?

Movie Cross-Links: See *THX 1138* in the Film Links at the end of this chapter for a vision of a robotic world not unlike the one championed by "The Robotniks." You also might watch movies like *Bicentennial Man, AntiTrust,* and *A. I. Artificial Intelligence* for a look at perspectives of art— or robots/androids, if you will—imitating life.

Life and Death on the Web
Joshua Quittner

A former police reporter for the *Albuquerque Dispatch,* JOSHUA QUITTNER often writes for *Wired* magazine and composes books with Michelle Statalla, his wife. Their most recent nonfiction work is *Masters of Deception: The Gang That Ruled Cyberspace.* Quittner writes a weekly column about the Internet for *Newsday;* the following article appeared in the "Netly News" column of *Time* magazine, April 7, 1997, with additional reporting by Karen Brophy, Noah Robischon, and Declan McCullagh. Although Quittner strongly emphasizes that the idea of the Internet being a "spiritual predator" is absurd, he also acknowledges that "the whole idea would be laughable if 39 people were not dead."

ALLUSIONS

Militias: Paramilitary groups—most recently, groups that claim that, as citizens, they have the right to bear arms and to group together for protection as a military unit.

Oklahoma City: Reference to the Oklahoma City federal building bombing in 1995.

TWA: Acronym for Trans World Airlines; the allusion is to the TWA airline crash in the summer of 1996.

Unabomber: A terrorist whose sociopathic killings took the form of package bombs set to explode when they were opened.

Waco: Texas site of the Branch Davidians' cult leader, David Koresh.

Conehead: Reference to the extraterrestrial Conehead family, who appeared frequently in satiric skits on *Saturday Night Live*.

1   Every time this country extrudes any significant bit of evil at its fringes, my editors dispatch me to the Internet to look for its source. This has been going on for four years now, and implicit in the assignment is the notion that anything menacing or subterranean must have its roots on the Net. Waco, Oklahoma City, the militias, the Unabomber, TWA 800. Each time I've dutifully logged on and gone hunting, but rarely have I bagged anything more than the usual Internet chatter.

2   That changed last week. Heaven's Gate left its fingerprints all over cyberspace: in postings broadcast to dozens of newsgroups, in recruitment chats with teenagers, in Websites designed for rich clients and in its own bizarre home page. Here was obsession, delusion and mass suicide played out in multimedia and hypertext—a horror, finally, best observed online.

3   Start with the Heaven's Gate Website, www.heavensgate.com, which must qualify as the most elaborate suicide note in history. From the blinking red ALERT headline of its celestial home page to its computer-generated painting of a resident of the kingdom of heaven, the site serves up 5 megabytes of soul-chilling blather. Hundreds of pages of millennialist writings, including transcripts of videotapes and the full text of a book called *Heaven's Gate*, lay out the cult's history and cosmology. There are a few special features as well. Buried in the invisible space at the bottom of the home page are hundreds of hidden words: UFO, space alien, extraterrestrial, misinformation, second coming, end times, alien abductions, Yoda, Yoga. Was this some kind of subliminal incantation? Or bait to draw in unsuspecting Web surfers searching the Internet for the key words of their obsessions?

4   Nothing is forgotten on the Net, and a little bit of cybersleuthing in its deeper recesses turned up plenty of evidence of past cult activity. One posting sent from a heavensgate.com E-mail address was "spammed" last September to dozens of Usenet newsgroups ranging from alt. conspiracy to alt.buddha.short.fat.guy. "Time to die for God?" it began. "Whether we like it or not, the Armageddon—the Mother of Holy Wars—has begun, and it will not cease until the plowing under is completed."

5   In one disturbing exchange, purportedly recorded in full, a cult member calling himself CandlShot struck up a conversation on the Internet Relay Chat system with an 18-year-old using the screen name JayBoy18. "Are you looking for work?" CandlShot began. "We are always looking for associates."

> **<CandlShot>**If you agreed to work with us, we would like to have
> you here with us, but we could accommodate you. Where do you live?

\<JayBoy18\>In the COLD state of Michigan.

\<CandlShot\>Actually, if you could not relocate, we are looking for associates in that area.

\<JayBoy18\>I couldn't relocate.

\<CandlShot\>That is understandable. However, you can still meet our needs. Do you live with family or friends? Actually, this is a conversation we should be having over the telephone. May I have your number so I may call you?

\<JayBoy18\>Um . . . no. You know how it is . . . you don't give out your number over the Net, besides . . . I just met you.

\<CandlShot\>You will not succeed unless you trust. Do you trust me enough to give me a set of numbers?

\<JayBoy18\>No, I'm afraid I don't. Sorry . . . how about this . . . I'll call you? I couldn't talk long, but we could get something done.

\<CandlShot\>No, I'm afraid that we cannot really have calls coming in at this time.

\<JayBoy18\>Well, you can E-mail me.

\<CandlShot\>That would be feasible.

6   While the young man gave his real E-mail address (bad idea), he cut the "interview" short when CandlShot tried to persuade him to reveal more details about himself (smart move).

7   A suicide book, correspondence from beyond the grave, aggressive proselytizing by someone who sounds like a Conehead—all of it frozen like a scorpion in amber for us to examine. What are we to make of this spectacle? Is the Internet somehow to blame? "We've known for years there are sexual predators on the Web," an authority on cults said on CNN. "Now it appears there may be spiritual predators as well."

8   Spiritual predators? Give me a break. Better yet, go look at this stuff yourself and tell me if you think it's dangerous. A Web page that has the power to suck people—against their will—into a suicide cult? The whole idea would be laughable if 39 people weren't dead. If you want to find out what killed them, however, you're going to have to click a lot deeper than www.heavensgate.com.

AFTERWARDS

Vocabulary

subterranean, extrude, bizarre, delusion, multimedia, megabytes, millennialist, transcripts, extraterrestrial, subliminal, incantation, cybersleuthing, proselytizing. Before you check the meanings for today's vocabulary in your dictionary, break them down into prefixes (e.g., "sub-" meaning "under") and their root (e.g., "terrain" meaning territory or land), and place both in your vocabulary log. How can a knowledge of prefixes assist you in predicting meaning for some words?

Content

1. What impression did the Heaven's Gate incident leave on cyberspace?

2. Who was Yoda? Why do you imagine the name was among the many key words found at the bottom of the Heaven's Gate homepage?

3. Look up www.heavensgate.com on the World Wide Web. Does the Web site still exist? If so, what does it contain?

Style and Structure

1. How does Quittner's opening paragraph build his readers' expectations and prepare them for his second paragraph, where the controlling idea of his composition becomes clear? What usually happens when his boss tells him to "go online" and find out information about a "significant bit of evil"?

2. Why do you think Quittner devotes so much space to reprinting an "Internet Relay" between a Heaven's Gate recruiter who called himself <CandlShot> and an eighteen-year-old from Michigan referred to as <JayBoy18>? What did he illustrate?

3. How does Quittner draw his discussion about "Life and Death on the Web" to a close? What does he imply? How many of the questions raised by the article have been addressed?

Collaborative Explorations

Select a topic that has provoked current social outrage or concern (a murder, a disaster, a court case), and then in groups of three, go online and research your topic. In particular, attempt to locate the source of current public information and understanding of your topic. Are you able to locate any significant information, or are most of your findings limited to "Internet chatter"?

Writing Assignments

1. What recent social or political event did the media sensationalize? Did newscasters promise constant updates that would get to the heart of the issue at hand (e.g., who or what is to blame for an airplane accident or celebrity scandal? What did they do or say? Can you recall the headlines in your local newspapers?) Write an essay in which you argue why readers and viewers should never believe what the media tell you without question. You might point out as many instances as you can

where the media jumped to conclusions to sell "copy," only to admit their reporting errors and to correct themselves at a later date.

2. Write an essay in which you argue for or against the notion that there are "spiritual predators" on the Web and/or that a Web page has "the power to suck people—against their will—into a [Heaven's Gate type of] suicide cult." Good, clear deductive and inductive reasoning, supported with concrete, representative evidence, will play a crucial role in your essay.

Thematic Reading Cross-Links: See "A Modern Inquisition" by Jack Kevorkian in Chapter 5, Media: Controversies and Celebrities, for another take on the use of the media and voluntary suicide.

Movie Cross-Links: See *The Net* in the Film Links at the end of this chapter for a movie that shows how the Internet could be used to erase a person's identity.

The Ultimate Technology Room

The Visual Connection: Photograph Writing Activities

On page 220 (bottom left) is a photo of an office called "The Ultimate Technology Room" by Colleen, its owner. Carefully study the details in the photo; to what extent do you believe she is fully justified in her claim? Include specific references to the technological devices in the photo to argue your position. (You also might consider what—if anything—is missing from Colleen's room that makes it less than "ultimate.")

Film Links: Cyberspace and Technology

1. Technology is often seen as giving human beings increased power over time and space. In one or more of the films below, trace this human quest for more power and its unforeseen consequences. What do the films tell us about the need to understand the importance of limited aspirations (technology often goes TOO far).

2. How do films about cyberspace and technological advancements speak to your hidden fears and secret fascination? How do such films relate to your own life and interests? Why do you imagine some of the films about technology or cyberspace project something dark, foreboding, and unforgiving? After generating a variety of ideas on this topic, narrow them down to a single focus—your thesis—and then analyze the central role of technology and/or cyberspace in one or more of the movies listed below.

3. How do forms of technology function as friends, assistants, and companions? Are they any substitute for another human being? Can a machine think (e.g., like HAL in *2001: A Space Odyssey*)? If so, is this a good or bad attribute? Support your claims with specific examples drawn from the following films, as well as more recent films on technology.

2001: A Space Odyssey (USA, Stanley Kubrick, 1968). Two astronauts match wits with a computer called Hal 9000.

THX 1138 (USA, George Lucas, 1971). In this future world, humans live underground and have replaced their names with acronyms and numbers.

China Syndrome (USA, James Bridges, 1979). A nuclear power plant executive strives to prevent a meltdown.

The Terminator/Terminator 2: Judgment Day (USA, James Cameron, 1984/1991). Cyborgs; back-and-forth time travel; nuclear holocaust; Arnold Schwarzenegger.

Back to the Future (USA, Robert Zemeckis, 1985). A kid named Marty travels back to 1955 in a DeLorean automobile.

The Net (USA, Irwin Winkler, 1995). A young woman discovers that computers have been used to erase her identity.

Hackers (USA, Iain Softley, 1995). Teenage computer freaks hack into oil company data system and discover conspiracy.

Contact (USA, Robert Zemeckis, 1997). A young astronomer decodes messages from aliens.

Gattaca (USA, Andrew Niccol, 1997). In a world ruled by bio-engineering, a man with flawed DNA schemes to find a way to get on the crew of a space expedition.

The Matrix (USA, Larry and Andy Wachowski, 1999). A software writer and hacker encounters some cyberspace rebels who show that there is more to Virtual Reality than he thinks.

Bicentennial Man (USA, Chris Columbus, 1999). An android designed to perform menial tasks begins to develop a personality.

AntiTrust (USA, Peter Howitt, 2001). A young computer programmer just out of college goes to work for a giant software company in the Pacific Northwest and discovers its president is not what he appears to be.

A. I. Artificial Intelligence (USA, Steven Spielberg, 2001). A robotic boy longs to be real.

Additional Writing Assignments

1. Write an essay comparing and contrasting people who use the Internet as their primary source of entertainment to individuals who find recreation and pleasure in "nontechnical" activities such as hiking, horseback riding, or mountain climbing.

2. Construct an argument of fact, defending the notion that "smaller is better" when it comes to personal computers, calculators, and telephones.

3. Define the term *cyberpunk* in a well-developed, thoroughly illustrated essay. What does a cyberpunk do? Where did the term originate?

4. Write an essay arguing either for or against the concept and practice of distance learning (classes given over the Internet). You might want to consider the theoretical benefits and limitations of this method of learning. Ultimately, assess whether you think distance learning would serve the student body at your college well.

5. In the same manner as Kurt Vonnegut's extended paragraph at the beginning of the chapter, write a composition in which you explain how and why you would rather lead a "natural" lifestyle than rigid, systematic existence in which time efficiency represents your most important priority.

Popular Culture

Observations and Opinions

I'm hip. I'm no square. I'm alert. I'm awake. I'm aware.
I'm on top of every scene, makin' the rounds, diggin' the sounds.
I read People magazine 'cause I'm hip.
Like dig. I'm in step. When it was hip to be hep, I was hep.
I don't blow, but I'm a fan.
Look at me swing, ring-a-ding-ding.
I even call my girlfriend man 'cause I'm hip.
Every Saturday night, with my suit buttoned
    tight and my suedes on
I get my kicks diggin' arty French flicks with my shades on.
I'm too much. I'm a gas. I am anything but middle-class.
When I hang around the band, poppin'
    my thumbs—diggin' the drums,
squares don't seem to understand why I flip—
    they're not hip—like I'm hip.
I'm hip. I'm alive. I enjoy any joint where there's jive.
I'm on top of every trend.
Look at me go, Vo-Dee-O-Do.
Sammy Davis knows my friend. I'm so hip.
I'm hip but not weird-like you notice, I don't wear a beard.
Beards were in but now they're out.
They had their day, but now they're passé;
just ask me if you're in doubt, 'cause I'm hip.
Now I'm deep into Zen, meditation, and macrobiotics, and
as soon as I can, I intend to get into narcotics.
'Cause I'm cool as cuc'. I'm cat. I'm a card. I'm a kook.
I get so much out of life. Really I do,
One more time play "Mack the Knife."
Let it rip. I may flip—'cause I'm hip.
oo oo I'm hip.

—DAVE FRISHBERG, "I'M HIP" FROM *THE DAVE FRISHBERG SONGBOOK*

Without deviation from the norm, progress is not possible.

— FRANK ZAPPA FROM *NEW YORK* MAGAZINE

My anxiety was born of some taboo I had long ago internalized about dancing not being masculine. The typical after-school and after-supper pastimes for boys in my suburban neighborhood were baseball and football. Forget that dancing can actually develop the timing and coordination needed to play second base, or that dancers have physiques that gym rats only dream about. Any parent signing his or her son up for dance class instead of (or even in addition to) Little League was practically subject to child-abuse charges—because invariably that boy would be subject to the cruel taunts of his peers.

— ROB HOERBURGER FROM "GOTTA DANCE!"

Groucho Marx once said that he wouldn't belong to any club that would have him as a member. In that pithy proclamation, he captured the essence of cool! It's something advertisers have been scrambling to do for some time now with their overuse of sloppy typefaces and belly-button pierced models.

— YVETTE DOSS FROM "FACE IT, MR. AD EXECUTIVE: THE ESSENCE OF COOL IS ETHNIC"

Observations and Opinions: Reading/Writing Activities

1. In your opinion, who or what determines "cool" or "hip" attitudes? How do the ironic lyrics from Dave Frishberg's "I'm Hip" provide a glimpse at real or imaginary traits of the cool, hip person?

2. Rob Hoerburger's quote from "Gotta Dance!" explains how and why the popular culture of his youth was a source of personal pain and anxiety. How does Frank Zappa's quote address trends, fads, and fashionable behavior? In what way might the "deviation" he mentions provide a positive change—maybe the source of "new" popular culture?

3. Reread the Observations and Opinions, "Face It, Mr. Ad Executive: The Essence of Cool Is Ethnic," by Yvette Doss. What advertisements and commercials have you seen that attempt to capture "the essence of cool"? Beginning with a focused topic sentence, write a journal entry about advertisements, commercials, and/or people who are simply "uncool" or "unfashionable."

Introduction

Popular culture is better known as "pop culture." The single syllable, pop, better expresses the informal, explosive, attention-getting nature of the culture itself. Pop culture is not an easily defined term because its meaning encompasses just about everything imaginable.

Because of advertising's ability to make products as unlikely as underarm deodorants and lawn mowers fashionable, just about every physical object has some place in pop culture. Look at any street corner in any large city in America and you will see a diversity of style statements that have their origins in pop culture. You would be likely to see a Chicago Bulls T-shirt, a Jerry Garcia tie, designer nails, a shaved head, baggy overalls, a plaid flannel shirt, Laurel Burch earrings, a Gucci bag, a cell phone, a handmade leather briefcase, a goatee, a three-piece pin-striped suit, a cowboy hat. All of these items have a functional purpose, but they are also emblems of pop culture. They have meaning; they are a way for individuals to express to the world a sense of personal identity and individuality. Ironically, this personal form of expression must use manufactured items that can be purchased by anyone who has the money to pay for them.

Pop culture is not, like traditional culture, a result of adaptations made to specific geographic places on the planet; rather, pop culture is driven by the marketplace. Although it is not exclusively commercial, its commerciality is the source of its power and the reason for its often low status. Pop culture has sometimes been considered "low culture"—meaning that it appeals to the "lower" (and less well-educated) classes and that it provokes "low" or "base" emotions. Pop culture was long viewed as sensationalistic, simplistic, and crude. Its cheapness— the masses were able to purchase it—made what pop culture expresses also seem cheap, yet it obviously appeals to basic human drives like sexuality, aggression, and sentimentality. Comic books, soap operas, top-forty music, and pulp fiction have all been considered trivial and vulgar at one time or another. This condescending attitude toward pop culture began to change in midcentury, however. Participation in mass culture became so pervasive after the development of radio, television, the long-playing record, and the paperback book (among other things) that the debate over "high" and "low" culture simply drifted away as everyone got caught up in the race to consume more and more goods. The ideals and values of pop culture became reflected in science, fiction, film, advertising, television, fashions, fads, and even religions. Nonetheless, the trendiness of pop culture makes us suspicious of it. It changes too rapidly, and marketing and advertising executives drive the changes.

Why are writers so interested in pop culture? We are inescapably a part of pop culture whether or not we want to be. Since writers observe and argue about the significance of events in their own experience, they necessarily draw on pop culture in order to understand and explain what is going on in the world around them. This generates expository and argumentative writing and the cultural discourse that we must have in order to steer our way into the future.

The essays in this chapter address the rise, fall, and continuance of different aspects of pop culture. At any one moment there are those who are in the know about the latest trends. They appear to be on the "cutting edge" of new ideas, attitudes, and behaviors. They change the way they talk, dress, and fix their hair. This could mean wearing bobby sox or a nose ring; it could mean listening to Carlos Santana, LeeAnn Rimes, Tori Amos, Bob Marley, Lauryn Hill, Bob Dylan, Sarah McLachlan, Keb' Mo', Leonard Cohen, or Alicia Keys; it could mean using words like "groovy," "chill out," or "whatever." This sense of being in the know defines "hipness." This term has its roots in the pop music world of the big band era when musicians who had adopted the swing style of playing were considered "hep." Later, "hep" changed vowels and became "hip." This gave us the hipster of the 1950s and the hippies of the 1960s. The words of Dave Frishberg's song "I'm Hip" give us an ironic impersonation of this attitude. Frishberg's hipster embraces both "macrobiotics" and "narcotics" in his zeal to embrace everything considered hip. Since the days of the hipster, the word has come to stand for a certain condition of awareness, especially associated with a state of mind described as "cool." People who are hip are cool.

In pop culture there is nothing worse than to be out of fashion, to suddenly find yourself out of step with the newest forms of verbal, physical, and material expression. Parents who criticized the Beatles for their long hair were immediately identified as unhip; thirty years later, to be wearing Adidas when everyone else had switched to Doc Martens was to risk subtle forms of social ostracism. Each generation creates its own pop emblems. Think of these terms: *soul, grunge, retro, hiphop, rap, new wave, punk, rave, heavy metal, outlaw, gangsta,* and so forth. Why did they emerge? What determines their cultural life span? Many of the following essays may offer clues to such questions.

Americans are slightly fanatical about sports. It is not possible to understand American pop culture without examining the role of sports. Sports were once described as a pastime, but they are now a part of everyone's daily life. Even those who are not interested in sports cannot avoid hearing about them. They're part of every news broadcast; whole cable networks are devoted to sports; talk-radio features them; cities and state legislatures must constantly debate how to pay for new stadiums. It has even changed the way we dress. In the past it was common for young boys to wear clothes with sports logos; now grown men and women, small children, and retirees can be seen striding across the mall in cross-training shoes, Sonics T-shirts, Sharks jerseys, Yankee hats, and Raider wrist-bands. Sports paraphernalia rule the world of everyday fashion.

In "Where the Wild Things Are," Barbara Ehrenreich notes that crowd behavior at modern sporting events, however raucous or absurd, stems from a rich historical tradition of participation in community ceremonies. Many people ignore notions of normal behavior or clothes; they paint themselves in team colors, wear grotesque hats, get crazy, and dress in outrageous costumes. Nonetheless, rather than suggesting that sports fans take things too far, she states, "We do a lot of complaining about the lack of 'community' in modern societies, but few have noted the absence of public and participatory festivities that can, however briefly, unite total strangers in ecstatic communion [at a sporting event]."

Dave Barry, by contrast, has been standing on the sidelines of American culture, and in "Why Sports Is a Drag," he satirically explains how all this sports-related behavior reveals some interesting differences between men and women. Of course, his satire pokes fun at people in positions of authority, mocks institutions, and parodies the pretentiousness of fads—just about anything you can think of that some people take too seriously. Like many satiric writers, Barry seeks to highlight human folly or extravagance in hopes that its recognition will lead to positive change.

"Grays on Trays," an essay by Martha L. Henning, uses snowboarding—regarded by many as an extreme sport primarily for young men—to argue that nothing could be farther from the truth. She argues that the young men who talk the talk and walk the walk conform to ritual behavior and thereby become the norm rather than define open doorways for self-expression and nonconformity.

In "Booming Amusement Parks: The Theme Is Extreme," T. Trent Gegax points out that as we move into the 21st century, America's love affair with entertainment has paved the way for what will become "a golden age of ersatz adventure—extreme theming, you might call it." In fact, some people, like the man who helped Walt Disney plan Disneyland, believe that in the future, "everything will be themed."

Rounding off the popular culture chapter is A. J. Jacobs in "Extremely Cool." He notes that many forms of extremism appear in the media today, from advertising to motion pictures. According to Jacobs, such extremism blends the subcultural attitudes of youth with the commercial marketing intentions for Generation X.

Pop culture used to be like a hundred-yard dash at a track meet. There were a few competitors who raced for the prize over a short distance, and the winners achieved universal acclaim. Today, pop culture is more like a marathon. The number of competitors has multiplied many times, and the race never seems to end. Because of reruns, videotapes, reissues of CDs, the vast storage capacities of computers, and CD-ROMs, many eras of pop culture exist simultaneously. Pop culture has entered into a new era in which it is possible to move around in time, to sample the past at will and reconstruct it in the present.

Gathering Thoughts: Prereading Inquiries

1. What is your perception of pop culture? Who or what has influenced your lifestyle?

2. If you were going to put works of American popular culture in a spacecraft that might later be discovered by intelligent beings on another planet, what representative samples would you choose to include? Explain the reasons for your choices.

3. What effect may the gap between generations have on pop culture?

4. When you hear the words "pop culture," what do you immediately think about?

5. What associations do you make between pop culture and your own life?

6. What causes fashions to change? How important are these changes?

7. How does pop culture affect personal relationships?

8. Does pop culture affect social problems like crime, drug use, and teenage pregnancy? If so, how? If not, explain.

9. Who benefits most from contemporary pop culture?

10. How has pop culture affected religion and politics?

Where the Wild Things Are

Barbara Ehrenreich

Born in 1941, **BARBARA EHRENREICH**, an award-winning reporter and essayist, has written articles for a very broad range of publications, including *The Atlantic Monthly, Esquire, The Nation*, the *New York Times*, the *New Republic*,

Vogue, the *Wall Street Journal*, and the *Washington Post* magazine. She presently serves as the essayist at the end of *Time* magazine. Politics and issues revolving around the mass media are constant targets of her prose. Among Ehrenreich's many books are *The Hearts of Men* (1983), *Fear of Falling* (1989), *The Worst Years of Our Lives* (1990), and *The Snarling Citizen* (1995). As the *Boston Globe* mentioned in its review of *The Worst Years of Our Lives*, "Ehrenreich's scorn withers, her humor stings and her radical light shines on." In the following essay that appeared in the June/July 2000 issue of *Civilization*, Ehrenreich defends what sometimes seems like the eccentric behavior of sports fans on the grounds that it stems from rich, historical, festive traditions.

ALLUSIONS

Protestant Reformation and Counter-Reformation: The Protestant Reformation spurred on by Martin Luther called for specific changes in the church, including (1) national, rather than Roman Catholic, control of church finances; (2) permission for the clergy to marry; and (3) several reforms that reduced the sacraments to Baptism, a reformed Mass, and the Holy Eucharist. The Catholic Church responded to these demands with the Counter-Reformation, which, among other things, created the Jesuit order to enforce church doctrine. Ultimately, the Reformation created a north-south split in Europe: the northern countries became Protestant, while the south remained Catholic. Both repressed public festivities on the grounds that they were "un-Christian."

A DEFENSE OF CHEESEHEADS, THE CHOP, AND ECSTATIC RELIGION IN THE STANDS

1   What today's demonstrative fans are telling us is that it cannot be suppressed forever. Sports fans don't usually attract much attention unless they get violent—hurling missiles at "enemy" players, rushing the field, brawling after the game. But in the last three decades, in a trend almost unnoticed by sports commentators and sociologists, fans have been expressing themselves in more colorful and peaceable ways, potentially even upstaging the games themselves. Soccer fans worldwide were generally the trendsetters, having been the first to paint their faces and decorate themselves head to toe in masks, ribbons, scarves, and massive headgear. These fans often bring music to the game—samba bands or African drums—and they sometimes march to stadiums in organized masses or leave in parades of heavily festooned, loudly honking cars. Most spectacularly, they engage in synchronized displays during the game, like the British "synchro-clap," in which the fans, as if schooled in the task, intersperse their songs and chants with precisely timed rhythmic clapping.

Spectators don't get much respect, at least compared to athletes, but you can't call them passive anymore.

2   In the last two decades, the trend toward participation has spread to American sports events, especially football, baseball, and basketball. Take face painting: Only a few years ago, ardent fans had to use magic markers or even house paint to lend their allegiances epidermal expression. Now there are at least half a dozen purveyors of skin-compatible colored makeup—and spokespersons for these companies describe the business as "really surprising" and "huge."

3   You can buy "team spirit" kits with colors appropriate to almost every known team, or you can be painted professionally at concessions located at stadium entrances. There are other forms of personal decoration, too, and these now go well beyond the team-colored scarf or sweatshirt to include color-coordinated nail polish, earrings, headgear—Cheeseheads, in the case of Green Bay Packer fans—and a new line of team-colored Afro wigs.

4   Americans have made their own unique contribution to the spectacle in the form of "the Wave," which was invented in 1981—though where, exactly, is a matter of intense dispute—and moved quickly from football to baseball and basketball. Another distinctly American mode of synchronized crowd display, much criticized by Native Americans, is "the chop" and its accompanying war chant, popularized by fans of the Atlanta Braves.

5   What motivates fans to become part of the show? Is this a case of team ardor run amok, or could there be deeper psychological forces at work? Sheer exhibitionism might explain some forms of display in their earliest stages—a painted bare chest, for example, can still catch the attention of cameras—but this cannot explain the thousandth painted face or about the massed synchronized activities. Nor, in a climate increasingly marked by free agency, is it easy to explain the ever-more flamboyant behavior of fans in terms of mounting team loyalty. With elite players free to market themselves to the highest bidder, and owners free to change lineups and move teams to new cities, fans may indeed be left with nobody to get excited about—except each other. In fact, Americans have been known to indulge in, say, face painting even when they have no direct stake in the game, as at soccer matches between teams representing foreign nations.

6   One possibility is that the fans are rebelling, however unconsciously, against their appointed role as spectators in sports that were once much more participatory. Medieval European football pitted whole villages against each other and involved "everyone . . . male and female, adult and child, rich and poor, laity and clergy," as Amherst College sports historian Allen Guttmann has written. He has speculated that today, "as sports become more commercialized and bureaucratized, fans may feel the need to say 'We're part of this, too.'"

7   But the specific forms of display undertaken by modern fans recall a tradition even broader and more ancient than sports: the organized festivities, both secular and religious, of preindustrial societies throughout the world. Almost universally, these have involved masking, costuming, dancing, and feasting, all of which are in chaotic abundance at today's sports stadiums. Face painting is a form of masking;

synchronized motions like the Wave a kind of dance. Medieval Europe boasted an especially robust tradition of communal festivity, with carnivals and other feast days taking up, in some regions, as much as one day out of every four in the year. When commentators complain that today's demonstrative fans are turning the game into a "carnival," they only betray their ignorance of history: Carnival was in fact the traditional setting for medieval sports such as wrestling, bull running, and archery.

8 Only scattered remnants of the European festive tradition survived into the modern era. Beginning in the 16th century, both secular and religious authorities, representing the Protestant Reformation and the Catholic Counter-Reformation, moved to suppress popular festivities on the grounds that they were disorderly, indecent, un-Christian, and, especially as the Industrial Revolution gained ground, an extravagant waste of time. Feast days were canceled, carnivals denied a venue, raucous celebrations were transformed into sober prayer vigils. Sports, at least the ones seen as plebeian, fell under the same attack: In 1608, a Manchester ordinance prohibited football, complaining of the harm done by a "company of lewd and disordered persons usinge that unlawfulle exercise of playing with the ffotebale in ye streets."

9 The result today is a global culture fairly desolate of joyous communal ritual. Sports enjoyed a revival in the late 19th century, but only because they were seen as a fine source of manly, nationalistic values; later they were encouraged largely as a tame form of "entertainment." In today's multi-billion-dollar sports industry, it no longer takes a village to score a touchdown.

10 We do a lot of complaining about the lack of "community" in modern societies, but few have noted the absence of public and participatory festivities that can, however briefly, unite total strangers in ecstatic communion. Emile Durkheim called this experience "collective effervescence," which he discerned in the ritual dances of Australian aborigines and postulated to be the emotional basis of all religion. A few religious denominations—Pentecostalism, for example—still offer a collective ecstatic experience, as did rock culture at its height. But the ecstatic religions tend to be marginal, and rock has been tamed for commercial consumption or driven into clubs as "raves." Hence, perhaps, the attempts by fans to transform sports events into an occasion for communal festivity—where else, in a culture of cubicles and malls, can you lose yourself so completely in a transient community of like-minded others?

11 Unfortunately, English lacks a word, or even a graceful phrase, for the desire for ebullient self-expression and excited merger with the crowd. Call it primitive religiosity of some sort of "carnival" instinct: what today's demonstrative fans are telling us is that it cannot be suppressed forever.

AFTERWARDS

Vocabulary

sociologists, festooned, interspersed, allegiances, epidermal, synchronized, flamboyant, communal, secular, effervescence, postulated, denominations, Pentecostalism, ecstatic, transient, ebullient. After you look up the vocabulary words in your dictionary, write their definitions down in your "vocabulary log," reread Ehrenreich's article, and consider what each word expresses in context. Would simpler words "lose" any connotative (associated) meanings? When? Where? Why? How?

Content

1. Ehrenreich mentions several possible factors that motivate sports fans to become actively involved in "the show." Name and analyze at least two of them.

2. Explain some of the reasons "only scattered remnants of the European festive tradition survived into the modern era."

3. What does Ehrenreich cite as America's unique contribution to a sports spectacle? In what way does wearing a cheesehead cap or painting one's body hearken to more ancient traditions and rituals at group gatherings?

Style and Structure

1. How does "A Defense of Cheeseheads, the Chop, and Ecstatic Religion in the Stands," the subheading for Ehrenreich's essay, frame the material she develops?

2. Analyze Ehrenreich's strategic purpose for comparing and contrasting modern to medieval sports/community events. What does she achieve by so doing?

3. How does Ehrenreich conclude her essay? In what way does it logically and reasonably bring her body paragraphs to a close?

Collaborative Explorations

Break the class up into four or five groups and have each group assess the sociological implications of Ehrenreich's essay. What, according to each group, draws people together and pulls others apart? How do sporting events fulfill a basic human need for expression—or do they? What recent international events beyond the world of sports have received a great deal of exposure? How did people confront and deal with social tensions as well as revel in some sort of victory or cause?

Writing Assignments

1. To what extent do you agree with Ehrenreich that our global culture today remains "fairly desolate of joyous communal ritual"? Take a position on this issue and write an essay defending your point of view.

2. Compare and contrast the advantages and disadvantages of watching sporting events on television to attending them in person. How does each setting differ in terms of ritual activities, group (crowd) dynamics, and ceremonial festivities? Overall, which do you prefer as a spectator and why?

Thematic Cross-Links: Compare the social celebration described in Ehrenreich's essay to that of Mehendi—henna painting—in Roohi Vora's essay, "The Magic of Mehendi: The Henna Painting Ceremony," in Chapter 12: The Body: Language, Ritual, and Wellness—A Casebook.

Movie Cross-Links: Check out crowd involvement in ancient sporting events by watching the portrayal of gladiators in *Spartacus* or *Gladiator*. For one filmmaker's futuristic look at the same, see Mel Gibson in *Mad Max Beyond Thunderdome*.

Why Sports Is a Drag
Dave Barry

Humorist **DAVE BARRY**, a Pulitzer Prize-winning journalist for the *Miami Herald*, frequently satirizes many aspects of modern American culture. His books include *Babies and Other Hazards of Sex* (1984), *Claw Your Way to the Top* (1986), *Homes and Other Black Holes* (1988), *Dave Barry Talks Back* (1992), *Dave Barry Does Japan* (1993), and *Dave Barry Is Not Making This Up* (1994). In addition to writing, Barry plays with The Rock Bottom Remainders, a rock group that includes such popular writers as Amy Tan and Stephen King. (Their motto is "We play music as well as Metallica writes novels.") Sports, a sacred cow for many Americans, becomes the object of Barry's satire in "Why Sports Is a Drag," an essay published in *Dave Barry's Greatest Hits* (1988).

ALLUSIONS

Howard Cosell: A famous sports announcer, Cosell had a habit of expressing simple observations in complicated ways.

Jane Fonda: An actress and one-time social activist, Fonda also made a number of very popular exercise tapes. She was once married to Atlanta Braves owner and media mogul Ted Turner.

Bill Mazeroski: A second baseman, Mazeroski played for the Pittsburgh Pirates in the 1960s.

Stan Albeck: Albeck coaches the New Jersey Nets, a professional basketball team.

1   Mankind's yearning to engage in sports is older than recorded history, dating back to the time, millions of years ago, when the first primitive man picked up a crude club and a round rock, tossed the rock into the air, and whomped the club into the sloping forehead of the first primitive umpire. What inner force drove this first athlete? Your guess is as good as mine. Better, probably, because you haven't had four beers. All I know is whatever the reason, Mankind is still nuts about sports. As Howard Cosell, who may not be the most likable person in the world but is certainly one of the most obnoxious, put it: "In terms of Mankind and sports, blah blah blah blah the 1954 Brooklyn Dodgers."

2   Notice that Howard and I both use the term "Mankind." Womankind really isn't into sports in the same way. I realize things have changed since my high-school days, when sports were considered unfeminine and your average girls' gym class consisted of six girls in those gym outfits colored Digestive Enzyme Green running around waving field-hockey sticks and squealing, and 127 girls on the sidelines in civilian clothing, claiming it was That Time of the Month. I realize that today you have a number of top female athletes such as Martina Navratilova who can run like deer and bench-press Chevrolet pickup trucks. But to be brutally frank, women as a group have a long way to go before they reach the level of intensity and dedication to sports that enables men to be such incredible jerks about it.

3   If you don't believe me, go to your local racquetball club and observe the difference between the way men and women play. Where I play, the women tend to gather on the court in groups of random sizes—sometimes three, sometimes five, as if it were a Jane Fonda workout—and the way they play is, one of them will hit the ball at the wall and the rest of them will admire the shot and compliment her quite sincerely, and then they all sort of relax, as if they're thinking, well, thank goodness that's over with, and they always seem very surprised when the ball comes back. If one of them has the presence of mind to take another swing, and if she actually hits the ball, everybody is very complimentary. If she misses it, the others all tell her what a good try she made, really, then they all laugh and act very relieved because they know they have some time to talk before the ball comes bouncing off that darned wall again.

4   Meanwhile, over in the next court, you will have two males wearing various knee braces and wrist bands and special leatheroid racquetball gloves, hurling themselves into the walls like musk oxen on Dexedrine, and after every single point one or both of them will yell "S——!" in the self-reproving tone of voice you might use if you had just accidentally shot your grandmother. American men tend to take their sports seriously, much more seriously than they take family matters or Asia.

5   This is why it's usually a mistake for men and women to play on teams together. I sometimes play in a coed slow-pitch softball league, where the rules say you have to have two women on the field. The teams always have one of the women play catcher, because in slow-pitch softball the batters hit just about every pitch, so it wouldn't really hurt you much if you had a deceased person as catcher. Our team usually puts the other

woman at second base, where the maximum possible number of males can get there on short notice to help out in case of emergency. As far as I can tell, our second basewoman is a pretty good baseball player, better than I am anyway, but there's no way to know for sure because if the ball gets anywhere near her, a male comes barging over from, say, right field, to deal with it. She's been on the team for three seasons now, but the males still don't trust her. They know that if she had to choose between catching a fly ball and saving an infant's life, deep in her soul, she would probably elect to save the infant's life, without even considering whether there were men on base.

6 This difference in attitude between men and women carries over to the area of talking about sports, especially sporting events that took place long ago. Take the 1960 World Series. If we were to look at it objectively, we would have to agree that the outcome of the 1960 World Series no longer matters. You could make a fairly strong case that it didn't really matter in 1960. Women know this, which is why you almost never hear them mention the 1960 World Series, whereas you take virtually any male over age 35 and even if he can't remember which of his children has diabetes, he can remember exactly how Pirates shortstop Bill Mazeroski hit the ninth-inning home run that beat the Yankees, and he will take every available opportunity to discuss it at length with other males.

7 See that? Out there in Readerland, you females just read right through that last sentence, nodding in agreement, but you males leaped from your chairs and shouted: "Mazeroski wasn't a SHORTSTOP! Mazeroski played SECOND BASE!" Every male in America has millions of perfectly good brain cells devoted to information like this. We can't help it. We have no perspective. I have a friend named Buzz, a successful businessman and the most rational person you ever want to meet, and the high point of his entire life is the time he got Stan Albeck, the coach of the New Jersey Nets, to look directly at him during a professional basketball game and make a very personal remark rhyming with "duck shoe." I should explain that Buzz and I have season tickets to the Philadelphia 76ers, so naturally we hate the Nets a great deal. It was a great honor when Albeck singled Buzz out of the crowd for recognition. The rest of us males congratulated Buzz as if he'd won the Nobel Prize for Physics.

8 It's silly, really, this male lack of perspective, and it can lead to unnecessary tragedy, such as soccer-riot deaths and the University of Texas. What is even more tragic is that women are losing perspective, too. Even as you read these words, women are writing vicious letters to the editor, expressing great fury at me for suggesting they don't take their racquetball seriously. Soon they will be droning on about the importance of relief pitching.

AFTERWARDS

Vocabulary

obnoxious, enzyme, Dexedrine, reproving, coed. Practice using four of the vocabulary words in context, placing them in separate sentences of parallel construction.

Content

1. Summarize Barry's article and show it to one of your peers. Were you able to capture Barry's sense of humor in your summary? Why or why not?

2. Contrast Barry's portrayal of men and women involved in sports. Does he seem to generalize, and if so, what might be his reason for doing so?

3. Why does Barry suggest that it is really a mistake for men and women to play on a team together? Does he really believe women can't play competitively with men? Justify your answer.

Style and Structure

1. How does Barry immediately call his opinion about sports into question? Why is he satisfied saying, "All I know is whatever the reason, Mankind is still nuts about sports"?

2. Why do you imagine Barry capitalizes the "m" in Mankind and the "w" in Womankind? What might be his strategic purpose? Does he seem to be signaling anything to his readers? Please explain your point of view.

3. Select and explain three or four instances of Barry's use of understatement or "tongue-in-cheek" (not totally serious) remarks. How do they reflect his attitude toward his subject matter?

Collaborative Explorations

In small groups, analyze the literal and implied meaning of Barry's article. Finally, compose a collaborative composition, analyzing how and why some readers might miss the point of Barry's essay if they were not familiar with irony and humor in writing.

Writing Assignments

1. Compose an essay refuting Barry's article "Why Sports Is a Drag." In particular, you may want to prove how and why what he says about women and sports, men and sports, or sports in general is untrue. Support what you claim with plenty of representative examples drawn from personal experience and popular culture today.

2. Inserting your own topic in the blank space, write an essay entitled "Why_____is a Drag." (Also, feel free to replace the word "drag" with thrill, joy, education, and so on.) Model your essay after Barry's article, experimenting with humor.

Thematic Reading Cross-Links: Compare the tone and use of satire in Barry's essay to that of Garrison Keillor in Chapter 6, Environments.

Movie Cross-Links: To gain an appreciation of Barry's satire, take a look at some films featuring popular spectator sports like *A League of Their Own, Bull Durham,* and *The Natural* (baseball); *Semi-Tough* and *North Dallas Forty* (football); *Rocky* and *The Great White Hope* (boxing); and *Fever Pitch* (soccer).

Grays on Trays

Martha L. Henning

MARTHA L. HENNING holds a Ph.D. in Rhetoric and Composition. Her book, *Beyond Understanding: Appeals to the Imagination, Passions, and Will in Mid-Nineteenth-Century American Women's Fiction*, urges readers to read more "holistically," with a change of mind that includes the multiple faculties available to nineteenth-century readers. She teaches writing and literature at Portland Community College, is an active figure at National Conferences on composition and rhetoric at two- and four-year colleges, and really does snowboard in skirts.

ALLUSIONS

Charles Darwin: A naturalist and author of *Origin of Species*—a book that out-lined his theory of evolution—Darwin challenged the contemporary beliefs about the creation of life on Earth and promoted the concept of natural selection: survival of the fittest.

Alpha male: The alpha male is the dominant male in a group—human or animal.

1   I bought my first board twelve years ago when I was in my early forties—that was a few years before I learned to avoid stereo-typing by wearing skirts. I did not begin snowboarding by choice. Rather, the decision came to me. Having packed the car the night before with skis, poles, boots, for the following morning's early start to the mountain, I awoke to discover my car window broken and skis stolen. I responded initially with the culturally constructed expectation, "oh gee, how terrible (or the like, riddled with appropriate expletives). I'll make a claim on my homeowner's insurance, replace my skis, and pretend that this event did not happen." Fortunately, however, I have other voices in my head; one spoke to me: "You've been skiing, now,

for more than a quarter of a century. Why do you keep doing it? You already know how." "Hummm," I pondered in that early morning parking lot, standing amid the shattered glass. "The situation is what it is. And my own reaction to this 'as-is' situation will create my own sense of reality here." At middle age, I contemplated whether I really was a bit old to continue dragging around all the clumsy ski equipment; wearing stiff, uncomfortable boots; and risking knee injuries or slices from too many edges of two "boards" that detached on unexpected impact. As the dawn cracked, I realized that some wannabe thief had Santa Claused me into the occasion to begin life anew—riding on, over, through, and in the general vicinity of snow.

2   Smiling good-bye to skiing, I embraced my first board—the sort that rides only in one direction, now considered antique. Soon it, too, was stolen. My second board seemed greatly improved at the time, but ten years later, it, too, was considered a historic curiosity. In a mere decade, the equipment so "advanced" that with step-in bindings, "Grays on Trays" (as some older boarders call ourselves) no longer need to shoo teen-age boys off the lift-top benches with bogus announcements of sitting privileges meant only for those over fifty. With all sorts of new technological advancement to the equipment, the sport progressively extends not *from* the norm, but *to* a norm. That is, with the opportunity to purchase equipment that makes riding easier, the sport is constructing social norms based, in part, not on the "labor intensive" methods of the past, but on methods comparatively more "capital intensive." For example, no longer having to sit to buckle boots to get going, boarders no longer need expend the labor of hoisting themselves off the snow to stand. In terms of the American long-honored term, "progress," for a price, boarders have "progressed" from the labor intensive necessity to stand up from a sitting position to the capital intensive ease of staying upright and slipping foot into binding to take off. Similarly, the production of snowboards has evolved from the several hand-labor intensive workshops of people's garages to the more capital-intensive factories of far fewer manufacturers. Such "progress" seems to reflect some very foundational principles of the market economy—corporate capitalism.

3   Embedded in the cultural climate of snowboarders themselves, we often see another principle of the market economy—corporate capitalism: competition. Our country's economy early predicated the competitive, aggressive, individualistic self-interest that Charles Darwin would later (1859) explain as "natural" of animals. As investors and/or snowboarders, male humans compete to become the Alpha male. The snowboarding featured in videos at sports bars, in advertisements, on billboards, in magazines—is that exhibiting those elements of competition basic to our country's economy. In a culture based on free enterprise, the person who "gets ahead" or becomes most noticeable is the person who is *most* competitive, aggressive, and individualistically self-interested. Simply put, the snowboarder who pulls the fattest tricks—goes the highest or most acrobatically or from and to the most dangerous places—is behaving precisely according to our culture's most cherished norms.

4   Such so-called "normal" competitive, aggressive, individualistic behavior creates the perceived needs for bounds: governments, laws, enforcement, etc. Hence

the signs, "out of bounds," designating the areas where the "biggest" air occurs. Rightfully, for a snowboarder to behave "out of bounds," that rider would have to refuse the Euro-American culturally constructed norm. A boarder rejecting the norms of competition, aggression, and individualism would be quite "out there" and indeed "extreme." Such a boarder would be rejecting all he or she had learned is dear to the heart of Americans as nurtured and instructed by countless hours of media. Once outside the cultural norms, that boarder might be free to construct "other" realities for the sport or even to align with tenets of "other" cultures. Such a neo-extreme rider, for example, might reassess and ponder behavior that he or she might like to foster to help promote a more ideal world. Such a rider might, for example, consider introducing onto the slopes clothing traditional to "other" cultures.

5   In our "dress for success" culture, where appearances and a tight undercurrent of labels have meaning, wearing unlabeled, frivolous, and colorful skirts can signify a refusal to play by the unspoken rules. Wearing skirts in environments recognized as having basis in inherent competition often elicits smiles and remarks of "far out." On bright sunny days, a snowboarder in a skirt adds a sense of celebration and cheer to the slope—especially as worn by my post-fifty year-old and rather large husband. On darker snowy days, a colorful skirt confronts the utility and practicality of the usual and redundant technologically advanced "equipment" clothing. Grays on Trays have already crossed certain cultural boundaries that tell us that the path of the snowboard should be limited to the youthful, daring, and strong. With the extra weight and diminished muscle structure that comes with being middle aged, adding a skirt just sweetens the scene a tad further.

6   In motion, a boarder can reject the norm in the style of her (or his) ride. Americans since Ben Franklin have been a humorless lot, preferring to get things done, to honor the cost-benefit analysis, to cut to the chase, to get from Point A to Point B. On a snowboard, one can reject this cultural trait by spinning in circles. One can dance around a bit. One can thwart the (rat) race by adding a sense of song. Indeed, a snowboarder can attempt by example and by physical inclusion to subvert the whole American corporate capitalist gig by connecting with others. Snowboarders can celebrate the obvious: no poles. Snowboarders have hands to hold with each other. Holding hands, riders can learn and promote trust and interdependence. Holding hands while spinning in circles down the currently dormant volcano is no serious matter. The greatest difficulty may well be in suppressing the giggles. A boarder can even cross the very tight—indeed spoken—cultural boundary with skiers—if so able and willing—by holding the ends of the skier's poles to spin into the occasional dance.

7   As an extreme sport, snowboarders can begin to shun the safety of the baggy-pant uniform. Likewise, riders can shun the comfort of our culture's "normal" behavior—moving beyond our inherited aggression, competition, and individualism. Challenging some of the many boundaries inherent in American culture, we can contribute to constructing an "other" world—traditional in constructs of kinship, tribalism, inter-dependence, sister- and brotherhood—by riding in commune with each other.

As friends and strangers join hands, we can, as individuals, celebrate the mountain, the gift of gravity, and our shared experience of life on this planet—together.

AFTERWARDS

Vocabulary

Expletives, norms, individualistic, neo-extreme, redundant, diminished, interdependence, corporate, constructs. Despite the use of many colloquial terms, the tone of Henning's essay tends to remain academic. In your opinion, why is this the case?

Content

1. When did Henning begin snowboarding? What situation inspired her to "begin life anew" as a snow sport enthusiast?

2. Why does Henning bring up the issue of "corporate capitalism" in her essay? How does it help develop her thesis that snowboarding is anything but extreme? To what extent do you find her argument convincing?

3. According to Henning, when would a snowboarder truly be "out there" and "extreme"? To what extent do you agree with her assessment and why?

Style and Structure

1. How does Henning use the contrast between two snow sports—skiing and snowboarding—to develop the controlling idea of her essay?

2. What strategic purpose might Henning have had for opening her essay with a narrative paragraph? What effect does it have on readers?

3. In what way does Henning's concluding paragraph pull together and refocus the ultimate point of her essay?

Collaborative Explorations

Many people criticize popular culture because of its commercial tendency. Is that fair? Do people say one thing and do another? Gather in groups and have the members jot down five items they purchased this past year and five things they did in the name of entertainment. Share your list with peers, comparing and contrasting responses. Make a master list including responses from all group members. Finally, present your list to the rest of the class, explaining pop culture's influence—or lack thereof—on the development of social attitudes and values.

Writing Assignments

1. In this chapter, Martha Henning and Dave Barry both address sports fans (see "Why Sports Is a Drag"). Henning focuses on snowboarding, a so-called extreme sport defined by its male practitioners. Barry, on the other hand, mocks the way sports are perceived by men and women—especially males. Write an essay analyzing how both authors satirize and explain sports for an ultimate purpose.

2. Write an argumentative essay proving or disproving Henning's claim that, "With all sorts of new technological advancement to the [snowboarding] equipment, the sport progressively extends not *from* the norm, but *to* a norm." A variation on this assignment would be to take any so-called extreme sport and argue that rather than departing from a norm, the extreme sport of your choice is moving toward or conforming to one.

Thematic Cross-Links: Refer back to the introduction to Chapter 4, Stereotypes and Social Barriers, for a discussion of how expectations sometimes go hand in hand with stereotypes. Both limit possibilities.

Movie Cross-Links: Consult your college documentary archives and check out one or two films on extreme sports (white-water canoeing, snowboarding, motocrossing, BMXing, skateboarding/inlining, surfing). Who seem to be the main sports participants? teenagers? young adults? middle-aged people? men? women? What do participants wear in the sport you view? How do they communicate (words, gestures, attitudes)?

Booming Amusement Parks: The Theme Is Extreme

T. Trent Gegax

T. TRENT GEGAX wrote the following article for the March 30, 1998, issue of *Newsweek* magazine in its "Millennium Notebook" column. Therein he examines the current status of amusement parks in the world in general and America in particular.

ALLUSIONS

Jurassic: Reference to the geological age of the dinosaurs, extending over a period from 208 to 44 million years ago.

ersatz: An inferior substitute for someone or something; phony.

Pegasus: A flying horse from Greek mythology.

Serengeti savanna: A subtropical plain in east Africa between Kenya and Tanzania.

Kenyan: A resident of Kenya, an east African country.

Catalonian: A resident of Catalonia, a state along the east coast of Spain.

1   After "Jurassic Park" ordinary amusement parks looked so . . . ordinary. But fear not, adrenaline junkies; at the total-immersion theme parks of the future, guests will get to play pulse-quickening roles. "The illusion of danger and close brushes with death are a reliable part of theme parks," says Bob Rogers, the theme-park industry's resident futurist, "and the experiences will become more and more intense."

2   We're about to enter a golden age of ersatz adventure—extreme theming, you might call it. "Everything will be themed," says Harrison Price, the park planner whom Walt tapped in 1953 to study the feasibility of Disneyland. "But it'll still be the same idea: storytelling, thrill and an entertaining design response." Theme parks' wildly successful formula, already copied by theme retail stores and restaurants, will work its way into museums and visitor centers. Airports, movie theaters, office buildings—all will "theme out." Even hospitals could get into the act. "We know how to create environments that manipulate people's feelings and health," says Rogers. "Why not apply this to the health industry?" Some well-established themes may start wheezing with age: boredom with theme machines like Hard Rock Café and Planet Hollywood could produce extreme mutations. Already, there's a hospital-themed London restaurant and a car-crash-themed American eatery.

3   As for traditional theme parks, they've never been healthier. Operators can't build them fast enough or raise prices high enough. Admission to Walt Disney World recently sped past the $40 mark. By 2010, more than 182 million parkgoers are expected to hit U.S. turnstiles, up from today's 161 million. To battle the long lines, parks will splinter into every conceivable niche—ethnic, age-based, economic and religious. Not that any of this portends the end of the classic scream ride. "The coaster will always be king," says Dennis Speigel, a park developer. Today's roller coasters go from 0 to 60 mph in 3.5 seconds and drop 200 feet. Tomorrow they'll go even faster and drop 500 feet. And every year, technology gets better at simulating reality. Improved holography coupled with heat blowers, for instance, will allow would-be daredevils to walk through walls of fire—virtually. "We're getting to the point where we're not unlike the movies," says Keith James, a park developer. "If you can imagine it and it can operate 13 hours a day, then you'll see it."

4   Disney's Animal Kingdom, set to open at Disney World next month, could stand in for a movie set. It blends live animals with audio-animatronic creatures ranging from the mythical (Pegasus and unicorn) to the prehistoric. The park's 500 acres of simulated Serengeti savanna suggests that theme parks will move beyond collecting animals to collecting entire ecosystems—and the storytelling ability with its organizational prowess, reproducing an African safari where the animals, unlike their Kenyan counterparts, always appear on cue. Trekkers will pay to venture into "the

bush," where they might stumble across poachers while tracking the matriarch of a herd of elephants.

5   Disney, in effect, is tapping into the adventure-travel boom, packaged (and priced) for the masses. "It's somewhere between watching it on TV and going there," analyst Bob Rogers says. Want photographs of big game to adorn your game-room walls? You don't have to drop $2,000 on a plane ride to Africa. You won't pick up a bug, there's no mysterious food and you'll recognize the toilets. And, the argument goes, places like Animal Kingdom will stem the tide of people pollution at the natural wonders they imitate.

6   And some theme parks are preserving human habitats. At the Port Adventure theme park, near Tarragona, Spain, real Catalonian fishermen spend their evenings drinking in fake cantinas—the kind that were destroyed when the old seaport fell to redevelopers. "Someday parks like this will be among the few places people can really drink in their history," Rogers says. And, as the occasional bar brawl confirms, there's still a place for a taste of real danger.

AFTERWARDS

Vocabulary

adrenaline, immersion, futurist, feasibility, holography, cantina. Take each vocabulary word and look up its definition first in a standard English dictionary and then in a thesaurus. What meanings are associated with each word? Finally, write an original sentence using each word.

Content

1. According to Gegax, what can Americans look forward to from future theme parks? Have the designers of such parks gone as far as possible in finding ways to entertain people, immersing them in experiences beyond compare?

2. What is the status of traditional theme parks in America? How might this be a barometer (measuring stick) for amusement parks yet to come? Explain.

3. To what extent will technology determine the direction of many theme parks in the future? Discuss some of the examples Gegax offers, as well as a few of your own.

Style and Structure

1. How does Gegax organize his essay? How does it lead naturally to his concluding paragraph?

2. Characterize the style of Gegax's essay. When addressing this question, consider his (1) word choice, (2) illustrations and examples, (3) concrete allusions, and (4) transitional devices and linking words.

3. In the concluding paragraph, Gegax ironically comments that "real Catalonian fishermen spend their evenings drinking in fake cantinas—the kind that were destroyed when the old seaports fell to redevelopers." How might such incidents place the positive attributes of amusement parks in a different light?

Collaborative Explorations

In small groups, do a historical survey of amusement parks in your state since the 1950s. From what social, musical, spiritual, or artistic source did each evolve? For instance, what inspired Dollywood in Tennessee, Marine World in California (and elsewhere), or Universal Studio's movie park in Florida? Have amusement park patrons changed over time? If so, why? Prepare a brief oral presentation to share with the rest of the class.

Writing Assignments

1. Compose a piece explaining how and why you think businesses have adopted many of the engaging visual traits of amusement parks (e.g., Fry's electronic stores are built like spaceships, Mayan temples, and Egyptian tombs). Why might a store or other business housed in a visually interesting building promote sales? Think about the hotels in Las Vegas that have adopted theme park images.

2. Write an essay wherein you disprove Gegax's thesis that amusement parks are alive and booming—a trend that is certain to continue into the 21st century. Begin by acknowledging that such parks are doing well right now. Then spend the rest of your essay arguing how and why such public interest and ongoing prosperity cannot last.

Thematic Reading Cross-Links: Refer back to Garrison Keillor's essay, "Minnesota's Sensible Plan," in Chapter 6, Environments—as well as Joshua Quittner's essay, "Life and Death on the Web" in Chapter 7, Cyberspace and Technology—to see how extremism extends itself into our daily lives and influences rational decisions.

Movie Cross-Links: See *Jurassic Park*, a movie mentioned in this essay about the ultimate amusement theme park. You might also look up *Westworld*, the story of a thematic vacation resort–amusement park—where adult fantasies are served by robots that begin to go berserk.

Extremely Cool
A. J. Jacobs

According to author/journalist **A. J. JACOBS**, extreme, in its purest sense, "should be dangerous, shock indulging, and envelope pushing," yet it is more than simply pop culture's current "happening" term, a term replacing former trendy words like "wicked" and "bad." Jacobs's article, "Extremely Cool," initially appeared in a Special Double Issue '96 of *Entertainment Weekly*.

ALLUSIONS

Barry Goldwater: Arizona senator and Republican presidential candidate in 1964.

Courtney Love: The lead singer for Hole (an alternative rock group) and a film actress.

Quentin Tarantino: Former video store clerk turned writer/director of *Reservoir Dogs* and *Pulp Fiction*—influential films in the early 1990s.

Charles Manson: Convicted mass murderer and cult leader of "the family" who remains a nightmarish symbol of the drug culture of the 1960s.

Che Guevara: Romanticized Cuban revolutionary; assassinated in Bolivia in 1970.

Lenny Bruce: A "hipster" comedian in the late 1950s and early 1960s known for taboo humor and shocking language.

Lollapalooza: A movable music festival held annually during the summer since 1991.

1   Perhaps you've seen this commercial: A twentysomething bald dude emits a glass shattering "Aaaaarrggh!" Heavy guitar riffs pummel your eardrums. A water-skier—on bare feet, no less—makes a death-defying leap off a monster ramp. What ultra-funky, Gen-X product are they peddling now? The latest Soundgarden album, perhaps? A new flavor of Fruitopia? Nope, this ad is pitching . . . a long-distance phone service from the NYNEX company. And here's the real marketing coup: The service is called Xtreme Dialing. Yes, folks, we have a winner! The suits at NYNEX, the Northeastern Baby Bell, have strrrrretched the word extreme to its most ludicrous form in pop culture thus far. But you can hardly blame them. As good capitalists, they're duty-bound to exploit the concept du jour; and for those who've spent the past year in a biosphere watching Blockbuster videos, extreme is just that. (Xtreme Dialing, by the way, has something to do with collect calls; we're still not clear.)

2   In its purest sense, something extreme should be dangerous, shock inducing, and envelope pushing. But pure or not, extreme is everywhere. On ESPN, you can watch extreme sports—a buffet of bone-crunching competitions ranging from bungee jumping to mountain biking. In *Twister*, you can root for the Extreme, Bill Paxton's

ballsy tornado chaser. In *New York* magazine, you'll spot a close contender for NYNEX's crown: recipes for Extreme Lemonade (just add pineapple juice!).

3   Still, extreme is more than just this week's happenin' term. A survey of today's pop culture indicates we may have entered the Age of Extreme. From Alanis Morissette's revenge ballads to Dennis Rodman's feather boa, from a website about exploding heads to Jim Carrey's martian facial contortion, moderation has finally met its match.

4   It's difficult to pinpoint when things started getting extreme. As with many bygone trendy words (see wicked and bad), extreme began its semantic life on the wrong side of the tracks. Traditionally, you avoided things extreme—think extreme poverty, extreme measures, or extreme unction. At the 1964 Republican National Convention, Barry Goldwater tried to give the word a makeover. "Extremism in the defense of liberty is no vice," he intoned. No dice. Goldwater lost the election to Lyndon B. Johnson by, uh, an extreme margin.

5   The true reform of the word began in the late '70s, when a pack of suicidal skiers, some sporting Day-Glo outfits and Mohawks, decided it might be fun to helicopter onto remote mountains and jump off 80-foot cliffs. Calling themselves extreme skiers, they had a snappy motto: "You fall, you die!" Extreme skiing gave birth to an entire genre of gonzo sports such as sky surfing, skateboard jumping, and the ugliest offshoot, Extreme Fighting, a bloody Cro-Magnon version of boxing that airs on pay per view.

6   These Che Guevaras of sports, covered with tattoos and scabs, fueled a fast-growing multimillion-dollar business (in 1995, 2.3 million snowboarders swarmed the slopes, up 92 percent from three years before). ESPN took note. The sports channel last year created the Extreme Games, a kind of weeklong athletic Lollapalooza that grabbed such good ratings the channel is now holding this in-your-face Olympics yearly instead of biannually, as originally planned. "We're a nation of thrill seekers," says Frank Farley, former president for the American Psychological Association and a recreational sports expert. "It's in tune with what we are."

7   Well, it's certainly in tune with what Madison Avenue craves. Fast, flashy, and oh so visual, extreme sports reel in that all-important Gen-X consumer. "They are an advertiser's wet dream," says Steven Daly, co-author of *alt.culture*, a book cataloging the '90s zeitgeist. "They're modern, contemporary, colorful, adventurous."

8   In 1993, Mountain Dew touched off the extreme-ad stampede with spots featuring cliff-jumping bikers; since then, the yellow fizz has become the fifth best-selling soft drink. This summer, Mountain Dew, along with such companies as MTV and Burton Snowboards, will sponsor the Extreme Network, a bizarre summer contest that equips half a million teens with low-cost beepers so they can receive messages from the likes of Evel Knievel and extreme-dial in for prizes. A torrent of other companies, from Kellogg's to Acura, have jumped on the bandwagon, packing their ads with hyperkinetic warriors. (See Tony the Tiger rock climbing. Major concussions are greeeeeat!)

9   From extreme sports, the word spread far and wide. Marketers on the World Wide Web, for instance, have started extreme clubs, 'zines, and the Extreme Résumé Drop, which automatically sends out your CV to 200 firms of your choice. Oh, the

rush! As Randall Rothenberg, former *New York Times* advertising columnist, says: "Extreme is to 1996 what new and improved was to 1963." And it's an apt comparison. Just as the latter catchphrase captured the wide-eyed optimism of the Kennedy era, extreme seems to suit our current culture.

10   More specifically, our popular culture. There isn't a corner of entertainment that doesn't have some high-decibel example of extremism. Just try *Pacific Blue*, the USA Network's *Baywatch* rip-off, an hour of buff dudes doing flips on their mountain bikes. MTV has *Singled Out*, an extreme version of *The Love Connection*, in which Jenny McCarthy shouts down hapless frat boys. And the birth of the Net has allowed everyone with a modem to indulge his most extreme compulsions, whether they be lust for Wilma Flintstone or a dweebish obsession with Dr. Who.

11   Then there are the extreme personalities that dot the landscape: Rodman dyes his hair the color of Tang, divulges gritty details about his sex life, and dynamites our traditional idea of how an athlete ought to strut his stuff. Quentin Tarantino lets loose with a platoon's worth of bullets in one over-the-top movie after another. And no doubt Courtney Love's mascara-smeared mug will one day appear next to the word extreme in your Funk & Wagnall's.

12   Perhaps we've thought of these various characters as odd or fresh, or maybe just incredibly annoying. But with the concept of extreme as a prism, these stars snap into focus: We embrace them not just for their talent but also because their attitude gives us the same adrenaline-fueled rush as extreme sports—sans helmet. They're the pop equivalent of street lugers: slightly dangerous, one step beyond.

13   Granted, boundary-busting entertainment is hardly a new idea. Just ask your parents, even your grandparents. It's traveled under pseudonyms such as hip or cool, showing up on Lenny Bruce's cursing lips and in Elvis' '70s excesses. Still, in today's pop culture, not only is there more of it, but the bar has been raised: The extreme has become more extreme than ever.

14   And more nihilistic, too. Unlike the just-do-it enthusiasm it engenders in the sports world, extreme often becomes something darker in pop culture. In publishing, right on the heels of A.M. Homes' *The End of Alice,* the graphic fictional story of a pedophile, comes Poppy Brite's *Exquisite Corpse*, a novel told from a serial killer's point of view. ("People need something to kick 'em in the ass a little," says Brite.) American moviegoers will get a taste of extreme filmmaking in July with *Trainspotting*, a British ode to heroin addiction that makes *Pulp Fiction* look tame, peppered as it is with shots of flying feces and a dead baby crawling on the ceiling. "Extreme is ironic, postmodern fun with a bit of a nasty edge," says Mark Gill, president of marketing for *Trainspotting*'s distributor, Miramax. "At the end of it all you leave having a good time."

15   In music, traditionally the most extreme medium, the Wonder bread Hootie & the Blowfish fad seems to have abated for the moment (their second album isn't breaking sales records). Filling their spot, Lollapalooza '96 band Psychotica waxes psychotic (the lead singer often appears in the buff on stage), Marilyn Manson conjures up images of Charles Manson, and the surviving members of the hoary extremist band the Sex Pistols are touring again.

16   Even Broadway, home to Velveeta productions such as *Cats* and genteel revivals like *The King and I*, has gone gaga for *Rent*, a cheddar-sharp tale of junkies and AIDS in New York's East Village. "We're not going to settle for the quiet puppet shows of yore," says Michael Marsden, a culture watcher and author. "The idea is to continually stun people. Entertainments that will survive are exaggerated ones that appeal to the senses in the fullest possible way."

17   If we are in the midst of an Extreme Invasion, what's driving it? Ask around and you'll get some appropriately extreme theories. Eric Perlman, the director of nine documentaries on extreme skiing, blames it on society's lack of a good war. "Men have a genetic and psychological need for speed, a need for danger," says Perlman. "And as the number of battles diminishes in the atomic age, we need a place to express them ourselves."

18   Or maybe it's about the plight of those deprived white folks. "All they have is a sort of soft culture," theorizes *alt.culture's* Daly. "Like that episode of Friends where Chandler and Joey got these La-Z-Boy recliners and reverted to this infantile state of neediness. If we take that as a symbol of white male culture, extreme sports are one way to feel real again, to get back your physicality."

19   Perhaps. But the most common theory lays the blame on that reliable old scapegoat: kids today. The thing is, kids today are different. Having been spoon-fed so many hours of Buzz Bin-intensity stimuli with minimal human contact, they like their entertainment fast, and they like it alone. "Extreme sports are done individually," says *Adweek* editor at large Barbara Lippert. "It's for the generation that likes to be by themselves and wired to the Net all night."

20   Of course, the very success of the word extreme spells its doom among the hipnoscenti. "It used to mean the total commitment of a samurai warrior," sighs director Perlman. "Now it's a drink with two types of fruit juice." (Yes, but one of them's pineapple!)

21   Today some extreme athletes are opting for other adjectives, calling their passion aggressive skiing or alternative sports. Even such a thoroughly mainstream outlet as ESPN has already shed the word: This year, the Extreme Games have been changed to the X Games. "We don't want to become passé," says Ron Semiao, the ESPN executive who created the contest. "In five years, extreme may become about as popular as the word mod or groovy."

22   Now, there's an idea for NYNEX: Groovy Dialing.

AFTERWARDS

Vocabulary

Gen-X, du jour, Day-Glo, Cro-Magnon, hipnoscenti, biosphere, decibel, nihilistic, pedophile. Select words describing human character or personality types, and then write an original sentence for each word, demonstrating your understanding of its proper application in written communication.

Content

1. What is the thesis of Jacobs's essay?

2. What does Jacobs's article suggest is the relationship between individualism and the pursuit of extremism?

3. To what extent do you think the author's numerous allusions enlighten some readers and possibly overwhelm others?

Style and Structure

1. Why do you imagine extremes often have a more dynamic impact on individuals than moderation? How might a tendency toward moderation inhibit "risk taking" in matters that might otherwise lead to outstanding accomplishments? How might "risk taking" become an end in itself by being self-destructive?

2. Discuss how Jacobs's references to specific people, places, and events enable him to develop his essay coherently and concretely. How might you use more specific references and examples to strengthen your own writing?

3. How does the author's essay structure lead his readers to the conclusion he wants them to reach? Be specific.

Collaborative Explorations

Take the vocabulary term *Gen-X* and research the word a bit. Have half of your group interview people their own age and the other half interview people their parents' age. (We are well aware of the fact that peers in your class may range anywhere from seventeen to seventy-five or older; what is needed here is a diverse look at one term. Therefore, you may have group one interview people between seventeen and twenty-five and the other group interview those twenty-six and older.) How does each group perceive the concept of Gen-X? How were your individual and collective opinions influenced and shaped?

Writing Assignments

1. Think about how "extremism" occurs not only in pop culture but also in religion and politics. Who would you consider an extremist? Write your own definition of this term and support it with specific examples.

2. In 1964, Republican presidential candidate Barry Goldwater said in one of his campaign speeches, "Extremism in defense of liberty is no vice." These words inspired some people and frightened others. How would

you interpret this sentence? Would you defend it as a political principle or attack it? Thoroughly support your argument with representative details and examples, along with clear reasoning and critical thinking.

Thematic Reading Cross-Links: For an insight into America's appetite for extremism in attire and body adornment, see Joe Woodward's "Pumped, Pierced, Painted and Pagan" from Chapter 12, The Body: Language, Ritual, and Wellness—A Casebook.

Movie Cross-Links: For portraits of extremes, see *Pulp Fiction* in the Film Links at the end of this chapter and *Blue Velvet* on the list of cult films at the end of Chapter 11, Movies.

The Visual Connection: Photograph Writing Activities

The Beatles: Sgt. Pepper's Lonely Hearts Club Band

1. In 1967, the Beatles released *Sgt. Pepper's Lonely Hearts Club Band*, an album that established new directions in music and demonstrated their awareness of popular culture, past and present. The artistic album cover paid tribute to artists, musicians, authors, actresses and actors, and many other people. Review the figures on the album cover on the previous page, and identify as many of them as you can. What role did specific individuals have in shaping the fine arts, humanities, social sciences, and so on? Write a short composition explaining what musician or musical group today, in your opinion, would write and record an album/CD with the impact of *Sgt. Pepper's Lonely Heart's Club Band* in terms of its enduring influence on music and popular culture as we move into the 21st century. Who would be the most likely pop culture figures on the CD cover of your modern equivalent of *Sgt. Pepper's Lonely Heart's Club Band?* Why?

2. Popular culture tends to be a part of our daily lives, and it manifests itself in many ways. For instance, take a look at the following photograph of the Goodyear Blimp. Apart from being a dirigible and an obvious advertisement for Goodyear Tires, what other associations do you have with it? When and where do you see blimps most often?

The Goodyear Blimp

Film Links: Popular Culture

1. Select a few movies from the Film Links list, view them, and jot down your initial impressions of them. How accurately do you think the films you watched depict the popular culture of the day? Who or what tended to shape your opinions? Using your common sense and identification with popular culture, write an analytical essay explaining why a film is or is not an accurate record of the pop culture it portrays.

2. Compare and contrast how popular culture is portrayed in two of the movies below; some suggested pairs would be *The Graduate* and *American Graffiti, Alice's Restaurant* and *Crumb, Play It Again Sam* and *Diner, Shampoo* and *After Hours*, and *Clueless* and *Pulp Fiction*.

3. Write an expository essay explaining how popular culture is identified, glamorized, and/or used in one or more of the following movies. How, for instance, does *American Graffiti* embody the spirit of the late 1950s and early 1960s? (Consider the values and "hangouts" of the characters, as well as the soundtrack for the film.) You may want to use some of the heuristics—questions—from Writing about Films listed in the Appendix at the end of the book to generate ideas and shape your analysis.

The Graduate (USA, Mike Nichols, 1967). A college grad is encouraged to go into plastics as a career but gets involved with Mrs. Robinson instead.

Alice's Restaurant (USA, Arthur Penn, 1970). Folk music, draft resistance, VW vans, dropping out of college—it was the 1960s, man.

American Graffiti (USA, George Lucas, 1973). High school grads in the early 1960s cruise their small downtown looking for something to do while listening to Wolfman Jack on their car radios.

Shampoo (USA, Hal Ashby, 1975). It's 1968; Richard Nixon is running for president, and an L.A. hairdresser is pursuing money and women all over town.

Diner (USA, Barry Levinson, 1982). A bunch of young guys like to hang out late in a Baltimore diner. They argue, commiserate, and strategize about many things.

After Hours (USA, Martin Scorsese, 1985). A yuppie-ish word processor finds himself in lower Manhattan with no money. His attempts to get home are frustrated by bizarre night-world characters.

Pulp Fiction (USA, Quentin Tarantino, 1994). Two chatty hitmen are linked to tawdry, violent lives that are caricatures of crime story stereotypes.

Crumb (USA, Terry Zwigoff, 1995). Documentary of underground cartoonist and his family, plagued by various forms of mental illness.

Clueless (USA, Amy Heckerling, 1995). Beverly Hills teen of the 1990s believes her matchmaking skills can bring her friends happiness. Loose adaptation of Jane Austen's *Emma*.

That Thing You Do (USA, Tom Hanks, 1996). In 1964, a rock band from a small town in Pennsylvania suddenly has a hit record.

Scream (USA, Wes Craven, 1996). A teen-slasher horror movie in which the teens make jokes about the conventions of teen-slasher horror movies.

Can't Hardly Wait (USA, Harry Elfont and Deborah Kaplan, 1998). A comedy about a graduation night party and the zany world of teen romance.

Ten Things I Hate about You (USA, Gil Junger, 1999). Sisters with opposite temperaments find romance at Stadium High School, in a loose adaptation of *The Taming of the Shrew*.

She's All That (USA, Robert Iscove, 1999). A comedy that poses the question, "What is the real meaning of a makeover?"

Legally Blonde (USA, Robert Luketic, 2001). A fizzy comedy about blondes, revenge, and Harvard Law School.

Additional Writing Assignments

1. Write an expository essay explaining alternative culture to an audience that has little or no real understanding of it. Use plenty of concrete examples to describe aspects of alternative culture vividly. (You may want to do some research in the way of readings and interviews before prewriting and drafting this assignment.)

2. Compare and contrast two or more lifestyles in the past forty years that are directly or indirectly a characteristic of various forms of pop culture.

3. Have you ever been criticized for the way you speak, walk, or behave? When people criticize you, what is the basis of their criticism? Write an essay defending your lifestyle.

4. Write an essay in which you defend the "anything goes" atmosphere driven by popular culture in the television marketplace, advertising, and films. Is the potential to make a lot of quick money by capitalizing on human vices or misery enough justification to disregard the long-term damage of human exploitation? Will truly unethical, inhumane people self-destruct in a competitive market based on attracting the maximum number of people? Use representative examples and careful logic as you build your argument.

5. What popular culture trends in the present do you think will continue into the future? Make a list of these trends and write an essay that makes a realistic prediction of future possibilities. You might think of things like food, fads, exercising machines, plastic surgery, dancing, movies, and so on.

Chapter Nine

Television

Observations and Opinions

A quarter of a century after the introduction of television into American society, a period that has seen the medium become so deeply ingrained in American life that in at least one state the television set has now attained the rank of a legal necessity, safe from repossession in case of debt along with clothes, cooking utensils, and the like, television viewing has become an enviable and ordinary part of daily life.

—MARIE WINN FROM "THE PLUG-IN DRUG: TV AND THE AMERICAN FAMILY"

I believe television is going to be the test of the modern world, and that in this new opportunity to see beyond the range of our vision, we shall discover either a new and unbearable disturbance of the general peace or a saving radiance to the sky. We shall stand or fall by television.

—E. B. WHITE FROM "REMOVAL"

Television in America, it would appear, is the soma of Huxley's Brave New World. But let me hasten to say that America's immersion in television is not to be taken as an attempt by a malevolent government or an avaricious corporate state to employ the age-old trick of distracting the masses with circuses. The problem is not that TV presents the masses with entertaining subject matter, but that television presents all subject matter as entertaining.

—NEIL POSTMAN FROM "AMUSING OURSELVES TO DEATH"

*When TV talks crime, people listen. A recent study conducted by
Michael J. Robinson, visiting scholar at the American Enterprise
Institute, and Maura Clancey, at the University of Maryland, shows
that "violent crimes are more memorable as news events than all
but the most dramatic political occurrences." Crimes considered
most newsworthy—children being molested in a Baltimore day-care
center; a paroled mugger shooting a New York transit cop—have
little in common with the routine petty crimes that dominate the
police blotter.*

—GEORGETTE BENNETT FROM "TV'S CRIME COVERAGE
IS TOO SCARY AND MISLEADING"

Observations and Opinions:
Reading/Writing Activities

1. When Winn states, "Television viewing has become an enviable and
   ordinary part of daily life" in the excerpt from "The Plug-in Drug:
   TV and the American Family," do you feel she speaks for you? Why or
   why not? Does she seem to have a particular audience in mind as she
   writes? Who?

2. Compare E. B. White's prophetic quote about television from
   "Removal" to Neil Postman's perception of television expressed in
   "Amusing Ourselves to Death." Why might Postman agree or disagree
   with White's statement, "We shall stand or fall by television"? Justify
   your position.

3. Although some people constantly criticize television, others heap
   compliments on it. Where do you stand? Do you watch television often?
   What sorts of programs do you watch? Why might Georgette Bennett's
   excerpt from "TV Crime Coverage Is Too Scary and Misleading" be a
   cause for alarm? Can we afford to ignore the social/political events in
   our lives, or would we live healthier, more balanced lives if we did not
   watch newscasts or tabloid news programs like *Hard Copy*, *America's
   Most Wanted*, and *Entertainment Tonight*? Write a paragraph in
   your journal in which you argue for the importance of television in your
   own life, as well as in the lives of those around you. Would television
   be easy to replace in our daily lives, or are we hopelessly addicted
   to it?

Introduction

Television has provoked mixed feelings since the first sets began to appear in viewers' homes in the late 1940s and became common in households during the 1950s. For some it is a whole new stage in human communication. Marshall McLuhan said it would create a "global village" that would break down the barriers that have so long led to misunderstanding and conflict between cultures and nations. Others saw its vast commercial potential for advertising products, stimulating demand, and creating new jobs. Some thought it could be used for educational purposes. Special channels were created for children's programs, university courses, language classes, and do-it-yourselfers. The civic-minded saw television as a way to spread democratic values and to encourage informed debate on important issues. Some of these ideas have become actualities.

On the other hand, television's critics have seen it as an invader, an alien electronic device whose effects are mostly negative. For those individuals, television puts an end to family conversation, to reading, to community participation. The constant barrage of commercials brainwashes viewers who become mind-numbed consumers of commodities, fads, and fashions with no sense of personal or social responsibility. Television is blamed for many social problems: illiteracy, violent crime, sexual immorality, corrupt politicians, cultural decline, and pervasive stupidity. Television turns citizens into couch potatoes. Intellectuals, teachers, and religious leaders encourage people not to watch it. It is accused of serving as a platform for liberal reformers and as a tool for conservative propagandists.

The debate goes on. The readings in this chapter will give you four more attempts to understand the role that television can and does play in our lives. Richard Zoglin assesses the effects of the ever-increasing number of cable channels and how cable television will allow for both trends and countertrends. Jane Whitney gives a firsthand account of her disillusionment as a talk-show host in the highly competitive "tell-all" format. Jonathan Rauch examines the phenomenon of "Reality TV" that has changed the viewing habits of people around the world. Rauch wonders how "real" any television program can be and what promotional agendas may be behind this new interest in supposedly "real" events and situations. Oscar Hijuelos contemplates how his image of his father has evolved over time after seeing a younger version of his father on *I Love Lucy*, an old television show (something you or your children may experience merely by reviewing home video recordings in years to come).

As you read these essays, you might think about your own habits as a television viewer. All forms of technology—the telephone, the automobile, the computer—serve as tools for solving problems but create unforeseen consequences as well.

The same is true for television. It has affected almost every aspect of our lives. Until fifty years ago or so, people lived without it. Could we do so again? Would we want to?

Gathering Thoughts: Prereading Inquiries

1. Does television encourage crime, violence, and deviant behavior?

2. Is watching television a positive social pastime? What are its good qualities, and who benefits from it most?

3. Are soap operas too explicit? Do they reflect life as you know it? Why are they so popular?

4. Who are the most influential people on television today? Do they provide youths with positive role models? Do you believe people model their behavior after celebrities on television, in film, or in music and art?

5. If you were a television producer, what sort of television program would you develop and why? What kind of program would you like to see on television?

6. Should we continue to censor movies shown on television? Is the ratings system useful?

7. What is appealing about watching a game show such as *Jeopardy*, *Wheel of Fortune*, or *The Weakest Link*?

8. How well does television reflect the population where you live? Are individuals from diverse ethnic backgrounds fairly represented on TV newscasts, sitcoms, and dramas? Does television exploit taboo subjects for ratings, or does it make an honest effort to address them with sensitivity and understanding?

9. What news programs do you watch? Are tabloid news programs like *Entertainment Tonight* informative? What do you learn by watching tabloid news?

10. Do you consider television "good company"? How often do you watch television with other people? Is television a mental distraction, or do people form serious bonds with television shows like soap operas and the characters within?

Beyond Your Wildest Dreams
Richard Zoglin

RICHARD ZOGLIN writes for many popular magazines, including *Time*. He authored the following article, "Beyond Our Wildest Dreams," for the special fall 1992 issue of *Time*, subtitled "Millennium Beyond the Year 2000." Georgia Harbison did additional reporting for the article.

ALLUSIONS

Kurt Vonnegut: Author of satiric science fiction such as *Cat's Cradle* and *Slaughterhouse Five* (see his article "Technology and Me" in Chapter 7).

Neil Postman: Academic media and social critic. His works include *Amusing Ourselves to Death* and *Technopoly*.

Philip Glass: Contemporary American composer of the operas *Einstein on the Beach* and *Sattyagraha*, film scores, and pop music.

Robert Brustein: Drama critic for *The New Republic*.

Jean Genet: French novelist and playwright.

> *"Here I am an educated person and a writer and I watch every channel, all 75 of them, simultaneously."*
>
> —KURT VONNEGUT

1   If it frightens you to think of how much TV has affected our cultural habits in just a few decades, then get ready for another zap to your system. In the future, what we know as TV will have been transmogrified from a box in the corner into a ubiquitous, wall-to-wall bath of infotainment. And the array of program choices, already so bewildering, will multiply almost to infinity. But that is the predictable part. The most tantalizing and scary prospect is what this electronic deluge will do to us. Will we become zombie consumers of Lethal Weapon 17, or connoisseurs of Greek drama on channel 894? Will our voracious image consumption erode our ability to read and speak, or will TV teach us new languages? Will we be happy in our comfy video cocoons, or yearn to escape from that cell and get our shoes muddy at an outdoor concert?

2   Two coming developments will take the video revolution to a new realm. Fiber-optic cable will bring hundreds, even thousands, of channels into the home. And

interactive computer technology will give formerly passive viewers almost total control over what they see, when they see it and what they do with it. People will be able to call up on their screen virtually everything the culture produces, from the latest Hollywood movie to lessons in chess, from an old episode of *The Twilight Zone* to this morning's newspaper, custom-edited for individual readers.

3   The array of choices will be so rich that TV may finally break out of the current malaise described by Bruce Springsteen in *57 Channels (And Nothing On)*. In his book *Life After Television*, George Gilder predicts that the merging of TV and computers will bring the demise of network mediocrity. "Big events—the Super Bowl or the election debates or the most compelling mass programs—will still command their audiences," he writes. "But all the media junk food and filler will tend to disappear. People will order what they want rather than settling for what is there."

4   Society will pay a price for that. As the mass audience disperses, there will be fewer cultural reference points, less common ground. "We have nothing to share now," laments Vonnegut. "There are thousands of things that a person sitting at home can see that nobody else is seeing. We have become lonelier because we no longer have a few central works of art to discuss."

5   Lonelier and less literate. Books will almost certainly become a more elitist and rarefied art form. The common currency of pop culture and public discourse will be the quick-cut, in-your-face style of TV sitcoms and music videos. "The visual image will be familiar, more communicative to people. But at the same time, there will be a general humiliation of language," says Neil Postman, chairman of New York University's communications department. Our connection with the real world may grow ever more tenuous as images increasingly supplant words and symbolic gestures overwhelm rational argument. The portent is ominous: How can an electorate conditioned by MTV ever have the patience to solve the budget deficit?

6   The couch potatoes of the future, whose every entertainment wish will be granted at the touch of a button, may have trouble interacting with one another in the real world. One hypothesis: people will become more self-centered, less attuned to their neighbors and society. Bridging the gap between cultures and races could become more difficult. Civility will suffer too. "Because most public events and entertainment will be experienced privately, people will lose a sense of how to behave in public," says Postman. "Even on the screen in movie theaters, they already have to tell people not to talk."

7   Yet the reassuring aspect of culture is that every stifling trend seems to produce a refreshing, subversive countertrend. At least a few people will grow tired of living like pampered moles and will want to go out to see a play or a concert. "If you spend the day watching your computer, you're not going to watch your television at night," contends Philip Glass, the avant-garde composer. "You'd rather go to the park and watch someone dancing." Live drama, predicts critic and iconoclastic director Robert Brustein, "will become what Jean Genet called 'the theater of the catacombs.' It will find small enclaves with the remainder of the faithful, like Christianity in the early days."

8   What will transform the content of culture most of all is the artistic world's great imponderable: individual genius. A prognosticator in the year 1500 would have had

no way of knowing that Shakespeare was just around the corner. A music seer in 1950 could not have guessed that Elvis Presley was warming up offstage. The next artistic revolutionary may already be waiting in the wings, ready to revitalize a tired art form or set the cultural world on a new course. And when the Next Big Thing hits, one question will hang most urgently in the air: What channel is it on?

AFTERWARDS

Vocabulary

transmogrified, ubiquitous, zombie, connoisseurs, voracious, malaise, mediocrity, elitist, tenuous, portent, ominous, civility, stifling, subversive, catacombs, enclaves, prognosticator. Reread how each of the above words was used in context. Then use five of them in original sentences about television.

Content

1. This article suggests that a single cause, the "video revolution," will lead to multiple effects in the future. What are they?

2. The article states that "every stifling trend" seems to produce a "subversive countertrend." What does this mean in the context of this article? Can you think of other examples?

3. Explain how the essay's title relates to its content. In what way does it create some reader expectations?

Style and Structure

1. This article consists of facts and predictions. How many factual statements can you identify? How many statements are purely hypothetical?

2. How does the author make use of quotes to make points and provide corroboration? Find each of the quotes and explain their impact.

3. Discuss the author's style of presenting information.

Collaborative Explorations

Form a small group and have each member list all the television programs he or she watches each week; then compare lists. Also, discuss channel surfing and how you watch several programs simultaneously. Discuss these questions: Does watching television develop any visual perception skills? Is there such a thing as video literacy? Are some people better at watching television than others? Does watching television lead to mindlessness, or can it sharpen mental acuity?

Writing Assignments

1. Write a personal essay in which you describe and defend your own television viewing habits. Explain how you use television. Show how television can both inform and entertain in ways that make it a positive addition to everyday life.

2. Write your own predictive essay. Given the current trends in all forms of electronic communication—computers, phones, television—make your own list of possible positive and negative consequences for the 21st century. Discuss specific current trends and project them into the future.

Thematic Reading Cross-Links: See the introduction to Chapter 7, Cyberspace and Technology, for background information on some of the technological advancements that could well change television as we know it into wall-to-wall "infotainment."

Movie Cross-Links: See *The Truman Show*, a movie about a man whose life is a twenty-four-hour-a-day TV show, listed in the Film Links at the end of this chapter.

When Talk Gets Too Cheap

Jane Whitney

An author, journalist, and former talk-show host, **Jane Whitney** originally wrote "When Talk Gets Too Cheap," an essay reminiscing about her days as a talk-show host, for the June 12, 1995, edition of *U.S. News and World Report*. From 1992 through 1994, Telepictures, Inc., produced *The Jane Whitney Show*, and at its height, the show reached 80 percent of the television stations and viewing audiences across the United States. Sadly, she reflects that audiences now look at dysfunctional talk-show guests as "entertainers" rather than "victims of exploitation."

ALLUSIONS

John Wayne Bobbitt: An abusive, philandering husband who was dismembered by his wife, Lorena.

Agent Orange: Chemical defoliant used in the Vietnam War.

General Colin Powell: Former head of the Joint Chiefs of Staff and current secretary of state.

Maya Angelou: African American poet/author of such works as *I Know Why the
Caged Bird Sings.*

Nielsen: Rating service used to determine advertising rates for television shows.

Lothario: Name of lover/hero from 18th-century drama.

1   I remember the precise moment when I realized I was a talk-show host who didn't
want to talk about what America wants to hear. I was interviewing tabloid Hall of
Famer John Wayne Bobbitt, whose willingness to trot out his new fiancée had
catapulted him back to the top of talk television's "most wanted" list after a brief
hiatus from the headlines.

2   Finding out whether Bobbitt's microsurgery had been a success wasn't part of
my agenda. All I wanted to know was why he persisted in basking in the halogen
glare of the media rather than moving on with his life. All the studio audience wanted
to know was whether he could still "do it." Disdainful of my probing of Bobbitt's
psyche, the audience started heckling me with all the deference of voyeurs at a wet
T-shirt contest. Defeated, I turned over the microphone to a young man wearing a
muscle shirt. "Are you, uh . . . you know . . . uh, can you still . . . uh, you know?" he
stuttered.

3   It was the would-be Mrs. Bobbitt who graciously spared him further suspense.
"John is a real man in every sense of the word," she said proudly. Bobbitt beamed.
The audience shrieked its approval. Amid the din, I wished I was standing in front of
a weather map doing the five-day forecast. So began the slow death of a career-long
dream.

4   I had cut my teeth on TV talk pre-Oprah—in the early '80s—when the fledgling
genre bestowed a kinder, gentler look at then closeted controversies like Agent
Orange and alcoholic teens. Back then, when people parceled out their privacy in
public, you got the feeling they were trying to fix what was broken in their lives. By
1991, when I returned from a stint as a network correspondent to start a syndicated
talk program, the audience was clamoring for raw conflict. Living-room
rubberneckers now demanded a whole new breed of talk-show guests. Substantive
storytellers were mostly relegated to the B team. Outrageous raconteurs were the
"people's choice."

5   A hit show could earn profits of $60 million a year. That pot of gold spurred
entertainment companies to launch not just one but two or three talk shows. Soon,
what had been a friendly rivalry became a cutthroat competition. The shows, once a
daily lesson in tolerance, metamorphosed into something approaching performance
art for "exploitalking" guests.

6   Suddenly, people who stopped me on the street wanted to know: "Where do you
get those people?" The truth is that most of our guests came to us. Wannabe panelists
jammed our 800 number to audition for "My Wife Is Obsessed with Pornography" or
"I Let My Husband Cheat Because I'm Pregnant."

7   Practically anyone willing to "confront" someone—her husband's mistress, his wife's lover, their promiscuous best friend—in a televised emotional ambush could snare a free ticket to national notoriety. Those who promised to reveal some intimate secret to an unsuspecting loved one got the kind of star treatment Gen. Colin Powell would get on "Meet the Press."

A Mother's Dread

8   For a show called "Revealing Your Double Life," we flew in a mother (her first plane ride) who'd been estranged from her son for two years without knowing why. He had asked to appear on the show to reveal that, thanks to impending sexual reassignment surgery, his mother was about to lose a son but gain a daughter. When I met her, the mother was weeping. "Do you know what's wrong?" she pleaded. "We were always so close. I don't know what's happened. Is he sick? Does he have AIDS?" She broke my heart. But to tip her son's secret before the cameras rolled would sabotage the surprise. I murmured assurances that everything would be all right. Of course, it wasn't. When her son made his televised entrance wearing a dress, she broke down and sobbed.

9   But their awkward reunion was eclipsed by the dueling confessions of a mother-daughter duo. The daughter, admired by her family for earning her college tuition by working in an old-age home, revealed that she in fact paid her way by topless dancing. Spurred on by her daughter's candor, the tearful mother admitted giving up an illegitimate baby for adoption.

10   The studio audience (and, as the ratings attested, its couchbound counterparts) lapped up every syllable. Rarely were guests chided for fessing up in public; they were routinely commended for their "courage" in coming clean—as if they had performed some public service. I could only rationalize that some guests saw the studio as a buffer zone, a safe haven that would cushion the aftershocks of exposing their secrets.

11   My safe haven theory is the only way I can explain what happened during "My Spouse Is Embarrassed by My Job." The show featured an angry husband named Michael unleashing a withering tirade against his wife, Andrea, for working as a maid. He ranted about how her job humiliated him and their two children. When he finally took a breath, we cut to a commercial to get Andrea a box of Kleenex.

12   By the time we came back, Michael had been transformed into a docile supplicant. Now, he wanted his wife of five years to know—"for the first time"—he didn't really earn his living as a computer engineer. Sure, he left home each day dressed in a three-piece suit. But he changed on his way to work. He confessed he was a janitor.

13   If Andrea had gone for his throat, any jury would have found it justifiable homicide. But not one audience member chastised Michael for ambushing his wife on television (although they did admonish him for leading a double life).

14   Increasingly, the audience and I saw the same guests through different lenses. They saw entertainment; I saw exhibitionism—albeit committed by consenting

adults. It was worse when children were hauled into the fray. Whenever possible, youngsters and especially infants were used to hook the viewer by upping the emotional ante. On one show, an 8-year-old boy listened wide-eyed as his aunt announced that he'd been abandoned by his mother because she "didn't want" him. On another, as a bitter ex-wife delivered a diatribe about her daughters' "deadbeat dad," the camera dollied in for close-ups of the girls in tears.

"Too Serious"

15   I wanted to believe that, like Phil Donahue, who still thrives juggling male strippers on Monday with poet Maya Angelou on Tuesday, you could have it both ways. I kept pitching shows that registered as Nielsen flatliners. They were "too serious" ("Women Addicted to Prescription Drugs"), "too controversial" ("Condoms in Schools") or, the kiss of death, too "MacNeil-Lehrer" ("The Cult of Victimization").

16   Why take a gamble on "Should Kids Be Tried as Adults?" when you can score a double-digit share with the TV-talk staple "My Mother Is a Slut"? Our PG-rated promospeak dubbed it "My Mother Is a Party Animal," but the reality was an R-rated free-for-all: fortysomething mothers, bulging out of bustiers, swapping invectives with their adult daughters, who bemoaned their mothers' promiscuity. Finally, incited by the mock outrage of their offspring and the audience, the moms triumphantly pulled condoms from their Victoria's Secret get-ups. In the world of TV talk, it was a Kodak moment.

17   I was rarely shocked by the outrageous stories folks shared. But I was dismayed that they opted for the electronic confessional rather than confide in a friend, a member of the clergy or a therapist. But then, what other medium sends the seductive message that by flaunting even the worst behavior, you can finagle 60 minutes of celebrity plus a shot at public absolution?

18   You don't have to be contrite, or even admit you did anything wrong. Sometimes it's enough just to show up. Take the three members of the California high school "Sex for Points" gang. The infamous bad boys from the Spur Posse parlayed their competition—bedding young girls—into a talk-show bidding war. The boys were courted like royalty by the TV-talk cognoscenti, including our show, which flew them to New York and had several staffers guard them. But when a rival show lured them from their hotel rooms with Knicks playoff tickets, the boys managed to give their chaperones the slip.

19   Eventually, the fickle Lotharios jumped the competition's ship and returned to us in search of a better offer. We herded them off in a limo for a night of partying. After their all-nighter, we were forced to buy them clean clothes to make their national TV debut.

20   Another time, we booked a couple named Sabrina and Kenneth who'd been caught having sex on a department store bed in their Louisiana hometown. They were the headliners on a show exploring "Teenage Public Displays of Affection," but they were clearly miscast as standard-bearers for sexually liberated youth. They reminded me of a shy couple who'd drift into a quiet corner at the senior prom. Their hands

locked in a death grip, they haltingly defended their "right" to "do it" wherever they pleased. Between them, they formed about five sentences. But their talk wasn't cheap. Since we'd won the right to their story with a hefty fee, they earned more per sentence than most nurses take home in a week.

21   Lately, there's been a lot of defensive talk that these shows can help people hear things in a different way, that at their best they shine light in dark corners. And that can happen. Such moments reminded me why I'd originally taken my job. I stood tall when a woman recounted how her visit to our studio led to her reconciliation with her son's wife. And when another mother credited us with inspiring her rapprochement with her lesbian daughter. Who knows how many others would rhapsodize that a talk show changed their lives?

22   But when human frailty is traded like a commodity in the name of entertainment, even a happy talk-show ending is tainted as a Pyrrhic victory. Just ask the mother who lost her son but gained a daughter on national television.

AFTERWARDS

Vocabulary

hiatus, halogen, deference, voyeurs, fledgling, genre, syndicated, clamoring, substantive, raconteurs, metamorphosed, promiscuous, notoriety, eclipsed, supplicant, chastised, admonish, exhibitionism, albeit, ante, diatribe, invectives, finagle, absolution, contrite, cognoscenti, rapprochement, rhapsodize, Pyrrhic. Locate definitions for the vocabulary words. Then, select and use at least ten of them in individual sentences—followed by rewrites of each sentence using synonyms in place of these vocabulary entries. When and where might one version of each sentence be more appropriate than another?

Content

1. What reasons does Whitney give for her frustrations with the TV talk show's format?

2. What harm does Whitney think public "confessions" can do? What examples does she give?

3. Why are producers of the talk shows reluctant to have guests discuss more serious topics? What difference does it make to them?

Style and Structure

1. How many specific talk-show topics does Whitney list? What conclusions can you draw from examining this list?

2. How does Whitney create a feeling of balance about her topic? Are all of her judgments negative? Explain.

3. How would you characterize Whitney's tone in this essay? What specific words contribute to this effect?

Collaborative Explorations

As a group, imagine that you are the producers of a TV talk show. Make a list of possible topics for a currently broadcast show. Discuss why the topics you select would be successful. Then, imagine you could produce a show of your own design. What kind of talk show would you (as a group) like to produce if ratings were not a concern?

Writing Assignments

1. Take a look at two or three talk shows, take notes on what is said and done, and draw your own conclusions. Write an essay in which you explain and analyze the effects of the show on yourself and the audience.

2. Write an essay in the form of a proposal in which you describe three programs that you would like to see produced on television. Given the possibilities of television as a medium for communication, show how it could be used as an enhancement of people's lives on both a personal and public level.

Thematic Reading Cross-Links: See Chapter 8, Popular Culture, for essays on people, places, and things that influence and entertain Americans.

Movie Cross-Links: See *Talk Radio* in the Film Links in Chapter 5, Media: Controversies and Celebrities, for an example of a talk-show host who goes too far to achieve higher ratings. Also see *The King of Comedy* in the Film Links at the end of this chapter for a portrait of a would-be talk-show host.

The Difference Between "Reality TV" and Reality

Jonathan Rauch

JONATHAN RAUCH is a senior writer for *National Journal* magazine and a writer in residence at the Brookings Institution in Washington. While the following essay by Rauch critiques *War Games*, a TBS Superstation "reality TV" special, it also comments on violence-based "Regular Guy" television programming.

ALLUSIONS

Turner Broadcasting System: Television network started by Ted Turner that later merged with Time/Warner and then AOL.

George F. Will: Syndicated conservative columnist.

Ken Burns: Producer of the PBS documentaries *Civil War, Baseball*, and *Jazz*.

1   The press kit for *War Games*, a TBS Superstation special, arrived not in anything as bland or conventional as an envelope, but in a canvas military-dispatch pouch, the sort of thing you might pick up for your kids at an army-surplus store. This was useful, since I was able to insert the *War Games* video into the pouch, sling the pouch over my shoulder, and manfully lug it down the hall to the VCR. I felt, even more than usual, like a Regular Guy, which apparently was the point.

2   *War Games*, a network official says in a press release, "fits perfectly into our strategy of providing exciting, high-profile and provocative original programming that appeals to the Regular Guy and the people in his life." With this show—"an exclusive inside view of the combat-readiness exercises that our own military uses to prepare for war"— "reality TV takes an exciting turn," says TBS. Eventually it had to happen: Guns and explosives, reality TV, and football would all converge in one mighty hormonal eruption.

3   TBS stands officially for Turner Broadcasting System, but Testosterone Broadcasting System would be more to the point. Superstation, which TBS bills as its flagship, and which reaches (according to its publicity) 81 million households, markets itself as "the TV haven for the Regular Guy." The Web site boasts of "Movies for Guys Who Like Movies" ("Every week we feature a movie with a macho edge. Are you man enough to take it?"), "Guy Sites" on the Web (featuring, when I visited, *www.beer.com*), exhaustive coverage of NASCAR racing, and *Gilligan's Island*. If you wonder what Regular Guys are doing at 5:30 every weekday morning, the answer is, watching *Gilligan's Island*. Must be that macho Skipper. *War Games*, by contrast, is what TBS hopes Regular Guys will watch during prime time. "We are already looking at this special as a pilot for a potential series," Jim Head, a TBS programming executive, says in the press release.

4   I like guns and explosives and reality TV and football every bit as much as the next openly gay, effete intellectual, which is to say, not very much. Well, *War Games* delivers plenty of bombs and bullets and planes, and the testosterone quotient is certainly up to specification. But in other respects the show is something of a surprise, not least to itself.

5   *War Games* runs for two hours. It was produced, TBS notes proudly, with the full cooperation of the Pentagon, which means that sandal-wearing peaceniks and devotees of adversarial journalism need not apply. As the Pentagon no doubt desired, the show features one exercise for each of the four military services. The exercises are covered by on-the-ground correspondents—one of whom is Anne Powell, daughter of retired General and now Secretary of State Colin Powell (how's that for fully cooperating with the Pentagon?)—and are also narrated by voice-over. Playing host to the proceedings, from a studio, is Howie Long, the football commentator and former Oakland Raiders defensive end.

6   George F. Will once remarked that football combines the two worst aspects of American life: violence punctuated by committee meetings. Football fans have always regarded their game as mock warfare; here it turns out that warfare is also mock football. Navy pilots protect an aircraft carrier "like linemen protect a quarterback," explains the voice-over. Says Howie Long of an Air Force exercise, "If Red Flag were a championship football game, the U.S. forces would be down by two touchdowns late in the fourth quarter." And so on, and on. If you find football disagreeable, or if you expect sophisticated analysis, or if you can't stand sports cliches, you are probably not part of the *War Games* target demographic.

7   And yet, much as (according to Bill Nye) Wagner's music is better than it sounds, *War Games* is better than it seems. Or better, at least, than it wants to seem. Or better, in any case, than it seems to want to seem. "This show is not a documentary," co-executive producer J. J. Jamieson (the other executive producer is John Barchilon) declares in the press kit. "It's not news. It's mostly entertainment, a little bit of sports, and a lot of action."

8   It is indeed a lot of action. In reality, military exercises can be long, slogging, dreary affairs. When a soldier is "hit" in an Army exercise, sensors on his uniform are triggered by a laser fired from an "enemy" gun; an alarm then goes off and the soldier sits or lies down. Nothing too visually gripping about that. In naval exercises, pilots chase not real submarines but submarine simulators, which look like bright-orange torpedoes. *War Games* therefore uses all the fast cutting, dramatic editing, animations, bomb's-eye-view simulations, sound effects, and graphics at its disposal. When a submarine-hunting pilot drops a torpedo, we might see the finger on the button, then a shot of a falling torpedo, then a radar screen, then a file shot of a real submarine, then an animation of a torpedo closing in, then the torpedo's view, then the tense faces of officers looking on, and so forth.

9   But here is the little joke—on the producers, on the audience, on TBS, on me. *War Games* is not "reality TV," because it is real. There is nothing real about putting a bunch of meticulously screened publicity hogs on an island, requiring them to engage in various contrived tests, and asking them to vote on who can stay until next week. Nor is there anything real about putting another bunch of meticulously screened publicity hogs on another island and exposing them to the temptations of seducers. Even putting people in a house to live full time under a camera's unblinking gaze is still, mercifully, a healthy distance from reality.

10   True, the war games in *War Games* are condensed and heightened and jazzed up with every MTV trick in the book. And the combatants are well aware of the cameras that shadow their every step, and of the correspondents who interview them for human-interest sidebars and post-game wrap-ups. And the Pentagon's cooperation probably ensures that if anything went horribly wrong—if someone, God forbid, really got killed—then that particular incident, however newsworthy, would not air before 81 million cable viewers. Yet, for all that, what one sees here is designed by the military to look and feel as much like real combat—the noise, the smoke, the surprises and chaos—as it can, with the result that couch potatoes and effete intellectuals see something more like the reality of modern professional warfare than TV has yet provided.

11   And so a unit of *BlueFox*, an Army force tasked to liberate a simulated town from guerrillas (really American forces trained in guerrilla tactics), finds that it must cross a barbed-wire coil at a run to reach the guerrillas before they kill their hostages. The commander, acting fast, orders a soldier to throw himself on the barbed wire and act as a human bridge while his comrades rush across. The comrades all cross safely, but the soldier is tangled in the wire long enough to be taken out by an enemy sniper. Imagine being him; or, worse, imagine being the commander who chose him.

12   The script is merely serviceable ("Sergeant Barron and his men get ready to race into the firestorm."). It is the combatants, in interviews and profiles, whose voices ring true. The catch in an airman's voice as he speaks of the buddy he lost on duty a few years ago tells you he is not reading lines. In the air, the pilots' voices crackling over the radio are preoccupied and intense, just as one expects, but too colorless and banal to pass a Hollywood script review. Particularly vivid are some of the women. "All right—let's kick ass!" barks Navy pilot Bridgette Brandhuber as she finishes briefing her crew before a mission. But in an interview, this same Lieutenant Brandhuber pauses to speak of the pressures of what she calls an "extremely male" environment. "Every so often," she says, "you have to have a girl day and get your hair done and do your nails and remember you're a girl."

13   The program's final exercise is a Marine mission in which all of the ordnance is real. "Things happen," we hear a colonel—a 33-year veteran—warn the troops. He speaks with both awe and sentimentality of "that young guy, that 18-,19-, 20-year-old young man. He gives his heart and soul to us." We see his point as, in the darkest hours of night, a 21-year-old sergeant exhorts his men to get moving: "I'm cold, too. I know we're all tired. Basically you can plan on getting absolutely no sleep tonight, all right? You've got to just dig down deep and deal with it, all right?"

14   Keep this under your hat, and for crying out loud don't tell TBS, but when I see a program whose correspondents and cameras document, up close and in detail, the people and processes of modern military exercises, I call that a documentary. Granted, this documentary is visually more sophisticated and hyperactive than anything Ken Burns has ever imagined, and less earnest by a long shot than anything on PBS. Also granted, the producers make no pretense of detachment: They admire, even love, their subjects. But a documentary is what this is. There, I've said it. TBS can sue me.

15   TBS must know perfectly well, of course, that it has made a documentary, albeit one without slow pans of old photographs or sententious narrators with British accents. But TBS also knows that the last thing the Regular Guy wants to watch is a documentary. So TBS is producing a documentary and, ironically, marketing it as reality TV—which, still more ironically, is the very opposite of a documentary.

16   On February 9, when a U.S. Navy submarine hit and sank a Japanese fishing trawler off Hawaii, the sub was giving a tour to civilians.

17   The accident was terrible, but the idea of giving tours to civilians is not. With the draft long forgotten, few American civilians have any real idea what modern warfare is like, or what professional soldiers and sailors and airmen do.

18   You could call *War Games* a big pink valentine for the military, and you would be right. But if *War Games* enables millions rather than dozens of Regular Guys to

witness military life up close and to do so out of harm's way and without causing shipwrecks—then more power to it.

19   Bottom line for effete intellectuals: *War Games* is good TV and good public-service journalism.

20   Bottom line for Regular Guys: Don't worry, it's not a documentary.

AFTERWARDS

Vocabulary

conventional, provocative, hormonal, effete, quotient, adversarial, demographic, meticulously, ordnance, sententious. Look up the definitions of these words. Notice which are adjectives and make a list of simpler, more commonplace words that could be used in their place.

Content

1. What do you think are some of the differences between reality and "reality TV"? How does the presence of cameras, microphones, and commentators possibly affect the "reality" that appears on the TV screen?

2. Why does Rauch call this program a "big pink valentine for the military"? How do programs like this help create good public relations for the military? Are there any aspects of the reality of service in the military that are not disclosed in programs like *War Games*?

3. Why do you think audiences are attracted to "Reality TV"? What other shows would you place in this category? How are they like documentaries? How are they different? Why are documentaries not as popular?

Structure

1. What evidence does Rauch give to support the claim that *War Games* are "good public service journalism"?

2. What sentences or words in this essay give it a slightly sarcastic tone? What does this tell you about the author's point of view?

3. Why is football often used as an analogy for war? Why does Rauch think it is ironic for *War Games* to present itself with a format like the broadcast of a football game? How is war *not* like a football game?

Collaborative Explorations

Form a group and invent your own "Reality TV" show. Think about what situations, either actual or fabricated as a game, would produce interactions between people that would provoke the interest of viewers. What do audiences want to see when they tune in to this kind of program? Think about who the potential audience is for this kind of show. Write up a proposal that would be a business plan for a new program. List all the components you can think of that would be necessary to actually do a show every week.

Writing Assignments

1. Choose another of the Reality TV programs on television and describe the way it presents reality to viewers. Does it borrow from the format of other types of television programs? Do the participants seem to be performing for the cameras at any point in the program? Explain the appeal of the program you've chosen.

2. Rauch suggests that this entertainment program is also a "public service" advertisement for the military. Look at other Reality TV programs and try to figure out what their intentions may be besides simply providing entertainment. Are they promoting certain fashion trends, lifestyles, or political ideas? Write an analytical essay in which you reveal these below-the-surface messages.

Thematic Cross-Links: Compare the ideas expressed in Rose Anna Higashi's essay, "Boycott America's Media: Take Back Your Thinking Skills" in Chapter 5, Media: Controversies and Celebrities, to those expressed in Rauch's analysis. How do both express concerns about "empty entertainment," and at what point do the authors seem to differ?

Movie Cross-Links: Compare Rauch's definition of "reality" with the TV reality depicted in *The Truman Show*.

The Mambo Kings Play Songs of Love
Oscar Hijuelos

Born in New York City in 1951, **OSCAR HIJUELOS** is a prolific writer, particularly on subjects related to family. His works include *Our House in the Last World* (1983), the Pulitzer Prize-winning *Mambo Kings Play Songs of Love* (1989), *Sisters of Emilo Montez O'Brien* (1993), and *Mr. Joe's Christmas* (1995). Among his many awards and honors are the 1985 Rome Fellowship of the American Academy and Institute of Art and Letters, a Guggenheim fellowship, and a grant from the National Endowment for the Humanities.

ALLUSIONS

I Love Lucy: One of the pioneer situation comedies on television, starring Desi Arnaz and Lucille Ball.

Ricky Ricardo: Television name for Desi Arnaz in *I Love Lucy*; Arnaz was married to Lucille Ball, who was called Lucy Ricardo on the show.

Tropicana: Nightclub where Ricky Ricardo played with his band.

mambo: A sexy Cuban dance.

Dracula: Novelist Bram Stoker's legendary vampire who makes his way from his castle in Transylvania to England.

Spencer Tracy: Academy Award-winning actor and star of the movie version of *The Old Man and the Sea.*

The Old Man and the Sea: Novelist Ernest Hemingway's Pulitzer Prize-winning novel detailing a struggle between an old Cuban fisherman and a marlin.

Ethel Mertz: Lucy Ricardo's best friend played by Vivian Vance, constantly plotting with Lucy against her own husband (William Frawley as Fred Mertz) as well as Lucy's husband, Ricky Ricardo.

canción: Spanish for song.

1   It was a Saturday afternoon on La Salle Street, years and years ago when I was a little kid, and around three o'clock Mrs. Shannon, the heavy Irish woman in her perpetually soup-stained dress, opened her back window and shouted out into the courtyard, "Hey, Cesar, yoo-hoo, I think you're on television, I swear it's you!" When I heard the opening strains of the *I Love Lucy* show I got excited because I knew she was referring to an item of eternity, that episode in which my dead father and my Uncle Cesar had appeared, playing Ricky Ricardo's singing cousins fresh off the farm in Oriente Province, Cuba, and north in New York for an engagement at Ricky's nightclub, the Tropicana.

2   This was close enough to the truth about their real lives—they were musicians and songwriters who had left Havana for New York in 1949, the year they formed the Mambo Kings, an orchestra that packed clubs, dance halls, and theaters around the East Coast—and, excitement of excitements, they even made a fabled journey in a flamingo-pink bus out to Sweet's Ballroom in San Francisco, playing on an all-star mambo night, a beautiful night of glory, beyond death, beyond pain, beyond all stillness.

3   Desi Arnaz had caught their act one night in a supper club on the West Side, and because they had perhaps already known each other from Havana or Oriente Province, where Arnaz, like the brothers, was born, it was natural that he ask them to sing on his show. He liked one of their songs in particular, a romantic bolero written by them, "Beautiful María of My Soul."

4   Some months later (I don't know how many, I wasn't five years old yet) they began to rehearse for the immortal appearance of my father on this show. For me, my

father's gentle rapping on Ricky Ricardo's door has always been a call from the beyond, as in Dracula films, or films of the walking dead, in which spirits ooze out from behind tombstones and through the cracked windows and rotted floors of gloomy antique halls: Lucille Ball, the lovely red-headed actress and comedienne who played Ricky's wife, was housecleaning when she heard the rapping of my father's knuckles against that door.

5   "I'm commmmmming," in her singsong voice.

6   Standing in her entrance, two men in white silk suits and butterfly-looking lace bow ties, black instrument cases by their side and black-brimmed white hats in their hands—my father, Nestor Castillo, thin and broad-shouldered, and Uncle Cesar, thickset and immense.

7   My uncle: "Mrs. Ricardo? My name is Alfonso and this is my brother Manny . . ."

8   And her face lights up and she says, "Oh, yes, the fellows from Cuba. Ricky told me all about you."

9   Then, just like that, they're sitting on the couch when Ricky Ricardo walks in and says something like, "Manny, Alfonso! Gee, it's really swell that you fellas could make it up here from Havana for the show."

10   That's when my father smiled. The first time I saw a rerun of this, I could remember other things about him—his lifting me up, his smell of cologne, his patting my head, his handing me a dime, his touching my face, his whistling, his taking me and my little sister, Leticia, for a walk in the park, and so many other moments happening in my thoughts simultaneously that it was like watching something momentous, say the Resurrection, as if Christ had stepped out of his sepulcher, flooding the world with light—what we were taught in the local church with the big red doors—because my father was now newly alive and could take off his hat and sit down on the couch in Ricky's living room, resting his black instrument case on his lap. He could play the trumpet, move his head, blink his eyes, nod, walk across the room, and say "Thank you" when offered a cup of coffee. For me, the room was suddenly bursting with a silvery radiance. And now I knew that we could see it again. Mrs. Shannon had called out into the courtyard alerting my uncle: I was already in his apartment.

11   With my heart racing, I turned on the big black-and-white television set in his living room and tried to wake him. My uncle had fallen asleep in the kitchen—having worked really late the night before, some job in a Bronx social club, singing and playing the horn with a pickup group of musicians. He was snoring, his shirt was open, a few buttons had popped out on his belly. Between the delicate-looking index and forefingers of his right hand, a Chesterfield cigarette burning down to the filter, that hand still holding a half glass of rye whiskey, which he used to drink like crazy because in recent years he had been suffering from bad dreams, saw apparitions, felt cursed, and, despite all the women he took to bed, found his life of bachelorhood solitary and wearisome. But I didn't know this at the time, I thought he was sleeping because he had worked so hard the night before, singing and playing the trumpet for seven or eight hours. I'm talking about a wedding party in a crowded, smoke-filled room (with bolted-shut fire doors), lasting from nine at night to four, five o'clock in the morning, the band playing one-, two-hour sets. I thought he just needed the rest.

How could I have known that he would come home and, in the name of unwinding, throw back a glass of rye, then a second, and then a third, and so on, until he'd plant his elbow on the table and use it to steady his chin, as he couldn't hold his head up otherwise. But that day I ran into the kitchen to wake him up so that he could see the episode, too, shaking him gently and tugging at his elbow, which was a mistake, because it was as if I had pulled loose the support columns of a five-hundred-year-old church: he simply fell over and crashed to the floor.

12   A commercial was running on the television, and so, as I knew I wouldn't have much time, I began to slap his face, pull on his burning red-hot ears, tugging on them until he finally opened one eye. In the act of focusing he apparently did not recognize me, because he asked, "Nestor, what are you doing here?"

13   "It's me, Uncle, it's Eugenio."

14   I said this in a really earnest tone of voice, just like that kid who hangs out with Spencer Tracy in the movie of *The Old Man and the Sea*, really believing in my uncle and clinging on to his every word in life, his every touch like nourishment from a realm of great beauty, far beyond me, his heart. I tugged at him again, and he opened his eyes. This time he recognized me.

15   He said, "You?"

16   "Yes, Uncle, get up! Please get up! You're on television again. Come on."

17   One thing I have to say about my Uncle Cesar, there was very little he wouldn't do for me in those days, and so he nodded, tried to push himself off the floor, got to his knees, had trouble balancing, and then fell backwards. His head must have hurt: his face was a wince of pain. Then he seemed to be sleeping again. From the living room came the voice of Ricky's wife, plotting as usual with her neighbor Ethel Mertz about how to get a part on Ricky's show at the Tropicana, and I knew that the brothers had already been to the apartment—that's when Mrs. Shannon had called out into the courtyard—that in about five more minutes my father and uncle would be standing on the stage of the Tropicana, ready to perform that song again. Ricky would take hold of the microphone and say, "Well, folks, and now I have a real treat for you. Ladies and gentlemen, Alfonso and Manny Reyes, let's hear it!" And soon my father and uncle would be standing side by side, living, breathing beings, for all the world to see, harmonizing in a duet of that canción.

18   As I shook my uncle, he opened his eyes and gave me his hand, hard and callused from his other job in those days, as superintendent, and he said, "Eugenio, help me. Help me."

19   I tugged with all my strength, but it was hopeless. Still he tried: with great effort he made it to one knee, and then, with his hand braced on the floor, he started to push himself up again. As I gave him another tug, he began miraculously to rise. Then he pushed my hand away and said, "I'll be okay, kid."

20   With one hand on the table and the other on the steam pipe, he pulled himself to his feet. For a moment he towered over me, wobbling as if powerful winds were

rushing through the apartment. Happily I led him down the hallway and into the living room, but he fell over again by the door—not fell over, but rushed forward as if the floor had abruptly tilted, as if he had been shot out of a cannon, and, wham, he hit the bookcase in the hall. He kept piles of records there, among them a number of the black and brittle 78s he had recorded with my father and their group, the Mambo Kings. These came crashing down, the bookcase's glass doors jerking open, the records shooting out and spinning like flying saucers in the movies and splintering into pieces. Then the bookcase followed, slamming into the floor beside him: the songs "Bésame Mucho," "Acércate Más," "Juventud," "Twilight in Havana," "Mambo Nine," "Mambo Number Eight," "Mambo for a Hot Night," and their fine version of "Beautiful María of My Soul"—all these were smashed up. This crash had a sobering effect on my uncle. Suddenly he got to one knee by himself, and then the other, stood, leaned against the wall, and shook his head.

21   "Bueno," he said.

22   He followed me into the living room and plopped down on the couch behind me. I sat on a big stuffed chair that we'd hauled up out of the basement. He squinted at the screen, watching himself and his younger brother, whom, despite their troubles, he loved very much. He seemed to be dreaming.

23   "Well, folks," Ricky Ricardo said, "and now I have a real treat for you . . ."

24   The two musicians in white silk suits and big butterfly-looking lace bow ties, marching toward the microphone, my uncle holding a guitar, my father a trumpet.

25   "Thank you, thank you. And now a little number that we composed . . ." And Cesar started to strum the guitar and my father lifted his trumpet to his lips, playing the opening of "Beautiful María of My Soul," a lovely, soaring melody line filling the room.

26   They were singing the song as it had been written—in Spanish. With the Ricky Ricardo Orchestra behind them, they came into a turnaround and began harmonizing a line that translates roughly into English as: "What delicious pain love has brought to me in the form of a woman." My father . . . He looked so alive!

27   "Uncle!"

28   Uncle Cesar had lit a cigarette and fallen asleep. His cigarette had slid out of his fingers and was now burning into the starched cuff of his white shirt. I put the cigarette out, and then my uncle, opening his eyes again, smiled. "Eugenio, do me a favor. Get me a drink."

29   "But, Uncle, don't you want to watch the show?"
30   He tried really hard to pay attention, to focus on it.
31   "Look, it's you and Poppy."
32   "Coño, sí . . ."

33   My father's face with his horsey grin, arching eyebrows, big fleshy ears—a family trait—that slight look of pain, his quivering vocal cords, how beautiful it all seemed to me then . . .

34   And so I rushed into the kitchen and came back with a glass of rye whiskey, charging as fast as I could without spilling it. Ricky had joined the brothers onstage. He was definitely pleased with their performance and showed it, because as the last note sounded he whipped up his hand and shouted "Olé!," a big lock of his thick black hair falling over his brows. Then they bowed and the audience applauded.

35   The show continued on its course. A few gags followed: a costumed bull with flowers wrapped around its horns came out dancing an Irish jig, its horn poking into Ricky's bottom and so exasperating him that his eyes bugged out, he slapped his forehead and started speaking a-thousand-words-a-second Spanish. But at that point it made no difference to me, the miracle had passed, the resurrection of a man, Our Lord's promise which I then believed, with its release from pain, release from the troubles of this world.

AFTERWARDS

Vocabulary

mambo, bolero, simultaneously, momentous, radiance, gags, exasperating. The vocabulary words for this essay consist primarily of concrete nouns or modifying words (adjectives and adverbs). How do they bring life and depth to Oscar Hijuelos's narrative? What might have been lost without them?

Content

1. Identify the speaker in "The Mambo Kings Play Songs of Love."

2. Summarize Hijuelos's narrative. What seems to be his overall purpose for writing it? Who does he write about? When? Where? Remember, a summary condenses a lot of information, omitting subpoints. It consists of a controlling idea (topic sentence or thesis statement) and the major discussion points, using transitions and linking devices to establish a clear relationship between them.

3. Briefly compare and contrast Hijuelos's portrayal of his father on the *I Love Lucy* rerun to the description of his uncle watching television—years later.

Style and Structure

1. Go through a paragraph or so, and note the different sentence structures Hijuelos uses to relate his tale. In your opinion, how does his sentence variety keep the essay interesting? Why?

2. Analyze the movement of Hijuelos's narrative, beginning with the first sentence, "It was a Saturday afternoon on La Salle Street, years and years ago when I was a little kid. . . ." to the last sentence, "But at that point it made no difference to me, the miracle had passed. . . ." What happens first, second, third, and so on?

3. How would you describe the mood or tone of Hijuelos's narrative? In what way does it indicate his attitude toward his subject matter?

Collaborative Explorations

Divide into groups of four or five people, and set aside a time you can all meet for about two and one-half hours. Then have one member of your group rent a copy of *The Mambo Kings* from your local video store, or, if your college media center owns a copy of it, check it out for an afternoon or evening. Watch the movie as a group, paying particular attention to scenes with Ricky Ricardo (played by his son, Desi Arnaz Jr.), the Tropicana Night Club, and the Ricky Ricardo Orchestra, and the "mambo kings" themselves. Following the movie, assess how well the director expressed the experience in Hijuelos's narrative, and write a brief one-page collaborative critique based on your group's conclusion. Finally, compare and contrast critiques in class.

Writing Assignments

1. Construct a narrative account of one of the first times you recall watching television, listening to the radio, phonograph, or CD player, carrying a "boom box," and so on. Each time you revise your composition, work a bit on increasing sentence variety.

2. Write an essay detailing a fond memory of your father, mother, family member, or parental figure when you were still a child. Is the subject of your essay aware of the importance you place on your memory of them? Use plenty of specific references and descriptions to "show" rather than just "tell" readers about your memory.

Thematic Reading Cross-Links: See Chapter 3, The American Family, for essays on father/child relationships.

Movie Cross-Links: See *Mambo Kings* in the Film Links for Chapter 4, Stereotypes and Social Barriers, for a movie adaptation of the novel from which this excerpt was taken.

The Visual Connection: Photograph Writing Activities

Does every picture tell a story? Consider the photographs of television sets for sale at *The Good Guys*, an electronics store specializing in selling all sorts and sizes of television sets and DVD and VHS players.

Plethora of Television Sets

Film Links: Television

1. Break the class down into groups of two or three, with each group selecting one film. Watch it together and take thorough notes regarding the narrative contents. When the film concludes, share your responses to it, justifying your insights when they conflict with others. How do you account for the variation in responses? Assemble one collaborative essay detailing your group experience.

2. Select a movie such as *Quiz Show* and use it as a starting point for analyzing how and why television has had such a history of conflict between entertainers and journalists and their corporate sponsors. How do commercial interests use the television medium to pursue their own self-interest regardless of the effect on the public? What are viewers interested in watching? Have the networks succeeded in giving the public what it wants?

3. Select one or more of the following films and think about how television is related to power. What kind of power does television give to those who are on it? to those who own it? to those who watch it? Write a definition of "media power" and explain its various aspects.

Network (USA, Sidney Lumet, 1976). Network anchorman behaves irrationally on the air and becomes a media cult hero.

My Favorite Year (USA, Richard Benjamin, 1982). The guest appearance of a swashbuckler movie star on a 1950s television comedy show causes consternation for the staff and chaos for the crew.

The King of Comedy (USA, Martin Scorsese, 1983). An avid TV viewer decides to kidnap a popular talk-show host.

Broadcast News (USA, James Brooks, 1987). A TV journalist rises in his career due mostly to his appearance and help from his friends.

Mr. Saturday Night (USA, Billy Crystal, 1992). The ups and downs of five decades in the life of a comedian.

Quiz Show (USA, Robert Redford, 1994). Based on 1950s TV scandal regarding rigged game shows.

To Die For (USA, Gus Van Sant, 1994). A beautiful young woman wills herself to be a successful television personality.

Up Close and Personal (USA, Jon Avnet, 1996). A veteran reporter decides to help a young woman make it as a journalist for a Miami TV station, but their relationship becomes more than merely professional.

The Truman Show (USA, Peter Weir, 1998). A man is raised on the set of a television show and doesn't know it.

Mad City (USA, Costa-Govras, 1997). An ambitious newsman turns a hostage situation into a media circus.

Wag the Dog (USA, Barry Levinson, 1997). A presidential advisor and a movie producer create a phony war using television to distract the public from a presidential sex scandal.

Holy Man (USA, Stephen Herek, 1998). A man on a spiritual pilgrimage meets and helps a home shopping network executive sell unnecessary items—a light satire.

Pleasantville (USA, Gary Ross, 1998). Two teenagers are transported to a 1950s sitcom that makes them think about social limitations and how to get beyond them.

Additional Writing Assignments

1. Critique one of the top four television shows, pointing out the strengths and weaknesses of it, and ultimately arriving at a concluding position. On a scale of one to ten, where would the show you critiqued be and why?

2. Advertising and television feature foul language and sexual explicitness (hailed by some as an honest presentation of popular culture) more than ever before. Write an essay arguing that television either is or is not responsible for declining morals and antisocial attitudes in the United States. Make sure you demonstrate all cause-and-effect relationships with specific examples followed by analysis.

3. Compare and contrast two situation comedies, two news broadcasts, two talk shows, and so on in order to determine which is better. How are they alike and different? Is the acting, reporting, or hosting of one show superior to that of another? How? Why?

4. In a paper illustrated with references to specific music videos and recording artists, argue that music videos are themselves a form of art. As you brainstorm this topic, ask yourself questions like, "What do music videos project? How?" In what way do individuals or music groups act out their songs? Why is such a presentation a satisfying form of entertainment on television? How might the music lift a visual collage to another level?

5. Make a list of what you consider the most influential television shows ever. Then, brainstorm or cluster each television program to freely associate their strengths and weaknesses. Finally, select three or four of the programs you brainstormed, and write an essay arguing how they influenced the direction and set a standard for popular television viewing at the end of the 20th and beginning of the 21st centuries.

Chapter Ten

Music

Observations and Opinions

In life, reggae singer Bob Marley disdained the impedimenta of what he called "Babylon"—modern Western civilization—such as lawyers, preachers, and barbers. His philosophy was a radical Caribbean romanticism, surcharged with the Biblical cult of Rastafarianism. His habits ran to regular indulgence in cigar-sized joints of powerful marijuana. Neither was conducive to an orthodox personal life. . . . when he was dying of cancer in 1981 at 36, he refused to make out a will. Preferring to believe that he would live forever, he ordered a new Mercedes Benz.

— Jerry Adler from "Marley's Ghost in Babylon"

In the minds of many Americans, for whom country music has always seemed an aberration in pop culture—the bastard stepchild of an otherwise forward-thinking music industry—this landlocked and fairly homogeneous city, presumably full of nothing but hillbillies, evangelists, rednecks, and racists, made perfect sense as the nexus of the country music establishment. If country music was cornball and ignorant, favored by southern Baptists, hicks, and "poor white trash," then Nashville, perched halfway between the Appalachian Mountains and the deep, rural South, was the heart of it.

— Victoria Starr from K. D. Lang: All You Get Is Me

Literally, "Tejano" means Texan, not just the music but the people as well. It is the soundtrack to MexAmerica. "Tejano," says Abraham Quintanilla, Selena's father and Astudillo's manager, "is

*a fusion, with all these influences: rock and roll, pop, country, rap,
jazz. We're Americans who happen to be of Mexican descent."*
                              —JOHN LELAND FROM "BORN ON THE BORDER"

*Rap remains almost completely dominated by black males and this
mind-set. Although women have been involved in rap since at least
the mid-80's, record companies have only recently begun to promote
them. As women rappers like Salt-n-Pepa, Monie Love, M. C. Lyte,
L. A. Star and Queen Latifah slowly gain more visibility, rap's
sexism may emerge as a subject for scrutiny. Indeed, the answer
may lie with women expressing in lyrics and videos the tensions
between the sexes in the black community.*
                    —MICHELLE WALLACE FROM "WHEN BLACK FEMINISM FACES
                                   THE MUSIC, AND THE MUSIC IS RAP"

Observation and Opinions: Reading/Writing Activities

1. In her quote from *k.d. lang: All You Get Is Me*, is Victoria Starr correct when she states that country music has always seemed an aberration in pop culture—the bastard child of an otherwise forward-thinking music industry? Discuss the reasoning that led you to your opinion.

2. Paraphrase Michelle Wallace's excerpt from "When Black Feminism Faces the Music, and the Music Is Rap." To your knowledge, has the sexism in rap emerged "as a subject for scrutiny"? Have female rappers gained more visibility?

3. Review the Observations and Opinions quotes and jot down a few notes regarding your knowledge of the following types of music: (1) reggae (see the Jerry Adler quotation), (2) country, (3) Tejano (see the John Leland quotation), (4) rap, (5) rock and roll, and (6) big band music. Feel free to jot down additional information on other types of music such as heavy metal, alternative, jazz, the blues, and so on. Finally, organize and revise all your notes, shaping them into a paragraph containing statements about music types (topic sentences), followed by specific definitions of each music type. You might concretely illustrate music types by referring to representative musicians, composers, and performers of the music under discussion. What are the elements that define each style?

Introduction

Just as essays provide readers with a way of comprehending and responding to topics, issues, and human conflicts, music connects with listeners and creates thoughts, feelings, and reflections through sound. In the first live music broadcast via satellite (a global transmission), the Beatles gathered in a London studio and sang "All You Need Is Love." When the Berlin Wall was torn down in 1989, the Germans played Beethoven's Ninth Symphony—emphasizing the last movement, "The Ode to Joy." Civil rights marchers sang "We Shall Overcome" as they faced off against hostile police during the 1960s. Music is as local as the Delta Blues of Mississippi John Hurt or as international as the ragas of Ravi Shankar. A song may address your personal identity or your national heritage. It may tantalize you with fantasies of love or exorcise the demons of disappointment and frustration. Any way you look at it, music surrounds you day and night.

People listen to music on the street, in their cars, in their living rooms, in concert halls, in the dentist's office, with headphones while jogging. Music is played at weddings and funerals, at parties, at graduation ceremonies, at halftime in football games, at dances, and in church. Some people listen to it in the dark on their bedside radios. What is it about music that makes it such a powerful and constant companion in our lives?

In this chapter, several writers reflect on this question. In addition, the comics artist Robert Crumb gives us pictures and captions in a comic strip essay on "Street Musicians." He suggests that these poorly paid, often ragtag and unknown performers may have been around since cities were first built around 4,000 years ago. They don't have much prestige, but they do tell us something about the personal need of some people to make their own music in their own way. In her recollection, "The Rites of the Dead," Susan Dobra re-creates the memory of a Grateful Dead concert, a special kind of event that developed over the thirty-year history of the band. The Deadheads who followed the band on tour and the loyal fans who turned out whenever the band came to town saw themselves as part of a loosely defined community of tie-dyed drummers, bootleg tapers, whirling dancers, old hippies, and uncategorized free spirits who were drawn by the promise of good music, good times, and good vibes.

In "Four and More: For Miles Davis," Quincy Troupe remembers the forty-year career of jazz trumpeter Miles Davis, who emerged with the bebop style of the 1940s and continuously evolved for the rest of his life, playing with such musicians as John Coltrane, Herbie Hancock, Tony Williams, and John McLaughlin. Troupe uses the intense rhythms of poetry to re-create the image, the mood, the style, the inspiration that great musicians communicate.

In "The Aesthetics of Rap," Dara Cook argues that rap and hip-hop performers are the poets of our time who speak to new realities in new ways. Though criticized for their outrageous language and blatant commerciality, rap and hip-hop performers are, according to Cook, a part of the same African American tradition that produced such poets as Langston Hughes and Nikki Giovanni.

Finally, student Willow Lamberson casts a satirical eye at pop music stars like Britney Spears and N'Sync. Lamberson wants to persuade us that this is "Fake Music" and that we should hold out for more authentic forms of expression.

These readings move from the personal to the political forms of expression in music, from the amateur to the professional, from the imperfect to the unexplainable. Music moves around in our culture like a living thing. The best we can do is follow its tracks.

Gathering Thoughts: Prereading Inquiries

1. What is your favorite type of music? What music wouldn't you listen to? Why?

2. When is the first time you can recall listening to music or singing?

3. Why do people clap their hands, nod their heads, and tap their feet when they listen to music? Is it a natural response or is it something people plan to do? (You might turn on some music at home or at school, and observe how people respond to music "unconsciously.")

4. How is "attitude" projected in music?

5. Why do you imagine wedding receptions and parties that offer no background music tend to be so dull?

6. What is the function of music in your life? Do you sing to yourself and/or others?

7. Divide a sheet of paper into three columns and make a list of (1) music that relaxes you, (2) music that inspires you, and (3) music that agitates or angers you.

8. What would a day be like without music of some kind? Why?

9. Is there a best time for listening to music?

10. Who are the most influential music groups or musicians in your life? Who do you think has made the greatest impact on the world with his, her, or their music? Why?

B. B. King's guitar, "Lucille"

Street Musicians
Robert Crumb

ROBERT CRUMB'S artistic career has been varied, beginning with the Once American Greetings Corporation, drawing greeting cards, and ultimately becoming the legendary cartoon artist of such counterculture comics as Mr. Natural and Zap Comix. The breadth of his work encompasses characters from Flakey Foot to the Vulture Demonesses, to Mode O'Day and Fritz the Cat. In addition, he has toured London in *Boswell's London Journal*, based on Boswell's literary classic, and debated the Buddhist philosophy of detachment in *Those Cute, Adorable Little Bearzy Wearzys*. Different from and yet similar to developing writers, Crumb remarks: "I go through long periods of agonizing over what I'm doing. I've never been a facile draftsman—I always have to struggle to figure out how to draw things." In "Street Musicians," Crumb offers a look at musicians from the streets of ancient Babylon to the K Street Mall in Sacramento, California. A condensed version of the comic appeared in the August 26/September 2, 1996, issue of *The New Yorker*; the following version represents its original form.

ALLUSIONS

Babylon: Capital of ancient Babylonia, which the exiled Jews found luxurious and corrupt. Today, any place full of vice, sin, and corruption is referred to as a "Babylon."

Blind Lemon Jefferson: A blues guitar player and singer.

Philistines: In the Old Testament, the Philistines were enemies of the Israelites (the descendants of Jacob who comprised the twelve tribes of Israel); today, people who are uncultured or ignorant are sometimes referred to as Philistines.

John Philip Sousa: Famous marching band composer; inventor of the sousaphone.

STREET MUSICIANS

STREET MUSICIANS HAVE BEEN AROUND AS LONG AS THERE HAVE BEEN STREETS. THERE WERE PROBABLY ITINERANT MUSIC MAKERS ON THE STREETS OF ANCIENT BABYLON!

IF YOU HAD LIVED IN ANY GOOD-SIZED TOWN IN THE SOUTHERN UNITED STATES DURING THE 1920s YOU MIGHT HAVE WALKED RIGHT BY THE LIKES OF BLIND LEMON JEFFERSON AND MANY OTHER GREAT EARLY BLUES SINGERS WHO MADE THEIR LIVING LARGELY FROM WORKING THE STREET.

THE MOST COMMON TYPE OF STREET MUSIC TO GREET YOUR EARS THESE DAYS IS THE YOUNG, WHITE SINGER-SONGWRITER WHO FLAILS ON A GUITAR AND BELTS OUT HIS CREATIONS WITH ALOT OF "FEELING."

OOHH OOOHH BLACK SNAKE CRAWLIN' IN MY ROOM

'CAUSE I'M A KINDRED SPIRIT OF THE EAGLE GONNA FLY UP ON TH' MOUNTAIN TOP YEAH

SOMETIMES THEY EVEN HAVE THEIR OWN SOUND SYSTEMS, WITH WHICH THEY CAN REALLY BE LOUD AND OBNOXIOUS. THESE GUYS ARE ALMOST NEVER ANY GOOD MUSICALLY. THEY HAVE MORE NERVE THAN TALENT OR SKILL. IT NEVER SEEMS TO OCCUR TO THEM TO PUT MORE HOURS IN PRACTICING AT HOME BEFORE GOING PUBLIC WITH THEIR NOISE. AND WHO GIVES A HOOT ABOUT THE PROFOUND MEANING OF THE LYRICS THEY'VE CONCOCTED? NOBODY EVER STANDS AROUND LONG ENOUGH TO GET THEIR "MESSAGE", EXCEPT MAYBE THEIR GIRLFRIENDS.

DONTCHA KNOW WE'RE ALL GOIN'DOWN IN A SHIP OF FOOLS BABY

OH BOY

ERK

SOME STREET MUSICIANS AREN'T EVEN REALLY MUSICIANS AT ALL, BUT CRAZY PEOPLE WHO STUMBLED ONTO THE IDEA THAT YOU CAN EXPRESS YOUR INNER TURMOIL BY BLOWING ON A HORN OR BANGING ON AN UNTUNED GUITAR, AND POSSIBLY PICK UP A LITTLE CHANGE DOING IT.

HONK

BLAT

SKREECH

...MAYBE THEY'RE PLAYING SOME KIND OF "FREE-FORM" JAZZ AND I'M JUST BEING CLOSE-MINDED.

STILL, MIRACLES *DO* HAPPEN, AND ONCE IN A WHILE—*NOT OFTEN*—ONE ENCOUNTERS *GREAT* MUSIC BEING PLAYED IN THE STREET. INVARIABLY, THE PERFORMER IS AN UNASSUMING INDIVIDUAL, SUCH AS THIS YOUNG RAGTIME GUITAR WIZARD WHO HAS BEEN PLAYING ON THE STREETS OF SAN FRANCISCO FOR TEN YEARS, AND CAN STILL BE FOUND THERE. HE PLAYS THE OLD TUNES NEITHER MECHANICALLY NOR SENTIMENTALLY, BUT WITH THE FORCE AND DRIVE OF OLD-TIME COUNTRY DANCE MUSIC. NEEDLESS TO ADD, THIS WONDERFUL MUSIC IS ENTIRELY LOST ON 99% OF THE MASS-MEDIA-HYPNOTIZED PHILISTINES PASSING BY.

FIFTEEN YEARS AGO I SAW A BLIND ACCORDIAN PLAYER OUTSIDE THE ENTRANCE TO THE SACRAMENTO STATE FAIR. A WOMAN, MAYBE HIS WIFE, WAS WITH HIM. I WAS STOPPED IN MY TRACKS BY HIS MUSIC, AND STOOD LISTENING FOR A LONG TIME. HE WAS PLAYING SOUZA MARCHES (ALL FIVE PARTS) AND SUCHLIKE TUNES *FLAWLESSLY*, YET WITH A SMOOTH, RELAXED RHYTHM.

AGAIN, CROWDS OF PEOPLE PASSED BY ON THEIR WAY INTO THE FAIRGROUNDS WITHOUT PAYING HIM THE SLIGHTEST NOTICE!

ONCE I SAW A BLIND GIRL IN FRONT OF MACY'S IN DOWNTOWN SAN FRANCISCO, SINGING AND PLAYING AN AUTOHARP ON HER LAP. IT WAS VERY NOISY ON THE STREET, AND SHE WAS BARELY AUDIBLE. I WAS MOST FASCINATED AND CAME CLOSE SO THAT I MIGHT HEAR HER BETTER.

SHE SANG OLD POPULAR SONGS IN A TINY, SWEET VOICE, STRUMMING CHORDS ON THE AUTOHARP... IN FACT IT WAS BEAUTIFUL MUSIC. BUT SENSING THAT SOMEONE WAS BENDING CLOSE TO LISTEN, SHE BLUSHED AND BROKE INTO GIGGLES.

TEE HEE

ONCE, ON THE SAD K STREET MALL IN SACRAMENTO I SAW A SKINNY LITTLE "OKIE" REDNECK GUY SINGING AND PLAYING IN A ROCKABILLY-BLUES STYLE.

HE WAS THE GENUINE ARTICLE, TRULY A RARE BIRD, AUTHENTIC, DEEPLY ROOTED IN THE TRADITION... I WAS AMAZED AND PROFOUNDLY MOVED BY HIS MUSIC. HIS CHEAP GUITAR WAS BATTERED AND GRIMY, AND HE LOOKED AS IF HE'D BEEN IN A FIGHT. HIS PANTS WERE TORN TO SHREDS. HE WAS A PITIFUL SIGHT, BUT FORTUNATELY FOR HIM HE WAS WITH A BIG, TOUGH BUT PROTECTIVE-LOOKING BLACK MAN.

I GAVE HIS PARTNER SOME MONEY, SAID I THOUGHT THE GUY WAS GREAT, THEN ASKED WHAT HAD HAPPENED TO HIM.

YEAH, HE'S GOOD, ISN'T HE, BUT HE DRINKS TOO MUCH... LAST NIGHT HE GOT DRUNK AN' PASSED OUT IN THE PARK AN' SOME PUNKS BEAT HIM UP, TORE HIS PANTS ALL UP LOOKIN' FOR MONEY... LUCKY THING I HAD TH' GUITAR PUT AWAY IN A SAFE PLACE...

LESS GO, BILL... WE GOT ENUFF FOR A PINT...

END
R. CRUMB '96

AFTERWARDS

Vocabulary

Outside of the allusions to specific names you may be unfamiliar with, Crumb's vocabulary is simple. Why would this be appropriate for a comic strip?

Content

1. Crumb seems critical of "crazy people," "white singer-songwriters," and "media-hypnotized Philistines," but is full of wonderment toward the other street musicians who appear "deeply rooted in tradition" and highly skillful. What are Crumb's musical values? What does he want us to appreciate about the musicians whom we might happen to hear on the street or anywhere else?

2. What cartoon figure impresses you the most and why? What does it convey?

3. Do you know any of the people upon whom Crumb built his "Street Musician" history? If so, what dimension has Crumb added to your knowledge of them? If you have never heard of people like Blind Lemon Jefferson, has Crumb given you an insight into Jefferson's legendary personality? Explain.

Style and Structure

1. Each cell of the comic is like a paragraph in an essay. How do the drawings take the place of words? What do they add to the meaning of the piece?

2. Express in your own words what Crumb is trying to tell us about street musicians. How does your narrative resemble the artist's meaning?

3. How does Crumb's style of drawing create a definite "mood" in his comic? In what way might the mood he captures in his pictures resemble the mood authors try to convey when they write character sketches of people?

Collaborative Explorations

In a small group, list all the places where you have seen street musicians. Make a list of the characteristics they have in common. Where are the good spots to play?

Why? Also, compare notes on the different styles of music and performances you have seen. Do your perceptions resemble Crumb's, or are they different?

Writing Assignments

1. Do you think cities should encourage street musicians to perform? (There are laws against it in many places because some merchants think it is bad for business.) Does playing on the street contribute something valuable to the life of a city, or is it just a way for a few musicians to pick up some quick cash?

2. Do you think music listeners have been "hypnotized" by the mass media? Has commercialism narrowed the forms of musical expression to a few repetitious categories? Describe your own musical preferences. What music makes you want to lean a little closer and listen intently?

Thematic Reading Cross-Links: See the introduction to and readings in Chapter 8: Popular Culture.

Movie Cross-Links: See *Crumb*, a documentary of the life of Robert Crumb, listed in Film Links at the end of Chapter 8: Popular Culture.

The Rites of the Dead
Susan Dobra

SUSAN DOBRA has a Ph.D. in rhetoric from the University of California, Berkeley, and continues to make timely contributions to the field. She also does some freelance writing. Dobra's related works on the Grateful Dead and popular culture include "His Job Is to Shed Light: The Grateful Dead's Place in the Bardic Tradition."

ALLUSIONS

Nepalese: A design, garment, and the like, originating in Nepal.

Rastafarian: A member of a biblically based cult.

Mount Tamalpais: A mountain, north of San Francisco in Marin County, that looks out over the city and the Bay Area.

1   On a summer evening in Berkeley, California, circa 1984, a tradition is about to recur. Across the usually staid campus of the University of California, ritually costumed celebrants, young and old, are arriving and beginning to gather in and around the stately Greek Theater. Pastels and intricate patterns of flowing garb flutter and fly in a warm breeze that whispers across campus from the Golden Gate, swirling through the gathering throng in quiet greeting. A boyish young man, his face tanned and radiating pristine health, reveals his calm yet clear anticipation; he blesses each passer-by with a quiet, "Welcome home, sister. Welcome back, brother." I return his beatific smile. Around me, the crowd is growing; we have been gathering since mid-day, arriving by foot or in cars, vans, or converted school buses, all bedecked with innumerable and intricate variations of the symbols of our tribe: skeletons and skulls, roses, lightning bolts. And tie-dye—brazenly multicolored tie-dyed everything, everywhere. Tonight, the rites of the Grateful Dead will be celebrated once again, and we, the Deadheads, are beginning the ritual preparations.

2   I stroll with a deliberate rhythm along the promenade outside the amphitheater, gazing knowingly into the eyes of those I pass. One of these is a woman my own age, older than the youthful women running past us, and calmer, centered in her demeanor. We nod as we pass, my eye enchanted by her elaborately beaded neckpiece as it sparkles in the sun. We have seen each other many times before, yet I do not know her name. I know that when she dances, her soul expands to encircle all those around her, and that her ecstatic beauty then is belied here and now by a face most would see as ordinary, one you probably wouldn't notice in the street on any normal day.

3   But this is no normal day. And the sidewalk is beginning to look like a multi-ringed circus or a medieval pageant: blankets cover the ground displaying beadwork, Guatemalan shirts, Nepalese vests, bumper stickers, t-shirts, hand-carved artifacts and crafts of many descriptions. Makeshift food concessions have sprung from the sides of gaily colored buses in the parking lots and side-streets nearby. Radiant women and thoughtful-looking men offer organic sandwiches: banana-honey-almond butter (on sprouted wheat) and avocado-cheese-sunflower-sprout (in homemade pita bread). A young girl glides by on a skateboard, her tinseled tiara glistening behind her, and a Rastafarian brother—a "dredhead"—sits on the grass relishing a sweet-smelling spliff. A slightly sad-looking fellow saunters by with index finger upraised, dreamily asking everyone and no one, "Got a miracle? I just need one ticket."

4   And there is music. Everywhere I walk in the promenade from one end of the theater's expansive front face to the other, I hear the very tastiest of Grateful Dead tunes—segments of concerts gone by preserved for posterity by industrious and ingenious tapers. Their melodies, harmonies, and dissonances blend each into the other as I pass; the sounds never clash, but yield to one another as if threads in one continuous tapestry of song.

5   I glance up at the sun to confirm that it is a few hours before the show. Time to begin wandering into the theater for many of us who have friends inside, loyally and lovingly saving blanketed spaces. As I near the gates, a gray-bearded security guard, his dark brown face glowing in welcome, calls out, "Show your ticket now. Everyone hold your own ticket. Jerry says we're going to have a good time tonight."

6   "Hey, Willie."

7   "How's it goin', Willie!"

8   "Don't stay out here too long, now, Willie. Be sure and come on in when the music starts." Loving fans greet him as they pass. Willie has been doing this now for longer than most of us have been coming to shows—before some were even born. I remember seeing him in a movie shot at a Dead show in 1974. The event was being recorded on film for future generations, and there, along with all the hippies, dippies, and trippers, was Willie, outside the front gate, greeting all comers with the gentle reminder to "hold your own ticket." I glitter my best glimmer at him, and pass in through the gates.

9   Inside, we are quickly and apologetically searched by young blue-coated staff people amid humorous exchanges about the contents of various packs and bags. They must know the multifarious and magical contents of many of these bags, but they trust us to use them wisely and responsibly, a reputation we've gained and upheld through the many years of cooperation with promoter-king Bill Graham and his people. It helps that Bill himself is a Deadhead. I pass through untouched.

10   And then we are inside the circular amphitheater. Here, the atmosphere is that of a family reunion. Brothers and sisters greet one another like they haven't seen each other in years—though it's probably only been since the last show—with loving embraces or happy screams. What was a warm profusion of color outside is an explosion of rainbows in here, dappling the floor in front of the stage and splashed throughout the rising circles of seats surrounding it. As more and more of the celebrants arrive, I watch as the theater begins to fill, gradually to the brim.

11   Along comes Calico, gray hair in characteristic braids, ethnic skirts fluttering as she walks purposefully through the crowd, happily returning smiles. Calico has spent most of the last two decades living in the Hog Farm commune with a group of Deadheads and other friends dedicated to service and good fun. A combination wise old crone and high priestess, she is proof positive to many of us that dancing to the Dead is the potion to eternal youth. We nod and pass.

12   I find my way slowly along cement walls, smiling at passing faces, familiar or not, united with all of them by a rising anticipation of sheer joy. A lion-eyed, curly-headed man a good ten years younger than me hands me a perfect long-stemmed red rose and tells me I look beautiful. We hug, connect hearts, and move on. Couples stroll and boppers bounce on by. Balloons drift and Frisbees fly. In the air, a palpable web of connection begins to form. I feel it subtly with my fingers, playing with it as if it were a spiral-shaped harp of myriad invisible strings.

13   Finding at last my dearest and closest friends and family awaiting me on the upper grass, I am enfolded by extended embraces and welcomed like a long-lost

traveler returning at last. We come together with a familiar readiness, settling in and making space for each other. I breathe in deeply and open my arms wide, embracing the entire congregation, the campus, the bay, the Golden Gate and Mount Tamalpais across the water, all of which I see from this lofty vantage. I prepare myself for the celebration, stretching into a salutation of the sun. I am drenched in the warmth of pure love.

14   Showtime draws closer. The crowd solidifies, undulating like a single, gracefully moving organism, taking on a personality all its own. We become a mass of movement, thousands of bodies all in motion yet all one entity. The sound is rising— from a murmur, to a buzz, now verging on a roar. And when at last the musicians take the stage, the place explodes. We greet them with unabashed adoration, screaming, hooting, whistling, beaming, and laughing like children. Even before the music starts we begin to sway expectantly, listening for the notes of the guitars' tune-up to begin, hoping for a hint of the first song, a glittering glimpse of what ecstasies the night ahead will hold.

15   I inhale deeply and look tenderly around me, feeling completely, perfectly at home. And the music begins.

AFTERWARDS

Vocabulary

demeanor, spliff, tapestry, glimmer, palpable, myriad. Once you have located the definitions of each vocabulary word, attempt to determine their origins. Consider the connotative qualities projected by each word to arrive at your conclusions.

Content

1. Susan Dobra describes arriving for a concert much as would a person who has gone on a pilgrimage and finally arrived at her destination. Christians made pilgrimages to the Holy Land in the Middle Ages and Muslims still make them to Mecca today. What is the purpose of a pilgrimage, and how does it fit with Dobra's description?

2. What is it about music that contributes to a sense of community? A music historian, Joachim Berendt, once described a choir as an image for the ideal human community. What do you think he meant by that? What is Dobra's vision of the community of Deadheads? Is she part of an audience or a tribal gathering?

3. Do you expect that all those who attended Grateful Dead concerts were as comfortable as Dobra? Have you ever attended a concert and not felt you were "in with the in crowd"? If so, explain the circumstances. Also, how do you think you would have felt at a Grateful Dead concert?

Style and Structure

1. How does Dobra use description to communicate feeling in this essay? What words or phrases strike you as particularly vivid?

2. How are details used in this essay in order to create a particular effect?

3. In what way does Dobra prepare us for the ending of her narrative?

Collaborative Explorations

With two or three other people make a list of some of the concerts you have attended. Place them in some categories that you make up yourself. What sort of a spectrum of experiences do these concerts represent? Make a list of the various reasons people go to concerts.

Writing Assignments

1. Write a personal narrative essay about a concert you attended, but rather than describe the music you heard, describe the people you encountered or observed.

2. The Grateful Dead were rooted in the counterculture of the 1960s. How do the music groups today reflect other decades? What are musical performances like today? What cultural values do they reflect? Explain in an essay.

Thematic Reading Cross-Links: Refer to Chapter 6, Environments, for essays on physical and social environments. Also see Chapter 8, Popular Culture—especially as it relates to Deadheads.

Movie Cross-Links: See the *Grateful Dead Movie* listed in Film Links at the end of this chapter.

Four and More: For Miles Davis
Quincy Troupe

An award-winning poet, **QUINCY TROUPE** is an equally distinguished prose stylist. His works include *Embryo* (1972), *Snake-Back Solos* (1979), and *Skulls Along the River* (1984). In addition to his poetry collections, Troupe collaborated with Miles Davis in *Miles: The Autobiography* (1989), edited *Giant Talk: A Third-World Anthology,* and wrote *The Inside Story of TV's*

"Roots" with David L. Wolper. Currently, Troupe is a professor in the literature program at the University of California, San Diego, and he is writing *The Footman's Chronicles*, a novel based on growing up in St. Louis with his father. Troupe published *Weather Reports* in 1991 and *Avalanche*, his fifth book of poetry, in 1996. *Soundings*, a collection of his essays, is also forthcoming. A versatile artist, Troupe made a CD and tape recording entitled *Root Doctor* (1994) wherein he read his own poems, accompanied by legendary jazz and blues guitarist Phil Upchurch. The title of the following poem from *Weather Reports* provides two important textual clues: (1) the subject matter (an allusion to a jazz composition by Miles Davis called "Four," from an album called *Four and More*), and (2) Miles Davis, the person for whom the poem is written.

ALLUSIONS

bebop: A style of modern jazz initiated in the 1940s by alto saxophonist Charlie Parker and trumpeter Dizzy Gillespie.

Miles Davis: A jazz trumpet player, renowned for his elegant, expressive style.

1.

a carrier of incandescent dreams, this
blade-thin, shadowman, jagged by lightning
crystal silhouette
prowling over blues-stained pavements
his life, lean, he drapes himself, his music, across edges
his blood held tight, within
he takes risks in staccato flights

& clean as darkness & bright as lightning
he reverses moments, where the sound becomes two cat eyes
penetrating the midnight hours, of moon pearl faces
lacing broken, mirrored waters
mississippi mean, as this sun-drenched trumpet-man
is mean, holding dreams high on any wind, light

his voice walking on eggshells

2.

& time comes as the wrinkles
of your mother's skin shrinks inward
the spirit flying towards that compelling
voice, light, calling
since time began, on the flip-side of spirit, you

miles, shredding placemats at each stage of your music
then go down river to explore
a new blues

the drum skin of your young years wearing
long, the enigmatic search
of your music
changing with every turning of the clock's hands
spinning your sound towards the diamond-point
in the river, lyrical, beyond edges
where light comes & goes

3.
O Silent Keeper of shadows
of the gutted, bloody roads filled with gloomy
ticking of time-clocks, time running down these roads
around hairpin turns, turning in on itself
during luminous moments
when love is found when love was sought
O Iridescent Keeper, of rainbowing laughter, arching
music from a gold-capped grin

Of a bluesman, holding, the sun between his teeth

is where you miles come from, playing roadhouse funk
funky soothsayer, of chewed-up moments played
clean, shekereman, at the crossroads of cardinal points
dropping dewdrop solos, of strut & slide
mean off into glide & stroll
talisman, hoodooing from bebop
trumpet voice walking on eggshells
mississippi river pouring from roots of your eyes

AFTERWARDS

Vocabulary

incandescent, staccato, enigmatic, luminous, iridescent, soothsayer, talisman.
Look up each word to discover which syllable(s) are stressed. Then, examine
how the sound of the words adds to the rhythm of the poem.

Content

1. Why is "mississippi" mentioned twice in the poem? What is the connection to the African American experience and music?

2. What does it mean to say Davis's "voice" is walking on eggshells?

3. What does this poem reveal about the cultural significance of music?

Style and Structure

1. If you read the poem out loud, you will get a feel for the rhythm of the language. How would you describe the effect of the rhythm? Is it like listening to Miles Davis's jazz improvisations? (If you have never heard Miles Davis play, you might look for CDs entitled *Kind of Blue, Workin'*, and *In a Silent Way*, among many others.)

2. The first section of the poem refers to Miles Davis in the third person ("his life," "his blood"); the second and third sections are addressed to Davis himself ("you miles," "your music"). What effect does this shift make in the poem?

3. Why does Troupe use the subtitle "For Miles Davis" for his poem? How does it help you read the poem? Justify your answer.

Collaborative Explorations

In a group of three or four people, have each person read the poem aloud as he or she hears it. How many different ways can you find to read it? How does this alter or affect the meaning of the poem?

Writing Assignments

1. Write an analysis of this poem in which you attempt to show how the poem communicates. What does Troupe do with language that is unconventional? fresh? creative? Print out the key words or phrases and explain their impact on you.

2. Choose a musician who has had a powerful impact on you in one way or another and write an impressionistic, poetic essay in which the language you use seems to resemble the music itself in some way.

Thematic Cross-Links: For other character portraits, see Alice Walker's essay, "My Father," and James Houston's essay, "How Playing Country Music Taught Me How to Love My Dad," from Chapter 3, The American Family.

Movie Cross-Links: See *Round Midnight*, a depiction of the life of a bebop musician, listed in the Film Links at the end of this chapter.

The Aesthetics of Rap

Dara Cook

Author and critic **DARA COOK'S** articles have appeared in many distinguished magazines, including the *Black Issues Book Review*. In the following essay, Cook explains how hip-hop could be considered poetry and argues that rap is indeed an aesthetic art form. "The Aesthetics of Rap" originally appeared in the March/April 2000 issue of *Black Issues Book Review*.

ALLUSIONS

Imamu Amiri Baraka: First published under the name LeRoi Jones, poet and playwright Baraka wrote *The Dutchman* and *The Blues People*.

Chester Himes: Author of crime novels, including *Cotton Comes to Harlem* and *Pinktoes*, which have been described as "savagely slapstick ghetto crime comedies."

Walter Mosely: Author of the crime novels *Gone Fishin'* and *Always Outnumbered Always Outgunned*.

John Edgar Wideman: The author of *Brother and Keepers* (1984) and *Fatheralong* (1994).

Paul Laurence Dunbar: A poet and novelist, Dunbar emerged as a prominent voice during the Harlem Renaissance of the 1920s.

Phyllis Wheatley: Born in West Africa, she was brought to America as a slave in 1761. She is the first African American woman published as a poet.

Jean Toomer: Part of the Harlem Renaissance, he published *Cane*, an experimental novel, in 1923.

1   Now canonized, the cutting-edge poets of the preceding generation are celebrating the lyrical brilliance of today's rappers, and vice-versa.

2   Possibly because of rap's commercial entertainment orientation, its coverage of such unsavory topics as criminality, drugs and sex, and its authorship by a largely disenfranchised part of society, rap music has enjoyed little perceived intellectual currency. Recognizing both the American tendency to discredit or ignore the creative genius of young African Americans and the poetic talent of some of today's rappers, established poets have served as the de facto ambassadors of "rap-as-poetry" to those of us who love rhythm, rhyme and verse.

3   "Hip-hop is a very important battlefield," poet Sonia Sanchez remarked during a reading at Eso Wan Books in Los Angeles. Born Wilsonia Driver in Birmingham, Alabama in 1934, Sanchez is an award-winning writer and professor. After

publishing poetry with such writers as Amiri Baraka, she released her first poetry collection, *Homecoming*, in 1969. Her works received critical acclaim, most notably the autobiography *A Blues Book for Blue Black Magical Women* (1973) and *Homegirls and Handgrenades* (Thunder's Mouth, 1984) which earned the prestigious American Book Award for poetry in 1985. In 1998, Temple University, where she has taught creative writing and black literature, awarded her an honorary Doctor of Humane Letters degree.

4   Her place secure in the canon of American poetry, Sanchez has done more than publicly endorse hip hop. She appeared in the 1997 Universal Records documentary, *Rakim* (aired on BET), hailing the rapper Rakim, an enormously gifted poet, and has even performed with him. The documentary shows Sanchez performing one of her favorite Rakim raps, "Casualties of War" (from Eric B. and Rakim's 1990 album, *Don't Sweat the Technique*, MCA Records) in one of her own poetry readings. Rakim's depiction of battle and its psychological consequences is a corporeal and vivid representation of fighting in the Gulf War, one that echoes those of Sanchez's generation in Vietnam.

5   Sanchez is one of the most outspoken advocates of hip-hop poetry. During the 1999 ABC *Nightline* program, "Tupac Lives," Sanchez acknowledged, "They are poets and no one wants to give them that kind of benefit of being poets. They want to say rappers and put them in another little group. But they certainly are an extension of many of the poets who came before."

6   Other established poets like Baraka have also accepted and promote rap as a form of poetry. Nikki Giovanni so embraced the expressive power of hip hop that she dedicated her 1997 collection *Love Poems* to the slain rapper Tupac Shakur.

7   "Tupac Shakur was a great leader," Sanchez has said. "He was a prophet. He delivered with the truth. When I read in the high schools and junior high schools, one of my poems for Pac; you can hear a pin drop. They stop whatever they're doing. I'm talking about in an assembly. The noise that they're making, they stop. And they lean back on the words like what you saying? What you saying about this man who is our man? Who is from our generation? Who told us the truth?"

8   But as radical poets of yesterday, now firmly established in the canon of contemporary poetry, recognize the gifts of rappers, hip hop poets themselves are, in a parallel move, embracing black literary traditions.

Def Breaks It Down 4U

9   Mos Def, 26, reclines in a hired Lincoln Town Car, dodging black market taxis and jaywalkers on Brooklyn's Flatbush Avenue as it edges toward the Music Emporium, where he is scheduled to sign copies of his debut solo rap opus, *Black on Both Sides*. The record store is only blocks away from Nkiru Books, Brooklyn NY's landmark black bookstore that Def and his partner-in-rhyme Talib Kweli, from the rap group Black Star, purchased last year.

10   Through Nkiru Books they intend to "stimulate interest in reading," Def says. Def hosts lectures and readings at Nkiru, and even performs there himself. Def

developed his ability to translate his senses into sentences from some of the most brilliant classic and contemporary African American writers, but lyrical novelists rather than poets. "Chester Himes is one of my strongest influences because he was documenting real street shit in a very eloquent way, in a way that was not heady; you got it. Walter Mosely and John Edgar Wideman do that a lot. They draw relationships to things that everybody experiences but they articulate them so freshly. Like in *Philadelphia Fire*, John Edgar Wideman talked about night and said, 'Spaces open which haven't been there before.' And it's true, things open in the night that don't happen at any part of the day: Spaces for opportunity, spaces for trouble. The hallmark of a good writer is to be able to make a deeper commentary or draw a relationship between things that we all may have noticed but may not have been able to articulate, or may not have noticed at all."

11   He credits his parents—his father runs a heating and cooling installation business with his brother, and his mother is a hospital technician—for his love of letters. "My parents read a lot," he remembers. "My father was the most interesting reader. He read everything—but I don't think he owned one fiction book. They were all nonfiction." Born Dante Beze in the Bedford Stuyvesant section of Brooklyn, he started rapping at the age of nine and has always loved performing and oration.

12   Since his first recording in 1994, Def has fed poetry-starved listeners an oeuvre of intricately crafted rhymes, one that echoes the rhythmic and metaphorical sentiments of Black Arts Movement poetry. "Sides" is one of the finest examples of contemporary poetry. His lyrics thematically and metaphorically cohere, his images are palpably powerful. His opening for the song "Hip Hop" is one example: "Speech is my hammer/bang my world into shape/Now let it fall."

13   Some rap lyrics, like those of Mos Def, are poetry—very good poetry. But the American public is reluctant to pay rap its poetic props. The closest the public at large has come to praising rap is to appreciate a few poets who imbue their works with hip-hop sensibilities, slang and rhythms, such as Paul Beatty, author of the 1994 poetry collection *Joker, Joker, Deuce* (Penguin) and the 1996 novel, *The White Boy Shuffle* (Henry Holt & Company).

14   Nevertheless, ambassadors of hip hop like Sanchez and fans of hip-hop's influences in literature have heralded hip hop's poetic crusaders. Def, when he formed *Black Star*, received praise from hip hop critics, college rap fans, and underground rap aficionados alike, who applauded their 1998 debut album, *Mos Def and Talib Kweli are Black Star* (Rawkus) for its intelligent, conscious lyrics. Now he is among the first rappers to be acknowledged as a poet.

15   Def speaks slowly and determinedly, exercising the same attention to diction in his speech as he does [in] his lyrics. He often punctuates his sentences with a smile that lights up his chiseled features, acknowledging to himself and cueing his listener that he has perfectly conveyed and completed his thoughts.

16   "Good poetry," Def explains, "must convey a sense of place, feeling, relationship. A longing, a yearning for something—of expression, of understanding. Not all rap lyrics do this . . . I think my most poetic rhyme is probably my opening

on "Respiration" (from his debut album). It goes, 'The new moon rode high in the crown of the metropolis./Shinin, like who on top of this?'

17   "You see, I live in Brooklyn, right on the water. And one night I was over by the water, just looking out on one of those nice, spring nights, and the moon was just smack dab in the middle of the sky. It was over everything. All of these skyscrapers, all of this steel and metal monuments to money—the moon was above all of it. The city sometimes, with all those peaks, looks like a crown. It was like the moon was in the metropolis' crown."

18   Def reads political literature extensively and takes exception to the surprise he frequently hears in response to this fact. Def compares this to America's historical reception of black literature. "It's no different from white folks being amazed by Paul Dunbar, Phyllis Wheatley, or being amazed that Jean Toomer came out with *Cane*. Why is it so incredible that young black people can articulate or have an awareness of things that happened more than twenty minutes ago or a year ago?"

19   An unusually close reader of the literature of black America, Def defends the intellectual gifts of young black America. Def particularly admires the poetry of his partner Kweli. He quotes an incredibly insightful verse of Kweli's on an unreleased single: "A day is measured by the sun, but the sun was made on the fourth day/Such mysterious ways/Without the sun, man, those must have been some serious days."

20   Common is another fellow rapper Def admires, citing Common's verse on "Respiration" which envisioned grief with a music production metaphor: "Threw dirt on the casket, the hurt, I couldn't mask it/Mixin' down emotions, struggle, I hadn't mastered/I choreograph seven steps to heaven."

21   However well respected by fellow rappers or even established poets, many of hip-hop's brightest lyrical lights are commercially dim. Rappers like Common struggle for commercial viability, not having yet sold the 500,000 copies per CD that spell gold. Perhaps because these artists' lyrics require an attentive ear and cognitive dexterity, the average music buyer overlooks these works for simpler and less demanding hip hop. Rappers with less intricate lyrics get the public eye and ear.

22   Def blames "American laziness" for the misconception of rap as intellectually bankrupt. "If you depend on *Time, Newsweek,* CNN and network TV for your information, and don't have your own relationship and experience to something, then that's what you'll believe. People aren't going any further than what they're seeing on TV. The very people that accuse you of not being able to think for yourself are not doing their own thinking," Def laments.

Can Poetry Go Gold or Platinum?

23   Nevertheless, some good poet/rappers, like Lauryn Hill and platinum-selling Nas, have enjoyed commercial success. Hill, who last year set the female record for most Grammys won in a single night, is a poet extraordinaire. Her lyrics on "Everything is Everything," from her 1998 Grammy-snatching solo debut, *The Miseducation of Lauryn Hill* (Sony Music), conjures the exaggerative, maternal enormity of Nikki Giovanni's poem "Ego Trippin".

24   On "Project Windows" from his latest album, *Nastradamus* (Columbia Records), Nas describes growing up in New York City's Queensbridge section with arresting lyricism: "At night the windows were speakers, pumpin' life out/A fight, people screamin' cause somebody pulled a knife out/So I look at this poem/I'm hooked to this tune/Every night the same melody/Hell sounded so heavenly."

25   Nas officially nods approvingly at conventional poetry by inviting poet Jessica Care Moore to perform the album's intro and outro.

26   Many dedicated readers of African American literature who revel in the creative accomplishments of the Harlem Renaissance and the Black Arts Movement, lament the absence of similar artistic movements today. Perhaps they should reconsider. *The Oxford Companion to Philosophy* says: "Poetry is at its best an all-in, maximally dense, simultaneous deployment of linguistic resources—sound and rhythm as well as sense, the bringing together of numerous strands of meaning, through metaphor and other figures, through ambiguities (often unresolved), controlled associations and resonance, allusions: all of these contributing to a well-integrated, unified effect."

27   Rap's economy, adherence to metaphor, simile, imagery, and ability to express the pain and triumph of a people with infectious cadence and an obsession with rhythm renders it poetry par excellence. Listen closely to hip-hop poets like Def, Hill, Nas, Common, Kweli and Rakim—our new millennial Barakas, Sanchezes, Jordans and Hugheses—and you will realize that one of the greatest poetic movements in recent history is happening right now, and it's called hip-hop.

AFTERWARDS

Vocabulary

Canonized, disenfranchisement, unsavory, currency, de facto, prestigious, corporeal, oeuvre, palpably, heralded, aficionados, cognitive, dexterity. Look up the above words noting their denotative and connative meanings. Also, make note of their meaning in languages other than English.

Content

1. How would you define *poetry*? Do the examples given in this essay fit with your definition? How many definitions of poetry can you find in this essay?

2. Rap and hip-hop have been criticized because of their commercialism. To what extent does the author succeed in convincing readers that, with these performers, commercial motivation is less important than artistic expression?

3. What representative examples does the author use to support her arguments? Does she explain the quotations thoroughly enough to demonstrate their significance?

Style and Structure

1. How does the author attempt to persuade the reader that hip hop is an authentic type of poetry? In your opinion, does she succeed?

2. How does the author's word choice help to elevate her discussion of rap? Identify the words or phrases that come from literary sources—not the language of the street.

3. What is the author's strategic purpose in comparing contemporary rappers with well-established African American writers?

Collaborative Explorations

Assign four to five people to a group and then have each member bring lyrics to a favorite song to the next class. At the next meeting, share the lyrics and determine whether or not they are *good poetry* and why.

Writing Assignments

1. Choose some form of music that you feel is underappreciated, and write an essay in which you show through examples that it is connected to a tradition of expression that has deep cultural roots.

2. Write an essay in which you argue and illustrate how and why rap has evolved from solely an African American to a mainstream experience that cuts across and includes many ethnic groups.

Thematic Cross-Links: See Michelle Wallace's quote from "When Black Feminism Faces the Music, and the Music Is Rap" in the Observations and Opinions section at the beginning of this chapter. She finds that the ongoing use of sexist lyrics in rap interferes with her consideration of it as an art form.

Movie Cross-Links: See *O Brother, Where Art Thou?*, listed in the Film Links at the end of this chapter, and make a list of the various types of "roots" music performed. Consider the poetic traditions that have come out of gospel, blues, and country music.

Fake Music

Willow Lamberson

WILLOW LAMBERSON is a student at South Puget Sound Community College in Olympia, Washington. In the following essay Lamberson takes a critical look at the "cult of music worship."

ALLUSIONS

Michelangelo: Michelangelo Buonarotti, Renaissance sculptor, painter, architect, and poet.

Wind in the Willows: English novel (1910) by Kenneth Grahame. Ostensibly a children's book, it is based on the adventures of the impetuous Mr. Toad.

1   Many people in our culture are in a kind of cult that involves something similar to "music worship." I don't know whether these people realize what they are doing or not, or if they realize that they are part of a vast scheme. There are people who recognize this cult-like thing for what it is, but unfortunately many seem to have a difficult time expressing what it is they know without coming across as narrow minded. The thought that there are so many people falling victim to this plot disturbs me, and it is my desire to warn you, lest you, too, fall victim to it.

2   The names of the masterminds behind the cult of music worship are unknown to me. The names of their tools are widely known, though, and they are many. As I am not terribly well-informed on all the various members of this cult-thing, I will only mention three of the main perpetrators with whom I am familiar: Britney Spears, N'SYNC, and the Backstreet Boys.

3   These pop icons, worshipped by their fans, are only puppets in the hands of their masters, and this is the thing that bothers me. The songs that they sing are written by someone else, someone who writes them for the sole purpose of making money. They aren't making music because that is what they love to do, but because they get paid to do it—not like the Beatles, or Radiohead, who created music because they just couldn't help it.

4   Think of "Baby One More Time" by Britney Spears, and then consider "The Sweetest Thing" by U2. These songs are so different: one so fake, the other so real. It's like the difference between a painting by Michelangelo and a paint-by-number. The U2 song is coming from them, from their own creative imaginations, their own experiences, their very selves.

5   The same person who writes Britney Spears's songs also writes songs for the Backstreet Boys and N'SYNC. I heard that this person recently received an award for his songwriting skills. That's good; I'm glad that credit is being given where credit is

due. Otherwise it would be like the Muppets getting credit for their performances, when in reality they're just little rag dolls that can't do anything by themselves. I enjoy the Muppets, as do many people, and some people have posters and other Muppet paraphernalia which they proudly display around their home. That's all fine and good, just as long as we understand and appreciate who the real artists are.

6   In the days of yore there were two types of musical artists: singers, and songwriters, but they each received recognition for their respective talents. For example, George Gershwin and his brother Ira Gershwin were both recognized as great popular songwriters in their day, and they had many hit songs. People knew whose songs they were listening to. There were also the popular singers who were given the songs of writers in order to present them to the public. Perhaps people were partial to certain singers because they liked their voice, or their style of singing, or the way they portrayed a song to the public. The point is, there were singers and songwriters and each received their due credit. If singers had no talent, they weren't popular. The same goes for a songwriter. Like Max in *The Sound of Music* said when George made a comment about Max getting the money while his singing group just gets the fame, "Tis unfair, I know. But one day all that will change—I shall get the fame too." I look forward to the day when the real talents in music are recognized.

7   I believe that the real musicians, the real artists, aren't truly part of pop culture, but that they are part of a sub-culture. They write music that they like, and it just gets popular. John Lennon of the Beatles said, "I met Paul and said, 'Do you want to join me band?' And then George came along, then Ringo. We were just a band who made it very very big, that's all." They were just your average guys who got together to play music. Over the years their music changed, reflecting the changes they were undergoing. Because their music was living, it could grow with them. When the Beatles broke up, John, Paul, George, and Ringo didn't stop making music. They kept on separately, because it was something that they loved to do, and they just couldn't stop. These were just four guys who had tremendous musical talent: the ability to write meaningful lyrics, to write beautiful music to accompany them, and to present it themselves in an artistic and powerful way. They had the ability to convey something from themselves through their music.

8   Think of some of the songs by the Beatles. They have feeling—something people can relate to—because the songs are born of experience. Their song "In My Life" (specifically the first verse) is something any person can relate to:

There are places I'll remember
All my life, though some have changed
Some forever, not for better
Some have gone, and some remain
All these places had their moments
With lovers and friends I still can recall
Some are dead and some are living
In my life I've loved them all

9   And is there anyone who has heard the song "Creep" by Radiohead and hasn't been able to relate to it? Especially the second verse and chorus:

> I don't care if it hurts
> I want to have control
> I want a perfect body
> I want a perfect soul
> I want you to notice
> When I'm not around
> You're so very special
> I wish I was special
> But I'm a creep
> I'm a weirdo
> What the hell am I doing here?
> I don't belong here

10   The songs are living, lasting. They come from something in a person that can't just be put there . . . it has to have been lived. And I believe that as long as people are on this earth, they will remember these songs. The Beatles are still remembered, still listened to, more than thirty years after they ceased to be a group. Or take U2, a group that's been around since the late seventies. They're still around, and they're still hugely popular. Do you think Britney Spears will still be popular in thirty years? Do you suppose that her songs from today will be getting her new fans from the kids of tomorrow? I don't believe so, for the simple reason that the only reason she is popular is because of the way she looks. If she were homely, would people like her? If you have ever examined the lyrics she sings I think you'll find that they're really lacking in purpose, because their purpose is not to express the soul, or emotions or to impart to the listener something of value, or an opinion, or even to just provide listening pleasure. Their purpose is to make money, and the performers are to provide viewing pleasure. To do this, they must have a catchy tune, or a danceable beat, or some sort of appeal to the targeted audience. However, the main appeal is in the singer presenting them. Attractive people are chosen to present the songs to the public, and they use their bodies to obtain fans. Where is the musical artistry of that?

11   I don't think that Britney Spears' songs have the ability to retain any of the popularity that they enjoy today. Do you think that this song has the ability to stand the test of time?

> Yeah yeah yeah yeah yeah
> Yeah yeah yeah yeah yeah yeah
> I think I did it again
> I made you believe we're more than just friends
> Oh baby
> It might seem like a crush

But it doesn't mean that I'm serious
'Cause to lose all my senses
That is just so typically me
Oh baby, baby
Oops! . . . I did it again
I played with your heart, got lost in the game
Oh baby, baby
Oops! . . . You think I'm in love
That I'm sent from above
I'm not that innocent

12   I believe that in a few short years her fifteen minutes of fame will be over, and she will join the ranks of the all-but-forgotten pop-stars of yesterday. And she and the others like her will be replaced with the newly made pop-icons of tomorrow. And so it goes, these pop-stars are easy to come by—not like one-of-a-kind groups like the Beatles, U2, or Radiohead. People might try to mimic them, but it's never the same as the real thing. It's like trying to replicate Mona Lisa's smile.

13   Britney Spears, Backstreet Boys, N'SYNC, whatever. They're all similar; they're all like performing monkeys. Since they are merely performers masquerading as artists, they are basically the equivalent of trained monkeys. Think of an organ-grinder with his monkey that dances for the crowd, then goes about with a little tin cup to collect from the audience. The monkey gives the cup filled with contributions to his master, who takes good care of his little monkey so that it will be sure to perform well and bring him more money. And the people adore the cute, comical little monkey. Is the picture clear? Britney Spears, performing for her adoring crowd, making loads of money for herself and her master . . . .

14   The people focus on the monkey, and the music is only the background. What will the monkey do today? The organ-grinder smiles inwardly, a thin, greedy smile. "The fools," he thinks. "They worship my monkey, and give it their money. They don't realize that there are millions of monkeys just like it. I could switch monkeys and they wouldn't know the difference. They could get their own monkey, and it would do just as well as mine. No, I'm glad they're fools. More money for me."

15   Do you see what's happening? They're cheapening music, making it crass. It causes me pain, and it stirs me to anger, because I love music. I admire people who have talent and a love of music as well. Music isn't just a livelihood, a means of making money. Music isn't a peripheral. Music is everywhere. Every culture has music. Even the whales have songs. Still, it's something you have to experience to understand. Like the composer Nobuo Uematsu said, "Can anyone express the emotions we get from music?" Have you ever heard a sound so haunting, so beautiful, that it made the hair on the back of your neck stand on end? That it moved you to tears? I have. As Rat says in *The Wind in the Willows*, "So beautiful and strange and new! Since it was to end so soon, I almost wish I had never heard it. For it has roused a longing in me that is pain, and nothing seems worth while but just to hear that sound once more and go on listening to it for ever."

16   The warped music that is being made for money may sound nice, but when you listen to it, remember its purpose. Think of where it comes from. It has no real message (other than *buy me, buy me, buy me . . .*), no real feeling. And it has but one purpose: to make money.

17   In conclusion, I believe that it's the whole money thing, the whole phoniness of pop music, that makes it disgusting to me. While some of it can be pleasant to listen to, on the whole I find it too repugnant to tolerate. You might like pop music. You might not care about its purpose. Or perhaps you didn't know that Britney Spears, the Backstreet Boys, and others don't write their own music. Perhaps you didn't know how they came about. And that's because they don't want you to know. They don't want you to think about that. They want you to believe that they are just as talented as any other musician. Because if you believe they are really working for it, you feel better about giving them your money.

18   In closing, all I ask is that you consider your reasons for listening to pop-music, if indeed you do listen to it. Some people scorn the pop groups because of their lack of talent. Some just hate that kind of music because they like an opposing style. Others overlook it and fork over their money to buy the albums and help keep the scheme going. Your personal preferences in music dictate what albums you buy. If you like that kind of music, then that's your choice. It just bothers me to no end that people worship trained monkeys. So think of the artists who are really working, putting themselves into their music. These are the ones who deserve our admiration, not the fake ones, the performing monkeys. And so I look forward to a day when, if a Spears song comes on the radio, we will all cry out in one voice what Telly Savalas said in *The Dirty Dozen,* "Keep that cheap wailin' slut quiet!"

AFTERWARDS

Vocabulary

perpetrators, paraphernalia, icons, replicate, masquerading, peripheral. Write a short paragraph in which you assess your own experience with "fake music," using at least three of the above vocabulary words.

Content

1. How would you describe the distinction that Lamberson makes between authentic music and fake music? Do you agree with this distinction?

2. What differences do you see in the language of the two songs—one by Britney Spears and one by Radiohead? What are the characteristics of the Radiohead song that make Lamberson see it as better?

3. How effective is Lamberson's analogy between an organ grinder's monkey and a pop singer?

Style and Structure

1. In the first paragraph of the essay, Lamberson establishes a tone of mock-seriousness that she continues throughout the essay. What specific words and phrases create this tone?

2. Comment on Lamberson's use of rhetorical questions to introduce new points in her essay. How do they prepare the reader for what follows?

3. How are the beginning and closing paragraphs used as framing devices for the whole essay?

Collaborative Explorations

Gather together in small groups, assigning one member as a recorder, and generate your own list of real and fake musicians and singers. Next to each individual your group identifies, list two or three characteristics justifying their place on the list. Have each group present its findings to the rest of the class.

Writing Assignments

1. In the same manner as Lamberson, write an essay comparing and contrasting the authenticity of two things. Think of other kinds of performers, like actors, dancers, or artists.

2. Construct an argumentative essay refuting Lamberson's scathing attack on pop singers. Be sure your argument contains sound reasoning and relevant examples. Try to show why pop music—no matter how silly it may seem—is an authentic part of everyday life.

Thematic Cross-Links: See the introduction to Chapter 5, Media: Controversies and Celebrities, for a look at some of the ways performers of "fake music" are able to market themselves.

Movie Cross-Links: Compare Willow Lamberson's point of view to the satire of commercialism and hype in *This Is Spinal Tap* listed in Film Links. Do the essay and the film make similar points?

The Visual Connection: Photograph Writing Activities

1. Look at the following photographs of Sarah McLachlan, Jimi Hendrix, Stevie Ray Vaughan, and Shemekia Copeland. What do you know about them? What is (or has been) their role in modern music? Divide a piece of paper into two columns. Then write a brief sketch of each individual, noting what you know for certain about the musical celebrity, or what the pictures themselves "tell" you. If you decide to write about the story each picture seems to tell, practice using qualifying words so that your reader can distinguish between fact and fiction.

Sarah McLachlan

Jimi Hendrix

Shemekia Copeland

Stevie Ray Vaughan

2. Go online, download a picture of one of your favorite musical performers, and write a brief narrative introducing his or her music to readers as if they were hearing about the musician for the first time. What would you want your audience to know about the musician? How would you describe his or her music? Is it pleasant, disturbing, melodic, or powerful? How well do you think his or her music will withstand the test of changing musical tastes? Will people listen to his or her music fifty years from now? Explain.

Film Links: Music

1. What do the films listed in number 3, below, tell you about music as a business? What is the conflict between music as a form of artistic expression and music as a commercial product? How is this conflict represented in these films?

2. Browse through a movie or video guide and get an idea of what these movies are about. Then select two films that portray rock and roll, country, jazz, and so forth and write a comparison/contrast paper about them. You might want to take a look at the guide to Writing about Movies in the Appendix to remind you what to look for in your analysis.

3. Evaluate one of the music documentaries from the following list or from a list of your own—one that has been approved by your instructor. An important part of your evaluation here will be to focus on how well the performance is documented. How well could you hear the music? Did the documentary include live performances? If so, what does a live performance lack on film? How does film enhance a live performance? How does the film capture the feeling of an "event"? Overall, was the documentary a success?

A Hard Day's Night (Britain, Richard Lester, 1964). Beatlemania from the inside out.

Monterey Pop (USA, D. A. Pennebaker, 1968). Influential concert documentary featuring Jimi Hendrix, Big Brother and the Holding Company, The Who, Otis Redding, The Mamas and the Papas, and Ravi Shankar.

Woodstock (USA, Michael Wadleigh, 1970). The counterculture in full flower: Richie Havens, Joe Cocker, Santana, Ten Years After, Country Joe and the Fish, Crosby, Stills and Nash, Joni Mitchell, Sha Na Na, Jimi Hendrix, and Jefferson Airplane.

The Last Waltz (USA, Martin Scorsese, 1975). Documentary of The Band's farewell concert: Van Morrison, Neil Young, Bob Dylan, Joni Mitchell, Ronnie Hawkins.

The Grateful Dead Movie (USA, Jerry Garcia and Leon Gast, 1976). Phantasmagorical montages, goofy animation, concert footage, dancing Deadheads. The Godzilla of San Francisco rock bands playing their favorite blend of old-timey blues, bluegrass, avant-garde, modal jazz,

R & B, psychedelic, funk, and Beat poetry in one continuous nonstop bus tour full of big grins, peace signs, and tie-dyed everything.

Coal Miner's Daughter (USA, Michael Apted, 1980). Story of Loretta Lynn's rise from Appalachian poverty to Grand Ol' Opry stardom.

This Is Spinal Tap (USA, Rob Reiner, 1984). Satiric documentary of a fictional heavy-metal rock band.

Sweet Dreams (USA, Karel Reisz, 1985). Biography of country singer Patsy Cline reveals conflicts between career and marriage.

Round Midnight (France/USA, Bertrand Tavernier, 1986). Portrait of jazz saxophonist living in Paris, based on the lives of Lester Young and Bud Powell.

La Bamba (USA, Luis Valdez, 1987). Life of Richie Valens, Latino rocker of the 1950s.

The Commitments (Ireland, Alan Parker, 1991). An Irish band makes a splash performing American soul music of the 1960s.

The Doors (USA, Oliver Stone, 1991). Biography of Jim Morrison and his quest to "break on through to the other side."

What's Love Got to Do with It? (USA, Brian Gibson, 1993). Tina Turner's tempestuous marriage and flamboyant career.

Run Lola Run (Germany, Tom Twykwer, 1999). Techno music provides the soundtrack for a hyper action crime drama with philosophical implications.

Buena Vista Social Club (USA, Wim Wenders, 1999). Guitarist Ry Cooder travels to Cuba to meet and perform with legendary Cuban musicians.

High Fidelity (USA/Britain, Stephen Frears, 2000). An owner of a record shop in Chicago tries to understand how music can help him explain his lack of success with women.

O Brother, Where Art Thou? (USA, Joel Coen, 2000). A comic odyssey of three escaped convicts is accompanied by a musical tour of blues, country, gospel, and bluegrass.

Additional Writing Assignments

1. Select a song with lyrics that seem to speak to you for one reason or another. Recite the lyrics out loud but don't sing them. Next, listen to

or sing the lyrics along with the music written for them. Then write an essay analyzing how (1) the lyrics themselves function a lot like the content of an essay and (2) the music provides tone, transitional devices, and style.

2. Compare and contrast instrumental music or classical music with the sort of music you have to listen to when a receptionist puts your telephone call on hold, when you have to wait in a doctor's office, as you shop in a mall or store, when you ride an elevator, and so on. What is the effect of having some music forced on you? How does that differ from listening to music of your own choice? How might a "situation" sour your attitude toward a type of music? (How is music different from Muzak?)

3. Classify and divide different subcategories of a music type (e.g., rock and roll might be divided into alternative, grunge, heavy metal, techno-synth, punk, and so on). What conclusions can you draw about the music type after your examination of its many different forms? Be sure to supply your readers with plenty of representative examples to make any theoretical assumptions you reach believable.

4. The longest running radio program in the history of the British Broadcasting Corporation (BBC) is called *Desert Island Discs*, and it has been running weekly since 1942. Each week various guests name eight recordings they would take with them to a desert island. If you could take only eight discs with you for an extended stay on a remote island (handily equipped with electricity), which would you take? Write an essay in which you name and describe the discs you would pack in your bag and explain your reasons for choosing each. Also explain the role that music plays in your life. When do you listen to it? What does it do for you? Do you need it?

5. "Classical" music covers a wide range of historical periods, styles, and forms—from Renaissance madrigals to Romantic symphonies, from Italian operas to 20th-century film scores. These pieces of music are usually called "compositions," just as essays are. Listen to a piece of classical music and try to describe the elements that give it form and structure. Like an essay, it is likely to have a beginning, a middle, and an end, thematic development, digressions, rhythm, emotional appeals, abstract ideas, and so forth. Write an essay in which you compare the composition of music to the composition of an essay. Also, explain some of the important differences. What, for example, can words do that pure sounds cannot? What can a melody communicate that words cannot?

Chapter Eleven

Movies

Opinions and Observations

For science fiction films may also be described as a popular mythology for the contemporary negative imagination about the impersonal. The other-world creatures that seek to take "us" over or are an "it," not a "they." The planetary invaders are usually zombielike. Their movements are either cool, mechanical, or lumbering, blobby. But it amounts to the same thing. If they are non-human in form, they proceed with an absolutely regular, unalterable movement (unalterable save by destruction). If they are human in form—dressed in space suits, etc.,—then they obey the most rigid military discipline, and display no personal characteristics whatsoever. And it is this regime of emotionlessness, of impersonality, of regimentation, which they will impose on earth if they are successful.

—Susan Sontag from "The Imagination of Disaster"

Wicked, scheming, creative, sexually potent and deadly to the male, the femme fatale is one of the few powerful female figures in classical Hollywood cinema. Originally a character constructed in French romantic literature, the femme fatale in film is particularly associated with film noir and the thrillers of the 1940s and 1950s. Like her predecessor, the vamp of the 1920s, the femme fatale was defined by her desirable but dangerous sexuality—which brings about the downfall of the male protagonist. Typically, the femme fatale combines sensuality with driving ambition or self-interest. She lures men into her web of intrigue and robs them of their will power and rationality, exploiting her irresistibility to make them collude with her schemes.

—E. Ann Kaplin from "Women in Film Noir"

There is something that might be called cinematic beauty. It can be expressed in a film, and it must be present in a film for that film to be a moving work. When it is very well expressed, one experiences a particularly deep emotion while watching that film. I believe it is this quality that inspires the filmmaker to make his film in the first place. In other words, I believe that the essence of the cinema lies in cinematic beauty.

—Akira Kurosawa From *Something Like an Autobiography*

The best case study in animation to illustrate the powerful influence society has over the types of films that are produced is the story of Betty Boop. She was a major cartoon character before the Production Code of 1934 was put into place, and her dramatic and fatal transformation illustrates how a product created under one set of standards often withers when placed in a new milieu. At the same time, the Code alone cannot explain why this dizzy little flapper degenerated so quickly.

—Dan Patanella from "Betty Boop
and the Production Code of 1934"

Observations and Opinions:
Reading/Writing Activities

1. Susan Sontag and E. Ann Kaplin both tend to provide definitions as they relate to films, with Sontag defining the nature of "science fiction" movies and Kaplin explaining a film type: the femme fatale. Jot down your own definitions for (1) two of your favorite movie genres (e.g., action, romance, comedy, drama, fantasy) and (2) two movie types (e.g., the hero, fool, gunslinger, private eye, spy, villain).

2. In the passage from *Something Like an Autobiography*, Akira Kurosawa offers some philosophical insights into what makes movies moving: cinematic beauty. In a paragraph or so, define the essential qualities you would look for if you were a director. What would make a film "work"? What sort of movies would you like to film and why? (What type of films do you watch? Why do you go see that kind of film?)

3. Do you know about the Production Code of 1934? Look it up online as well as other articles on Betty Boop. Then share your information with the rest of your class. To what extent would you agree with Patanella's

belief that "a product created under one set of standards often withers when placed in a new milieu"?

Introduction

Films have a double nature. On the one hand, they are the most realistic art form ever invented. They give us twenty-four photographs a second to look at, and they create the powerful illusion made by "moving pictures." These images not only represent the actual world, but they blow it up into giant images on the screen of a movie theater. Audiences all over the world find it easy to believe what they see in movies. No matter how far-fetched the image, it is still right there before our eyes, and we accept it on some level as real. On the other hand, films are like dreams. Moviegoers go into a dark theater and sit in a seat that allows them to temporarily withdraw from the world. Going to the movies is like going to bed—your body is passive and you are isolated from the world around you—except that your eyes are open and you are sitting in a public place. Each movie viewer feels alone with the images on the screen; movies feel personal, like each one was made just for us. The images in films tap the psychological depths of our own memories.

Films are more than just personal dreams; they also represent the collective dreams of whole societies and cultures. Films are not viewed by solitary individuals but might be viewed by millions all over the world. Some films tap into deeper levels of perception and draw people to them. Certain actors become cultural icons because of the power they have over audiences. Think of how fans look to the "stars" to guide them, how the personal lives of movie actors influence those who watch them.

In "Popcorn Psychology" Andrew Day suggests that movie posters are the first invitation to enter the fantasy world of film. He examines the facial expressions and postures that entice potential moviegoers to buy a ticket. In the next reading selection, "Modern Day Minstrel Shows," Stanley Crouch attacks the negative racial stereotypes that have persisted in films despite the apparent social progress that has taken place in the last fifty years. Crouch suggests that films may retard social progress by continuing to exploit familiar, and therefore commercial, ways of categorizing members of minority groups.

Jessica Yellin explores how the film industry's sensitivity to political correctness and wariness about racial profiling have affected the characterization of movie villains in "See No Evil: Where Have All the Villains Gone?" She suggests American moviemakers need to create villains and other stereotyped evildoers in order to provide antagonists for action/adventure films.

Finally, film director Martin Scorsese traces his obsession with movies back to his childhood when movie-going experiences were always related to family.

He would draw his own movies after school and look forward to the day he could challenge the accepted practices of the profession; however, the Golden Age of the studio system of filmmaking changed. As a result, when Scorsese finally made movies, he laments that "even though I thought along the lines of the movies I loved as a child, the movies I made came from a different place."

How does film criticism relate to the composition process? Movies are universally familiar and accessible. As such, they offer superb topics or issues for examination, analysis, and discussion. Indeed, film criticism is a way to get beneath the surface of a movie and connect it to those deeper psychological, cultural, and mythic levels of perception that make movies—and all other art forms—meaningful.

Gathering Thoughts: Prereading Inquiries

1. What films have had the greatest impact on you as a viewer? Make a list of them and briefly describe how each film affected you.

2. What makes you want to see a movie? commercials? previews of coming attractions? word of mouth? newspaper reviews? big-name stars? What are you looking for in a movie? Explain the kind of experience you want.

3. How does owning a VCR or laser disc change the way you look at movies? Do you enjoy watching movies more at home than in the theater? Do you watch a greater variety of movies than, say, your grandparents because videotapes are cheap to rent? How often do you watch a movie over and over again?

4. Why do movie stars become cultural icons (significant figures)? Think of movie stars from the Hollywood studio era (Bette Davis, Spencer Tracy, Clark Gable, Humphrey Bogart) and stars of more recent years (Tom Hanks, Meryl Streep, John Travolta, Whoopi Goldberg, Brad Pitt, Harrison Ford). What do they tell us about American culture? How do they function as symbols?

5. What properties are unique to the film medium? How is a film different from a novel, a play, a song, or an opera? Make a list of film traits that distinguish it from other forms of artistic expression. What can a film do that other art forms cannot?

6. How is music used in film? Do you ever buy soundtrack recordings? How many different functions does music have in films?

7. The movie industry reaps huge profits each year from "block-busters." Movies like *Star Wars*, *Jurassic Park*, *Terminator*, *Men in Black*, *Independence Day*, *Twister*, and *Titanic* have changed the way movies are made nowadays. What have been the positive and negative effects of the "blockbuster" phenomenon? Are movies better than ever, or have commercial formulas drastically reduced the variety of films released each year?

8. What foreign films have you seen? Besides the language differences, how are movies made in other countries across the globe different from American movies? Do foreign films challenge our expectations about movie viewing? Explain.

9. Marketing surveys have shown that "R"-rated movies are likely to draw the largest audiences. Why is this? What does this say about the rating system on movie production? Do you think marketing pressures encourage filmmakers to insert more violence and sex in their films—just to ensure that the movies receive an "R" rating? If you were a marketing manager whose major concern was making money (not how you did so), what would you tell moviemakers and why?

10. Some films are about "serious" subjects like capital punishment *(Dead Man Walking)*, while others are strictly for entertainment *(Die Hard)*. Make a list of films you would put in each category. What "serious" subjects have been dealt with in films before?

Popcorn Psychology: Movie Posters Make Eye Contact, Sell Tickets

Andrew Day

ANDREW DAY is a staff writer for *Civilization* magazine. In the following essay which appeared in the April/May 1999 edition of *Civilization*, Day explains that what film posters project and what people notice amount to a lot more than coincidence. Every detail on movie posters is calculated, leaving nothing to chance.

ALLUSIONS

Rachel Leigh Cook: Actress who appeared in *The Naked Man*, *The Hi-Line*, and *Antitrust*.

Freddie Prinze, Jr.: Actor who appeared in *I Know What You Did Last Summer*, *Head Over Heels*, and *Summer Catch*.

1   How do movie studios come up with designs for the posters they use to lure us into theaters? Bonnie Seigler, co-organizer of a recent American Institute of Graphic Arts conference on design for film and television, laughs and says it's simple: "Film advertisers will tell you that every poster has got to have a gun or a naked woman on it—period."

2   It's not that simple, according to John Fahy, Miramax's creative director and vice president of advertising, who says that at least in the case of his studio, each poster is intended to tell you something substantive about the film it advertises. He notes that one of the more subtle, but effective, techniques poster designers use in trying to show what a film is about is to show its stars looking in a particular direction, or at something specific. Horror movie posters, for example, sometimes show actors looking off to the side, or over their shoulders, practically inviting you to help search for whatever's about to get them. Not surprisingly, a poster for a romantic film will often show its two leads looking into one another's eyes. Posters for films about lofty subjects commonly show characters looking up and off in the distance, to let you know they're thinking about something really important. Lately, though, you may have noticed that many posters at the multiplex show the stars looking somewhere else: right at you. You'll most often see this in posters for films put out by the major Hollywood studios, but their smaller competitors do it also—as in the poster for Miramax's romantic comedy *She's All That*, in which leading lady Rachel Leigh Cook stares straight ahead, rather than toward co-star Freddie Prinze, Jr. According to Mary Corliss, curator of the film poster collection at the Museum of Modern Art, this sort of thing was less common during Hollywood's so-called golden days of the 1930s and '40s. Back then, a poster was supposed to show characters interacting with one another, thereby conveying a sense of the film's premise. And although studios were just as interested as they are now in using stars to sell tickets, Corliss says poster designers were less likely to show stars looking at their fans because the actors were supposed to be larger than life—aloof and unattainable.

3   Now that we know everything about every star's personal affairs, those days are past, and this fact may be reflected in today's movie poster designs. Hollywood actors now are just like us, or at least a little like us; perhaps film advertisers are trying to lure us into the cinema by convincing us that we have a personal link to the people we pay to watch. In posters, stars still sell tickets, but differently than before: They tell you very little about the movies they promote. They simply show actors and actresses eyeing you so as to say, "Fork over for a ticket, and you get to spend two hours alone with me, in the dark."

AFTERWARDS

Vocabulary

substantive, subtle, lofty, curator, interacting, premise, aloof. Use a dictionary to look up synonyms for all these words.

Content

1. What kind of information in a movie poster could be considered "substantive"? What does a poster appeal to in its audience?

2. Find a site with movie posters on the Internet using tips included in the exercise following the writing assignments for "Popcorn Psychology." Then analyze a cross section of movie posters by looking at the facial expressions and the body language. What do they suggest about the relationship between the men and women depicted? What specific details are significant in making your assessment?

3. What premises are built into the posters you found? How does your selection of posters characterize a certain aspect of male/female relations? What kind of story does the design of the posters suggest?

Style and Structure

1. Describe the composition of some of the posters you located on the Internet. Look at how words and images are used and explain how the form is related to the content.

2. What difference does it make to you, as a potential moviegoer, whether the actors in the poster are looking at each other or looking outward toward the audience?

3. How do advertisements like movie posters suggest meanings rather than explicitly state them? What are they trying to reveal—without revealing too much?

Collaborative Explorations

Form a group and examine and discuss the movie ads in a newspaper. Think of various categories that the ads could be put in according to movie genre or method of composition. Write a description of the traits of each category. Try to draw some conclusions about the nature of movie advertising. Have things changed much since Bonnie Seigler said, "Film advertisers will tell you that every poster has got to have a gun or a naked woman on it—period."

Writing Assignments

1. Write an essay in which you consider various types of advertising and the promises that are made about the kind of experience the product or service will provide. Then draw some conclusions about the relationship between ads and audiences. How do we, as consumers, learn to read them? How do they deliver or fail to deliver on their promises?

2. Look at some movie poster or ads and at some CD covers and write a comparison/contrast essay in which you examine the advertising strategies uses to sell movies and music. How do they entice consumers to take an interest in their form of expression? How do movies and music overlap? You might want to consider looking at some sound-track CDs.

Thematic Cross-Links: Where and when do photographs of posters advertising movies come close to telling the "real story" they suggest? Contrast the way tabloids use photographs to attract attention and infer cause and effect relationships as discussed in Carol Squiers's essay, "Diana and the Paparazzi" from Chapter 5, Media: Controversies and Celebrities, to the way Day asserts the film industry employs psychology in designing movie posters for the same purpose.

Movie Cross-Links: See *Casablanca*, or *Annie Hall*, or *Buffalo 66*, or *Eyes Wide Shut* (following the apparatus for Day's essay), and see if the poster adequately represents the contents of the film.

Using the Internet

After reading "Popcorn Psychology," follow up by doing your own research project on movie posters and the changing patterns for communicating to audiences about the content of the films.

Use www.google.com or www.altavista.com as your search engine.

When you get to the portal site, click on "Images." Then type in the title of one of the films, and it will take you to various sites where usually more than one image of movie posters for that film are displayed. In some cases, posters made for international distribution are displayed as well.

For comparison we have chosen five successful films from each decade between 1930 and 2000 that display the kinds of male/female images that Day describes. Use these film titles to search online to find their posters.

Think about the impact these images are intended to have. What ideas or feelings are condensed into the advertisements? How has movie poster advertising changed over the decades? Think about how you would design a movie poster for a film you have seen. What factors would you take into consideration while planning your design?

1930s

City Lights (1931)
It Happened One Night (1934)
The Thin Man (1934)
Ninotchka (1939)
Gone with the Wind (1939)

1940s

Rebecca (1940)
Casablanca (1942)
Sullivan's Travels (1942)
Laura (1944)
Out of the Past (1947)

1950s

A Streetcar Named Desire (1951)
The African Queen (1951)
Singin' in the Rain (1952)
(1966)
From Here to Eternity (1953)
Roman Holiday (1953)

1960s

The Apartment (1960)
The Hustler (1961)
Who's Afraid of Virginia Woolf

The Graduate (1967)
Bonnie and Clyde (1967)

1970s

The Last Picture Show (1971)
Harold and Maude (1971)
Rocky (1976)
Annie Hall (1977)
Days of Heaven (1978)

1980s

Raging Bull (1980)
Blade Runner (1982)
The Terminator (1984)
Lost in America (1985)
Die Hard (1988)

1990s

Pulp Fiction (1994)
Braveheart (1995)
L.A. Confidential (1997)
Run Lola Run (1998)
Matrix (1999)

Modern Day Minstrel Shows
Stanley Crouch

STANLEY CROUCH *is an essayist, novelist, playwright, and jazz historian who has consistently displayed a strong adversarial voice when he focuses on conventional wisdom of any kind. Crouch writes with an informed but unpredictable point of view. He was featured in Ken Burns's video documentary* Jazz.

ALLUSIONS

Sidney Poitier: African American actor and director whose performances in *The Defiant Ones* (1958), *Lilies of the Field* (1963), *Guess Who's Coming To Dinner* (1967), and *To Sir, With Love* (1967) helped to break down racial barriers in American cinema.

Blaxploitation: A film genre that emerged in the 1970s which marketed films made by black artists for black audiences. These films included *Shaft* (1970), *Across 110th St.* (1972), *Superfly* (1972), and *Coffy* (1973) and featured soul music and jazz soundtracks by artists such as Quincy Jones, Isaac Hayes, Earth, Wind and Fire, Curtis Mayfield and J. J. Johnson.

Malcolm X: Born Malcolm Little, Malcolm X changed his surname when he joined the Black Muslims, where he emerged as an articulate advocate for civil rights and black empowerment. He later broke with the Black Muslims and was assassinated by a member of that group in 1965. *The Autobiography of Malcolm X* is a major work of African American literature.

Eldridge Cleaver: One of the founders of the Black Panther Party and the author of *Soul on Ice* (1968), which is the story of his political awakening. In his lifetime Cleaver served time in prison for rape, became a world-famous author, founded a political party, spent time in exile in Algeria, fought off a cocaine addiction, joined the Republican party and became a born-again Christian. He died in 1992.

Huey P. Newton: One of the founders of the Black Panther Party, Newton was convicted of manslaughter in the death of an Oakland police officer. He emerged as a charismatic symbol of Black Power while in prison as a result of the "Free Huey" movement. He was later indicted for murder, fled to Cuba, and then returned to Oakland to face trial. He was eventually acquitted.

1   There has been a long and far from glorious history of the Afro-American character in the mass entertainment of images on the wall that is the film industry. From one

end of the country to the other, early film audiences sat in darkened rooms and looked at what were almost always the butts of jokes, the buffoons preferred above all others. If a screenwriter or a director could think of nothing else and needed some immediate comic relief, the answer to the dilemma was often send in the Negro clown.

2   The appeal of the Negro clown, like that of the cowboy, was both familiar and exotic. The Negro clown's weird outfits, his talk, his walk, his singing and his dancing were as far out of the ordinary as the ten-gallon hats, six-gun belts, chaps and horses of the cowboy. With the comic arrival of the Negro, as with the cowboy, the audience was taken into another world, not one outside the United States and not one of which audiences were unfamiliar, but one that had the quality of a homemade fantasy. In all its variations, comic or dramatic, that fact of Afro-American appeal has remained a constant.

3   Most of the early depictions of black Americans on film stretched backwards into the conventions that arrived in the 1830s with the minstrel shows, when the national stage got its first serious injection of vitality, finding the music, the dance, and the comedy associated with the Negro irresistible. We still see variations on what became common when white men blacked up their faces and showed us the "authentic" darkie.

4   The minstrel figure was often a man who stretched himself outside of his natural position in society and became a fool as he attempted to give a speech on a sophisticated subject. The result was one mispronounced and misused word after another, the speaker sometimes becoming so flabbergasted that he nearly passed out and had to be dragged offstage.

5   Then there was the black-faced chump who was so gullible he could be bamboozled by just about anybody. There was also the razor-toting Negro known as Zip Coon, a caustic cartoon of a man who had blood in his eyes and was as irritable as a sore-headed bear.

6   Since then, we have seen many things pushed up on the screen that are supposed to represent "real" black Americans, most of them either variations on one kind of buffoon or another, one kind of Zip Coon or another. Some of the largest profits in film and television history have been made on stories that would have been impossible without black characters; for instance, *Birth of a Nation, Gone With The Wind,* and *Roots.*

7   But, even when things move forward, toward more three-dimensionally human characterizations, things will slide backwards. There will be high points in the work of a Sidney Poitier; in the range of characters that stretched from the mayor to lawyers to cops to criminals to citizens in long-running "Hill Street Blues" television series; the largely reasonable and decidedly funny work done on "The Cosby Show"; and the better work of the black actor or actress you might want to point out. Then we will suddenly find the Afro-American image face down in the buffoon barrel or the gutter.

8   The problem is neither black people in comedies nor black people depicted as criminals, since there are black people who are comical and there are black people who are criminals. It just seems that the old-time religion of simple-minded stereotypes periodically rises back up.

9   Then Hollywood gives us another variation on the minstrel update that took high profile in the 1970s with blaxploitation: street hustlers, thugs and sluts are posed as "real" black people, while those who have command of the English language and work with their brains instead of with their backs—or on their backs—are supposedly inauthentic.

10   We have most recently seen this over and over again in the street trash videos of the gangster rappers who (in concert with their record companies) are so ruthless in their pursuit of money, and who are at such a loss for any sense of civilization that they reiterate every stereotype that racists have promoted for years. They are the biggest Uncle Toms and coons in entertainment history.

11   Much of this, ironically, is the result of the "street brother" becoming the emblem of "black reality" after the Black Power deification of Malcolm X and the rise of activists Eldridge Cleaver and Huey Newton. All three of those men were social failures—criminal misfits and saber rattlers—who resented and were jealous of the accomplishments of the black middle class.

12   But the fact that the complexity of Afro-American life remains so far from the screen is a problem that goes beyond race. We so rarely see human complexity of any sort, regardless of skin tone. Bruce Willis, Arnold Schwarzenegger, Sylvester Stallone and Mel Gibson make their money in exactly the same way that Wesley Snipes has come to make his—in formulaic action films. Denzel Washington may well be the Sidney Poitier of the moment, but the extraordinarily rich possibilities some of his roles suggest and that some of the better films capture is not what Hollywood is about. Hollywood is about one thing and one thing only—that's profit.

13   The challenge remains the same as it always has—making solid films that do good enough business to justify quality writing and quality production. One thing we can count on is the fact that those who hold the purse strings in Hollywood have no commitment to anything other than success. They will just as quickly make good films with black characters as they will make superficial ones. Because they don't care, there is no opposition. All we need now is a string of high quality successes and the cinematic sea will surely change. Until another trend takes over.

AFTERWARDS

Vocabulary

buffoons, bamboozled, caustic, reiterate, saber rattlers. Look up the definitions for each of the vocabulary words and then determine an antonym (word conveying the opposite meaning) and synonym (word conveying the same meaning) for each.

Content

1. What factors does Crouch think keep the "complexity of Afro-American life" from being expressed in films? How is racial stereotyping connected with commercialism, according to Crouch?

2. Crouch suggests that certain filmmakers, political activists, and rappers have benefited from the "street brothers" as the most "authentic" image of the Afro-American. What other images would Crouch like to see? Why is he so incensed that some Afro-Americans would use images of "street hustlers, thugs and sluts" to market their films, books, and music?

3. What do you think Crouch means by "quality writing and quality production"? What are "three dimensionally human characterizations"? What examples can you think of from the films you have seen that would be described in these words? What is Crouch looking for in films but is not often finding?

Style and Structure

1. How does Crouch make use of historical examples to support his discussion points? Make a list of these examples and find more information about them.

2. Word choice (or diction) is very important in a discussion of racial identity. Crouch uses words with both positive and negative connotations. He uses "Afro-American," "Negro," and "black" more or less interchangeably and brings up racist words like "darkie" and "coon." He also uses "Uncle Tom" to refer to rappers. Look at each sentence in which the words appear and describe the impact they have on you. What emotions do they evoke?

3. Underline the most important points in this essay and explain how they are logically related to one another.

Collaborative Explorations

Form a group and have each member think of a film that contains racial stereotypes. Identify these stereotypes and discuss why they are used in these films. Do they make the films more commercial, as Crouch suggests? How do these images fit into the "formulaic" nature of entertainment? As a group, compose a statement about the use of racial stereotypes in entertainment.

Writing Assignments

1. Choose any film or television show in which members of various racial or ethnic groups are represented. Make a list of the characters and the traits revealed about them in the story. Write an essay in which you decide whether or not the film or show relies on stereotyping. Explain how you recognize it when you see it.

2. Write your critique of a stereotype that you think creates an unjustified negative impression. Explain where you think this stereotype originated and why it continues to be a part of film. Give examples from several films to illustrate your points.

Thematic Cross-Links: Contrast Crouch's exposition about African Americans in the film industry to Toni Morrison's essay, "On the Backs of Blacks," in Chapter 4, Stereotypes and Social Barriers, for a historical look at how media sources throughout history have shaped race talk and perpetuated symbols demonizing African Americans.

Movie Cross-Links: See *Bamboozled*, Spike Lee's film (listed at the end of Chapter 4, Stereotypes and Social Barriers) and compare how Lee also uses the minstrel show stereotypes to criticize race relations in the present.

See No Evil: Where Have All the Villains Gone?

Jessica Yellin

JESSICA YELLIN is a general assignment reporter for FOX13 News in Tampa Bay, Florida. Born and raised in Los Angeles, Yellin is a graduate of Harvard University. Beginning her career as a reporter, she wrote for *George*, *Details*, *Entertainment Weekly*, and the *Los Angeles Times*. She also worked as an editor at the *Los Angeles* magazine. In 1998, Yellin began a broadcast career as a general assignment reporter and morning anchor for Central Florida News 13 in Orlando, Florida. The following essay, written for the January 1998 edition of *George*, focuses on villains in America's motion picture industry.

ALLUSIONS

The Avengers: A British satiric spy series from the 1960s.

The Manchurian Candidate: A Cold War melodramatic film about an American soldier brainwashed to become an assassin.

Fail-Safe: A Cold War thriller about an accidental nuclear exchange of weapons between superpowers.

Dr. Strangelove: A satiric black comedy about absurd events and the motivation behind them that provokes a nuclear showdown.

1   W ith the demise of the Soviet Union, Hollywood found itself out in the cold with no one to hate. Now, all of a sudden, it's warmed up to a new crop of bad guys—ranging from giant bugs to supernovas.

2   No one ever said it was easy to save the world, but these days what's an action hero to do? Hunt down Dr. Evil and his nuclear missile? Not likely. In the new James Bond film, *Tomorrow Never Dies*, rather than confront the usual psychotic arms dealer, 007 takes on a media mogul who's stirring up World War III just to boost his television ratings. In Uma Thurman and Ralph Fiennes's film version of *The Avengers*, due out this summer, the superstars battle a man who's taken control of—no kidding—the weather. Granted, venal cable operators and British weathermeisters aren't the first things that come to mind when you think of bad guys—but then, not much does anymore.

3   Back in the halcyon days of the Cold War, studios had only to allude to some vague commie conspiracy and you'd have classic political thrillers like *The Manchurian Candidate*, *Fail-Safe*, and *Dr. Strangelove*. But when the Red Menace democratized, Hollywood was left hard up for convincing enemies. In the scramble for new evil forces, producers tried South Africans (*Lethal Weapon 2*), but then F. W. de Klerk and company abolished apartheid. Next came the Japanese (*Black Rain*, *Rising Sun*), until the yen stopped inspiring terror in Western hearts. Finally, Arab terrorists made a showing (painfully, in *True Lies*), until accusations of anti-Arabism put the brakes on that.

4   The villains du jour are wacko Russian splinter groups in possession of nuclear missiles (*The Peacemaker*, *Air Force One*) or the Chinese (*Red Corner*). But sadly, the Russkies just don't make for a decent villain anymore, and Hollywood's thirst for capturing China's lucrative movie market may dissuade it from vilifying the Chinese.

5   To dodge controversy, more producers are doing what Hollywood does so well: steering clear of real-world politics. Increasingly, moviemakers are focusing on the fantastic, crafting demons out of everything from the environment to gigantic ants. DreamWorks, Disney, and MGM all have nature-scare films in the works (comets, asteroids, and supernovas threaten Armageddon). This year, expect to see the return of monster movies (Loch Ness-like water creatures, *King Kong*, *Godzilla*, and such); insect flicks (killer ants); and, best of all, more of that ultimate, broad appeal antagonist: the Devil himself. In the cyberpunk apocalypse films *Gattaca* and *The Postman*, the villains are either inanimate objects (computers or scientific progress gone bad) or people who haven't been born yet. The return of future-shock films, as well as the creature double feature, could be seen as a nod to the effectiveness of '80s anti-defamation leagues. Bugs, comets, Satan, and the not-yet born all have limited constituencies and they're not likely to protest.

6   But movies don't have to be politics free. "You can use any type of villain as long as it's an individual," says *Jackal* producer Jim Jacks. "If it's about a whole group, that's when it becomes a problem." Given this logic, the most natural enemy to come along would be the contemporary American ideologue—the kind of demon-among-us who might, for example, blow up a federal building in Oklahoma. But don't count on it. Hollywood is loath to alienate any market—skinheads included.

AFTERWARDS

Vocabulary

mogul, venal, halcyon, allude, apartheid, lucrative. Look up the roots for the vocabulary words in Yellin's essay.

Content

1. Look up the origin of the word "villain" and note its various meanings. Write your own definition of a villain and explain its application by giving examples from films you have seen.

2. Consider the examples that Yellin provides and think of some examples of your own. Bearing both in mind, why do you think the images of villains have evolved over time? What are some images of villains from past decades? Think of how wars and other political conflicts influence who is identified as a villain. Who would you choose as a villain in a film you would make?

3. What is the difference between a villain that's "individual" and one that represents a "whole group"? Why does producer Jim Jacks think that villains need to be individuals? What is the danger of creating a villain—especially when considering how a film will be marketed?

Style and Structure

1. Explain the purpose of the historical perspective to make points about the nature of movie villains.

2. In what way does Yellin's concluding sentence answer the question posed by her title?

3. Examine the use of cause and effect in this essay. Does Yellin imply that movies create villains in the public consciousness, or do the villains emerge from actual events that are then exploited by filmmakers?

Collaborative Explorations

Brainstorm lists of villains, past and present, in collaborative groups. Then have each group compare the characteristics they find satisfying and essential for any antagonistic character. You might keep this list for a later writing assignment.

Writing Assignments

1. Write an essay agreeing or disagreeing with Yellin's statement, "Hollywood is loath to alienate any market." Support your argument by analyzing villains as they appear in recent films.

2. Describe the characteristics of an intriguing villain. Why must a villain be highly individualized to be interesting? Write a paper in which you explain why audiences love to hate villains. Give some examples of villains that have become popular and some villains who have fallen short of celebrity.

Thematic Cross-Links: See Ray Hanania's essay, "One of the Bad Guys," in Chapter 4, Stereotypes and Social Barriers, for a discussion on fair depictions of social enemies in film. Do you think political correctness in the depiction of villains in film will be redefined in the aftermath of the September 11, 2001, terrorist attacks on the Pentagon in Washington, D.C. and the World Trade Center in New York?

Movie Cross-Links: Consider how villains are represented in *Broken Arrow*, *Little Big Man*, and *Invasion of the Body Snatchers*, listed in the Film Links for this chapter.

A Box Filled with Magic

Martin Scorsese

MARTIN SCORSESE has directed *Who's That Knocking at My Door?* (1968), *Mean Streets* (1973), *Alice Doesn't Live Here Anymore* (1974), *Taxi Driver* (1976), *New York, New York* (1977), *The Last Waltz* (1978), *Raging Bull* (1980), *The King of Comedy* (1982), *After Hours* (1985), *The Color of Money* (1986), *The Last Temptation of Christ* (1988), *Goodfellas* (1990), *Cape Fear* (1991), *The Age of Innocence* (1993), *Casino* (1995), and *Kundun* (1997). He has also been an active spokesman for the cause of film preservation. He wrote "A Box Filled with Magic," an essay in which he explains his roots in the film industry—the Golden Age of Hollywood—as well as what films mean to him today for the *Newsweek* extra issue published in the summer of 1998.

ALLUSIONS

Robert Donat: British actor who appeared in *The 39 Steps* (1935).

Maria Schell: Austrian actress who appeared in *Voyage of the Damned* (1976).

Otto Preminger: American director of *Laura* (1944) and *Anatomy of a Murder* (1959).

Fred Zinnemann: American director of *High Noon* (1952) and *From Here to Eternity* (1953).

Billy Wilder: American director of *Double Indemnity* (1944), *Sunset Boulevard* (1950), and *Some Like It Hot* (1959).

Stanley Kramer: American director of *The Defiant Ones* (1959) and *Inherit the Wind* (1960).

Elia Kazan: American director of *A Streetcar Named Desire* (1951) and *On the Waterfront* (1954).

Roberto Rossellini: Italian director of *Open City* (1945) and *Paisan* (1946).

Vittorio De Sica: Italian director of *The Bicycle Thief* (1948) and *Two Women* (1961).

Ingmar Bergman: Swedish director of *Wild Strawberries* (1957) and *Persona* (1966).

Andzrej Wajda: Polish director of *Kanal* (1956) and *Danton* (1982).

Shirley Clarke: American director of *The Connection* (1961).

John Cassavetes: American director of *Shadows* (1960) and *Woman Under the Influence* (1974).

Orson Welles: American director of *Citizen Kane* (1940) and *Touch of Evil* (1958).

1   I've always linked my moviegoing experiences to my family. My parents weren't educated. There were no books in our house. I was constantly ill with asthma, and the only activity we could share was going to the movies. We lived in Little Italy in downtown Manhattan, and I remember the neighborhood movie theaters well, with their tantalizing posters promising dreams, and a rich array of second- and third-run movies. Admission was 18 cents for children. The first film I remember seeing by title was *Duel in the Sun.* I was 4 years old. My mother said she took me to see it because I liked Westerns, but actually it had been condemned by the church, and I suspect that's the real reason she took me. The movie was overpowering with its hallucinatory color imagery, violent music, hysterical melodrama and intense sexuality. I wasn't ever the same after that.

2   When I was a boy, there wasn't much direct communication between my father and me. But at the movie theater, the two of us shared the remarkable images and

strong emotions that emanated from the giant screen, emotions we couldn't otherwise articulate to each other. Together we saw such pictures as *The Red Shoes*, *I Shot Jesse James*, *Rear Window*, *The Thing*, *The Day the Earth Stood Still*, *The Bad and the Beautiful*, Jean Renoir's *The River*, *Sunset Boulevard*, *The Greatest Show on Earth*, a re-release of *The Public Enemy*, *War of the Worlds*, *The Heiress* and *Shane*. They left such an impression on me that today, much of the desire and need to express myself on film comes from that early loving experience with my father. Movies fulfilled a desire to communicate with those I loved.

3   The impulse to make movies began in 1951 when my father took me to see a British film, *The Magic Box*, directed by John Boulting. It starred the wonderful actor Robert Donat as William Friese-Greene, one of the unsung pioneers of the invention of cinema. A photographer at the turn of the century, Friese-Greene was obsessed with making pictures move. In a scene that was pivotal to my life, he demonstrates the concept of moving pictures to his girlfriend, played by Maria Schell. He picks up a book she's reading in the garden and flips through its pages. On each page is a drawing of stick figures he'd made in the margins. The images of a little girl and a dog were static when seen separately, but when he flipped the pages, they moved. This was miraculous to me as a child. Friese-Greene explained that this phenomenon was called "the persistence of vision." Through this principle an optical illusion is created that makes the pictures appear to move. I went home and tried it myself with telephone books. I was transfixed. I wanted to make movies.

4   I wanted to create images that reflected the life around me: what I saw in the streets, at home and, in particular, in my church. There I found the images very powerful, transcendent and, at times, lurid and erotic. The church in my neighborhood was a historic one: the first Catholic cathedral in New York, St. Patrick's Old Cathedral, built in 1809. Imposing and grand, it provided a refuge from the streets. And it was, in its own way, a very theatrical place. Light coming through the stained-glass windows created color and drenched the atmosphere. Gilded chalices and monstrances and incense added to the effect. I was fascinated by the plaster statues of Saint Teresa of Avila and Saint Rocco, and by the giant crucifix over the altar. Candles were lit in front of two large plaster tableaux. One of them depicted souls in purgatory, naked bodies caressed by bright orange and yellow flames, looking up to heaven where angels were dripping the most precious blood of the crucified Jesus from a golden chalice. The other tableau was a life-size figure of Jesus, his body wounded and broken, lying dead in his sepulcher.

5   There was also a statue of Saint Lucy, my father's favorite saint—he had eye ailments and she was the patron saint of eyes. My mother told the story of Saint Lucy this way: a young girl with beautiful eyes was pursued by a man who was obsessed with her to the point of violence. But her virtue was so great that she plucked out her eyes and defiled her beauty to put an end to his pursuit. God rewarded her by giving her back her eyes. The statue showed Lucy's beautiful face with her wonderful, innocent eyes gazing up to heaven. In her outstretched hand was a gilded plate, and on it were two human eyes. These images, as well as those from my home and my

neighborhood, all found their way into the drawings I had started to make, drawings that—only in my imagination—moved. Later they found their way into my movies.

6   After going to the movies, I'd listen to my family talk about what we had seen together. Often I'd hear them say, "It was good, but you know what would've really happened in that story . . ." And they'd discuss what they thought would have been a more interesting scenario, usually a much more realistic one. Then my father would add, resignedly, "But they can't do that in movies." I often thought, "What if they could?" And as I got older, I wondered, "What if I could?" That impulse was so strong that I secretly drew my own movies after school. They were series of frames—like comic strips or storyboards—with opening credits and stories that were inspired by different Hollywood genres, including epics.

7   Years later, when I started to make movies for real, I found I couldn't be a part of the cinema that created that strong emotional bond between my father and me—entertainment from the "golden age" of Hollywood. The studio system had started to fall apart in the 1950s and had completely disintegrated by the time I began making movies in the '70s. So even though I thought along the lines of the movies I'd loved as a child, the movies I made came from a different place. Entertainment became secondary. (Even when I tried to make a film like those of the great era—*New York, New York* in 1977—it turned out quite differently.) When I accepted the fact that I wouldn't make old-style movies, I reconciled the situation by having my father and mother become a part of my films. My mother cooked for the cast and crew, my father helped out in the costume department and often they both played small parts.

8   The 1950s, when the old system was changing, had a strong artistic impact on me. Something new was happening in the movies. Censorship broke down with the films of Otto Preminger, Fred Zinnemann, Billy Wilder, Stanley Kramer and others. They attacked the taboos. I think what struck me most in these movies was a new emotional power and honesty. And of foremost importance, the fourth wall between the audience and the camera was knocked down by the films of Elia Kazan. The acting of Marlon Brando, Montgomery Clift, James Dean was revelatory in its naturalness. I was mesmerized by *On the Waterfront*. For the first time I saw on the screen people I knew in real life, similar to those in my world of the Lower East Side. They reflected emotions and realities I knew intimately. At the end of the '50s, I thought if I were ever to make movies, I would want to create scenes as emotionally powerful and memorable as those in Kazan's films.

9   By 1960 my film viewing changed. I had seen foreign films on TV, particularly Italian films by Roberto Rossellini and Vittorio De Sica. A new cinema was being created abroad, by Ingmar Bergman and Andrzej Wajda and, of course, in the New Wave works coming from Italy, France and England. Add to that the "discovery" of Japanese cinema in the West, and the new American cinema shepherded by critic Jonas Mekas—experimental cinema and the new narrative films of Shirley Clarke and John Cassavetes. When I look back now, I realize that it was seeing Cassavetes's *Shadows* and a re-release of Orson Welles's *Citizen Kane* at the same time that were the defining moments for me. Over coffee afterward with fellow film students at New York University, I knew I really had to make movies. And today the impact both films

made on me is still powerful. In a way I think some of the approaches in my own films are attempts to reconcile the disparate styles of those two seminal filmmakers. At the same time, I found I had one foot in European cinema and still can't seem to retract it.

10   Up to now I have not lost the intense desire to say something in film or, at times, the sheer exhilaration of working in the medium; nor have I lost the sense of challenging myself against the work of the great masters. From working on the script and designing shots in preproduction to mixing the score in postproduction, each stage of moviemaking is a collaborative process. On the set itself, there's an excitement that comes from working with great collaborators. It ranges from raucous fun in scenes where actors perform freely, playing off each other like musicians in a band, to moments of almost religious serenity. In a sense, I've been able to re-create my early movie-viewing experience by making movies with a film family.

11   But the quiet concentration and sense of fulfillment I felt drawing my own movies as a child I can now find only in the editing room. It's where you deal with the very essence of film. When you take two pieces of film, one piece moves and the other piece moves, and when they are cut together, the cut itself creates another kind of movement—an emotional and psychological movement in the mind's eye that creates an emotional and psychological reaction, shared by the filmmaker and the audience. After 25 years, I think of each film as a new chance, an opportunity to explore new and different ways of expression. Still, I may never entirely get beyond the simple amazement of watching still pictures move and come to life.

AFTERWARDS

Vocabulary

tantalizing, array, imagery, melodrama, hysterical, phenomenon, persistence, transfixed, transcendent, lurid, gilded, chalices, monstrance, tableaux, purgatory, genres, reconciled, mesmerized, disparate, seminal, raucous. Many of these words have their roots in languages other than English. Look them up and check the meanings of the roots; then place them in your vocabulary log for future reference.

Content

1. Explain what Scorsese means when he says, "Movies fulfilled a desire to communicate with those I loved." How does watching a movie together create a form of communication?

2. How did religious imagery affect Martin Scorsese's imagination when he was young? Explain.

3. What connection does Scorsese make between viewing movies as a child and his desire to make them as an adult? What effects has movie viewing had on his life?

4. Look up Saint Teresa, Saint Rocco, and Saint Lucy in a dictionary of Roman Catholic saints in your library. What does each saint patronize? How were these saints significant to Scorsese as a child?

Style and Structure

1. Scorsese's essay recalls stages in his development as a filmmaker. How many stages are there, and how would you label them?

2. How does Scorsese take his discussion of family and religion to a conclusion in the second-to-last paragraph in the essay?

3. In which paragraphs does Scorsese make use of lists to show what he is talking about? How strategically effective are the lists?

Collaborative Explorations

Form a small group and have each member make a list of the first movies he or she remembers seeing. Compare lists. Try to remember who you saw the films with and what memories and emotions they bring to mind. Draw some conclusions from your discussion about how movies play a role in our development in early life.

Writing Assignments

1. Think about a long-held interest of your own that is similar to Scorsese's interest in movies. Are you a fan of anything? Do you have a hobby? Do you participate in music or sports? How have these interests shaped your life? How do they help you understand yourself and communicate with others? Write an autobiographical piece in which you discuss some of these early influences in your life.

2. Scorsese seems to remember parts of his life by recalling the films he was watching at any particular time. Think of periods in your own life and the songs you listened to, the TV programs you watched, the movies you saw. Write an essay about your own life and reflect on these influences. How and why are they meaningful to you?

Thematic Reading Cross-Links: See Chapter 3, The American Family, for other readings touching upon influential parent-child relationships.

Movie Cross-Links: See the films listed in Scorsese's biographical note. Also, see the films by directors listed in "Allusions."

The Visual Connection: Photograph Writing Activities

1. During the 1940s, neighborhood theaters like the one pictured below presented a bill of feature-length films, cartoons, and a newsreel. Weekly movie attendance averaged over 100 million per week. Moviegoing was a social event and a family activity. This was the kind of theater that Martin Scorsese recalls going to with his parents in "A Box Filled with Magic." Think about how the movie theater shown on the next page is different from the movie theaters today. How has moviegoing changed? Write your own description of what it's like to go to the movies today.

Capitol Theater, March 30, 1941

Film Links: Movies

1. Most of the films listed here are movies about movies. Select one or more and explain what is revealed to you about the filmmaking process and the nature of the film business. What are the components of the process? How does the collaborative nature of the filmmaking process make it complicated? What are some of the obstacles that must be overcome in order for a successful film to be produced? What makes a film a "success"? Explain in an essay.

2. Choose films with an asterisk from the following list and think about how movies about movies cause you to reflect on the nature of the medium in ways that, say, action films or horror films do not. Why do you think filmmakers are motivated to make films that reveal the behind-the-scenes world of producers, directors, and writers? How does knowing more about film production change the way you think about films in general? Write an argumentative essay in which you persuade a reader that knowledge of the filmmaking process enhances the film-viewing experience.

Casablanca (USA, Michael Curtiz, 1941). On the eve of World War II, an American who owns a nightclub in German-occupied Casablanca finds himself embroiled with the French Resistance and a former lover.

Annie Hall (USA, Woody Allen, 1975). A New York comedy writer falls in love with a would-be photographer from Wisconsin who shares his neurotic obsessions.

*Sunset Boulevard** (USA, Billy Wilder, 1950). A screenwriter is seduced by the gothic charms of a former silent movie star.

*The Day of the Locust** (USA, John Schlesinger, 1975). The 1930s present a backdrop for disenchanted Hollywood grotesques and people who feel cheated of the American Dream.

*The Stuntman** (USA, Richard Rush, 1980). How real is the reality created by movies? A director making a film explores this question.

*The Purple Rose of Cairo** (USA, Woody Allen, 1985). A character in a movie walks off the screen and runs away with a woman in the audience.

Blood Simple (USA, Joel Coen, 1985). A sleazy private detective is hired to commit murder.

*Barton Fink** (USA, Joel Coen, 1991). A New York playwright comes to Hollywood to write a script and finds himself in an hallucinatory world.

*Hearts of Darkness: A Filmmaker's Apocalypse** (USA, Max Bahr, 1991). Documentary shot during the making of *Apocalypse Now*.

The Player* (USA, Robert Altman, 1992). A slick Hollywood producer kills a screenwriter he believes is stalking him and then has second thoughts.

Ed Wood* (USA, Tim Burton, 1994). Biography of incompetent but persistent director whose films are so bad they're famous.

Living in Oblivion* (USA, Tom DiCillo, 1994). A director of a low-budget film struggles with cast and crew to get one scene shot in a day.

Get Shorty* (USA, Barry Sonnenfeld, 1995). Small-time Miami mobster goes to Hollywood to collect on a bad debt and decides to become a movie producer.

L.A. Confidential (USA, Curtis Hanson, 1998). A high-minded young detective unearths corruption within his own department.

Buffalo 66 (USA, Vincent Gallo, 1998). When Billy Brown is released from prison, he decides to go see his parents. On the way he kidnaps a woman and persuades her to pretend to be his wife.

Eyes Wide Shut (Britain, Stanley Kubrick, 1999). When a doctor's wife confesses that she has had sexual designs upon other men, the doctor goes on his own exploration of the darker side of sensuality.

Additional Writing Assignments

1. Make a list of four or five great "double-bill" pairs of films that would go together well for one reason or another. Then, write a comparison-and-contrast paper in which you analyze how the films relate to each other.

2. Choose a well-known director—Alfred Hitchcock, Stanley Kubrick, Susan Seidelman, Frances Ford Coppola, Spike Lee, George Lucas—and watch four or five of the director's films. Also, you might look for works on the director in the library. Read the director's biography and the circumstances that led to the production of the films you have seen. Finally, write an essay in which you show how certain thematic patterns can be found in a director's works.

3. Between 1940 and 1944, the following actresses won Oscars for Best Actress: Ginger Rogers, *Kitty Foyle*; Joan Fontaine, *Suspicion*; Greer Garson, *Mrs. Miniver*; Jennifer Jones, *The Song of Bernadette*; and Ingrid Bergman, *Gaslight*. Fifty years later, the following actresses won Oscars for Best Actress: Kathy Bates, *Misery*; Jody Foster, *The Silence of the Lambs*; Emma Thompson, *Howard's End*; Holly Hunter, *The Piano*; and Jessica Lange, *Blue Sky*. Choose one film from each list and

make some observations about the images of women in American films. What do the actresses of the 1990s have in common with the actresses of the 1940s? How are they significantly different?

4. Examine the role of Native Americans in any combination of the following films:

Broken Arrow (USA, Delmore Daves, 1950). A U.S. Army scout makes peace with Cochise and the Apaches.

Jim Thorpe—All American (USA, Michael Curtiz, 1951). Bio of Native American athlete who starred in Olympics and pro football.

Little Big Man (USA, Arthur Penn, 1970). Story of Jack Crabb, a white man raised by Indians. A revision of the story of Little Big Horn.

Windwalker (USA, Keith Merrill, 1980). An old chief recalls his long life. Native languages of Crow and Cheyenne used throughout.

Powwow Highway (USA, Joanelle Romero and Jonathan Wacks, 1989). Two Native Americans drive in an old Chevy to New Mexico and observe life on various reservations.

Dances with Wolves (USA, Kevin Costner, 1990). A lone soldier becomes a member of the Lakota Sioux tribe in 1870.

Black Robe (Canada, Bruce Beresford, 1991). A Jesuit travels north into Huron country in 1634.

The Last of His Tribe (USA, Henry Hook, 1992). The true story of Ishi, the last member of the Yahi tribe, discovered in 1911.

Thunderheart (USA, Michael Apted, 1992). An FBI agent who is part Sioux investigates a murder on the Oglala Sioux reservation and learns some things about reservation politics and native beliefs.

The Last of the Mohicans (USA, Michael Mann, 1992). The fifth remake of Cooper's novel.

Smoke Signals (USA, Chris Eyre, 1998). Two Native Americans journey to Phoenix seeking to retrieve the ashes of their deceased father, who had abandoned his family ten years earlier.

How accurate do you think any of these films are in their portrayal of Native American culture? What stereotypes does each film contain? How is the relationship to Euro-American culture characterized?

5. Some films have achieved success by becoming known as "cult films"; that is, they may have achieved mixed reviews and little commercial success when first released, but they were later rediscovered by particular segments of the film-viewing audience who found them fascinating and worthy of many reviewings. Examples of some cult films would be:

Invasion of the Body Snatchers (USA, Don Siegel, 1956). A doctor returns to a small town after a brief absence and finds everything is just the same—only different.

Dr. Strangelove, or How I Learned to Stop Worrying and Love the Bomb (USA, Stanley Kubrick, 1964). Black comedy about atom bombs, B-52s, and paranoia during the darkest days of the Cold War.

The King of Hearts (France, Philippe de Broca, 1966). The inmates of a mental asylum take over a town during World War I.

Bedazzled (Britain, Stanley Donen, 1967). A fry cook sells his soul to the devil in exchange for seven wishes.

Bonnie and Clyde (USA, Arthur Penn, 1967). Real-life bank robbers are turned into antiheroes in this influential retake on the gangster film.

Easy Rider (USA, Dennis Hopper, 1969). Two bikers hit the road in search of connection to the counterculture and find something else.

Performance (Britain, Nicolas Roeg, 1970). A criminal hides out in a house occupied by a decadent rock star.

A Clockwork Orange (Britain, Stanley Kubrick, 1971). Futuristic fable of Alex and his "droogs," street punks who hang out in milk bars.

Harold and Maude (USA, Hal Ashby, 1971). A suicidal youth forms an attachment to an eighty-year-old woman.

Blazing Saddles (USA, Mel Brooks, 1974). Black Bart, a convict, becomes a sheriff. Satire on Westerns.

The Man Who Fell to Earth (USA, Nicolas Roeg, 1976). An alien comes to earth seeking water but finds booze, business, and television instead.

Blade Runner (USA, Ridley Scott, 1982). A 21st-century cop searches for "replicants"—robots programmed to believe they are human.

Repo Man (USA, Alex Cox, 1983). Various alienated humans encounter aliens from outer space who may also be in the repo business.

Blue Velvet (USA, David Lynch, 1986). A college student finds a severed ear, and this leads to a bizarre world hidden beneath the surface of an ordinary lumber town.

Slacker (USA, Richard Linklater, 1991). Adventures of various people hanging around Austin, Texas, without much to do but talk.

View one or more of these films and draw some of your own conclusions about what it is that makes some films "offbeat" but interesting. How and why are these films different from "mainstream" movies?

The Body: Language, Ritual, and Wellness—A Casebook

Observations and Opinions

Now Suzanne takes your hand and she leads you to the river
She is wearing rags & feathers from Salvation Army counters
And the sun pours down like honey on Our Lady of the Harbour
And she shows you where to look among the garbage & the flowers
There are heroes in the seaweed, there are children in the morning
They are leaning out for love, & they will lean that way forever
While Suzanne holds the mirror
And you want to travel with her, and you want to travel blind
And you know that she will trust you,
For you've touched her perfect body with your mind

—LEONARD COHEN FROM "SUZANNE"

Eccentrics are people who take a boundless joy in life, immoderate
men and women who refuse to violate their ideals. Their minds are
always buzzing with ideas. They may fail in a particular endeavor,
but society wins by their example, and by what can be salvaged from
the exotic ideas and seemingly unanswerable questions that they
propagate with such enormous energy. At the root of eccentricity is
a healthy and determined irreverence. It is utterly harmless, and a
source of decency, tolerance, and respect for different views
and people.

—DAVID WEEKS AND JAMIE JAMES FROM *ECCENTRICS*

Every culture creates a concept of the "natural body," and each modifies it through piercing, painting, and hairstyles.

—PAULA PERLMUTTER FROM THE *JOURNAL OF SCHOOL HEALTH*

The cultural status of tattooing evolved steadily from an antisocial activity in the 1960s to a trendy fashion statement of the 1990s. As a well-established art form, tattooing has undergone dramatic changes the past three decades. In the 1970s, artists trained in traditional fine art disciplines began to embrace tattooing and brought them [tattoos] sophisticated imagery and techniques.

—KELLI MCCORMACK FROM "YOUTH AND TATTOOS"

Observations and Opinions: Reading/Writing Activities

1. Leonard Cohen touches upon all aspects of this chapter: the body proper, the body (spiritual rather than corporal), body language, ritual events, and wellness. Analyze parts of Cohen's excerpt from his poem, "Suzanne," noting the possible meaning conveyed by images.

2. Each generation could be considered a culture in itself. What would be your generation's concept of the "natural body"? What examples can you offer? Does your generation tend to modify its sense of the "natural body" through various forms of body art and/or enhancement?

3. Do you or any of your friends enjoy a certain cultural status as a result of a tattoo or the label of eccentric? Reread and explain Kelli McCormack's excerpt from "Youth and Tattoos" and David Weeks and Jamie James's statements from *Eccentrics*.

Introduction

Popular culture has an intangible dimension that extends to attitudes, behaviors, and lifestyles. Our preoccupation with the body, particularly its wellness and beauty, deserves special consideration. Americans seem drawn to anything that promises to give them an edge in self-expression, personal appearance, increased vitality, and physical strength.

The human body has been called a temple; it can function as a shrine, inviting homage through preening, physical exercise, mental calisthenics, body enhancement, clothing choice, and body adornment (tattoos, piercings). However we appear to others—serious, indifferent, somber, or lighthearted—this appearance is tied to certain assumptions about how we are supposed to look. Whatever we may feel inside, the perceptions of others are shaped by attitudes found in popular culture.

This chapter is a casebook study of the human body—particularly as it relates to language, rituals, and health. These essays shift the focus to topics and issues about the construction of the "self" and its relation to the physical body.

Popular culture provides us with various codes that allow us to attribute significance to what we do; therefore, clothing styles, body language, ritual preparation, and physical condition express who and what we are. The way people present themselves to others expresses their values. A shaved head, long hair, tattooed arms, pierced tongue, heavy make-up, and leather clothing make some kind of statement about a person. They express a personal style of living and view of the world. The social world is a sort of ritualized drama in which people express their role and their character through the behavior they exhibit and the costumes they choose. Just as actors grow beards, or lose weight, or dye their hair in order to better create a role, so all of us create social roles for ourselves through the way we shape and adorn our bodies.

Linda Hogan's essay, "All My Relations," describes the rituals involved in a sweat lodge ceremony that are "part of a healing and restoration." This body purification ritual reinvigorates her and others as she becomes one with "the nurturing silence that is relationship with ourselves."

Roohi Vora also describes a ritual ceremony with relation to body beauty and wellness in "The Magic of Mehendi: The Henna Painting Ceremony." She discusses the origins of mehendi/henna painting and its significance in Pakistani and Indian ceremonies like weddings, as well as henna's growing impact on American youth. Like Hogan, she describes a ceremony that has deeper cultural roots and significance than might appear on the surface. Vora explains that the traditional sacred practice of mehendi acts as an invitation to "grace, happiness, and good fortune in the marriage." While the implications of henna body painting—a sort of skin blessing—might be lost on America's youth, their appreciation and application of it as a form of body art, beauty, and personal expression find an eager audience.

"Foreign Bodies," an online article by Soppie Phipps from the *FleshZine Newsletter*, addresses several issues about body piercing. In addition to describing various types of piercings, she alludes to the "deep-seated root in tribal cultures." Body piercing is part of a recurring phenomenon in pop culture called neo-primitivism, a set of assumptions suggesting that individuals can express their detachment from mainstream culture by imitating the cultural practices of small-scale tribal societies that existed before the emergence of cities 3,000 years ago.

Student Nicole Overman examines the demeaning causes and dangerous effects of social pressures to look like a *Baywatch* Barbie. She begins by questioning "the drive behind the popular craze of breast implants." Just "what makes a normal woman with a perfectly healthy body cut herself up?" she asks prior to illustrating that "people kill themselves to accomplish the Pamela Anderson Barbie Doll look so they can be accepted as beautiful in today's society."

Joe Woodward concludes this chapter with "Pumped, Pierced, Painted and Pagan." Like Nicole Overman, he begins his essay by expressing concern about the increased desire among women for body enhancement. However, he expands his initial observation to include all forms of body art or enhancement—of which he does not approve. For instance, he states that all "kinds of cosmetic self-mutilation are unsurprising in our post-Christian culture. In fact, they are the ultimate in retro, a throwback to paganism." The rituals of one religious tradition do not necessarily overlap those of other traditions. Woodward expresses the skepticism and criticism that conservatives sometimes feel when pop culture easily embraces fashion trends that have symbolic and countercultural significance.

Gathering Thoughts: Prereading Inquiries

Consider the following questions and respond to them informally in your journal or writing log. You might return to these questions after reading this chapter and note what, if anything, you understand from a different point of view and how and why some responses were confirmed by the section authors, individual assignments, and collaborative activities.

1. What does it mean to be well in body and mind?

2. How does one's appearance serve as self-expression? When might it be the result of something beyond his/her control? Freewrite about each in your journal, noting how people's clothing can accentuate or subdue body language.

3. Brainstorm a list of physical as well as mental activities you ritually perform on a daily basis. What are the steps in each type of daily ritual? How many steps did you cite that have something to do with body wellness?

4. Is there any particular time of the day, week, month, or year where you feel like dressing special or using make-up (men as well as women)? When? Where? Why?

5. Reflecting on your personal experiences with and observations of others, how do people with a good attitude towards other people behave? How do they talk, walk, gesture, and stand?

6. Describe the mannerisms of a snob, an insecure person, a confident leader, and a show-off. How might a simple gesture say more than words?

7. Some people become obsessed with enhancing their bodies one way or another. Outside of weightlifters, who can you think of that would fit that description? Are these people ever really satisfied with their appearance?

8. What do you immediately conclude about a person with tattoos or body piercings? Do you view either or both as an expression of the self or merely the cool thing to do?

9. How are some people actually cruel to their bodies and why? What sort of things do they do in the name of beauty, competition, and physical and mental fitness?

10. Why might some people consider various forms of body language and body adornment (gestures, jewelry, tattoos, body piercings, scarring, body painting) a declaration of antisocial behavior?

All My Relations

Linda Hogan

A Guggenheim Award winner and major voice in Native American literature, **LINDA HOGAN** was born in Denver, Colorado, spent her youth in Oklahoma, and, in 1978, obtained an M.A. degree from the University of Colorado at Boulder. Since then, Hogan has played a prominent role in the development of contemporary Native American poetry, particularly in its relationship to environmental and antinuclear issues. As a poet, short story writer, novelist, playwright, and essayist, she continues to add to her considerable literary output. Hogan's fiction includes *Seeing Through the Sun* (1985), an American Book Award Winner; *Mean Spirit* (1990); *Red Clay*, a combined poetry/short story collection (1991); *Solar Storms* (1995); and *Power* (1998). Among her nonfictional works are *Eclipse* (1983), a poetry collection; *Dwellings: A*

Spiritual History of the Living World (1995), essays on the philosophy of nature and the environment; and *The Woman Who Watches over the World: A Native Memoir* (2001), an autobiography.

1   It is a sunny, clear day outside, almost hot, and a slight breeze comes through the room from the front door. We sit at the table and talk. As is usual in an Indian household, food preparation began as soon as we arrived and now there is the snap of potatoes frying in the black skillet, the sweet smell of white bread overwhelming even the grease, and the welcome black coffee. A ringer washer stands against the wall of the kitchen, and the counter space is taken up with dishes, pans, and boxes of food.

2   I am asked if I still read books and I admit that I do. Reading is not "traditional" and education has long been suspect in communities that were broken, in part, by that system, but we laugh at my confession because a television set plays in the next room.

3   In the living room there are two single beds. People from reservations, travelers needing help, are frequent guests here. The man who will put together the ceremony I have come to request sits on one, dozing. A girl takes him a plate of food. He eats. He is a man I have respected for many years, for his commitment to the people, for his intelligence, for his spiritual and political involvement in concerns vital to Indian people and nations. Next to him sits a girl eating potato chips, and from this room we hear the sounds of the freeway.

4   After eating and sitting, it is time for me to talk to him, to tell him why we have come here. I have brought him tobacco and he nods and listens as I tell him about the help we need.

5   I know this telling is the first part of the ceremony, my part in it. It is a story, really, that finds its way into language, and story is at the very crux of healing, at the heart of every ceremony and ritual in the older America.

6   The ceremony itself includes not just our own prayers and stories of what brought us to it, but includes the unspoken records of history, the mythic past, and all the other lives connected to ours, our family, nations, and all other creatures.

7   I am sent home to prepare. I tie fifty tobacco ties, green. This I do with Bull Durham tobacco, squares of cotton which are tied with twine and left strung together. These are called prayer ties. I spend the time preparing in silence and alone. Each tie has a prayer in it. I will also need wood for the fire, meat and bread for food.

8   On the day of the ceremony, we meet in the next town and leave my car in public parking. My daughters and I climb into the back seat. The man who will help us is drumming and singing in front of us. His wife drives and chats. He doesn't speak. He is moving between the worlds, beginning already to step over the boundaries of what we think, in daily and ordinary terms, is real and present. He is already feeling, hearing, knowing what else is there, that which is around us daily but too often unacknowledged, a larger life than our own small ones. We pass billboards and little towns and gas stations. An eagle flies overhead. It is "a good sign," we all agree. We stop to watch it.

9   We stop again, later, at a convenience store to fill the gas tank and to buy soda. The leader still drums and is silent. He is going into the drum, going into the center,

even here as we drive west on the highway, even with our conversations about other people, family.

10   It is a hot balmy day, and by the time we reach the site where the ceremony is to take place, we are slow and sleepy with the brightness and warmth of the sun. In some tribes, men and women participate in separate sweat lodge ceremonies, but here, men, women, and children all come together to sweat. The children are cooling off in the creek. A woman stirs the fire that lives inside a circle of black rocks, pots beside her, a jar of oil, a kettle, a can of coffee. The leaves of the trees are thick and green.

11   In the background, the sweat lodge structure stands. Birds are on it. It is still skeletal. A woman and man are beginning to place old rugs and blankets over the bent cottonwood frame. A great fire is already burning and the lava stones that will be the source of heat for the sweat, are being fired in it.

12   A few people sit outside on lawn chairs and cast-off couches that have the stuffing coming out. We sip coffee and talk about the food, about recent events. A man tells us that a friend gave him money for a new car. The creek sounds restful. Another man falls asleep. My young daughter splashes in the water. Heat waves rise up behind us from the fire that is preparing the stones. My tobacco ties are placed inside, on the framework of the lodge.

13   By late afternoon we are ready, one at a time, to enter the enclosure. The hot lava stones are placed inside. They remind us of earth's red and fiery core, and of the spark inside all life. After the flap, which serves as a door, is closed, water is poured over the stones and the hot steam rises around us. In a sweat lodge ceremony, the entire world is brought inside the enclosure. The soft odor of smoking cedar accompanies this arrival of everything. It is all called in. The animals come from the warm and sunny distances. Water from dark lakes is there. Wind. Young, lithe willow branches bent overhead remember their lives rooted in ground, the sun their leaves took in. They remember that minerals and water rose up their trunks, and birds nested in their leaves, and that planets turned above their brief, slender lives. The thunder clouds travel in from far regions of earth. Wind arrives from the four directions. It has moved through caves and breathed through our bodies. It is the same air elk have inhaled, air that passed through the lungs of a grizzly bear. The sky is there, with all the stars whose lights we see long after the stars themselves have gone back to nothing. It is a place grown intense and holy. It is a place of immense community and of humbled solitude; we sit together in our aloneness and speak, one at a time, our deepest language of need, hope, loss, and survival. We remember that all things are connected.

14   Remembering this is the purpose of the ceremony. It is part of a healing and restoration. It is the mending of a broken connection between us and the rest. The participants in a ceremony say the words, "All my relations," before and after we pray; those words create a relationship with other people, with animals, with the land. To have health it is necessary to keep all these relations in mind.

15   The intention of a ceremony is to put a person back together by restructuring the human mind. This reorganization is accomplished by a kind of inner map, a geography of the human spirit and the rest of the world. We make whole our broken

off pieces of self and world. Within ourselves, we bring together the fragments of our lives in a sacred act of renewal, and we reestablish our connections with others. The ceremony is a point of return. It takes us toward the place of balance, our place in the community of all things. It is an event that sets us back upright. But it is not a finished thing. The real ceremony begins where the formal one ends, when we take up a new way, our minds and hearts filled with the vision of earth that holds us within it, in compassionate relationship to and with our world.

16   We speak. We sing. We swallow water and breathe smoke. By the end of the ceremony, it is as if skin contains land and birds. The places within us have become filled. As inside the enclosure of the lodge, the animals and ancestors move into the human body, into skin and blood. The land merges with us. The stones come to dwell inside the person. Gold rolling hills take up residence, their tall grasses blowing. The red light of canyons is there. The black skies of night that wheel above our heads come to live inside the skull. We who easily grow apart from the world are returned to the great store of life all around us and there is the deepest sense of being at home here in this intimate kinship. There is no real aloneness. There is solitude and the nurturing silence that is relationship with ourselves, but even then we are part of something larger.

17   After a sweat lodge ceremony, the enclosure is abandoned. Quieter now, we prepare to drive home. We pack up the kettles, the coffee pot. The prayer ties are placed in nearby trees. Some of the other people prepare to go to work, go home, or cook a dinner. We drive home. Everything returns to ordinary use. A spider weaves a web from one of the cottonwood poles to another. Crows sit inside the framework. It's evening. The crickets are singing. All my relations.

AFTERWARDS

Vocabulary

Hogan uses simple vocabulary words to relate her experience at the cleansing ceremony. Paraphrase one of her paragraphs, replacing all monosyllabic with multisyllabic words. Why might simple vocabulary words, rather than elevated diction of your paraphrase, suit the purpose of Hogan's essay best?

Content

1. What visual images come to mind as you read Hogan's reflective essay?

2. What are the components of the cleansing ceremony? For instance, what is a prayer tie, and why is it significant?

3. Why do ceremony participants say "all my relations" before and after they pray? What do the words create, and why are they important to good health?

Style and Structure

1. How does Hogan's narrative style place her readers at the event, viewing what she observes, experiencing what she experiences?

2. How is the sweat lodge experience in Hogan's essay a "spiritual healing ceremony?

3. Hogan uses several short sentences in her essay (e.g., "We speak. We sing."). What mood do they establish, and how is it appropriate for a cleansing ceremony in a sweat lodge?

Collaborative Explorations

Though passive constructions are usually discouraged in formal writing, Hogan uses many of them in her essay. As a group, carefully consider Hogan's ultimate goal in her essay, and discuss why the passive voice, which shifts the focus from the actor to an action itself, might be more appropriate than the active voice, which stresses the person performing the action. Test your group's conclusions by doing a comparative study of one of the essay's paragraphs as written by Hogan and the same paragraph rewritten in the active voice by group members.

Writing Assignments

1. Brainstorm the word "wellness" or word group "good health." What do you associate with either? Why? Write an essay, presenting plenty of concrete examples, wherein you explain the process of achieving "wellness" or "good health" physically, spiritually, or psychologically.

2. Write an essay describing a particular ceremony. Make a specific point about the ceremony to provide a controlling idea or direction for your composition. Then develop your essay using plenty of concrete nouns and active verbs, enabling readers to visualize what you explain. You might also want to use words that appeal to the senses (sight, sound, taste, touch, smell).

Thematic Cross-Links: For an interesting contrast of behavior at a social celebration, see Barbara Ehrenreich's, "Where the Wild Things Are," in Chapter 8, Popular Culture. Also see "O Furo" from Chapter 6, Environments, which depicts another type of cleansing ceremony.

Movie Cross-Links: See *Windwalker* and *Smoke Signals*, both listed in the Film Links at the end of Chapter 11, Movies, for a glimpse into Native American culture in film.

The Magic of Mehendi:
The Henna Painting Ceremony

Roohi Vora

Currently completing a Master's in English at San Jose State University, ROOHI VORA holds a BSc. (Bachelor in Science) and an M.B.B.S (Bachelor in Medicine and Surgery) from Pakistan. She is working as a research assistant at San Jose State, as well as a professor's assistant at Evergreen Valley College in San Jose. Her poetry and short stories have appeared in *Leaf by Leaf*, a college literary magazine. In the following essay, Vora describes the magic of a henna painting ceremony and its association with tradition and culture in the East. The essay also reflects on the popularity of henna painting practices, in recent years, in the West.

1   It is an evening of festivity. To the uplifting beat of *dholki* (a drumlike instrument), a group of young Pakistani girls sing popular Urdu and Punjabi wedding songs, while others dance the *bhangra* (folk dance). The bridegroom's family arrives at the home of my friend Farah, the bride, to celebrate Mehendi *Rasam* (ceremony). As the evening progresses, mehendi is applied to her hands and feet. Dressed in yellow shalwar kameez with a dupatta (stole) covering her bent head, she is the model of a traditional bride in preparation for her new life. The yellow color implies simplicity before marriage, traditionally worn by all brides before adorning mehendi for the wedding day. Unadorned and pale, Farah sits on a little stool, her hands and feet spread out in front of her as delicate designs are traced on her palms and soles by the mehendi *walles* (ladies specializing in the task). The friends and family members also participate by adorning their hands with intricate patterns using only the best mehendi paste.

2   As the mehendi enriches the hands and feet of the bride and her friends with its vibrant red color, its rich fragrance—a heady combination of earth, clay, chalk, and damp green leaves—fills the air. The mood is set for a sacred practice intended not just to beautify the body, but to invite grace, happiness, and good fortune in the marriage, and the future home and family of the bride, my very dear friend. Mehendi is a kind of talisman, a true blessing upon the skin. Such is the significance of a traditional mehendi ceremony at a typical Pakistani wedding.

3   The art of mehendi or henna painting is an ancient custom. Having been practiced for many thousands of years in North Africa (Morocco, Egypt), SW Asia, India, and Pakistan; it has become popular in North America only in recent years. It was brought to India from Egypt around 712 A.D. as a gift from ancient Egyptians. Mehendi is the word used in the Hindi language to describe henna—the Persian name for a small flowering shrub with green leaves and a thorny bark. The small leaves of this plant are dried, crushed, and mixed with oils to make a paste. This paste yields a natural orange to reddish brown color, which is then used to create patterns, especially on the palm of the hand and sole of the foot—a ritual to celebrate the

wedding day of the bride. The more adventurous brides like to have the back of their hands and arms, and their feet up to their ankles painted as well. Mehendi and henna are often used interchangeably and mean the same thing.

4   Henna decorates a bride's hands and feet in order to beautify her, but most importantly, at a marriage ceremony, mehendi brings happiness to the bride and her future family. It is considered an *acha shagoon* (good omen) for a prosperous life—one of the many aspects of mehendi. Women use it as a cosmetic to paint their nails, and dye their hair a rich coppery red by leaving mehendi in their hair for hours at end to achieve the desired reddish brown color. My mother-in-law used it in place of nail polish to color her nails a shade of bright orange. Henna's cooling and conditioning properties make it a popular and favorite product amongst women during summer months. Mehendi revitalizes the hair and makes it shine, conditioning it at the same time. My great Grandma at the age of eighty, boasted of long, silky hair, attributing their glow to the frequent use of henna. Ever so often I would sit on a dari (carpet) with other cousins, in the dalan (courtyard) of her big house, watching her perform the ritual of spreading the henna paste with her fingers, forking her way evenly through her shiny long hair.

5   Although predominantly used by women, henna has carved itself a creative niche among men also. Many men dye their beards and moustaches red. This practice is especially common amongst *maulvis* (Moslem preachers), who follow the footsteps of Prophet Mohammed. In Saudi Arabia, Prophet Mohammed (May Peace Be Upon Him) dyed his hair with henna, a sanctioned practice that became popular among his followers in 632 BC.

6   Whether used for decorative or dyeing purposes, the application of henna requires much patience and practice. Different occasions like Eid, birthday parties, or social get-togethers, are an excuse for women and girls to get together and apply henna on their hands. On the night before Eid known as "Chand Raat" excitement abounds. Muslim women invite their friends to celebrate the sighting of the new moon at the end of Ramazan and start preparations for the Eid day. The celebration involves putting mehendi on each other's hands and cooking sweets and desserts. This practice has become popular among the Pakistani and Indian Muslim ladies in the San Francisco Bay area. Henna for these occasions can be obtained in powder as well as liquid form found enclosed in a plastic cone. The powdered henna extract is made into a paste by mixing with it with oils, whereas the plastic cone is thoroughly prepared, ready for use. One needs a small stick with a sharp tip for the paste. The tip is dipped in to the henna before it can be applied to the skin to trace a design. The end of the cone can be cut to a fine point and mehendi squeezed from it to form the desired pattern on the hand. Many pattern books are available, but the best way to enjoy putting on mehendi is to be creative and come up with one's own designs, for mehendi is a form of self-expression and communication.

7   The whole process of henna painting may take up to an hour, but to get a rich red color, one has to sit for hours after the application, and henna has to dry completely on hands and other body parts. It is best to keep hands and feet warm and moist for a darker color and longer lasting results. Some women dab lemon-sugar solutions on the skin to keep it moist, others drink hot tea to keep warm. I remember having used

a hair dryer to warm my hands after applying henna. The color of henna usually lasts one to three weeks. Washing with soap, or rubbing hands with chemicals helps the color to fade away more quickly.

8   Henna painting has become more popular among the young in the US ever since pop diva Madonna started to decorate her body with exotic henna patterns. This practice of application of an ancient art has taken the world by storm. The growing Indian and Pakistani community in the United States has also helped propagate this art. Henna has become a form of expression for youngsters, who are using it in many creative ways that were unknown in the East. It has become an alternate choice to the art of tattooing. Henna decorates the front and back of the neck area, as well as the forearm, and the belly button. I believe the art of henna painting has a healthy impact on the younger generation. It is creative, painless, temporary, and has a magical appeal. Women find it charming to look at, and its unique fragrance attracts attention everywhere. Henna painting introduces us to a flexible art. One can choose one's own designs and draw personal images to make a statement.

9   Henna has a magical quality that links it to the ancient world. When applied to the body it emits a radiant red color and bathes it in fragrance. A graceful art, henna-painting takes one back to the customs and traditions that have kept its secrets alive. When the hand is being painted one is transported to the enchanting world of henna where old customs and practices reign supreme. It emerges as a prayer—a form of good luck, ceremonial and sacred—making one aware of life's many fundamental mysteries.

AFTERWARDS

Vocabulary

In what way do all the vocabulary words in Vora's essay tend to relate to fashion or other aspects of popular culture? Once you have found definitions for words you either do not know or do not use, write an entire paragraph on the topic of fashion trends going into the 21st century; use a minimum of six vocabulary words from this essay in your paragraph.

Content

1. Relate the significance of mehendi—the henna painting ceremony—at weddings and other gatherings in Pakistani and Indian culture.

2. List some of the most common uses of henna mentioned by Vora. Do you know of others?

3. What stimulated the current fascination and interest in henna painting among American youths? Have you ever seen peers on campus with henna designs on their hands?

Style and Structure

1. Describe the overall tone of Vora's essay; is it somber, happy, instructive, humorous, or enthusiastic? How is her tone ideally suited to her essay?

2. In what way do the first two paragraphs in Vora's essay establish a visual, festive atmosphere for her discussion of henna painting? How do they prepare readers for the body of her essay wherein she explains henna paintings in more detail?

3. How, why, when, and where does Vora employ process analysis in her discussion of henna painting? What makes the strategy particularly well suited for developing material in context?

Collaborative Explorations

With three or four peers, brainstorm some sort of definition for the word "beauty." Bring your definition with you when you then go to your campus computer-assisted classroom. Next, look up both "mehendi" and "henna" painting online. Print out articles about them, as well as any photographs of henna designs/painting on human hands and feet. Finally, explain how and why mehendi does or does not fit your group's sense of beauty through body art.

Writing Assignments

1. Review Vora's essay and refresh your memory on the many ways henna enhances concepts of beauty and fashion during ceremonial situations and daily life. Next, brainstorm the pros and cons of getting a permanent tattoo. Which do you find more appealing, practical, or provocative—henna paintings or tattoos? What are the advantages and disadvantages of each? Ultimately, write an essay comparing and contrasting tattoos and henna painting, arguing for one or the other as the ultimate form of body art.

2. Write a process analysis essay explaining the best method for applying make-up, preparing for an interview, wrapping or polishing fingernails or toenails, washing the body, and so on. You might want to open your essay with comments about traditions related to your topic. Then, move from general material to a focused thesis statement that will serve as the controlling idea as you develop your paper. Also, use plenty of concrete nouns and active verbs to enable readers to visualize the process at hand.

Thematic Cross-Links: See "Extremely Cool" in Chapter 8, Popular Culture, for insight into the nature of popular culture and why the sacred ceremony of henna painting has become a fashionable form of body art among American youths.

Movie Cross-Links: For an example of what appears to be henna art in a popular movie, see the full body designs on the Princess at the beginning of *The Mummy* (1999).

Foreign Bodies

Soppie Phipps

A zine, an electronic or paper publication, can be about anything, and since it is an independent publication, there is neither censorship nor control over subject matter. In the following essay, originally from the online zine, *FleshZine*, SOPPIE PHIPPS examines the "lengths some people will go to with their body adornment." In so doing, Phipps blends process analysis (how something is or was done) with description and illustration. For further information about body adornment (tattoos, body piercings)—as well as an array of zines reflecting social and political attitudes and trends in popular culture—you may want to consult your college library or online publications. Some representative photographic examples of popular kinds of body piercing appear following this essay.

1   As a new and somewhat hesitant fan of body piercing, I have become increasingly intrigued at the lengths some people will go to with their body adornment—recently I have encountered people with more holes in their ears than I can count. But this is no longer unusual. These days, you are much more likely to encounter people with a large bone through the nose, in your local Tesco's; and "ear-plugs" seem to be increasingly popular. On frequent occasions I have been left with several questions in my mind. For instance, how does the body react to having foreign objects inserted into it? Recently I have read some conflicting views on body piercing, so needing to know more, I spoke to our resident experts on the subject; Phil Barry (chairman of the E.P.P.A.), and Pauline Clarke (producer of "Piercing World").

2   Firstly, it is generally recommended that you stick to using surgical stainless steel or high carat gold, as some people have a tendency to react to silver or other low-grade metals in unsatisfactory ways. This should be no problem as there is an increasingly large selection of suitable jewelry on the market. Many piercers tend to sell these items from their studios, and there are always stalls selling top quality

ornaments at the various conventions and expo's. Sometimes it is possible to have pieces specially made to order, ensuring maximum comfort and fit for the more sensitive areas of the body. It is recommended that you buy jewelry specially designed for body piercing, as this is the safest. The nasal and ear piercings tend to be a little less likely to react to "fashion" jewelry, and once the initial piercing has healed up completely (about 3–6 weeks), you can change the gold keepers to other earrings of your choice. However, it is worth bearing in mind that the sensitivity to low-grade metals is a purely individual matter—it will vary from person to person, so what one can tolerate may cause a reaction in someone else.

3   At the moment, body piercing appears to be getting more and more creative, despite having a deep-seated root in tribal cultures. Pauline told me that the tongue piercing is becoming increasingly popular among young people, whilst Phil reckons the eyebrow adornment is the thing of the moment: he's doing about one of these a day—grunge metal has a lot to answer for!! I must confess I am not heavily pierced. I'm told that there is nothing uncomfortable about wearing a metal ring or bar through the tongue although I guess it might get in the way whilst eating, so be prepared to modify your diet for a while! The membrane does swell initially, so care must be taken that the barbell fitted has some extra length either side to allow for this, as there will be problems with healing otherwise. Having said this, the mouth is remarkably quick healing, so this is a fairly straightforward operation. This means once the jewelry is removed, healing will begin immediately—if kept out for an hour or so, it will probably be quite difficult to replace.

4   Some of you may have spotted the recent article in "The Independent" about navel piercing. Whilst I applaud the paper for bringing an "underground" interest to the light of the general public, I was immediately dubious of their answers to some of the issues raised. One point stated was that a navel that sticks out cannot be pierced. This, according to our panel, is a matter of opinion. A belly button of this type can easily be done, but afterwards discomfort may be felt, purely because clothing etc. is more likely to irritate it. So don't let that put you off, just look after it! This having been said, the newspaper was probably voicing one individual's opinion, and that should be respected.

5   Another piercing that I've heard odd views about is the one located in the web between the thumb and forefinger. Various people I have come across, have said that this is the only piercing that will not "heal." Technically, there is no real reason for this, so long as it is carried out properly. Again, the area will swell, so it is important that the jewelry inserted allows for this and does not pinch, causing further aggravation. It is also important neither to go too deep (and clip the muscle) or too shallow (the jewelry may rip out); a professional will be able to gauge this accurately. You may experience initial discomfort, as constant action and exposure may cause slight irritation. Healing time is not long—between 3–6 weeks. Whilst some people have no trouble accepting this type of piercing, others will never be able to accept metal here—it's a purely personal thing.

6   Talking of healing, other piercings I'm told will never heal fully are the "Prince Albert" and the "ampalang." This is due to the fluids secreted in this area which keep

the piercing lubricated. The clitoral piercing is one that a piercer may refuse to do. If carried out incorrectly, the needle can sever the main nerve, and by doing so, can cause irreparable damage. Neither Phil nor Pauline have experience of any piercings being rejected by the body, although it is possible for piercings to "migrate." The piercing can either be pushed forward or grow backwards into the skin. In these cases it is probably best to remove the metal and start again. This happens sometimes when perhaps the needle has not been positioned correctly—causing the piercing to be either too deep or too shallow, or the wrong jewelry has been selected; although it can happen for no reason whatsoever—you can never be entirely sure. It is suggested that navels are pierced from top to bottom, whilst nipples are best from left to right. This is for aesthetic and practical purposes—they seem to heal up better this way. Most problems are created by people who don't really know what they are doing. Be especially wary of anyone who offers to use a piercing gun on places other than the ears and nose. The gun is designed for these purposes only. The gun's post is too short for any other use. If used incorrectly, the gun can cause swelling and discomfort where the butterfly (back fastener) pinches the skin. On a positive note, I have not heard of anyone dying from being pierced, but care should be taken to keep the piercing clean and germ-free, as failure to do so could lead to infection. As far as after-care is concerned, common sense would suggest keeping the area clean. This can be done using mild salt water or hydrogen peroxide (commonly available in [a pharmacy]) diluted 50%, though this should not be used on the genital areas, as they are more sensitive. Keep an eye on newly pierced areas to make sure healing is taking place and nothing is wrong.

7   NEVER attempt to carry out piercings yourself (unless you are prepared to suffer the consequences)—we at Flesh Canvas strongly recommend you seek the service and advice of a registered qualified professional. It would seem that as long as each operation is carried out under correct conditions, the world is your oyster— the only limit is your imagination!

AFTERWARDS

Vocabulary

expo's, membrane, whilst, dubious, aesthetic. In context, highlight Phipps's use of unfamiliar vocabulary in "Foreign Bodies." Then, use your thesaurus to locate synonyms (words having the same meaning) for each of them. Finally, brainstorm another list of descriptive words, which might be used when discussing body piercing and tattoos.

Content

1. What is your attitude toward body piercing and why? Who or what helped form your attitude toward body modification?

2. Does the article suggest why people would want to have their bodies pierced? What insights do you have on body piercing? Why have people you know elected to ornament their bodies?

3. Explain the potential health hazards or issues related to body piercing. Why doesn't Phipps seem to think that there are real health risks involved in body piercing?

Style and Structure

1. How does the author create an immediate link with her readers who may be interested in but not very knowledgeable about "body adornment"?

2. Tone is often an effective tool for any writer, for it reflects an author's attitude toward his/her subject. What is the tone of Phipps's essay? How does it appropriately communicate enthusiasm to a specific audience—body piercing fans who read her online article in *FleshZine?* Do you imagine the tone of her article would change if addressed to another audience? Explain.

3. The expository or explanatory nature of Phipps's essay both informs and explains details about body piecing to her readers. How does she move smoothly from one discussion point to another? What writing tools does she use?

Collaborative Explorations

To what extent have images been used to define youth movements or cultural attitudes? In small groups, brainstorm as many examples of countercultures as you can, and determine which countercultures owe their present public perception and individual acceptance to sensationalized forms of mass media. How might human emotions like fear, regret, and resentment distort the truth and cause people to jump to conclusions about countercultures? What advantage or disadvantage might there be in the media's representing people and events as they are rather than as they appear?

Writing Assignments

1. Interview persons who have had their body pierced and inquire about their motivation for getting their body pierced. Develop your essay by examining the benefits and disadvantages of body piercing.

2. How would you make a case for or against body piercing—or any other form of "body modification" (e.g., tattoos)? Think of the personal, social, and health arguments that would be most persuasive.

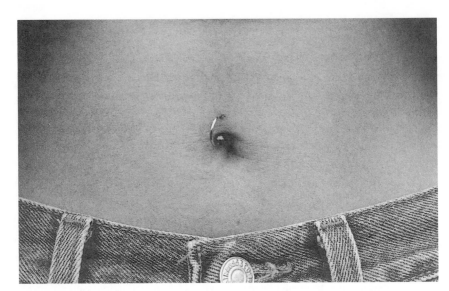

Belly Button Ring

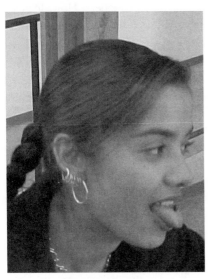

Multiple Earlobe Rings
and Tongue Spike/Stud

Lip Ring and Tongue Spike/Stud

> *Thematic Reading Cross-Links:*   See Joshua Quittner's, "Life and Death on the Web," in Chapter 7, Cyberspace and Technology, for another view on the persuasive power of fashion trends and cults.
>
> *Movie Cross-Links:*   For an example of a film about body adornment, see *The Illustrated Man* listed in the Film Links at the end of this chapter.

Striving to Be a Baywatch *Barbie*

Nicole Overman

In the following essay, student **NICOLE OVERMAN** considers the serious implications of breast implants. Part satire on how social attitudes lend themselves to marketing the perfect woman—Barbie—and the sort of beachwear worn by models on *Baywatch*, Overman's essay is also cautionary and exposes the potential dangers of plastic surgery.

ALLUSIONS

Baywatch: A popular television series in the 1990s featuring buxom, leggy Barbie doll-like models, small bathing suits, and beachfront melodramas.

Hooters: A restaurant chain known for its big-breasted waitresses.

1   What do Pamela Anderson Lee, all the big-busted beauties from *Baywatch*, Jenny McCarthy, and the waitresses at Hooters have in common? All these models are the ideals for women in today's society. These are the molds women set out to fit. Society has created its own image of beauty and everyone spends their own lives conforming to it. People kill themselves to accomplish the Pamela Anderson Barbie Doll look so they can be accepted as beautiful in today's society. Unfortunately, filling these D cups is easier said than done. According to Cynthia Kling's article in *Harpers Bazaar*, "Breast Obsessed," "Nine out of ten women can't achieve this perfect look naturally, but only through the plastic surgeon's artistry." What is the drive behind the popular craze of breast implants? What makes a normal woman with a perfectly healthy body cut herself up?

2   Silicone breast implants started as early as the mid 40's. According to the article "How Silicon Ended Up in Women's Breasts," published in *Ms.* magazine by John Byrne, the silicone implants were used to enlarge the breasts of Asian prostitutes so they would be more appealing to American men. Now, big breasts are no longer just a part of the prostitute or adult entertainment world, they are used to sell everything

from cars and gum to clothes and makeup. Alexandra Jacobs' article published in *Entertainment Weekly*, "Baring Her Pain," states over 150,000 women undergo breast augmentation every year.

3   The cosmetic surgery business has boomed since demand has increased so much. Society views women with perfect bodies as having big breasts. Some breast-obsessed men and their comments can be a reason some women want breast implants. Some women feel that they are inadequate, as if their body isn't good enough. In order to please their boyfriend, lover, or husband, some women go and get breast implants. Some women begin to feel that in order to be loved, they have to look like a supermodel off the cover of *Vogue*. They have good reason to. Everywhere they look, they see women with big chests—in ads, in the movies, and on television.

4   Everywhere you turn you see beautiful, skinny, well-developed women taunting other women to resemble how they look. They are everywhere; on all the magazines at the checkout counter, making women envious of what they don't have. They are in movies and on television shows; the guy always gets the beautiful, thin, big-busted woman. Isn't that why *Baywatch* is so popular? Almost the whole cast has huge breasts, some of them fake, but it's all the same on television.

5   The same kind of women are on all the advertisements. Advertisements selling everything in the world—cars, cigarettes, clothes, and makeup—use these models to sell their products. Advertisers know that most men love to look at beautiful women, so they use that to their advantage. Some commercials exploit women so they can sell their products. Most of the beer and cigarette commercials are the perfect examples. The men drinking or smoking are always with the beautiful women. The second they crack open that beer all the beautiful women appear. This is what advertisers use to lure consumers to buy their brand of beer. Some car advertisements do the same— exploit beautiful women so they can sell some cars. The odds are against women; everywhere they turn, they're faced with the image they are supposed to live up to.

6   As a result of society's views on when a woman is beautiful, women often have very low self-esteem. They think they aren't worth anything the way they are, so they have breast implants to be accepted. Many women are risking their health to conform to society's ideal of a beautiful woman. Some men's harmful comments don't help any; it just drives them faster to get breast implants. All they want to do is have their lovers be impressed with their bodies and enjoy looking at them like they do the models on television. Employment is another factor that drives women to enlarge their breasts. In some cases the more beautiful you are, the more likely you are to get the job. Big breasts are essential in some jobs including modeling, acting, cheerleading, and waitressing at Hooters, as well as some jobs in the business world. It is rare to see a small-chested woman waitressing at any restaurant, or starring on any television show. Many women have breast implants so they can get the part in a movie, make the cheerleading team, or climb that executive ladder.

7   There are generally two types of women who have breast implants: the 80% who do it for cosmetic reasons and the 20% who do it for reconstructive reasons, says the *Journal of the American Medical Association*. Women either do it for themselves, or do it for those around them. The women who do it to please themselves are the ones

who are generally happy after the surgery. Many cancer patients seek breast implants after having mastectomies. It makes them complete again and boosts their confidence. These are the women who are happy with their new breasts. Also, women who genuinely want breast implants for themselves, without being pressured by society, are the ones who love their new breasts.

8   The other side of the coin isn't as happy. The other 80% of the women do it because they have been subjected to society's influence. "Women feel that they should look like the women on the cover of *Cosmo*," says talk show host Jenny Jones, "but those are not realistic role models." The women going in for the operations don't want to see that. They think that after the operation their husbands will love them more, they'll get the part in the movie, they'll be on the front cover of *Cosmo*, or they'll get that job they've always wanted. For some those are the wrong reasons to get breast implants. They end up with lower self-esteem than before they changed their breast size.

9   The effects of breast implants can be terrifying. According to interviews in *Ms.* magazine with women who have undergone breast implant surgery, many women felt effects like crippling fatigue, joint pain, and irritable skin which leads to skin rashes. For some it was as serious as being infected with inflammatory rheumatoid arthritis, burning lungs, seizures, and axonal polyneuropathy, a condition that prevents brain signals from reaching the nerves. When breast implants used to be made with silicone, most of the breast implants went terribly wrong. The implants often broke or became rock hard. Some of them even started moving up towards the neck or armpit. There was nothing women could do but to remove them which cost more than inserting them and left them with less than when they started. According to Linda Marsa's article, "The Breast Implant Backlash," in *The Working Woman*, there have been over 440,000 lawsuits against the makers of these implants, and those are just the women who have come forward. There are still many more silent sufferers.

10   Besides the damaging effect on a women's health, there are psychological effects that go along with breast implants. Most women got the implants to become more attractive to men. After the surgery some of these women aren't very impressed. They get a lot more attention, but it often isn't the attention they are looking for. Some of the men who are giving the attention aren't interested in the body, mind and personality as a whole; they are just interested in the two fake sacs of silicone. This attention often causes their self-esteem to go down instead of up which was what the implants were originally intended to do. Often women seeking beauty in the eyes of society get breast implants, but still aren't happy in the end. This is because they still aren't perfect in their eyes; there is still more to fix. Until they have the perfect body, which is almost impossible to obtain, they will never be happy.

11   When you get right down to it, 36 D's are something men like to look at, but something they don't want to get intimate with. In *Men's Health*, out of 62 percent of men that have been intimate with a woman with breast implants, 50 percent said it was a total turn off. It was good to look at, but when it came to touching them, it was a different story. One man described it as "touching tennis balls." In *Men's Health*, 57 percent of men said that they would discourage their partner from having

implants. "Quality, not quantity rules," they say. This is what women need to hear; they need to hear that men love them for who they are.

12   Some women are speaking out and taking action to challenge society's views. Jenny Jones has founded the Image Foundation which helps women with implant problems. In the future Jones wants to provide books and videotapes to schools to teach girls and boys that they don't have to conform to someone else's idea of beauty. This is the attitude and action we need if we are to conquer this problem. This ideal of beauty being judged by breast size is something that needs to stop. It only damages women, their confidence, and their bodies. Our breast size isn't something we can control; we need to accept the ones we have. Women need to learn to be happy with what they have and not try to change what's natural. In a perfect society this would happen; women would value themselves for who they really are, not for how big their package is. To accomplish this, society needs to stop defining a woman by how big her breasts are.

AFTERWARDS

Vocabulary

Go through this essay and note how the author defines unknown vocabulary and other references in context.

Content

1. Explain how "Striving to Be a *Baywatch* Barbie," the title of Overman's essay, immediately focuses her readers on two influential, familiar symbols of popular culture. That is, why do you think Overman intentionally avoided mentioning the real topic of her essay, the causes for and effects of breast implants, in her title?

2. Where does the author seem to stand in relation to her topic? Does she seem to see herself as a victim of popular culture? Why or why not?

3. According to Overman, why might receiving breast implants become a terrifying experience? What health issues, physical and psychological, are at risk?

Style and Structure

1. How does Overman structure her essay? What does she discuss first? second? third?

2. Overman often refers to professional journals and popular magazines about silicone breast implants. How do these references, along with short quotations, strengthen her arguments regarding (1) the reasons women seek breast implants and (2) the dangers of breast implants?

3. In what way does her concluding paragraph place all of her discussion points into perspective with the controlling idea—the thesis—of her essay?

Collaborative Explorations

Break up into groups and devise ten interview questions about (1) plastic surgery and (2) breast implants. Begin by determining a definite purpose for your interviews. For instance, perhaps your group might want to establish some sort of profile of people who wanted or needed plastic surgery. Avoid making any assumptions or passing any judgments here. Next, with interview questions in hand, have each group member interview at least five people in the community in general and your college campus in particular. It might be a good idea "conditionally" to phrase your interview questions. (Under what circumstances would you consider plastic surgery? or if you could receive free plastic surgery, why or why wouldn't you accept the offer?) When your group gets together again, give each member a chance to present his or her interview results with others. Ultimately, assemble some sort of collaborative essay addressing the initial purpose for your interviewing people. (You may want to review interview techniques at the end of Chapter 3, The American Family.)

Writing Assignments

1. Write an essay explaining the difficulties you faced some time in your life when you attempted to live up to a particular standard of behavior, to keep up with the most recent trends in fashion, or to resemble popular film and music celebrities. Did your aspirations or role-playing also empower you? If so, how and why? Thoroughly develop your composition, blending illustrations and examples with cause and effect reasoning. Model your essay title after Nicole Overman's composition, "Striving to Be a Baywatch Barbie" ("Striving to Be a Power Ranger," "Striving to Be an ER Intern," "Striving to Be Like Oprah Winfrey," "Striving to Be a Superstar," and so on).

2. How does society in general and the media in particular appeal to different genders, different age groups, and different lifestyles? Generate some ideas on this issue by prewriting on: (1) genuine human needs, (2) understandable human desires, and (3) human needs and desires as created and marketed by the media. Using the first two prewritings to maintain a perspective on your topic, turn to your third prewriting, focus your dominant response to it in a thesis statement, and argue a thesis in a fully developed essay.

> *Thematic Reading Cross-Links:*   Refer back to "Foreign Bodies," earlier in this chapter, for a comparative look at body modification (piercing) and plastic surgery—especially breast implants. Popular culture encourages both, despite the dangers.
>
> *Movie Cross-Links:*   See the movie *Brazil*, a movie depicting a nightmare world dominated by bureaucracy and media, in the Film Links list in Chapter 5. The dark humor in the story line includes the obsession of several people with "beauty" and the painful lengths they will go to obtain it artificially.

Pumped, Pierced, Painted and Pagan

Joe Woodward

JOE WOODWARD'S article initially appeared in the August 17, 1998, edition of *The Report Newsmagazine*, a conservative Canadian publication that emphasizes family and faith.

ALLUSIONS

Tribalism: A way of life based on adherence to rituals and traditions of a small-scale society.

Paganism: A term that usually denotes non-Christian or pre-Christian religious beliefs or practices.

1   Plastic surgeon Benjamin Shore was a little flustered last year when a 30-something female patient returned to his office, requesting that her breast implants be redone. A year earlier, he had given her a large set of "double-D cup" saline implants, 500 cubic centimetres or half-a-litre in size. Now she was back, wanting 800 cc implants. "She wasn't an exotic dancer," says the Brampton, Ont., physician. "She was just a woman who wanted to feel good about herself, and she thought this would do it." But her case also proved to be the last time he co-operated in such an extravagance. "Six months later, she was back, wanting the smaller implants," he recounts. "With all that weight on her chest, whenever she lay on her back, she couldn't breathe."

2   Though plastic surgeons are voicing some discomfort with the trend, unnaturally large and clearly artificial breasts represent the cutting edge of feminine fashion. The August edition of the fashion magazine *Allure* surveyed American plastic surgeons,

asking the age-old question, "what do women want?" And according to the doctors, "women today don't want to look natural but supernatural." The size of the average implant has grown three to four times, and more telling yet, women are voicing a preference for high, round implants, over more anatomically-correct teardrop-shapes. The new ideal has become the gravity-defying "half grapefruit" breast, popularized by the chiseled and sculpted former star of *Baywatch*, Pamela Anderson: absurdly large, firm as a football, and plainly artificial.

3   The growth of the breast augmentation industry has clearly outstripped the needs of mastectomy patients and women genuinely short-changed by nature. During the Dow-Corning implant fiasco, culminating in the 1992 ban against silicon implants, the market briefly sagged. But the consumer horror stories about scarring and supposed links to diseases like fibromyalgia had less effect than might have been expected. Consumer confidence was restored by the introduction of alternative saline implants, and the procedure's popularity again began to soar. In the past six years, the annual number of breast augmentations has climbed 400%, to over 120,000 in the United States and 10,000 in Canada.

4   But the desire for unnatural aesthetics is not limited to mammoth mammaries; tattooing, body-piercing and scarification are equally hot trends in body fashion. Experts say all these kinds of cosmetic self-mutilation are unsurprising in our post-Christian culture. In fact, they are the ultimate in retro, a throwback to paganism. Edmontonian Sarai Jorgenson, 23, has accumulated seven tattoos on her breasts, neck, shoulders, back and stomach; and at the moment she has 19 piercings, mostly (though not exclusively) on her face. She wears her naturally blonde hair in green, purple or blue, with black dreadlocks, and people she went to high school with no longer recognize her on the street. She got her first tattoo at 15—a panther she later covered with a butterfly—and her first piercings at 18. "I was a shy person; I had low self-esteem," Ms. Jorgenson recounts. "But I love my body now; I think it's beautiful."

5   Ms. Jorgenson's first youthful forays into body art may have been hesitant; but her intentions now are fully and confidently thought out. "It's like Rufus Camphausen writes in his book, *The Return of the Tribal*, body art is the recovery of a practice 30,000 years old," she says. "We're simply developing modern medical ways of performing a natural human function." She laughs at the suggestion that her purpose is simply attention-seeking. "Like, I do this so people will insult me on the street?" she guffaws, shaking her array of silver rings. "Like, I want to make it really hard to find a job? No. I do this because I think it's beautiful. I look at the women in *Cosmopolitan*, and they look ridiculous. I look at the women in *Savage* magazine, women who look like me, and I think they're beautiful."

6   The Edmonton waitress just recently began her next body project, stretching her earlobes and nasal septum, and she has already lengthened her lobes three-quarters of an inch. She has no plans to pump up her breasts, both of which she says are adorned with nipple rings. Some time ago, she tried a little scarification, but like most white people, she cannot form the kinds of "keloid scars" that give scarified black people their "gorgeous" lumpy skin patterns. If scars are out for her, she might eventually try the Hindu practice of tongue-splitting, something just now catching on

in Los Angeles. "What I'm doing is, I'm taking what I was born with and making it into what I want it to be," she explains patiently. "These are all just different forms of modifying my body. They're no stranger than steroid muscles or silicon breasts."

7   "The vast majority of women still want breasts that look natural," Dr. Shore reports. "But in the 1970s, that would have meant 100 cc to 120 cc implants. Today, what's considered natural are 375 cc to 450 cc implants. And I'd say about 10% of [Ontario] women now want them so much bigger than that, and so much higher, they're plainly artificial." Despite feminist claims about male oppression, however, he reports that "less than 1%" of women take such leaps into the unnatural from the prompting of husbands or boyfriends. "In almost every case, this is something the woman herself wants to do for herself," he muses. "I'm amazed whenever I have to say to a woman, that would look unnatural, or that would look artificial, and she still says, 'that's okay, that's what I want.' So I just won't take on those patients anymore."

8   Calgary plastic surgeon Gregory Waslen thinks that demand for "monster breasts" is largely a geographical phenomenon, oddly prevalent in grapefruit-growing states. "We're not California or Florida, here," he argues. "There's always a part of the market that wants something beyond the normal, but I'd guess that's no more than 2% of Alberta patients." In the normal 250 cc to 400 cc (C to D cup) range, breast augmentation now garners a 92% satisfaction rate from its patients, he says. Admittedly, up to 10% of Alberta patients and 50% of American patients subsequently return to their doctors for yet bigger breasts. The trend toward the gargantuan is simply a fad driven by shows like *Baywatch*, in Dr. Waslen's opinion, and it will soon run into its natural upper limit, a limit set by the frequency of "full-figure" backache.

9   According to the *Allure* survey, however, California's plastic surgeons have some doubts they will be able to hold the line at 1,000 cc implants, or full litre breasts. And magnifying the trend toward the unnatural, a small but growing proportion of women are asking for simultaneous breast implants and the liposuction of their hips, in the attempt to manufacture a body boyishly lean below the ribcage and bovine-bosomy above. They are apparently undeterred by a 3% to 5% complication rate (from internal scarring) for the breast augmentation alone.

10   New York University psychology professor Paul Vitz, author of *Psychology as Religion*, suspects that monstrous breast augmentation is a fad. However, that sort of fad—cosmetic mutilation—has now been able to enter into the mainstream culture only because of the revival of paganism and the eclipse of the once-dominant Judeo-Christian ethic. "With the exception of [male] circumcision, Orthodox Judaism forbids any alteration of the body, even embalming," he says. "And the Christian tradition has been almost as strict." As the apostle Paul warns in 1 Corinthians 3, "Know you not that you are temples of God . . . and if any man defiles the temple of God, him shall God destroy." While modest pierced ear studs were traditionally thought permissible, the injunction against "defiling the temple" was understood to forbid everything from tattoos to sexual sterilization.

11   "There's a different understanding of the body in pagan or animistic cultures," says psychologist Vitz. In Christian cultures, he explains, the physical appetites must be disciplined, but the body is an essential part of human godliness. In pagan

cultures, the body is something separate, alien to each person's "inner divinity," yet it belongs entirely to the person or tribe, to do with as they see fit. "As a result, the pagans take a far more extreme and violent attitude toward the domination of the body, as something needing artistic modification or transformation." This "customizing" of the body is not a private activity, however. The tribal group almost always dictates the form of such bodily modifications for anyone who belongs. So the customized bodies are not only painful, but usually highly visible.

12   "Clearly, all the unnatural breast enhancement today is seeking an effect that is entirely visible," says Dr. Vitz. "Breasts cease to be maternal objects. They even become less and less objects of sexual touch. They've become the 'high kitsch' of an image culture," and primarily signs of status, like the silver rings around an African woman's neck. A century ago, energetic western women might become obsessed with inner moral perfection and fall victim to moral scrupulosity, he continues. Today, however, they seek some vague aesthetic perfection and end up collecting more and more visible abnormalities, like collagen-enhanced lips. "Unnatural breasts aren't the only new cosmetic mutilations," he adds. The new paganism encourages everything from liposuction to body-piercing and scarification.

13   Tattooing today is almost as common as ear-piercing, says Roman Corkery, an artist with Calgary's "Symbols of Strength" tattoo and body-piercing studio. And as popular as tattooing is, the demand for body piercing has begun to surpass it. "Moms come in with their little 15-year-old daughters, getting little navel rings, then four of their friends come in, then eight more," he marvels. Daily, Mr. Corkery's mid-sized studio averages eight tattoos and a dozen piercings. Body piercing has given tattoos a real race into the mainstream, because its results are less permanent and cheaper. The holes themselves eventually vanish once the jewellery is removed; and piercing runs $20 to $50, while tattoos cost $100 to $500. Scarification and branding, still in the experimental stage in the U.S., have not yet arrived in Alberta.

14   Good statistics on the growth of these "body arts" are impossible to find, says Caroline Jeffries, owner of the To the Point piercing and Smiling Buddha tattoo studios. But until 15 years ago, Calgary supported only one full-time tattoo parlour; today it boasts a dozen. The first body piercing shop opened in 1991; now there are six. Not accounting for repeat customers, Calgary's 800,000 population may generate as many as 40,000 visits yearly to either sort of establishment.

15   As tattooing has entered the mainstream, the images of demons, knives and nudes have given way to pictures of dolphins, flowers and Canadian flags, says body artist Corkery. And a high proportion of the women opt for a simple "ankle chain" or "woven armband" pattern. Likewise the majority of piercing enthusiasts opt for multi-earrings or a discreet nose stud. A more adventurous (or randy) minority— roughly 20% of the piercings at "Symbols of Strength"—are on the tongue and 5% to 10% are on the nipples or genitalia. Now available in both Britain and the U.S., but still a fringe interest even there, are the new Teflon and coral "inserts," used primarily to provide "devil's horns" that bond directly onto the customer's skull under the skin.

16   Anthropologist Claudia Launhardt, who teaches at Trinity Western University in Langley, B.C., agrees that the trend toward cosmetic self-mutilation reflects society's

turn toward paganism. The forms of mutilation are consistent with traditional tribal practices the world over. Mutilations can indicate group membership and allegiance, like the tattoos of the Japanese yakuza criminal underworld. It can also assert a measure of social dependence. For example, the Manchu Chinese elites of the 19th century bound the feet of female infants almost from birth, partly because small feet were held to be marks of great beauty, but also because it rendered upper-class women almost incapable of walking.

17   However, there is one crucial difference between traditional tribal mutilations and (at least so far) the modern western equivalents, Prof. Launhardt insists. In tribal societies, the tribe, not the individual, confers the membership, dependence or the status of a particular mutilation.

18   "Here, so far, what we have is merely fashion or fad, because the individuals decide how they would like to change their bodies," Prof. Launhardt explains. "In a tribal society, the elders or the laws must say whether a warrior, having killed a lion, can now have a particular tattoo, or whether a woman, possessing so many cattle, can wear a certain kind of lip disk. These things are very real and binding marks of a person's status for life." In that sense, breast enhancement is much more tribal than modern body piercing, she argues, because bulbous breasts are an attempt to ape the rich and the famous of Hollywood. In Canada, although medically indicated reconstructive breast surgery is ordinarily covered by medicare, the usual fee for cosmetic work ranges from $4,000 to $4,500.

19   Cosmetic mutilation has certain repetitive features worldwide that may soon be reproduced in North America. For example, the Haida of the Pacific Northwest, the Kayapo of the Amazon and the Mursi of southern Ethiopia all wore "lip plates," stretching the lower lip either with or without puncturing it. "But the wealth of the material [used in lip plates] was important to the status conveyed, whether it be gold in the Amazon or ivory in Africa." Likewise, from childhood, both the Kikiyu of Africa and the Lao of northern Thailand stretched the necks of their high-born females with silver rings; their necks became so long, they needed the rings to support their heads.

20   Anthropologist Launhardt adds that in primitive cultures, cosmetic mutilation is often a badge of courage and ability to withstand pain. "Having killed a lion, a Dinka tribesman may be allowed a particular, very painful kind of tattoo," she explains. "Having proven his courage, the tattoo becomes the testimony to the pain he can bear." In North America, however, pain is generally something to be avoided at all costs, so mutilation did not become mainstream until modern anaesthesia made it relatively painless. "As our modern mutilations are made less painful," she predicts, "some people will be driven to find ever more extreme forms of mutilation."

21   And so they are: body artists in Los Angeles and New York are now experimenting with "skin braiding." Three long strips are cut from the flesh and left attached to the body only at the top. The strips are then braided and reattached at the bottom. The result is supposed to heal as a permanent skin braid.

22   Medical missionary John Patrick of Ottawa, a fellow of the Centre for Renewal in Public Policy, says that he has seen very little cosmetic mutilation during his many

recent trips to central Africa. "Most of that has vanished," he reports. "They're new Christians leaving a pagan tradition, just as we're new pagans, leaving a Christian tradition." Yet he marvels at the rapid resurgence of self-mutilation in the West. "It seems to prove that, even when shorn of all hope, human beings still have a natural sense of the necessity of atonement."

23   For his part, Calgary plastic surgeon Peter Whidden sees little hope of resisting the invasion of the monster breasts. "I'd agree that, so far, maybe only 2% of the women here want huge, unnatural breasts," he says. "But these fads move north a lot faster than we like to think. There's a burlesque subculture developing, and I don't think we can stop it. Still, after 30 years of practice, I'm not going to start deforming little girls, even if they want me to."

AFTERWARDS

Vocabulary

Flustered, extravagance, augmentation, mastectomy, fiasco, fibromyalgia, aesthetics, mammaries, accumulated, forays, guffaws, septum, gargantuan, liposuction, animistic, defiling, scrupulosity, discreet, allegiance, bulbous, mutilation, anesthesia, burlesque. After looking up the vocabulary words, go back through Woodward's article and note how they were used in context. Next, take a piece of paper, and divide it into two columns; label column one "Words with Positive Connotations," and label column two, "Words with Negative Connotations." Finally, place each vocabulary word under one column or another, parenthetically noting positive or negative connotations for each. What might Woodward's word choice suggest about his attitude toward body art or modification?

Content

1. Why does Woodward claim that enhancing one's body—tattooing, scarring, and body piercing—are throwbacks to pagan society? Doesn't he make some assumptions about the diverse cultural values of people in North America—if not the world?

2. What marks the major difference between what Woodward refers to as "traditional tribal mutilations and (at least so far) the modern western equivalents"?

3. Traditionally, with whom do you associate tattoos or piercings? According to Woodward, how do popular tattoos today contrast with those of yesteryear? To what extent would you attribute changes to popular culture or the fact that tattooing has "entered the mainstream"?

Style and Structure

1. How does the alliteration in Woodward's title capture your interest and clearly establish a sense of what may follow in his essay?

2. Woodward tries to maintain a certain level of objectivity in his essay; he never comes right out and says body piercing is bad or breast enhancement is ugly. Instead, he keeps referring to all forms of body modification as primitive or pagan. How does this affect his presentation of material? Does he strike you as impartial? Why or why not?

3. What seems to be Woodward's strategic purpose for devoting the first three paragraphs to modern breast enhancement operations prior to a discussion of what he refers to as the "desire for unnatural aesthetics" such as tattooing, body piercing, and scarification? When and where does his discussion of breast augmentation operations reappear? How does he tie all parts of the essay together?

Collaborative Explorations

Woodward himself noted that some of the women he interviewed stated they had low self-esteem before body modification. In fact, after piercings and tattoos, one woman said "I love my body now; I think it's beautiful." As a group activity, expand upon his observations and others' testimonies regarding the relationship between positive self-esteem and body modification. Your collaborative study should include research on men as well as women. Based on your findings, prepare a short presentation for the rest of the class to share your insights. To take this a step further, encourage peers to use some of your written-up interviews as resource materials for their own compositions.

Writing Assignments

1. If body art, especially tattooing, is nothing more than reverting to paganism, why do so many individuals opt to get tattoos of Christian icons such as the Virgin Mary, Jesus Christ, a cross, or a Christian saint? Write an argumentative essay refuting Woodword's claim that body art and modification—which he refers to as mutilation—amounts to little more than paganism gone wild. In preparation for this assignment, you might want to interview a wide range of people who chose to adorn themselves with tattoos—as well as owners and artists at tattoo parlors themselves.

2. In your opinion, how and why does body piercing—including tongue spikes—alter one's physical appearance for better or worse? To generate

some ideas on this issue, take a look at the following photos featuring different kinds of body modification.

Thematic Cross-Links: Refer back to "Striving to Be a *Baywatch* Barbie," earlier in this chapter, for another essay on body modification, its dangers, and its practitioners.

Movie Cross-Links: See Ray Bradbury's *The Illustrated Man* listed in Film Links for this chapter.

The Visual Connection: Photograph Writing Activities

1. The following photo portrays a tattoo artist engaged in his craft. Carefully study the photograph, noting his physical attributes, dress, body language, and concentration as he creates a design on his human canvas. Does he fit your notion of a typical tattooer, or do the photographic details move beyond a stereotype and suggest more?

Tattoo Artist

2. Look at the following patterns of henna painting closely. If you were given a choice to make up your own henna pattern, what would you choose? Write an essay expressing why you chose your particular pattern, where you would apply it, and what meaning it would have for you—keeping in mind henna's spiritual significance and/or place in popular culture.

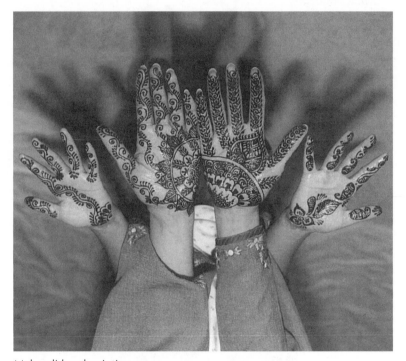

Mehendi hand painting

Film Links: The Body: Language, Rituals, and Wellness

1. Science fiction films often take actual situations, exaggerate them, and project them into the future. Consider how *Gattaca* uses the idea of bioengineering to make us reconsider the ideal physical human perfection. Also, consider how *Blade Runner* makes use of the idea of cloning to make us rethink the consequences of creating replicated beings. Choose either one of these two films and write your own analysis of these issues and the complex statement each film makes about them.

2. Compare the 1950s and the 1980s versions of *The Fly*. This horror film deals with a serious issue in a grotesque way. Like the short story "The

Metamorphosis" by Franz Kafka, *The Fly* shows what happens when a human being is changed into an insect. This could be interpreted as showing the psychological consequences of any change to the appearance of the body. In an essay, discuss the psychological realities that are expressed in sensational visual metaphors in these horror films.

3. Select any two films below and analyze individual character development by comparing and contrasting the evolution of personalities as observed through body language. Consider how physical behavior reveals internal states of being.

The Illustrated Man (USA, Jack Smight, 1969). Story of a chance meeting of a young wanderer and a strange, tattooed man—many of whose tattoos tell stories in and of themselves.

Smoke Signals (USA, Chris Eyre, 1998). Two young Native Americans leave the "rez" in search of a lost father and the rituals that can sustain them in the modern world.

Ghost Dog (USA, Jim Jarmusch, 1998). The rituals of the samurai code provide structure for the life of a very unconventional hit man.

American History X (USA, Tony Kaye, 1998). A skinhead becomes a part of a complex world of gangs and prisoners who express themselves through violent rituals and tattooed bodies.

American Beauty (USA, Sam Mendes, 1999). A middle-aged man takes up weight-lifting as part of his search for his lost youth.

The Mummy (USA, Stephen Sommers, 1999). A mummified priest raises havoc with Egyptologists. A goofy remake of 1932 original.

Run Lola Run (Germany, Tom Tykwer, 2000). Lola becomes a body in constant motion to save the life of her boyfriend.

Miss Congeniality (USA, Donald Petrie, 2001). A tomboyish FBI agent goes undercover as a contestant in a beauty contest and discovers another side of herself.

Brazil (UK, Terry Gilliam, 1985). A man in a technocratic society tries to correct a police error and is accused of being a terrorist; meanwhile, people search for their identity, engaging in plastic surgery and makeovers.

Additional Writing Assignments

1. Go to the library or online and find information on the use of body piercing and tattooing in tribal societies. You might start by looking at

textbooks on cultural anthropology. Write an essay in which you explain why other cultures modify their bodies. How are they different from the followers of popular culture, and how are they similar?

2. Write an essay arguing that body language as a form of communication speaks louder than words. While you may include discussion of body adornment in your essay, you should also think about the various ways you convey attitude.

3. In an essay using informative process analysis techniques as the main method of development, show how the food we eat and the exercise we receive corresponds directly to body wellness.

4. Some authors seem to recast modern forms of body beautification, such as tattoos, body piercings, and mehendi drawings, in the light of body mutilation. Using this extremely conservative reasoning and point of view, why wouldn't removing hair on the human body be a form of mutilation as well (e.g., cutting hair, shaving one's facial hair, under arms, legs)? Write an essay arguing that in the 21st century, what some regard as body mutilation amounts to little more than body modification to suit personal preferences, improve hygiene, or become one with fashion trends.

5. What popular culture trends that celebrate the human body in the present do you think will continue into the future? Make a list of these trends and write an essay that makes a realistic prediction of future possibilities. You might think of things like food, fads, exercising machines, plastic surgery, dancing, and movies.

Writing about Films

Films have been called "moving pictures" or "movies" since their earliest days because thousands of images pass before our eyes when we watch them tell some kind of story. There is an art to doing this. It takes the collaboration of dozens, sometimes hundreds, of people to produce a film. When you, the viewer, finish looking at a film, you can think about how it made you feel, what it made you think about. Films are probably the most popular form of entertainment in the world because they have such power to affect an audience. The large screen, the dramatic situations, the photography, the action, the special effects, and the sound track all combine to create a riveting experience. You can use this experience as a starting point for your own reflections and as a way to start writing.

Professional film reviewers and critics get paid to analyze films. This kind of writing aims to dissect a film, take it apart, and evaluate it. This is not the only way to respond to films. Most people respond to the effect of the story itself, just as people listen to songs and enjoy them even though they may not know anything about music theory or recording techniques. Movies and songs create a kind of chemical reaction in our brains. They are just illusions, but they are powerful and make us think about all kinds of things. After all, we all have our own tastes. No one likes all movies or all songs.

We usually like a movie because it speaks to us in some way. The chemical reaction comes about when we identify with the movie in some way. We can see ourselves in the situations portrayed on the screen. These celluloid fantasies awaken our imaginations and allow us to see ourselves in whatever situation comes up on the screen. Our minds and emotions get stretched a bit; they get a workout. A good movie can leave one feeling exhilarated, or emotionally exhausted, wrung out. A movie like *Schindler's List* or *Titanic* can provoke sorrow and tears; a movie like *What's Eating Gilbert Grape?* can help you understand how families fall apart and how they get back together. There is no end to what you can learn from movies because they are like giant fun-house mirrors that reflect life in strange and exaggerated ways.

When you finish watching a film—any film—there are questions you can ask yourself that will sharpen your perception and understanding of what you have just seen. Your ability to respond to a film will also be enhanced if you get in the habit of taking notes. This isn't very easy to do in a movie theater, but it can be done at home quite easily where you can stop and start a film, or simply watch it more than once, on your VCR or DVD player. Finally, there are some vocabulary words that apply specifically to films. The more you learn about the language of cinema, the better able you are to put your observations and ideas into words. You have to know what things are called if you want to talk about them. This appendix contains a discussion of two crucial terms—shot and scene—that you should become familiar with, some tips on how to take notes, and a guideline of questions that will generate writing responses.

Two Terms

Shot

A shot is a continuous, unedited piece of film, the basic unit of storytelling in film. When shots are spliced together, they create a scene. Most of us have taken "snapshots" that are frozen moments of time. A shot in a film is created in the same way: a certain amount of film is exposed to the light. When the camera operator closes the shutter, the shot's over. It could last for less than a second or for several minutes. There are thousands of shots in an average movie. Each one has an impact of some kind on the eye of the viewer. A camera can move during a shot. It can zoom in and out; it can pan left or right; it can be pushed on a dolly or raised up and down on a crane. This camera movement is still only one shot if the camera just keeps running without interruption. The shot ends with a cut.

Scene

This is not a very precise term, but it is a useful concept to help you remember what you've seen. A scene is a series of shots composed around a location or dramatic incident. Think of the beginning of *The Godfather*. Vito Corleone's daughter is about to get married. The first twenty-six minutes of this movie take place in two locations: Vito Corleone's study where various people come to request favors and outside in the yard where the wedding party is taking place. The movie cuts back and forth between these two locations. There is the dark, private world of the Godfather where he listens to the problems of his friends and relatives and figures out what he can do to help them. There is the open, colorful, social world of the party with its singing, dancing, and lighthearted banter. These two scenes contrast with one another visually and set up the clash of values that will define the whole film: the conflict between business and family. If you recognize these scenes, then you can better understand how the story is put together. Each scene contributes vital information that either reveals character or advances the plot. Most movies are made up of somewhere between seventy to ninety scenes, though this number varies widely depending on the kind of story that is being told.

How to Take Notes on a Film

Once you understand what a scene is, you can use this concept to organize your notes by numbering the scenes as you go along. As you watch a film, you should number each scene and jot down some observations that will help you remember what happened in that scene. So, for opening scenes of *The Godfather* you would write something like:

1. Study: Vito Corleone receives a visit from the father of a girl who has been beaten up. He wants the Don to get revenge on the man who did it.

2. Party: Guests dance while the mother of the bride sings Italian songs. Santino flirts with a bridesmaid.

3. Study: Corleone discusses a business offer from one of the other Mafia families with Tom Hagen, his adopted son. The Don doesn't want to get involved with drugs.

4. Party: Michael Corleone, the youngest son, arrives in his army uniform with a date. He tries to explain his family to her.

Using this method, you can keep track of what happens in a movie and see the sequence of the scenes. This can be helpful later, especially with films that move back and forth in time, as *The Godfather, Part II* does. If you don't take any notes at all when watching a film, it is very difficult to remember what you have seen. Taking notes will also improve your concentration. You will see more that takes place on the screen because your attention will be focused on noticing the details.

Questions and Guidelines for Writing

These are questions that can be used with any film. The idea is to start writing by going through a list of prompts that will get your thinking started.

1. What happens?

   Here you might use your notes to write a plot summary. This is a very good way to solidify in your own mind the details and shape of the story.

   How does the film communicate? What is the exact sequence of events? How is the story told?

Does the film use flashbacks, dreams, voiceovers, multiple points of view, or fantasies? When, where, and why do you think the director uses these techniques?

2. What does this film mean to me? Why do I like or dislike it?

Whatever you think about the film, your writing should have a definite point of view and not merely summarize the film. The writing should be thoughtful, fitting, and to the point. Look upon this as an opportunity to find out what you think and to bounce your ideas off other people who have looked at and thought about the same film as you.

3. What does the film tell us about the society or culture we live in?

You can say what the film reveals about American culture, what it reveals about specific personal, social, historical, or political issues that are important to you. Usually, we have several reasons for liking a film. Try to explain what yours are.

You can analyze the cultural elements that create a larger meaning for a film. Here you need to think about explicit and implicit values represented in the film.

All films assume certain beliefs to be true and assume the audience can be expected to respond in certain ways. When you look at the cultural elements of a film, you attempt to reveal these basic assumptions and show how they shape the reality of the film and how they influence an audience.

If you look at a film—even one that claims to be merely entertainment—as an attempt to persuade an audience that certain social, political, religious, and/or sexual values are important, reasonable, or natural—then your job as a writer is to reveal these values and weigh their significance.

4. What is this movie really about?

What were the possible intentions of the screenwriter and director?

What themes or issues are at stake here?

Does the film make some kind of coherent statement? Is it full of contradictions?

5. What are the best scenes in the film? Why?

You can analyze the film as a drama and say something about what the conflicts reveal; you can discuss how the interior lives of the characters are revealed by dialogue, action, costumes, lighting, and so on.

List three memorable scenes in the film and describe the impact they had on you.

6. **What kind of story is it?**

You can think about what type of film you've chosen. You should describe the characteristics of this type of film and then show how your particular film is consistent or inconsistent with this definition.

Most video stores organize tapes by category. In which section would you place your film and why? Some film types include comedy, drama, romance, melodrama, horror, science fiction, action/adventure, mystery, musical, documentary, detective, western, war, suspense/thriller, political, alternative, cult, and religious.

Some films combine types. *Star Wars*, for example, has elements taken from romance, science fiction, westerns, and samurai movies.

7. **Which actors give the best performances? Why?**

What did the actors do or say that made an impact upon you?

What elements go into creating a great performance? Does it seem authentic?

8. **What images stay with you after the film is over? Why?**

Sometimes photographic images from a film linger in the imagination like powerful dreams. Think about how you remember a film. What images stick with you? Why? Try to explain in words what they mean to you.

For the Writing Instructor

Composition and Films: Frequently Asked Questions

What kind of preparation is required to present a film?

Treat a film as you would a written text. Review it and make up a set of questions that might lead to a discussion before seeing the film. Discuss the issues the film raises in advance of seeing it. Also, point out some features of the film in advance so that the students are looking for something as they watch.

How much do you need to know about film technique to use films in class?

Narrative films are fictional stories and lend themselves to the same kinds of critical approaches that are used with literary works. The cinematic techniques in films do not need to be part of the critique of a film. The films have been placed on the lists at the end of each chapter because of their thematic content. It might be useful to have students write out questions in advance that they think would help in analyzing a film. Just a few of these questions would be enough to generate discussion about how films communicate.

Is it worth the class time?

For classes that run fifty minutes, the average film will take two to three class sessions to view. This can be a productive use of class time a few times in a semester/quarter if the students are given questions and assignments to work on outside of class based on each day's viewing. Students should get in the habit of taking notes while watching a film. For homework they could type and organize their notes. This enhances class discussion and gives them some written material to work from if they write about the film as a whole.

Should the films be viewed at home instead?

We have listed at least ten films with each chapter. Students can choose any number of films to view at home and then write about. If students view films at home, they should have some sort of heuristic devised by the instructor or use the one provided in this Appendix. If students view films at home, they can view them multiple times and take much more extensive notes and become much more familiar with the details of the film.

What about showing excerpts?

Sometimes a fifteen- or twenty-minute clip from a film can be a great way to highlight the major theme or themes in each chapter of *Projections*, a starting point, if you will, for generating discussion and writing. These clips can be used to illustrate a wide range of situations that make sense if they are set up verbally in advance. Showing even shorter clips from a variety of films could also encourage students to rent them and write about them at home.

Are films too visual to be used in writing classes?

Most students today have spent more time looking at television and movies than they have reading. This experience is part of the culture they bring into the classroom. Learning a few film terms can enable them to talk about it, but they are often surprisingly sophisticated at noticing visual cues that are embedded in films and television shows. Encouraging students to read about what they have seen is a strong motivational device to encourage them to read more on their own. Students generally enjoy reading about subjects they already know something about, and, in many cases, have formed their own critical points of view. Many students, in fact, carry on quite detailed discussion about shows like *X Files* or any of the various versions of *Star Trek*.

What kind of assignments can you give related to a film?

The film appendix gives some specific questions, and each chapter has questions related to the films. The films are meant to supplement the readings in each chapter. The readings could be paired with the films in various ways in order to stimulate critical thinking by making comparisons and contrasts. Students can respond to films with personal essays that reflect on the role movies in general play in their lives; or students can write more analytical essays about the conflicts in the films and what they mean. They can always look at films as expressions of culture at a certain moment in time. They can write about what they think the film expresses.

Note to Instructors: Following other methods of immersing students in a theme, drawing what they already know and believe about them to the surface, we have included a section called Introducing Thematic Chapters through Film Clips in the Instructors' Manual. This feature offers an apparatus based on a film representative of the theme, including where to find a good clip, a prewriting assignment of the clip you plan to show, a summary of the action preceding it, and a set-up for the film clip itself. Thus, each thematic chapter in the Instructor's Manual offers a template you can use to prepare to show any film clip in a composition class.

Glossary of Literary, Rhetorical, and Cultural Terms

ABSTRACT WORDS: Words that define ideas, concepts, and attitudes (love, hate, ethics, indifference, honesty, pride) and tend to be interpreted differently from person to person.

ADVERBIAL CONJUNCTIONS: Joining words that are part adverb and part conjunction. Adverbial conjunctions are strong joining words, so they are appropriate for opening sentences or following a semicolon in a compound sentence to relate independent clauses.

additionally	consequently	eventually
frequently	furthermore	however
moreover	nevertheless	nonetheless
regardless	subsequently	therefore

ALLEGORY: A narrative in which all of the elements are symbolic. Some contemporary allegories include C. S. Lewis's *Chronicles of Narnia* books, George Orwell's *Animal Farm*, Arthur Miller's *The Crucible*, and William Golding's *Lord of the Flies*.

ALLUSION: A term used when making reference to a famous literary, historical, or social figure or event. Alluding to the Kennedy administration in the White House as "Camelot" conjures up visions of Arthurian romances and "the once and future king" who will return to unite a troubled country.

ANALOGY: An extended comparison where an unfamiliar topic is explained by noting its similarity to something familiar. For instance, we might write how and why popular culture is like a fun-house mirror, reflecting and distorting the real world.

ANALYSIS: To come to a conclusion about something through close inspection and observation. Analysis often includes separating a topic or an issue into smaller parts in order to reach a more thorough understanding of the whole.

ANECDOTE: A short story used to illustrate a point.

ANTAGONIST: A character in drama or fiction who rivals or opposes the central character (protagonist) in a work. The antagonist need not always be a person; nature itself—such as the ocean in Ernest Hemingway's *The Old Man and the Sea*, or HAL, the computer, in Arthur C. Clark's *2001: A Space Odyssey*—can function as the antagonist.

ARCHETYPES: Controlling paradigms (models) or metaphors for the human experience—both mind and body—frequently represented in art, literature, dreams, and ritual. Psychologists like Carl Jung have seen the value in exploring archetypes since "to understand an archetype is to recognize a pattern of behavior, and possibly how to relate or deal with it." Common archetypes include the *trickster*, the *caretaker*, the *sage*, the *healer*, the *savior*, the *ruler (king, queen)*, the *orphan*, and the *fool*.

AUDIENCE: The readers for whom the writer writes (friends, family, coworkers, professors, public servants, relatives). Writers must consider whether their audience knows a little or a lot about a topic, as well as whether it would be best to present material informally or formally.

BRAINSTORMING: Solving a problem individually or collectively by considering and/or rejecting ideas. In a composition, a writer uses brainstorming to generate ideas and determine a focus on a topic or an issue for writing paragraphs and essays.

CAUSE AND EFFECT: A rhetorical strategy that explains "why" in a composition. Simply using words such as "because," "since," and "therefore" indicates causal relationships. There are frequently multiple causes to a single effect, and a single cause can have multiple effects. Furthermore, an effect is not caused by a previously occurring event just because the first event occurred before it in time. Just because a musician receives a speeding ticket on the way to a concert does not mean the concert caused the speeding ticket. Cause and effect relationships in writing are very common.

CLICHÉ: A trite, tired, or unimaginative use of language. Generally, replace clichés with fresh, vivid expressions that leave concrete, powerful impressions on your readers.

> **Example:** "Been there—done that," or "I'm as happy as a lark." (How many of your readers have really ever seen a "happy" lark? Have you ever observed one, or are you merely familiar with the expression?)

COHERENCE: The smooth integration and flow of ideas within sentences and paragraphs. Writers achieve coherence in their work by using transitions and linking devices—words or word groups that indicate the relationship between other words, phrases, clauses, or entire paragraphs. (See also Transitions).

COLLOQUIALISMS: Informal expressions, somewhere between slang and formal expressions. Colloquialisms are acceptable in speech but not desirable in formal writing. Examples of colloquial expressions might include "I hear ya" instead of "I understand," or "As if!" instead of "What are you thinking?" or "This cannot be true," or "I find this incredibly difficult to believe."

COMPARISON AND CONTRAST: A rhetorical strategy that sorts out differences and notes similarities between people, places, and things. Though not an end in itself, comparison and contrast is a *means to an end*. The point of comparisons is to use them to reach some sort of conclusion. In comparing two types of transportation, a writer might be able to conclude which form of transportation was healthier, which form of transportation was the most economical, or which form of transportation was the most ecologically responsible. In successful comparative papers, authors often exhaustively research the differences and the similarities between items. Then, and only then, can they fully justify their conclusions.

COMPLEX SENTENCE: A sentence structure consisting of an independent clause and one or more dependent clauses. An independent clause, which contains a subject, a verb, and a complete thought, could be punctuated as a complete sentence. It becomes *dependent* when preceded by a subordinate conjunction (a dependent word). Subordinate conjunctions include words like:

after	although	among	as
because	before	beyond	despite
during	even though	except	if
since	though	until	wherever
when	whenever	while	without

Example: independent clause: the ballerina danced around the banana tree
dependent clause: *until* the rain stopped

Obviously, the dependent clause would be a sentence fragment if punctuated with a period after "stopped." The subordinating conjunction *until* makes the entire clause dependent on an independent clause for completion. Combined with the independent clause above, the dependent clause makes perfect sense and might read something like: *"The ballerina danced around the banana tree until the rain stopped."* Whenever a dependent clause opens a sentence, follow it with a comma.

Example: While Lisa telephoned her mother, her husband made dinner.

A dependent clause at the end of the sentence needs no punctuation because the subordinate conjunction clarifies its relationship to the preceding independent clause.

Example: The first violinist for the San Francisco Philharmonic performed at every major engagement until she retired in Billings, Montana.

COMPOUND SENTENCES: A sentence consisting of two or more independent clauses (complete sentences) combined into a single structure by separating the two independent clauses with a comma and a coordinating conjunction, a semi-colon, or a semicolon and an adverbial conjunction. Note the three ways to punctuate the following compound sentence:

Example: Megan applied for a medical internship, but she did not get the position.

Megan applied for a medical internship; she did not get the position.

Megan applied for a medical internship; however, she did not get the position.

COMPOUND/COMPLEX SENTENCE: A sentence structure consisting of at least two independent clauses and one or more dependent clauses. The clauses need not appear in any particular order to qualify as compound/complex, although compound/complex sentences that open with a dependent clause should be followed by a comma. Back-to-back independent clauses should be punctuated with a comma and one of the seven coordinating conjunctions, a semicolon, or a semicolon followed by an adverbial conjunction and a comma.

Example: Drusilla and Ashly rented an apartment in downtown Chicago (independent clause) because Drusilla worked at the Palmer House, and (dependent clause) Ashly was a tour guide at the Chicago Art Institute. (independent clause)

Example: If Julian Samson buys a new car, (dependent clause) Heather, his daughter, will drive his old Volkswgon Bug, and (independent clause) she will give her motorbike to her younger brother. (independent clause)

CONCRETE WORDS: Words may stand by themselves and can be understood because they are perceived through the five senses: touch, taste, sight, smell, and sound. For instance, a person can touch, see, and smell a flower; therefore, the word *flower* is concrete. See Louise Erdrich's visual narrative, "Beneath the House," in Chapter 3 for an excellent example of concrete words at work.

CONNOTATION: The meanings or implications associated with a particular word beyond its literal definition. The phrase *flying saucers*, for instance, carries connotations of little green Martians or intergalactic creatures from *Star Wars*, *ET*, or *Independence Day*. A connotation may be like excess baggage, so be as precise as possible when you write to avoid suggesting something you did not intend. For instance, refer to a "flying saucer" as an unidentified flying object (UFO).

COORDINATING CONJUNCTIONS: Joining words. There are seven—and only seven—coordinating conjunctions: *and, but, for, or, nor, so, yet.* When you write and revise your work, you will frequently use these words to indicate the equal importance, but varying relationship, between words or clauses. Your comma and coordinating conjunction function as a single unit to correctly punctuate two complete thoughts into a single sentence.

Example: Eight inches of snow had already fallen in just an hour, so we braced ourselves for the storm.

DEFINITION: A brief exposition designed to explain the meaning of a term or concept. Sometimes an author will spend an entire essay defining a term. The rhetorical strategy of definition limits a focus, narrows a topic, clarifies a point of view, or establishes a frame of reference. If key terms are carefully defined, both the writer and the reader will stay focused on the controlling idea or thesis of an essay and avoid digressions and misunderstandings.

DENOTATION: The literal or standard dictionary definition of a word, understood without emotional influences or associations. "Success," for instance, indicates an accomplishment—nothing more, nothing less.

DICTION: An author's word choice. High diction consists of elevated or elaborate speech, formal language, and, quite often, polysyllabic words. Diction also deals with word usage (concrete/abstract expressions, denotation/connotation, colloquialisms).

DIVISION AND CLASSIFICATION: A rhetorical strategy that takes the subject and breaks it down into smaller, more comprehensible units. In the process, writers consider subject matter from diverse points of view until they have found the most appropriate categories for division. After dividing the subject matter into smaller units, writers will then be free to examine each point in detail. Division and classification is probably one of the most familiar methods of essay development. Most material in an essay outline or the table of contents in a book, for instance, has been divided and classified.

DOCUMENTATION: Acknowledging primary and secondary sources of information through "parenthetical references" and a list of "works cited."

DOUBLESPEAK: A verbal smoke screen that covers up or masks unpleasant facts and details (e.g., referring to "revenue enhancement" instead of tax increase or "collateral damage" to refer to casualties of war).

EVIDENCE: Personal experience, observations of others, professional testimonies, and/or authoritative studies that clarify or support statements or accusations. In fiction, evidence often takes on the face of clues or information that motivates an action or resolves a mystery. In nonfiction, facts and examples support, and thereby prove, the validity of what you claim.

FIGURES OF SPEECH: Referring to people, places, and things in a nonliteral sense. The most common forms of figures of speech include the use of metaphor, simile, hyperbole, and personification.

HYPERBOLE: An exaggeration for emphasis. For example, "I am so tired that I could sleep for a week," or "Angela's piggy bank contained a million dollars."

IDIOMS: The use of words unique to a particular group or language. Idiomatic expressions are often neither grammatical nor logical, but they are "understood" when used (e.g., "hitting the books," which idiomatically means "to study" but literally refers to striking books). Idioms are difficult or impossible to translate into another language.

ILLUSTRATION: Showing, rather than telling, a reader what statements and claims mean. When illustrating discussion points, writers will use concrete examples from their personal experiences, observations, and readings. By using plenty of representative examples to illustrate and support what is said, writers validate their premises and help readers to visualize discussion points by showing—not just telling.

IMAGERY: Concrete expressions that appeal to the five senses, often employing the use of figurative speech to produce mental pictures.

IRONY: A literary device dependent on two separate and contrasting levels of meaning or experience. Verbal irony exists when the opposite of what was intended is expressed. Situational irony results when the opposite of what was expected takes place, leaving those involved powerless. Dramatic irony places characters in a state of ignorance, while you, the reader or viewer, are aware of what is about to take place.

METAPHOR: A figurative comparison without the use of "like" or "as." For instance, a simile would state: *The snow floated like lotus blossoms in the wind.* A metaphor would simply state: *The snow was lotus blossoms.*

MOOD: The emotional or emotion-intellectual attitude that an author takes towards a work (e.g., gloomy, ironic, optimistic, pessimistic, cheerful). The salutation in a letter is one of the many instances where a writer attempts to immediately establish a tone with his or her readers.

PARALLELISM: Constructing word groups into consistent, balanced patterns, using the same grammatical forms. Parallelism offers an excellent rhetorical scheme for condensing material using an economy of words. To achieve parallel structure, arrange your information into similar grammatical constructions, balancing a noun with a noun, a verb with a verb, an adjective with an adjective and so on (e.g., Tall, quick, and graceful, Roxanna glided across the ice on her silver skates). The possibilities for condensing paragraphs and sentences are endless with parallel structure, and the results of your efforts will not go unrewarded.

PARAPHRASE: Putting someone else's writings or ideas into your own words. (See Chapter 1, The Reading/Studying Process.)

PERSONA: Literally, a *mask* used in the form of a character or voice as the speaker of an essay or short story. An author's persona may change to suit his or her audience. Frequently, the attitudes of the persona differ from those of the author.

PERSONIFICATION: Giving human characteristics and attributes to inanimate objects (airplanes, rocks, air, fire, water, trees) and nonhuman animals (cats, owls, lizards, horses).

> **Example:** The wind groaned mournfully while the mighty oak trees imitated its lamentations.

POINT OF VIEW: The perspective from which an essay or story is written. In formal writing, point of view is expressed in the first person, wherein the author uses the pronoun "I"; or the third person, which is a more objective form of writing, wherein the writer uses "he," "she," or "it" as the narrator. Point of view may also refer to an author's attitude toward his or her subject matter.

PLOT: The sequence of events or story line in a dramatic work or a piece of fiction, as well as some verse. As Aristotle put it, plot is "the imitation of an action" and "the arrangement of the incidents."

PROCESS ANALYSIS: A rhetorical strategy that answers the question "how" in composition. There are two basic types of process analysis essays: informative process analysis, which shows how something happens or how something has occurred (the evolution of life according to both Charles Darwin and the Bible), and directive process analysis, which indicates "how to do" something (how to make a snow angel, how to build a cabinet).

PROSE: A general term applied to all forms of writing that do not follow any regular rhythmic pattern (such as poetry). We usually think of prose as writing consisting of sentences and poetry as writing consisting of "lines."

PROTAGONIST: The main character in a fictional or dramatic work.

SATIRE: An attack on human vices and follies. Satire places people, places, and things in ridicule or contempt for amusement—ideally to correct behavior or to improve attitudes and bring about necessary change.

SETTING: The social or historical or geographic background in fiction or drama. Setting may also include seasons, locations (e.g., city office or farm house), and occasions (a wedding, the Day of the Dead, the Mardi Gras, Independence Day).

SIMILE: A comparative figure of speech using "like" and "as" prior to nouns.

> **Example:** Dylan looked *like* a cherub.

> **Example:** The shoppers surged through Macy's open doors *as* violently as the raging sea.

SIMPLE SENTENCES: Sentence constructions with a basic subject-verb core: bees sting, people speak, wood floats, airplanes fly. Granted, two-word sentences are not very common, and most simple sentences also contain direct and indirect objects or complements.

> **Example:** The toy poodle ran across the living room rug, fiercely barking and growling at everyone and everything it approached.

Stripped of additional information regarding what the poodle did, the subject-verb core reads *"The toy poodle ran."* A complete thought in a simple sentence may contain a compound (more than one) subject, a compound verb, or both a compound subject and compound verb.

> **Example:** Francisco and Irma both learned how to play the Celtic harp last year. (compound subject and single verb)

> **Example:** Kikki read Toni Morrison's *Jazz* and wrote a paper about it. (single subject and compound verb)

> **Example:** Dianne, Mary, and Euridice drove across the United States, visited several state capitals, and wrote in their travel journals every day during the summer of 1998. (compound subject and compound verb)

SPEAKER: The narrator providing the point of view from which something is experienced in a story or a poem. In addition to narrating a literary work, the speaker may present privileged information—insights that come from his or her sphere of knowledge.

STRATEGY: Plan of action or method used for approaching, analyzing, and writing about a topic or an issue. Rhetorical modes are strategies or techniques for explaining topics and issues in writing.

SUMMARY: Condensation of another author's work into a shorter composition. A summary is usually one-fourth as long as an original piece of writing, and it simply seeks to highlight major points—the general idea—of a work without getting into a lot of detail. A summary of a literary piece may help the reader to grasp a firm sense of "the whole." For a detailed discussion of writing summaries see Chapter 1, The Reading/Studying Process.

SYNTAX: The arrangement of words in a sentence. Their respective placement in each sentence may add clarity. For instance, you would say, "Ringo played drums for the Beatles" rather than "Drums Beatles for the Ringo played."

THESIS: The main or controlling idea of an essay.

TONE: Mood projecting a writer's attitude toward his or her subject or audience, indicated through the carefully selected use of words. Sarcasm and sincerity, for instance, project very different attitudes about a subject to readers.

TOPIC SENTENCE: The main idea of a paragraph, much like a thesis, though not as broad. A topic sentence usually leads off a paragraph, and the sentences that follow should support the point with specific facts and details in order to provide unity for the paragraph.

TRANSITIONS: Words or word groups that assist a writer or a speaker in moving from one point to the next. Transitional expressions signal changes in direction, shifts in time, and the results of relationships between words, phrases, clauses, sentences, and paragraphs. Some common transitions include *after,* *before, therefore, however, moreover, nevertheless, thus.* The following is a more exhaustive transition list that details the function of specific transitional expressions.

> *ADDITION TRANSITIONS:*   first of all, second, third, finally, last of all, in addition, moreover, furthermore
>
> *CHANGE OF DIRECTION TRANSITIONS:*   but, consequently, however, yet, in contrast, otherwise, still, on the contrary, on the other hand, nevertheless, nonetheless
>
> *CONCLUSION TRANSITIONS:*   therefore, consequently, thus, as a result, then, in summary, in conclusion, last of all, finally, in short
>
> *EMPHASIS TRANSITIONS:*   furthermore, moreover, most of all, principally, especially, most importantly, especially significant
>
> *ILLUSTRATION TRANSITIONS:*   for example, for instance, specifically, such as, as an illustration
>
> *SPATIAL TRANSITIONS:*   above, below, inside, outside, here, there, beyond, behind, between, over, under
>
> *TIME TRANSITIONS:*   first, second, third, then, next, after, as, before, while, during, now, finally, meanwhile, subsequently

UNDERSTATEMENT: Intentionally undervaluing or overplaying something to create emphasis.

> **Example:** Hilda was certainly not unhappy to see her mother after thirty years.

UNITY: The state of having composed parts that have connections among themselves and coherence. A writer unifies a piece of nonfiction by making a point—usually the thesis or topic sentence—and sticking to the controlling idea he or she has established without digressing from that major discussion point. In other words, paragraphs should stick to supporting the thesis in a paper, and sentences should back up the topic sentence in paragraphs to unify your writing.

VOICE: The form of the verb, either active or passive, in writing. In the active voice, the subject does the acting (e.g., The actress *read* her lines), and in the passive voice the subject receives the action of the verb (e.g., The lines *were read* by the actress).

Index

Credits